The American Express pocket guide to

GREECE

Peter Sheldon

Mitchell Beazley

The Author
Peter Sheldon has lived in Greece for many years and knows the whole country intimately. He is a past director of the British School in Crete and now lectures at the British Council in Athens. He has written guides to most Mediterranean countries including four guides to Greece, and has for several years written for the Greek National Tourist Organization.

Acknowledgements
The author and publishers would like to thank the following for their invaluable help and advice: Dr Roderick Beaton, Isabel Carlisle, Diana Durant, Pamela Fiori, The Greek National Tourist Organization, Paul Holberton, Ila Stanger.

Following the 1981 general election in Greece, the national tourist authority was renamed the Greek National Tourist Organization (GNTO) – the name used throughout this book. However, the old title, National Tourist Organization of Greece (NTOG), is also widely used.

Quotations
The author and publishers are grateful to Faber and Faber Publishers (UK) and E. P. Dutton, Inc. (USA) for their kind permission to reprint the quotation from *Prospero's Cell* by Lawrence Durrell (p172).

Few travel books are without errors, and no guidebook can ever be completely up to date, for telephone numbers and opening hours change without warning, and hotels and restaurants come under new management, which can affect standards. While every effort has been made to ensure that all information is accurate at the time of going to press, the publishers will be glad to receive any corrections and suggestions for improvements, which can be incorporated in the next edition.

Editor David Townsend Jones
Executive Editor Hal Robinson
Chief Sub-Editor Susan Chapman
Researcher Catherine Jackson
Editorial assistants Lynne Lynch, Sue McKinstry, Paddy Poynder

Art Editor Eric Drewery
Designer Sarah Jackson
Illustrators Jeremy Ford (David Lewis Artists), Illustra Design Ltd., Rodney Paull

Editor-in-Chief Susannah Read
Executive Art Editor Douglas Wilson
Production Julian Deeming, Sarah Goodden

Edited and designed by
Mitchell Beazley International Limited
87–89 Shaftesbury Avenue
London W1V 7AD

© Mitchell Beazley Publishers 1983
Text © Peter Sheldon

ISBN 0 85533 399 5

Maps in 4-colour by Clyde Surveys Ltd., Maidenhead, England.
Typeset by Vantage Photosetting Co. Ltd., Southampton, England.
Printed and bound in Hong Kong by Mandarin Offset International Ltd.

Contents

How to use this book

The American Express Pocket Guide to Greece is an encyclopaedia of travel information, organized in the sections listed on the previous page. There is also a comprehensive **index** (pages 230–240) and full-colour **maps** at the end of the book.

For easy reference, all major sections (**Sights and places of interest, Hotels, Restaurants**) and other sections as far as possible are arranged alphabetically. For the organization of the book as a whole, see *Contents*. Note particularly that there are two separate A–Z sections in the description of Greece: the *Mainland and Peloponnese A–Z* (usually abbreviated to *Mainland A–Z*) and the *Greek Islands A–Z* (usually abbreviated to *Islands A–Z*). For places that do not have individual entries, see the *Index*.

Abbreviations

As far as possible only standard abbreviations have been used. These include days of the week and months, points of the compass (N, S, E and W), street names (Ave., Sq.) Saint (St), C for century, and measurements.

Bold type

Bold type is used in running text primarily for emphasis, to draw attention to something of special interest or importance. It is also used in this way to pick out places – shops or minor museums, for instance – that do not have full entries of their own. In such cases it is often followed in brackets by the address, telephone number, and details of opening times, printed in italics.

Cross-references

A special type has been used for cross-references. Whenever a place or section title is printed in sans serif italics (for example *Athens/Sights* or *Basic information*) in the text, this indicates that you can turn to the appropriate heading in the book for further information. For added convenience, the running heads, printed at the top corner of the page, always correspond with these cross-references.

How entries are organized

Thássos ☆

Map 4C8. 30km (19 miles) SE of Kavala. 24km (15 miles) long by 19km (12 miles) wide. Getting there: By ferry, from Keramoti and Kavala. Getting around: By bus to all villages. Taxi and garage facilities available. Population: 10,000.

The vales and mountains of Thassos are thickly wooded, with chestnuts, plane trees, pines and firs climbing almost all the way up the 1,203m (3,947ft) of Mt. Ypsario. Geologically, botanically and climatically they are part of Macedonia rather than of the Aegean, a continuation of Mt. Symvolo which rises behind the mainland town of *Kavala* (see *Mainland A–Z*), formerly a colony of Thassos, and of distant Mt. Pangeo, whence came its gold and resulting prosperity. The island was colonized from Paros in 750BC.

The closest good beach to **Thassos**, the main village, is 3km (2 miles) to the E at **Makry Ammos** (Long Sand) but most of it is reserved for the Makry Ammos bungalows (see below).

Cross-references always refer either to sections of the book – *Basic information* or *Planning* for example – or to individual entries in one or other of the A–Z sections, such as *Delphi* (in the *Mainland A–Z*), or *Mykonos* (in the *Islands A–Z*). Ordinary italics are used to identify sub-sections. For instance: see *Mythology* in *Culture, history and background*.

Map references

Each page of the colour maps at the end of the book has a page number (2–16) and each map is divided into a grid of squares, which are identified vertically by letters (A, B, C, D, etc.) and horizontally by numbers (1, 2, 3, 4, etc.). A map reference identifies the page and square in which the street or place can be found – thus **Olympia** is located in the square identified as Map **10**H4.

Price bands

Price bands are denoted by the symbols ▢ ▥ ▦ ▩ and ▨ which signify cheap, inexpensive, moderately priced, expensive and very expensive, respectively. In the cases of hotels and restaurants these correspond approximately with the following actual prices, which are typical at the time of printing. Although actual prices will inevitably increase, often by 20–30% a year, in most cases the relative price category – for example expensive or cheap – will be likely to remain more or less the same.

Price bands	Corresponding to approximate prices	
	for **hotels** *double room with bath, usually with breakfast*	for **restaurants** *meal for one with service and tax*
▢ cheap	700–1,300dr	260–455dr
▥ inexpensive	800–1,800dr	325–650dr
▦ moderate	1,250–2,650dr	520–975dr
▩ expensive	2,200–3,650dr	650–1,300dr
▨ very expensive	3,000–11,300dr	1,300–2,210dr

Bold blue type for entry headings.

Blue italics for address, practical information and symbols, encapsulating standard information and special recommendations. For list of symbols see p6.

Black text for description.
Bold type used for emphasis.
Sans serif italics used for cross-references to other entries.

Entries for hotels, restaurants, shops, etc. follow the same organization, and are usually printed across a narrow measure.
In hotels, symbols indicating special facilities appear at the end of the entry.

Dorian Inn
Pireos 15, Athens 112
☎ *52–39–782* ✆ *214779. Map* *16D1* ▦ 🖃 *146* ▦ 🚗 🅿 ⇌
🆎 🆑 ⊕ ⊛ *VISA*

Location: On a busy main road, in central Athens though at the wrong end of it. One of the large concentration of middle-priced hotels round Omonia Sq. The public rooms are small, but the air-conditioned private rooms are ample. Above-average service in the restaurant.
⇌

Key to symbols

- ☎ Telephone
- ⊙ Telex
- ★ Not to be missed
- ☆ Worth a visit
- ♣ Good value (in its class)
- *i* Tourist information
- 🚗 Car parking
- Ⓗ Hotel
- 🏠 Simple (hotel)
- 🏨 Luxury (hotel)
- □ Cheap
- ▥ Inexpensive
- ▨ Moderately priced
- ▧ Expensive
- ▨ Very expensive
- ♘ Number of rooms
- 🛏 Rooms with private bathroom
- ▤ Air-conditioning
- 🏡 Residential terms available
- AE American Express
- CB Carte Blanche
- ⊙ Diners Club
- ⊙ Master Card
- VISA Visa
- 🚙 Garage
- 🍽 Own restaurant
- 🍴 Meal obligatory
- ◔ Quiet hotel
- ⬍ Lift
- ♿ Facilities for the disabled
- □ TV in each room
- ☎ Telephone in each room

- ♨ Garden available
- ≼ Outstanding views
- ⇌ Swimming pool
- 🏖 Good beach nearby
- ♐ Tennis court(s)
- ✓ Golf course
- 🏇 Riding facilities
- 🎣 Fishing facilities
- 👥 Conference facilities
- Ⓡ Restaurant
- 🍴 Simple (restaurant)
- △ Luxury (restaurant)
- ⌷ À la carte available
- ▬ Set (fixed price) menu available
- ⊏ Good for wines
- ⌂ Open-air dining available
- 🏛 Building of architectural interest
- † Church or Cathedral
- ▣ Entrance free
- ▨ Entrance fee payable
- ▧ Entrance expensive
- 📷̸ Photography not permitted
- 𝒦 Guided tour available
- 𝒦̄ Guided tour compulsory
- 🖳 Cafeteria
- ⋎ Bar
- ◉ Disco
- ◪ Nightclub
- ♠ Casino/gambling
- ♫ Live music
- ≀≀ Dancing
- ▨ Revue

Before you go

Documents required

Nationals of EEC countries require only a passport or identity card for a stay not exceeding three months; for a longer stay, and for nationals of all other countries, a valid passport is needed. Visas are required by nationals of the Eastern bloc and some African, South American and Asian countries. To stay longer than three months, all foreign visitors have to apply for a residence permit from the Aliens' Centre, Halkokondyli 9, Athens ☎ (01) 36 – 22 – 601, or from the police visa service.

Health regulations require vaccination certificates against cholera, smallpox and yellow fever for people arriving from infected areas.

If you are intending to drive, an international driving licence will be required unless you are a national of an EEC country, in which case a valid national licence suffices. The vehicle registration certificate is essential, as is international third party insurance (green card). Anyone who brings a car to Greece and intends to stay longer than four months should obtain a *carnet de passages en douane* from the automobile club of the country where the car is registered.

Travel and medical insurance

Insure against loss of deposits paid to airlines, shipping companies, hotels or tour operators, and against emergency costs, such as special tickets home and extra nights in a hotel.

If you are a UK national, entitled to full UK benefits, you are entitled to the same health cover as Greek citizens. UK residents must obtain form E111 from the Department of Health and Social Security before leaving home. However, you should be warned that the national health facilities in Greece are not as comprehensive as in other countries, and generally speaking services are not up to European standards. If you want private treatment you will have to pay, so it is important to be insured adequately. Advice about this can be obtained from your travel agent.

Money

The unit of currency is the drachma (pl. drachmes), abbreviated to dr. There are coins for ½dr, 1dr, 2dr, 5dr, 10dr, 20dr and 50dr, and notes for 50dr, 100dr, 500dr and 1,000dr.

There is no limit to the amount of foreign currency you can import into Greece, although amounts over US $500 or the equivalent must be declared and a certificate obtained, which will be required for subsequent export. No more than 1,500dr may be imported or exported.

It is unwise to carry large sums of money and travellers cheques are a good safeguard against theft. Credit cards are accepted in most large establishments but it is best to carry an alternative means of payment as well.

Customs

Any items clearly intended for personal use may be brought into Greece free of charge. Duty-free allowances are given below.
Tobacco goods 200 cigarettes *or* 100 cigarillos *or* 50 cigars *or* 250g tobacco.
Alcoholic drinks 1 litre spirits *or* strong liquor (over 22% alcohol by volume) *or* 2 litres alcoholic drink under 22% alcohol, *plus* 2 litres still table wine.

7

Basic information

Perfume 50g/60cc/2 fl oz; toilet water, 250cc/9 fl oz.
Other goods Goods to the value of £28.

For a detailed list covering electrical goods and defining personal effects, you should contact the Greek Embassy or the Greek National Tourist Organisation (GNTO in English; *EOT – Ellenikós Organismós Tourismóu* in Greek).

When returning, there are no limitations on the goods you can export, with the important exception of antiquities and works of art acquired in Greece.

Getting there

By air: The availability and cost of flights to Greece vary enormously depending on the season. Athens is well served by a wide range of international airlines, and less regular scheduled flights fly to Thessaloniki. In the summer domestic flights connect these two airports with Corfu, Kos, Rhodes and Crete. Fares on scheduled flights are expensive, and can only be reduced by buying an advance excursion ticket which restricts the length of the visit. Internal flights are relatively cheap.

In the summer there are numerous charter flights to all parts of Greece at a fraction of the scheduled fare. To satisfy Greek law they are sold as part of a package including accommodation. These flights also carry time restrictions: a minimum of three days, which must include a weekend, and a maximum of four weeks. Make sure you are dealing with a reputable travel agent and know what you are buying.

By train: Fewer trans-European expresses run than in former days, and travelling to Greece by train is not to be recommended unless you are a rail enthusiast. The journey to Athens takes three days and nights from London or Paris, two from Munich or Venice and one from Belgrade, and is more expensive than a charter flight.

By bus: There are about ten companies operating between London and Athens by various routes. The journey takes three or four days and nights, with one or more nights spent in the bus. Although considerably cheaper than a charter flight, it is only recommended for the adventurous.

By car: The quickest (but most expensive) route from N and W Europe is through Italy to the ferry ports of Ancona, Bari or Brindisi, then by boat to Corfu, Igoumenitsa or Patra. If you are driving all the way you will have to take the slow road through Yugoslavia and enter Greece at either Evzoni or Niki.

By yacht/ship: It is possible to catch a ferry at Venice, Naples or Ancona to Piraeus; longer routes include Southampton or New York to Piraeus, although sailings are infrequent. If you are entering Greek waters in a yacht you should proceed to one of the 25 or so ports, indicated by your yacht club or yacht broker, which have passport and customs control facilities.

Climate

Although the tourist season is Apr–Oct, the heat can be unpleasant in July and Aug, especially in Athens, often reaching 32°C(90°F) in the shade and only falling to 24°C(75°F) at night. On the islands, however, the *meltémi* wind can make life more comfortable. The most pleasant warm weather occurs in Mar–May, before the sun has burnt the vegetation, and Sept–Oct, when the sea is still warm. Winter tends to be changeable, with heavy rain and long warm periods of sunshine. It is rarely cold enough for snow to settle, except in the mountains.

8

Clothes

Informal clothes are acceptable almost everywhere in Greece and, if weather permits, bikinis or shorts are enough on the coast and islands. Monasteries require ladies to wear skirts rather than trousers, and to cover their arms. Only a few very expensive restaurants demand a tie, as very few people dress for dinner. In winter take a coat and umbrella and be prepared for the changeable weather.

Poste restante

Correspondence marked 'Poste restante' can be sent to any post office in Greece. For collecting mail, some form of identification will be required and a small fee is charged. Post offices are closed on Sat and Sun as well as on the numerous public holidays. The major travel companies, such as American Express and Thomas Cook (Wagons-Lits), will also accept mail for their clients. The addition of anything (such as 'Esq.') to the addressee's name on the first line can cause confusion, so is best avoided.

Getting around

The Greek train, bus and boat services complement each other well and if you use them you will see aspects of the Greek way of life that you might otherwise miss. It is an advantage to have a car, however, to get to the more remote areas of the mainland.

Flying

Olympic Airways, the country's only internal airline, runs services between the major cities and tourist centres, costing roughly two to three times the bus fare. It is also possible to hire air taxis from Athens Airport.

The airport itself is just outside Athens and is divided into two parts; the W half serves Olympic Airways only and operates its own bus service to the company's terminal at Syngrou Ave. 96; the E half serves foreign airlines and operates a bus service to Syntagma Sq. There is a connecting bus service between the two parts of the airport, but it is extremely slow.

Buses

For visitors, buses run by tour operators such as American Express, CHAT tours and Wagons-Lits/Cooks are of greatest interest. All are comfortable and air-conditioned.

For long distance journeys between major towns buses are cheap and on the whole efficiently organized, although in remote areas the buses themselves are often ancient. There are two bus organizations, the OSE (state railway) which operates from railway stations, and the KTEL (a group of private bus companies) which operates primarily from bus terminals, although it is also possible to board the bus at the roadside (stop it by raising your hand) if you are sure it is the correct KTEL for that particular district (*nomós*). Whichever company you travel with, it is advisable to book seats well in advance (from OSE or KTEL offices and bus terminals). Although some buses have air conditioning this does little to ease the discomfort on a crowded bus.

Local buses are often market buses with a once-a-day service taking the locals to and from the nearest town. They usually leave early in the morning and return in the evening. These buses are invariably crowded and get increasingly more so as passengers are picked up from the roadside.

Railway services

The railways in Greece are not widely used by tourists, except for the main Athens-Thessaloniki line. This operates from Stathmos Athinou (Athens station), which is still popularly known as Larissa station. The other part of the Hellenic Railway Organization (OSE) operating from Athens serves the Peloponnese from Stathmos Peloponissou (Peloponissou station). It is narrow-gauge and is the slower of the two systems. Buffet and restaurant cars are available on most mainline routes, as are first-class seats for a 50% surcharge. A 20% discount is allowed on a return ticket. Reservations for any route can be made through OSE, Karolou 1, Athens, or at a travel agent. English is spoken at the central ticket office, Sina 6, Athens ☎ 36–24–402/6. Athens possesses one electric railway, from Piraeus to Kifissia; part of this runs under the town centre, justifying the label 'subway'.

Taxis

Taxis are plentiful in most major towns and can also be found in small villages; finding a helpful taxi driver on the other hand is more a matter of luck. To judge by their apparent ignorance of addresses or of alternative ways to reach a destination many seem to have been in the city little longer than the tourist; and they may also refuse to drive in a direction they do not fancy. Metered taxis (the vast majority), which are painted yellow or light grey, rarely seem to have the sign lit to indicate availability, especially during the ever-longer rush hours. They are also inclined to pack in passengers, charging each the full fare; this is illegal and can be reported to the tourist police. A few drivers are genuinely helpful, however; often these are people who have worked abroad and have bought their own cabs. Unfortunately, however, there is no distinguishing the helpful from unhelpful in advance.

Although you might try to hail a passing cab or pick one up at the few taxi-stands, it saves trouble if you let your hotel porter make the arrangements. For longer outings – although it is fairly expensive – hire a large unmetered black cab, parked near the luxury hotels; the driver will speak elementary English.

Getting around by car

When Heraklitos of Ephesos (576–480BC) formulated his alarming discovery that everything is in a state of flux, he could not have foreseen traffic jams in present-day Greek towns. Although the number of private cars has increased 15 times during the last 15yr and despite prohibitive duties and taxes which have doubled the price of cars and, furthermore, even if the 100,000 trucks and buses are included, the ratio of vehicles to population is still well below the EEC average; the accident rate, however, is disproportionately high. Moreover, due to the spectacular rise in prosperity throughout the country, especially among farmers, cars are no longer concentrated in the two main towns, although you could easily believe the opposite if you have the misfortune to be caught in the Athens or Thessaloniki rush hours.

Driving in the two main cities demands iron nerves. Ill-tempered traffic jams are enlivened by the honking of horns, which is as strictly forbidden as the removal of silencers and the races between powerful motorbikes, locally called *kamikaze*, which, unlike their Japanese prototypes, are more lethal to pedestrians than to the riders. Several hundred convictions for traffic offences per day make no evident impact. When buses are on strike, private cars are allowed to take paying passengers, and chaos results; when the thousands of taxis strike, which is more frequent, it is bliss for the harassed pedestrians and private drivers, but a problem if one has to catch a plane or boat. Red lights are frequently ignored, with motorcyclists, buses and taxis in descending order the worst offenders.

The speed limit in towns is 50kph(31mph) and because of the density of traffic it is almost impossible to exceed it. Similarly, because of the condition of the country roads, it is unlikely that you will be able to exceed the 110kph(68mph) limit elsewhere.

Parking near the town centre is impossible, even in smaller towns, and problems are increased because garages and parking lots almost invariably refuse casual customers. Road signs forbidding parking must be observed, and it is not advisable to park on the pavement.

In contrast, motoring in the countryside is a joy; there are so many sights inviting you to stop that this more than makes up for the bad driving habits of the Greeks. Resign yourself to finding the slowest truck ambling along in the fast lane; this is readily accepted by the driver's compatriots who overtake him on both sides. At crossroads, size often comes before right of way and the smaller vehicle gets the worst of a collision.

It is compulsory for both the driver and the front-seat passenger to wear seat belts and for children to sit in the back seat. International road signs are in use. Vehicles drive on the right. EEC rules of the road apply, but do be flexible in the interpretation of them. Expect to pay tolls on the major Athens–Patra and Athens–Thessaloniki roads.

Despite the problems, there is one great redeeming feature when driving in Greece, and that is the extraordinary helpfulness of Greek drivers in case of a breakdown or some other trouble. Not only does the ELPA assist cars with foreign number plates free of charge, but when you are stuck in mud, sand or snow, carloads of willing Greeks will tumble out to give you a helping hand. And when you have been towed or have limped under your own steam to a garage, of which there are plenty throughout the country, Greek mechanics are almost invariably quick and efficient at their jobs.

Hiring a car

If you are not too daunted by the prospect of driving in Greece and want to hire a car, lists of car hire firms are readily available in the English-language newspaper or from a travel agent and from the GNTO both in your country of origin and in Greece. It is essential that you have an internationally valid driving licence and are over 23 years old. International companies are well represented in most major towns. The larger companies can arrange for a car to be at the airport, harbour or station for you to pick up when you arrive.

Because of high taxes it is expensive to hire a car. Often the quoted price does not include tax and the total may be substantially higher. It may be possible to negotiate a reduction, however, especially in the off-peak season. When hiring a car from a small town, always check its condition before you sign the contract. Rental is usually charged by the day with

11

a surcharge for more than 100km (62.5 miles), or by the week with unlimited distance. International car hire companies will accept payment by credit card.

Mopeds and bicycles

Mopeds and bicycles can be hired and are ideal means of transport in the more remote mainland areas and on the islands. Ask locally for addresses of hire companies.

Getting around on foot

In the major towns the traffic is so unpredictable that pedestrians must be especially careful. In the country, however, the walker is respected and the worst dangers are natural ones – bees, snakes, scorpions, and twisted ankles. Sheepdogs are also keen to protect their territory and can be vicious. It is wise to have a companion when walking.

Boats

Fairly frequent car and passenger services from Piraeus go to the islands and most of the coastal towns. Major travel agents such as American Express or Thomas Cook can supply information on all ferries; individual ferry companies tend to give details of their own services only. Times should always be checked again locally on the day of departure; in any case it is wise to arrive in good time because it is not unknown for berths to be sold more than once, and although you can nearly always get your money back the delay can be critical. First, second and deck classes are available. Cabins can be obtained on overnight journeys. Organized cruises are an excellent way to visit the islands – the GNTO can supply a list of tour operators who specialize in these. It is also possible to hire a boat, with or without crew, for sailing alone or as part of a flotilla.

On-the-spot information

Public holidays

Jan 1; Epiphany, Jan 6; Shrove Monday, usually early Mar; Annunciation, outbreak of the Greek War of Independence, Mar 25; Orthodox Good Friday to Easter Monday (up to four weeks later than Easter in the rest of Europe); May Day, May 1 (when this falls within the Easter weekend it is compensated for on the following Tues); Whit Monday, 50 days after Easter; Assumption of the Virgin, Aug 15; Ohi Day, rejection of the Italian ultimatum in 1940, Oct 28; Dec 25–26. Shops, banks, museums and some restaurants close on these days.

Time zones

Greece is in the same time zone as Eastern Europe, i.e. almost always 1hr ahead of EEC countries but 2hr ahead of GMT.

Banks and currency exchange

Money and travellers cheques are best exchanged at banks, which are open Mon–Fri 8.00–14.00 and sometimes later in the afternoons. On Sun and holidays some banks are open at airports, ports and border crossings. In Athens the National Bank of Greece, at the corner of Syntagma Sq. and Stadiou, remains open for money exchange Mon–Fri 8.00–21.00, Sat–Sun 8.00–20.00. There are no exchange offices, but travellers cheques, credit cards, personal cheques with a

Eurocheque card and dollar bills are accepted by hotels in the three top categories (L, A, B – see *Accommodation* in *Planning*) and even by some of the cheaper hotels in main towns and resorts; by the leading restaurants in larger towns, but not in the countryside, nor by cheaper establishments; and by the luxury and tourist shops in major centres. When using credit cards, however, be warned that some lesser restaurants, bars and shops which advertise that they accept credit cards have been known to overcharge customers who pay in this way; worse, the amount charged might be altered subsequently. Irregularities such as these should be reported to the tourist police.

Shopping and business hours
Shopping hours are a science unto themselves but, as a rule, shops open Mon, Wed, Sat 8.00–14.30, Tues, Thurs, Fri 8.00–13.30 and 17.00–20.00. Food stores, barbers, hairdressers and beauty parlours close later in the evening, open on Sat afternoons between 16.00–22.00 with variations, but close on Fri afternoons. All times are liable to vary between regions. Office hours vary depending on the size of the company and a siesta is often taken in the middle of the day. Most offices close on Wed and Sat afternoons.

Rush hours
Rush hours only affect the major cities but there they can be chaotic. Taxis are impossible to find and public transport appallingly crowded. Driving your own car should be avoided if at all possible. Times vary from place to place and the duration seems to be increasing, but as a rough guide expect peaks to coincide with the start and finish of shopping and office hours.

Post and telephone services
The post office (ELTA) and the telephone system (OTE) are independent of each other.

Post offices are usually open Mon–Fri 8.00–13.00, 15.00–19.00. The central office in Athens is open Mon–Fri 8.00–20.00. Stamps can also be bought in kiosks and in shops selling postcards. Letters can be posted in yellow letter boxes marked ΕΣΟΤΕΡΙΚΟΝ (Interior) for destinations within Greece and ΕΞΟΤΕΡΙΚΟΝ (Exterior) for foreign mail.

The postal service is notoriously slow, particularly during the summer when the system is overloaded, so it is best to use the telephone or send a telegram for urgent messages. Telegrams can be sent from post offices or from OTE centres. Parcels are not delivered and must be collected from the post office.

Local telephone calls can be made from coin-operated phone boxes (insert a coin before dialling; the coin will be refunded if you don't get through), or from kiosks, cafes or bars, where you pay the owner a set rate. Long distance calls must be made from an OTE office in a large town or a post office in a small town. In both cases you make your call from a booth then pay for it at the counter. Rates are slightly cheaper between 21.00–5.00. Patience is needed when telephoning some rural and island areas as the system is not necessarily operated 24hr a day.

Athens is currently changing from six-digit telephone numbers to seven-digit numbers, and this will tend to cause confusion until the new system is fully installed.

Public lavatories
Public lavatories (*toualéta*) are rare except in airports, stations and main squares, and they are often far from perfect. It is possible, however, to use the facilities at cafes and hotels but

even these may be fairly basic. There are usually symbols on the doors but it is as well to know that ΓΥΝΑΙΚΩΝ (*Gynaikón*) means 'women' and ΑΝΔΡΩΝ (*Andrón*) means 'men'. It is advisable to carry tissues with you.

Electric current
This is generally 220V AC. In more remote places, however, especially the islands, it is often still 110V DC, so check before you go and take an adaptor.

Laws and regulations
The Greek authorities are particularly strict about the use or smuggling of drugs and heavy penalties are enforced. Nude bathing, except on a few nudist beaches, is illegal and culprits can be arrested or fined. Topless sunbathing carries less severe penalties – and on the more expensive hotel beaches or on beaches near Athens it may merely be frowned upon or laughed at. Hitch-hiking is not illegal and therefore is easier and more enjoyable than in most countries. Smoking is forbidden in public places such as cinemas, theatres and on local buses.

Customs and etiquette
Because of the Mediterranean climate, a siesta is usually taken between 14.30–16.30. This is especially common in summer, when everything except for the traffic in central Athens comes to a halt and nothing should be disturbed. Restaurants stay open at lunchtime from 12.30–15.30 (sometimes 15.00 in package tour hotels); in the evenings they are open between 19.30–24.00; tavernas open and close at least an hour later. Most hotels serve evening meals only until 22.00.

A certain amount of formality is observed when meeting and parting: shaking hands is general, kissing on cheeks only applies between intimate friends.

Queues are formed occasionally, though you have to fight to keep your place and then join the mad rush as the queue disintegrates on the arrival of the bus or train.

Tipping
Tipping is generally expected, except by taxi drivers who will happily accept a small token of appreciation but who probably own their cars and round up the fare to the next zero anyway. Hotel and restaurant bills include a 15% service charge but menus often list two prices; the price excluding service only applies if you are taking your food in a container to eat outside. It is customary to leave an extra 10% to be divided among the staff in the better restaurants and hotels; in cheaper restaurants and in tavernas approximately 5–10% *must* be left on the table for the assistant waiter and not on the plate on which the bill is presented, where it will be taken by the head waiter. If the service is exceptional, of course, the head waiter may deserve a few extra drachmes too.

At Christmas and Easter, restaurant service charges are increased by 20% for two weeks; taxis likewise charge a holiday bonus; in cafes and bars, leave an extra 5%. Cabin and dining-room stewards on cruise ships should be tipped in proportion to the duration of the cruise. It is debatable whether tipping in advance will improve the service so follow your own preference.

Anything under 20–30% at barbers or hairdressers might give you an undesired new look next time round. Cinema and theatre ushers, cloakroom attendants and porters all expect their *obol* – only passing to the nether world is free. It is wise to carry a good supply of coins with you at all times.

Disabled travellers

Disabled visitors to Greece should not expect the specially
adapted facilities that are becoming common in other countries.
The GNTO list of tour operators includes the names and
addresses of companies that may be able to make arrangements
for disabled travellers.

Local publications

The English-language newspaper is the *Athens News*, which
reports local news and includes information on local events. *The
Athenian*, a monthly journal, is useful for up-to-date
entertainment and restaurant reviews. The GNTO publishes
several leaflets in English on different topics. For local events,
The Week in Athens is a useful and reliable source of
information. It is also possible to buy official, monthly
timetables, *Greek Travel Pages* and *Key Travel Guide*, for
detailed planning of journeys.

Tourist police

The tourist police have the same power as the ordinary police
but are also specially briefed to help the visitor. They can be
recognized by the shoulder flash 'Tourist police' on their
uniforms. Many of them also wear badges indicating the
languages they speak. They are often the best source of advice
about accommodation, although they are not obliged to find
you somewhere to stay, and you must make your own booking
arrangements once they have given you some suggestions.

Useful addresses

Tourist information

Greek National Tourist Organization (GNTO)   Syntagma Sq.,
Karageorgi Servias 2, Athens ☎(01) 32–22–545; Elleniko
Airport, East Terminal, Athens ☎(01) 97–99–500
Tourist police (for complaints)   Syngrou Ave. 7, Athens
☎(01) 92–39–224. In smaller towns and resorts where there is
no GNTO office contact the tourist police for any information
that you require
Olympic Airways   Town terminal: Syngrou Ave. 96, Athens
☎(01) 92–92–251; Ticket offices: Othonos 6, Syntagma Sq.,
Athens ☎(01) 92–92–555 (international), or
☎(01) 92–92–444 (domestic)
Hilton Hotel   ☎(01) 92–92–445
Automobile and Tourist Club of Greece (ELPA)   Tower of
Athens, Messogio 2, Athens ☎(01) 77–91–615

Tour operators

American Express   Ermou 2, Athens ☎(01) 32–44–975
CHAT tours   Stadiou 4, Athens ☎(01) 32–22–886
Thomas Cook and *Wagons-Lits/Cooks*   Karageorgi Servias 2,
Athens ☎(01) 32–28–650 and 32–42–281

Main post offices (tahidromío)

Eolou 100, Athens
Syntagma Sq., Athens

Major places of worship

St Andrew's American/Protestant Church   Sina 66, Athens
St Denis' Roman Catholic Cathedral   Venizelou 24, Athens
St Paul's English Church   Filellinon 29, Athens
Synagogue   Melidoni 5, Athens.

15

Basic information

Consulates in Athens

Australia   Messogio 15, Athens 609 ☎(01) 36–04–611/5
Austria   Alexandras Ave. 26, Athens 148 ☎(01) 82–16–800
Belgium   Sekeri 3, Athens 134 ☎(01) 36–17–886/7
Canada   Ioannou Gennadiou 4, Athens 140 ☎(01) 739–511
Denmark   Dragatsianou 6, Athens 138 ☎(01) 32–46–611
Finland   Valaoritou 17, Athens 138 ☎(01) 36–18–411
France   Amalias Ave. 36, Athens 134 ☎(01) 32–30–476
Germany, West (FDR)   Loukianou 3, Athens 139
☎(01) 724–801
Ireland   Vassileos Konstantinou 7, Athens 138
☎(01) 732–771
Italy   Sekeri 2, Athens 138 ☎(01) 36–13–444
Japan   Vassilissis Sofias Ave. 64, Athens 140
☎(01) 733–732/3/5
Netherlands   Vassileos Konstantinou 5–7, Athens 138
☎(01) 739–701
New Zealand   An. Tsoha 15–17, Athens 618
☎(01) 64–10–311
Norway   Vassileos Konstantinou 7, Athens 138
☎(01) 746–173
South Africa   Vassilissis Sofias Ave. 69, Athens 140
☎(01) 749–806
Spain   Vassilissis Sofias Ave. 29, Athens 138
☎(01) 714–885/724–242
Sweden   Vassileos Konstantinou 7, Athens 138
☎(01) 724–504
Switzerland   Iassiou 2, Athens 140 ☎(01) 730–364/5/6
United Kingdom   Ploutarchou 1, Athens 139 ☎(01) 736–211
United States of America   Vassilissis Sofias Ave. 91, Athens 602
☎(01) 712–951/718–561

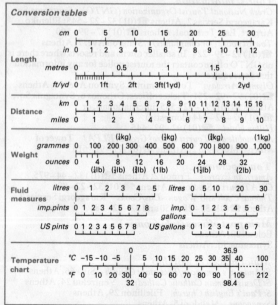

16

Emergency information

Emergency services
Police (cities) ☎100
First Aid (Red Cross) ☎166
In Greece, the most readily available source of assistance in
an emergency is the reception desk of your hotel.

Other emergencies
Gendarmerie (suburbs and country) ☎109
Emergency road service ☎104
Tourist police (Athens) ☎171
   For other towns see *A–Z* entries.

Medical emergencies
In Athens, the First Aid Centre (☎166) can tell you which
hospital is admitting casualties that day. The ELPIS dental
hospital answers emergency calls between 22.00–6.00
☎(01) 64–30–001. In other areas emergency telephone
numbers are displayed near public telephones.

Late-night chemists
In Athens ☎107 for a list of all-night pharmacies, or look in
the *Athens News*. In other areas, a list of late-night
pharmacies is displayed in all chemists' windows.

Motoring accidents
—If anyone is injured the police will intervene and,
   particularly if a pedestrian or cyclist has been hit, the
   driver may be arrested, even if clearly innocent. Ask for
   immediate assistance from your consulate.
—Exchange names, addresses, car details and insurance
   companies' names and addresses with other driver(s)
   concerned.
—If you are clearly responsible it may save time and trouble
   to say so. Contact the police, but if no one is injured they
   may show reluctance to be involved.
—Ask witnesses for their names and addresses, and for a
   statement.

Car breakdowns
—Pull into the roadside.
—Put on flashing hazard warning lights and place a warning
   triangle 50m(55yd) behind the car.
—☎104 for ELPA (Automobile and Touring Club of
   Greece) which assists foreign drivers free of charge and
   officers speak English.

Lost passport/travellers cheques
Passport: Report the loss immediately to the police and
contact your consulate (see opposite page) for emergency
travel documents.
Travellers cheques: Contact the local police immediately,
then contact the issuing bank, or the address given by the
issuing company.

Emergency phrases
Help! *Voítheia!*
There has been an accident.   *Égine éne dystýhima.*
Where is the nearest telephone/hospital?   *Poú ínai tó
   plisiéstero tiléfono/nosokomío?*
Call a doctor/ambulance!   *Kaléste éna iatró/asthenofóro!*
Call the police!   *Kaléste tín astynomía!*

Introduction

Visitors used to come to Greece for the glory that was; now they come to glory on the beaches. Far from being incompatible, however, the two may be enjoyably combined, though sightseeing, obviously, is less strenuous in the cooler seasons. But even when swimming is out, sunbathing is in, all over this peninsula jutting from the Balkans into the Eastern Mediterranean. Four-fifths of Greece's 131,944sq.km (50,944sq. miles) are mountainous, only two-fifths cultivable, and there are 15,020km (9,387 miles) of coastline (much of it on 1,425 islands scattered over the Aegean and Ionian seas) – more than enough for a lifetime of holidays, certainly enough for the holiday of a lifetime. . . .

Small wonder, then, that the number of tourists visiting Greece every year is little short of two-thirds of the country's population. Tourism has overtaken even shipping as the country's largest industry, though the merchant fleet, at 43 million tons, ranks third in the world's fleets – first, if all ships owned under flags of convenience by those fabulous shipping tycoons are included.

Though the country's vegetation is determined by the dry climate and soil, men and goats share responsibility for destroying the great forests of antiquity. Beeches, chestnuts, oaks, plane trees, pines and firs, however, still cover the more remote mountain ranges, while bay, juniper and myrtle are spread thinly over sparse heaths encircled by barren peaks. Wild flowers and scented herbs abound in the mountains, and, on the gentler slopes, graceful cypress trees stand guard over vast orchards and groves of citrus and olive.

Such variety, however, in land- and seascape is matched, indeed surpassed, by the art and architecture of Greece, whose splendour recalls 600yr of Antiquity (Archaic, Classical, Hellenistic and Roman), and the 2,000yr periods preceding and following that highpoint of human achievement.

The 9.7 million individualists who inhabit the present-day Hellenic Republic take pride in their great ancestors, while standing in equal need of preserving their self-regard. The unpredictable caprices of the hero-prima donna Achilles, sulking in his tent, and the wiles of Odysseus, too cunning for his own good, have remained twin prototypes of the Greek character since they were first illuminated by the genius of Homer, nearly 3,000yr ago. They have continued to defy all manner of racial inter-breeding, and remain manifest both in public and private behaviour.

Deep down, for example, every Greek knows he is better than any other Greek. He may loudly claim for Greece the invention of democracy, but he has little use for egalitarianism, considering himself just a little more equal than others. Greeks, however, may be dominated but are rarely blinded by their egos; and if their sense of humour occasionally lacks subtlety, their good nature and zest for living make up for this to a large degree.

As a nation, the Greeks look to politics, not to their native ancient drama, for high tragedy and low comedy. But for maximum enjoyment, frequent changes of protagonists are required – though the chorus keeps on repeating the same stale old lines. Could it be that the Greeks, after all their vicissitudes, have thus found the ultimate secret of achieving continuity through change?

Time chart

c.4000–3000BC	Neolithic settlements on the mainland, mainly in Thessaly. Matriarchates.
c.3500	Crete occupied from Asia Minor.
c.3000–1400	Minoan civilization in Crete. The Palace Periods. Priest-kings.
c.1450	Destruction of Knossos and Phaestos in Crete. End of Minoan Empire.
c.1450–1200	Achaean principalities under feudal overlordship of Mycenae, in the Peloponnese.
c.1230–1220	Trojan War: a host of Greek princes united under Agamemnon of Mycenae.
c.1200–800	Dorian invasion. Destruction of Mycenaean cities. The Dark Ages.
c.800–700	The Reawakening, starting in Aeolia (the islands) and Ionia (Asia Minor). Monarchies overthrown and landed oligarchies established throughout Greece, except in Sparta, where the semi-legendary Lykurgos created a unique totalitarian system. Sparta began to be the leading military power. Fame of the Delphic oracle established.
776	First Olympic Games.
700–600	The Greek city states colonized European shores of the Mediterranean. Aristocratic oligarchies replaced by tyrannies – the rule of one tyrant – a link between oligarchy and democracy.
650–550	Corinth and Aegina the main trading powers.
593–560	Solon's social reforms, intended to prevent tyranny and based on rational compromise ("Nothing in excess"), failed to prevent civil war in Athens.
560–510	Enlightened tyranny of Pisistratos and his sons, Hippias and Hipparchos, imposed Solon's reforms.
530–515	Temple of Apollo at Delphi rebuilt by the rival Alkmaeonid family, which altogether dominated Athenian politics for 200yr.
514–510	Hipparchos assassinated. Manipulated by the Alkmaeonid Klisthenes, the Delphic oracle commanded the Spartans to overthrow Hippias. Spartan invasion, and expulsion of Hippias from Athens.
510–500	Democratic reforms of Klisthenes in Athens.
499–493	The Ionian Revolt. The Greek towns of Asia Minor, assisted by Athens, rose against the Persians.
492–490	Two Persian expeditions sent in revenge against Athens. The first was wrecked in a storm off Mt. Athos, the second defeated at Marathon.
481–478	Most Greek states united under the command of Sparta to resist the Persian army of the Great King, Xerxes. Battle of Thermopylae. Xerxes in Athens: destruction of the Acropolis. Naval battles of Salamis and Mykale won by the Greeks. The decisive battle of Plataea won by the Greeks. Themistokles of Athens founded the Delian League to liberate the Greek towns of Asia Minor.
478–458	Under leadership of Kimon, Athens transformed the Delian League into an Athenian empire. Ostracism of Themistokles who *in absentia* was condemned to death. Rise of the Alkmaeonid Perikles and ostracism of Kimon.

19

Culture, history and background

	Roman Empire to Byzantium, which he renamed and embellished with Greek statuary. Christianity became the state religion.
379–395	The Edict of Theodosius the Great proscribing paganism. The sanctuaries of Delphi and Olympia closed. The Roman Empire divided; the eastern part would become the future Byzantine Empire.
395	Gothic raids into Greece.
467–477	Vandal raids.
527–565	The Academy in Athens closed by Justinian I. Greek superseded Latin as the official language. Temples converted into churches, or despoiled.
577	Beginning of continued invasions by Avars and Slavs. The latter settled in increasing numbers in Greece, until only a few Greek towns remained scattered in a Slav countryside.
976–1025	Emperor Basil II ('the Bulgar slayer') re-established effective imperial rule.
1040–84	Repeated invasions by Sicilian Normans.
1054	Schism between the Roman and Greek Churches.
1204–06	The Fourth Crusade captured and sacked Constantinople. Establishment of the Latin Empire. Occupation of many islands by Venice.
1206–61	The Latin Empire disintegrated. Michael Palaeologos reconquered Constantinople.
1261– 1387	Feudal anarchy. The Palaeologues regained some territory in Greece; the ephemeral Serbian Empire extended into Thessaly; unpaid Catalan mercenaries pillaged the countryside.
1387– 1453	The Turks overthrew the Bulgarian, Serbian, and finally the Byzantine, empires.
1453	Fall of Constantinople to the Turks.
1460– 1500	The Peloponnese surrendered to the Turks by the Byzantines. Venice kept the Ionian Islands.
1687	Accidental damage to the Parthenon during the Venetian siege of Athens by Admiral Morosini.
1770	Abortive Greek revolt.
1797– 1815	The Ionian Islands, freed from Venice, became Russian, French, then British.
1800–22	Rise and fall of Ali Pasha.
1821	Mar 25: Greek Independence declared.
1821–29	War of Independence.
1823–24	Lord Byron elected commander of the Greek forces. Death of Byron at Messolongi.
1825	Turkish rule restored over the Peloponnese by the intervention of Ibrahim Pasha of Egypt.
1827	Count John Capodistrias, former foreign secretary of the Russian Tsar, elected as first president of Greece. Battle of Navarino: destruction of Turkish fleet.
1831	Assassination of Capodistrias led to anarchy.
1832	Independence of Greece. Election of Prince Otho of Bavaria as king.
1833–62	Arrival of King Otho at Nafplio, capital of the new kingdom, with numerous Bavarians. Capital transferred to Athens. Bavarian Council of Regency followed by personal government when Otho refused to call a National Assembly. Bloodless revolution. New constitution and dismissal of the Bavarian officials. Unsuccessful Greek attempt to

	seize Epiros and Thessaly. An Anglo-French fleet occupied Piraeus. Army revolt: Otho resigned.
1863–81	The young Danish Prince George I became 'King of the Hellenes'. Constant Christian uprisings in the Balkans caused a Russo-Turkish war, which Russia won. The Conference of Constantinople awarded Thessaly to Greece, and self-government to Crete.
1896	First revived Olympic Games held in Athens.
1897– 1913	Another Cretan rising provoked war with Turkey, who reoccupied Thessaly. Anglo-French intervention. The Turks were granted N Thessaly in exchange for autonomy for Crete under Prince George of Greece. Union of Crete with Greece proclaimed by the Cretan statesman Venizelos who became prime minister of Greece. Formation of Balkan League against Turkey. First Balkan War: Greek army occupied Epiros and Macedonia. George I murdered. Second Balkan War between allied Balkan states and Bulgaria. Treaty of Bucharest doubled area of Greece.
1914–24	Opposing King Constantine's neutrality in World War I, Venizelos proclaimed a provisional government. Constantine forced into exile by the Allies. Alexander, his son, became king. Greece, under Venizelos, entered the war on the Allied side. Death of Alexander. Overwhelming plebiscite vote for King Constantine. Venizelos exiled. Defeat of the Greek army in Asia Minor. Revolt by colonels forced Constantine's abdication in favour of his son, George II. Venizelos represented Greece at the Lausanne Peace Conference. Greece renounced E Thrace and Smyrna. Exchange of populations: two million Greeks for 370,000 Moslems.
1924–35	Departure of King George II. The armed forces proclaimed a republic, but military dictatorship was followed by parliamentary rule under Venizelos.
1935	Monarchy restored after 97% plebiscite majority.
1936–41	Dictatorship of Metaxas after the failure of constitutional government.
1940	Italian invasion of Greece in World War II.
1941	Landing and evacuation of British Expeditionary Force on mainland and Crete.
1941–44	German-Italian-Bulgarian occupation of Greece.
1944–45	Greece in Western bloc; first Communist rebellion.
1947–49	Second Communist rebellion; American support for government under the Truman Doctrine.
1949–64	Period of recovery under Marshal Papagos; NATO membership.
1964–67	Succession of unstable governments.
1967–74	Establishment of a junta of colonels. King Constantine left Greece. Numerous plebiscites, the last voting for a republic. Proclamation of a republic and lifting of martial law. Following riots, coup d'état by a hard core of officers.
1974	Intervention in Cyprus brought Greece to the brink of war with Turkey. Parliamentary democracy under the former conservative prime minister Karamanlis replaced military dictatorship, and a plebiscite confirmed the republic.
1981	EEC membership. A socialist government elected.

Art and architecture

All periods are approximate and often overlap.

Art and architecture in pre-Archaic Greece

Palaeolithic (*600,000–7000BC*)   Continuing discoveries of bones, tools and utensils, mostly in caves, push back ever further the evidence of early Man in Greece.

Neolithic (*7000–2700BC*)   Development of cultivation and stock-breeding. Clay vases and statuettes. Citadels built at Sesklo and Dimini, near Volos in Thessaly.

Bronze Age (*2800–1100BC*)   The introduction from the east of the use of metal underlay the rise of the first three major civilizations, the Cycladic, Minoan and Helladic.

Cycladic (*2700–1400BC*)   Influences absorbed through trading encouraged the development of original art forms throughout the Cyclades, especially on Kea, Milos and Paros, with marble and clay idols, and vases in animal shapes or with geometric ornamentation.

Crete: Early Minoan (*2600–1900BC*)   Multi-coloured stone vases found in vaulted graves. Advanced use of metalwork.

Crete: Middle Minoan (*1900–1550BC*)   The Palace Period. Large, luxurious palaces at Knossos, Phaestos and Malia destroyed by earthquake and rebuilt on even grander scale. Exquisite *Kamarés* pottery, polychrome decoration, floral and geometric designs. Linear A script.

Crete: Late Minoan (*1550–1450BC*)   Continuation of Palace Period, with even more refined frescoes. Villas built at Agia Triada, Praisos and on island of Thira. Linear B script. Vases decorated with marine flora and fauna. Main finds are in the Archaeological Museum at Iraklio.

Helladic (*2800–1400BC*)   Centred on Attica, Boeotia and Evia, the Helladic evolved under Minoan influence into the **Mycenaean** civilization. This climaxed by 1300BC with the building of the citadels of Mycenae, Tirynth and Pylos in the Peloponnese, and Gla and Thebes in Boeotia – all stark, militarized adaptations of Minoan palaces. Superb gold masks found in the royal shaft graves. Circular domed beehive tombs. Main finds are in the National Archaeological Museum in Athens.

Geometric (*1000–700BC*)   (Also called **Homeric**.) Slow reawakening after the Dark Ages which followed Dorian invasion of Greece. Introduction of universal alphabet of Phoenician origin. Red terra cotta vases. Human and animal statuettes.

After the Geometric Period it is easier to trace the development of architecture separately from that of the other visual arts. The latter are described first.

Sculpture, painting and ceramics from 700BC

Archaic (*700–480BC*)   The characteristic features of Greek art developed as Dorian simplicity merged with orientalized Ionian elements. Sculptors long continued to maintain the traditional Egyptian style of attaching rigid limbs to the body, both in *xoána* (wooden idols) and in sometimes colossal *kouroi* – nude, vigorous youths carved in soft stone or marble. Only at the end of the period were hands and feet allowed some freedom of movement, though faces continued to wear a conventional smile. More attractive are the *korae*, which are almond-eyed maidens clothed in artistic folds.

Culture, history and background

The new art forms spread slowly from Ionia via the islands to Argos, Athens, Corinth and Sikyon. Best examples of this period are in the Acropolis Museum in Athens and the museum at Delphi.

Rich, oriental decorations of sphinxes, sirens, flowers and ornaments prevailed on ceramics from the islands, especially on Rhodes, then spread to Corinth and Athens, where they were eventually replaced by vases with black figures on a red background, depicting mythological and domestic scenes. Finally, red figures on a black background, greatly refined in style, were developed, establishing the undisputed artistic pre-eminence of Athens. Best examples are in the museum at Corinth and the National Archaeological Museum in Athens.

Classical (*480–338BC*)   The great architectural masterpieces of this period provided a magnificent setting for the chryselephantine (gold and ivory), bronze and marble sculptures of Myron, Paeonias, Phidias and Polykletos during the 5thC BC, Skopas, Praxiteles and Timotheos in the 4thC BC, and the paintings of Mikon and Polygnotos. Terra cotta statuettes from Tanagra excelled in realism and elegance. Polychrome decorations and fine vases with white backgrounds

Gold cup, c.1500BC, found near Sparta. The Minoan style and theme suggest a Cretan artist working on the mainland.

Detail from **Athenian black figure vase**, c.540BC, by Exekias, whose compositions influenced Western painting.

A rare surviving bronze of the 5thC BC: the **statue of a warrior**, found in a shipwreck off Riace, S. Italy.

Hermes with the Child Dionysos, c.330BC, a marble statue by Praxiteles, found at Olympia in 1877.

were created by Athenian potters, and good examples are in the National Archaeological Museum at Athens.

Hellenistic (338–146BC) To the classical purity of Greece, the conquests of Alexander the Great introduced the rich, Corinthian style and the often colossal scale of sculpture characteristic of the new centres of civilization in Asia Minor and Egypt. Highlights of this period included the bronzes of Lysippos, chryselephantine statues of Leochares, and portraits and allegories of Apelles and Protogenes. Only Roman copies survive of the paintings; and the most important sculptures are in Berlin, Istanbul, London and Paris.

In Greece itself, Athens for a while conceded pre-eminence to Rhodes, where Chares of Lindos fashioned the famous *Colossus*. Athens later regained its dominance through the archaic-influenced Neo-Attic school.

The tombs of Vergina and Derveni, whose gold and silver treasures are the pride of the Archaeological Museum at Thessaloniki, illustrate the Baroque, Rococo and classicistic phases which coexisted in classical Greece. Though by now Greece was an artistic and political backwater, rival Hellenistic dynasties continued to dedicate outstanding masterpieces in its temples. The school of Pergamon, dominant for some 50yr, provided the sculpture with which the kings of Pergamon enhanced Athens. Linear and floral motifs predominated on vases, with a black or white background, often in relief.

Roman (146BC–AD525) Despite flourishing artistic activity, this was a largely imitative period. Sculpture represented the classical gods, and portraits of the Roman emperors were modelled on Hellenistic kings. Some more original works are statues of Hadrian's favourite, Antinous, and of matrons characteristic of the period.

Byzantine and post-Byzantine (From AD525) Byzantine art forms included the ikon, mosaics and frescoes. Paradoxically dating from after the fall of Byzantium, the best Byzantine paintings in Greece are the ikons of the Macedonian school (14th–16thC) and the Cretan school (16th–18thC), with important examples of both in the monasteries of Mt. Athos.

Architecture in Greece from 700BC

Archaic (700–480BC) During this period the Greek temple, with its sloping roof and pediments, and portico of columns with Doric or Ionic capitals, completed its evolution from the Mycenaean royal hall. Wood and mudbrick were replaced by limestone and marble, stuccoed and painted. Towns moved to the plain below the acropolis, usually leaving it to become a religious sanctuary. Architectural landmarks include the Temple of Apollo in Corinth, the Heraions of Argos, Olympia and Samos, and the Sanctuary of Brauron.

Classical (480–338BC) The glory that was Greece is largely concentrated in this period of 150yr, during which the architects Iktinos, Kallikrates, Mnesikles and others endowed Athens with masterpieces in the Doric and Ionic styles. Other sites are temples at Aegina, Bassae, Delos, Delphi, Olympia and Sounio, and the fortified cities of Megalopoli and Messini in the Peloponnese. Perfect acoustics were achieved in amphitheatres such as that at Epidaurus.

Hellenistic (338–146BC) Alexander the Great's conquests in Asia Minor and Egypt led to the introduction of the grandiose, Corinthian order. Delos has the largest choice of remains from this period, though the excavation of Pella, the Macedonian

Culture, history and background

capital, promises even more important finds. In Athens, the kings of Pergamon built the Stoas of Attalos and Eumenes.

Roman (146BC–AD525) After the destruction of Corinth and the Roman dictator Sulla's plundering of Athens' artistic treasures, Julius Caesar inaugurated a new era with the rebuilding of Corinth, though this was soon outshone by a settlement for veteran soldiers at Philippi, built by Augustus. Nikopolis, founded by Augustus, and Athens, enlarged with imposing public buildings by Hadrian, have the most important Roman ruins in Greece. Hadrian and his close friend, the banker Herodes Atticus, also financed the decoration of the main Greek sanctuaries in the Roman Corinthian style.

The temples were closed following the introduction of Christianity, and secular styles were adapted to religious use in large, brick basilicas.

Byzantine, Frankish, Venetian and Turkish *(AD521–1821)* In the 6thC AD, Justinian converted several temples into churches after extensively adapting their interiors. In this way several important buildings, including the Parthenon and Theseion, were preserved. He is also credited with founding several monasteries on the sites of pagan churches, for example at Daphni and Kaisariani, and he built a series of fortresses stretching from the Ionian to the Black Sea, most notably at Ioanina.

The traditional cross-in-square plan of later Byzantine churches evolved from the basic rectangular basilica. This was crowned either by a single dome, as at Daphni, or, more often, by several small cupolas, and the stone masonry was usually broken by decorative lines of brick or tiles. Local variations on this traditional plan prevailed till the fall of the Byzantine Empire and were resumed in the Neo-Byzantine churches of modern Greece.

The interior followed strict rules. The ikonostasis, a screen either of sculptured marble or of wood with paintings of the saints, railed off the altar which was visible only through a central opening. For lack of money, mosaics were replaced from the 13thC by frescoes. The central image of Christ *Pantokrátor* (Almighty) filled the central dome above images of the Apostles. Images of the Virgin in the apse behind the altar,

The 11thC church at **Daphni** typifies the single-dome cross-in-square plan.

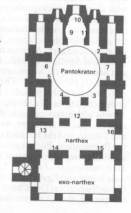

Key to mosaics
1 Annunciation; 2 Nativity; 3 Baptism; 4 Transfiguration; 5 Entry into Jerusalem; 6 Crucifixion; 7 Resurrection; 8 Thomas; 9 Michael; 10 Virgin with Child; 11 Gabriel; 12 Assumption of the Virgin; 13 Last Supper; 14 Judas' Betrayal; 15 Prayer of Joachim and Anna; 16 Presentation of the Virgin

and scenes from the Gospels and hosts of almost identical saints all over the church, were also characteristic.

Church building never stopped, even during the unceasing invasions of the early Middle Ages: the Church of Panagia Ekatontapyliani on Paros provides the most original example. But most of the tiny churches which survive in towns, and the large monasteries in remote, sheltered places, date from the 10thC revival under the Macedonian dynasty.

During the Despotates of Epiros and Mystra important churches were built in their respective capitals, Arta (13thC) and Mystra (14th–15thC). The Franks and Venetians are remembered mostly for their fortifications, which were often built on earlier foundations. In keeping with their feudal system, the Franks constructed powerful private castles, of which the best preserved example is the 13thC Kastel Tornese in the Peloponnese; at Mystra, the 13thC Frankish castle towers above the Gothic Palace of the Despots.

The Venetians surrounded whole towns with immense walls, as at Akro-Corinth and Nafplio. At the latter they also built some churches and as on Corfu, tall, elegant houses. From the 15thC on, the Turks repaired the Venetian walls, converted numerous churches into mosques, built a few of their own – especially in Crete, Macedonia and Thrace – and added some elegant fountains.

Aegean architecture (*1300–1870*) Climatic as well as historical considerations gave rise to distinctive local styles, only the most significant of which are mentioned below.

The basic cubic house with its flat roof or vault evolved during the decline of the Byzantine Empire, but the practice of whitewashing is recent, when it became no longer essential for fear of pirates to blend in with the surrounding rocks. The vaulted churches, often with blue cupolas, have been shared for centuries by the Orthodox and Catholic faiths, mainly in the Cyclades. The main building materials, soft stone and clay, produce a pleasing uniformity.

The Knights of St John introduced a Western European medieval style on Rhodes, during their period of rule from 1310–1522.

Architecture in the Peloponnese (*1450–1870*) In the Mani, the height of the nearly 800 towers was intended to reflect the status of their constantly feuding occupiers. These grim reminders of a bloody past are crumbling away, except at Vathia, now restored as a traditional settlement, and at Areopoli.

Architecture on the mainland (*1650–1870*) Architectural landmarks include the *arhontiká*, or mansions of wealthy merchants, in which wooden beams were put to both decorative and functional use. The towns of Kastoria, Siatista and Thessaloniki in Macedonia, Ioanina and Metsovo in Epiros, and the villages on Mt. Pilio in Thessaly, are all characteristic of this period.

Othonian architecture (*1832–1910*) The Neo-Classical German architects who followed King Otho to Greece created a domestic Othonian style. One- or two-storey stuccoed houses were built with shallow porches, Ionic columns, ornamental wrought-iron balconies, and terra cotta roof-edgings and statues. Prevalent in Athens and southern Greece until the 1950s, most of these buildings have since been replaced by featureless blocks of flats though some remain in the countryside.

The Greek temple

Intended to accommodate only a deity and priests, the temple was too small for worshippers, and there was an outside altar for public ceremonies. After various experiments, the rectangular plan built in the Doric or Ionic order prevailed by the 7thC BC. Though called after the two main Greek tribes, the orders were at first geographically determined, the Ionic order predominating in Asia Minor and the Doric on the Greek mainland. In the middle of the 4thC BC, the Corinthian order was introduced, lavishly ornamented with carved foliage, but it was never as distinctive as the other two, being essentially a variation of Ionic.

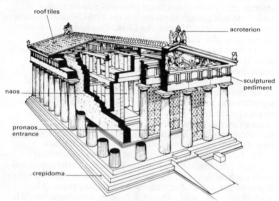

roof tiles

acroterion

naos

sculptured pediment

pronaos entrance

crepidoma

Temple of Aphaia, Egina: cutaway reconstruction.

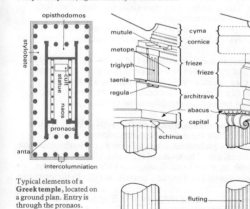

opisthodomos

stylobate

cult statue

naos

pronaos

anta

intercolumniation

Typical elements of a **Greek temple**, located on a ground plan. Entry is through the pronaos.

mutule

metope

triglyph

taenia

regula

cyma

cornice

frieze

frieze

dentils

architrave

abacus

capital

fascia

echinus

volute

fluting

torus

base

plinth

stylobate

Elements of the **Doric** (left) and **Ionic** (right) Orders. The proportions and the details differ but the fundamental divisions are constant.

Mythology

The ancient Greeks created their gods in the likeness of men. Their vices and virtues were painted only slightly larger than lifesize. Even their immortality was not inherent, but depended on eating and drinking ambrosia and nectar.

The earliest inhabitants of Greece had worshipped and sacrificed men to the **Great Goddess** until towards 1000BC, when successive Hellenic invasions finally destroyed the prehistoric matriarchal society and established male supremacy. They also worshipped local nature divinities – river gods, satyrs and wood nymphs – whose attributes the invaders' gods gradually took over. Later these were identified with various oriental deities, assimilated by the Romans and, in the early Christian period, the powers of some of the minor gods were even associated with certain saints. In the following outline, alternative names are given in brackets.

Creation started from **Chaos. Gaea** (*Earth*) gave birth to **Ouranos** (*Uranus, Heaven*), whose prolific weeping for shame at his mother's nakedness created the Mediterranean and Black Sea, dividing the earth disc into two equal parts surrounded by the River **Okeanos** (*Ocean*), while scattered tears accounted for rivers, lakes, the world's flora and even its fauna. At the centre of the Earth lay Greece. And at her centre, the navel of the Earth, was *Delphi*.

The world was first populated with the incestuous and hideous offspring of Gaea and Ouranos. The three hundred-handed **Giants** and three **Cyclopes** disappointed Ouranos who cast them into **Tartaros** (*Hell*). Then came seven male and female **Titans** who were persuaded by their mother, Earth, to castrate Ouranos their father. They divided the world between them under the leadership of the youngest, **Kronos** (*Time*). Because Kronos refused to liberate his brothers – the Giants and Cyclopes – from Tartaros, Gaea cursed him in turn to be overthrown by his children. To avoid this fate he attempted to devour them all, but his sister, **Rea**, who was also their mother, substituted a stone for the sixth child, **Zeus**.

Zeus was brought up in a cave at Dikti on *Crete*, with his goat-footed foster brother **Pan**, by the goat **Amalthea**. Returning to the paternal household as cup-bearer Zeus administered an emetic, supplied by his mother Rea, to Kronos, causing the latter to disgorge the substitute stone – which became the prized possession of the Delphic oracle – and the five undigested older brothers, at whose hands Kronos then met his fate.

After the fulfilment of Gaea's curse, the brothers Zeus, **Poseidon** and **Hades** divided heaven, the sea and the Underworld between them. The Cyclopes, now released, gave Zeus his thunderbolts, which he used to defeat a final revolt of the Titans as they attacked **Mt. Olympos** by piling **Pelion** (Mt. Pilio) on **Ossa** to scale it. Zeus set about establishing his dynasty by first raping his mother Rea, then his sister **Hera**, whom he subsequently wed. Their marriage was not successful, however, and despite Hera's borrowing of Aphrodite's girdle to arouse her husband, only **Ares, Hebes** and **Hephaestos** were born in wedlock. **Aphrodite** herself and **Athena** were born miraculously; and the twins **Apollo** and **Artemis, Hermes** and **Dionysos**, all Zeus' illegitimate offspring, joined their half-siblings on Olympos.

The following is a brief alphabetical account of Zeus' companions on Olympos and of his brothers, Hades and Poseidon.

29

Aphrodite (*Venus*)

Aphrodite is first encountered as she emerges naked and fully grown from the sea at Cyprus, from where she sailed in a shell to *Kythira*. She only gradually came to conform to the stricter Greek behaviour and in *Corinth* she remained associated with the sacred prostitutes. Little remains of the sanctuary at **Akro-Corinth**, however. The statue found in 1820 at *Milos*, now in Paris in the Louvre, is the best-known ancient representation of her.

Even among the Olympians, Aphrodite excelled in capriciousness and inconstancy, and as a penalty she was married to her unattractive half-brother **Hephaestos**. Among her offspring were double-sexed **Hermaphroditos** and **Eros** (*Cupid*).

Apollo (*Phoebos*)

Hera forbade Mother Earth to provide a place for **Leto** (*Latona*) to give birth to the fruits of her union with **Zeus**, and sent a monstrous sea serpent, **Python**, to pursue the expectant mother. **Poseidon** offered the floating island of *Delos* where the twins **Artemis** and **Apollo** were born. Apollo grew up in the land of the **Hyperboreans**, identified as the British Isles, then returned to kill Python, who was guarding the sacred cave at *Delphi*, an act commemorated in the quadrennial Pythian games.

Apollo is also associated with public health – oddly, perhaps, because his silver arrows were a cause of epidemics. He also merges with the sun god, **Ilios** (*Helius*) who, heralded by **Eros** (*Dawn*), drove a fiery chariot daily across the sky and sailed back at night on **Okeanos**.

Ares (*Mars*)

Though a legitimate son of **Zeus**, the god of war was several times defeated – twice by his half-sister **Athena**, and once by **Herakles**. Impetuous and good-looking, but nevertheless unpopular among both gods and mortals, he had only minor temples dedicated to him and no major sanctuary or shrine. As Roman Mars, he came into his own, however, appropriately at *Nikopoli*.

Artemis (*Diana*)

The first-born of Leto's twins, she somewhat precociously assisted at the birth of her brother, **Apollo**, the following day. The great huntress took nightly baths but spared none of those who had the fortune, or misfortune, to observe her nakedness. Thus perished **Endymion**, the handsome shepherd; **Orion**, the fellow hunter; the aspiring suitors **Aktaeon** and **Meleager**; and even **Niobe**, a boastful mother.

As Apollo became identified with **Ilios**, so Artemis assumed the duties of the moon goddess **Selene**. She was associated with Apollo's cult at *Delos*. At Ephesos, despite her fervently defended virginity, she was identified with the luxuriously oriental **Cybele**, depicted with row upon row of breasts. Similar fertility properties were revered at *Vraona* (Brauron). At Aulis she was the stern huntress; she was the sterner **Epipyrgidia** (*Protectress of the Fortress*) in Pisistratos' first temple on the Acropolis in *Athens*; and she was the blood-thirsty Artemis **Orthia** (*Upright*) in *Sparta*, where Lykurgos replaced human sacrifice with ritual scourging.

Athena (*Minerva*)

As **Pallas** (*Wielder of the Spear*), she fought only in just causes. Her real strength lay in peaceful domestic occupations, however, and for this she triumphed over **Poseidon** for the

patronage of *Athens*. In *Delphi*, as Athena **Pronoia**
(*Providence*), she took the depreciated place of Gaea. In *Sparta*
she shared with **Artemis** the respect of antiquity's most
masculine society, and no town lacked a shrine in her honour.
As **Lindia**, in a succession of temples at Lindos on *Rhodes*, her
fame was such that Alexander wore her mantle in battle. But on
the Acropolis in *Athens* she ruled supreme, as **Nike** (*Victory*),
Parthenos (*Virgin*), **Polias** (*Protectress*) and **Promachos**
(*Leader in Battle*), to whom Alexander dedicated the gilded
shields taken from the Persians. She was also goddess of
wisdom, and stayed aloof from the petty jealousies of Olympos.

Demeter (*Ceres*)

Originally the main successor to the **Great Goddess**, the
goddess of earth and fertility participated wholeheartedly in the
stormy amours of her family. She was raped by **Poseidon** and
bore **Zeus** a daughter, **Persephone** (*Proserpina*), whom **Hades**
abducted to the Underworld. As pleas to Zeus, who had no
authority there, were useless, Demeter forbade trees to fruit
and grain to ripen, so that it needed mother Rea's diplomacy to
prevent the extinction of all life on earth. In compromise,
Hades allowed Persephone, after spending the winter months
in the Underworld with him, to spend spring and summer on
earth with her mother.

The mysteries of Demeter were the oldest and most respected
of Greco-Roman times, but her sanctuary at *Eleusis* is now
sadly neglected.

Dionysos (*Bacchus*)

Dionysos' orgiastic career on earth centred on his discovery of
wine, the enjoyment of which he promoted throughout the
world in the company of drunken satyrs and maenads. But
another aspect of the god, though still connected with the cult of
wine, was his patronage of the dramatic arts, manifest in the
annual Dionysia spring festival at *Athens*.

While sailing to the Cyclades this curiously human god was
captured by pirates and bound to the mast. But his divinity
reasserted itself as ivy and vines began to grow over the ship,
and lions played at the god's feet to the music of flutes. As the
pirates fled overboard they were turned into dolphins.
Dionysos sailed on to *Naxos* where he married **Ariadne**, who
had been abandoned there by **Theseus**. This strange god was
also the presiding deity at *Delphi* during Apollo's absence in
winter, and at *Delos* Hellenistic mosaics show him associated
with a panther.

Hades (*Pluto*)

Although not an Olympian, Kronos' eldest son was so absolute
in his domain that he alone became synonymous with it.
Antiquity knew several gates to the Underworld, but the souls
of the dead were led by **Hermes** to the river Styx in the
Peloponnese, where they were ferried across by **Charon**. In the
Underworld they were judged by **Minos**, **Radamanthys** – sons
of **Zeus** by **Europa** – and **Aeakos**. The second was in charge of
Asians, the third of Europeans, and Minos held a court of
appeal.

For many it might have been preferable to remain among
those unprovided with a coin, placed beneath the tongue, to pay
for judgement, because even the **Asphodel Fields**, purgatory
for minor sins, were guarded by the three-headed hellhound
Kerberos (*Cerberus*). But at least the souls could drink from the
twin pools of **Lethe** (*Oblivion*) and **Mnemosyne**
(*Remembrance*), strangely enough identified with two springs at

Livadia. Grave offenders were thrown into Tartaros; the blameless went to the **Elysian Fields**.

Appropriately, Hades' best-known temple stood before the grottos at *Eleusis*, from which his chariot had emerged when he abducted his niece **Persephone**.

Hebe (Juventas, Youth)
The acknowledged daughter of **Zeus** and **Hera**, she was never considered a true Olympian, and even lost her role as her father's cup-bearer to **Ganymede**, who Zeus abducted by adopting the guise of an eagle – an event represented in a terra cotta in the *Olympia* museum. She was married off to **Herakles**.

Hephaestos (Vulcan)
The ungainly god of fire, Hephaestos, was thrown from Olympos by his disappointed mother Hera, and was fostered by **Thetis**, who played a part among gods and men quite out of proportion with her status as an ordinary sea nymph. He developed such skill as a metal-worker that he was welcomed back among the Olympians, but only until he dared to release his neglectful mother from the chains in which she had been hung for attempting to rebel against the rule of **Zeus**. Cast out once again, he fell to earth on *Limnos* and broke both his legs, which made him permanently lame. Despite his marriage to Aphrodite, he was never recalled and specialized thereafter in forging armour and arms for the divine and human elite, ably assisted by the **Cyclopes**. The Hephaesteion in *Athens* was dedicated to the patron of metal smiths, despite its frieze depicting the exploits of **Theseus**.

Hera (Juno)
Until about the 8thC BC, the Queen of Heaven, who was also the protectress of marriage, rivalled her brother-husband in power and surpassed him in the number of sanctuaries dedicated to her – particularly after she had replaced her sister **Demeter** as successor of the **Great Goddess**. For their first 100yr, the Olympic Games were dedicated to her; her temple at *Samos* was the most splendid in Greece; and more than one Heraion was the scene of an important prehistoric event, such as the election of **Agamemnon** as leader of the Achaeans against Troy.

Hermes (Mercury)
As patron of merchants, travellers and thieves, Hermes must often have been invoked by opposite interests: he was herald and messenger of the gods; as **Psychopompos** he guided departing souls to the Underworld; as **Logios** he granted eloquence and convincing lies; treaties were under his care; and as **Trismegistos** (*Three Times Great*) he was the god of science and mysteries. Praxiteles' *Hermes* in the *Olympia* museum is the outstanding 4thC BC marble statue in Greece. Plinths with the god's head and phallus once stood at crossroads.

Hestia (Vesta)
The gentle purity of the protectress of the hearth, the prototype of placid maiden aunts, was so little appreciated that she lost her place among the Olympians to orgiastic **Dionysos**. Her sacred hearth stood in *Olympia*'s Prytanion.

Poseidon (Neptune)
Though, like his brother **Hades**, supreme in his own element, the sea, he was an Olympian as he partook in earthly affairs – especially as the dreaded earthshaker, to whom as many sanctuaries were dedicated as to the sea god. He was exceedingly bad-tempered but, nevertheless, as amorous as his brother **Zeus**, with whom he shared their sister **Demeter** and

their mother. Both brothers courted **Thetis**, Poseidon for once with honourable intentions, but both feared the prophecy that her son would overshadow his father. This prophecy was fulfilled when she married King Peleus and bore him a son, **Achilles** – all Olympians honoured her wedding feast at Iolkos, where uninvited **Eris** threw a golden apple of discord which started the Trojan War.

Poseidon competed with **Hera** for Argos, with **Dionysos** for the island of Naxos, and with **Athena** for *Athens*, where the marks of his trident in the Erechtheion enjoyed as much esteem as Athena's olive tree. His main sanctuaries were at Isthmia and *Sounio*. The bronze found at Cape Artemision, now in the National Archaeological Museum in *Athens*, is one of antiquity's most impressive statues.

Even after having been frightened into swearing obedience, Zeus' family found countless ways to circumvent his will, as their foregoing biographical sketches show. He was further restricted by the **Moirae** (*Fates*), though how far Zeus determined fate and how far he was subject to it is uncertain.

Other mythological figures

Deukalion's flood was survived by **Deukalion** himself and his wife, **Pyrra**. When their ark came ashore on Mt. Parnassos they threw stones – the 'bones' of Mother Earth – behind them: those cast by Deukalion became men, those by Pyrra, women. Added to this unorthodox renewal of humanity was one true son, **Hellen**, ancestor of the Hellenic race. His sons **Aeolos** and **Doros** and grandsons **Achaios** and **Ion** were the progenitors of the respective tribes.

Poseidon as well as Hellen had a son called **Aeolos**, who was entrusted with keeping the winds imprisoned in caves, until his father should strike his trident into the cliffs to release the required breeze or storm.

Asklipios (*Aesculapius*) was also an important figure. The son of **Apollo** and the Thessalian princess **Koronis**, he was delivered by divine surgery after his mother had deceived her god and had been fatally wounded by an arrow from indignant Artemis as a result. Like so many of the divine half-breeds, including **Achilles**, **Herakles** and **Jason**, Asklipios was brought up by the wise centaur **Cheiron** on *Mt. Pilio*, where he came to surpass his teacher in medical knowledge. He accompanied his fellow pupils on the Argonauts' expedition to Kolchis, then on his return settled at *Epidaurus*.

When Asklipios went beyond curing the living and restored the dead to life, **Hades** complained to **Zeus** about this interference, and it was brought to an end by a thunderbolt. Asklipios was translated to higher spheres, and medical science developed at his increasingly popular shrines. **Hygia**, goddess of health, continued the good work among the living.

Collective deities were also important to the Greeks. The **Charitae** (*The Three Graces*) were mainly decorative; the **Mousae** (*The Nine Muses*) inspired the arts and met as an academy under Apollo's chairmanship on Mt. Helikon; and the **Moirae** (*The Three Fates*) predestined the lot of the newborn. The **Eumenides** (*Erinyae, The Three Furies*) haunted evil doers, and were appeased in a cave on the Areopagos in *Athens*; while **Nemesis**, goddess of vengeance, maintained a reasonable balance between good and evil among mortals, and was worshipped at a temple at *Ramnous*.

Orientation map

N

ALBANIA

YUGOSLAVIA

Seres

Dran

MACEDONIA

Florina

Thessaloniki

Kastoria

Veria

36

37 Halkidiki

38

41

Mount
Olympos

35
34

39

40

42

23

EPIROS

THESSALY

Ioanina

Kalambaka

Larissa

Corfu

Corfu

Igoumenitsa

Parga

Volos

32

Skiathos

IONIAN ISLANDS

Paxi

Preveza

33

31

SPORADES

30

Lefkada

CENTRAL
GREECE

Agrinio

Delphi

Evia

Ionian
Sea

Ithaka

Messolongi 14

Halkida

Kefalonia

Patra

Gulf of Corinth

Attica

Eleusis

ATHE

Kastel
Tornese 16

Corinth

Daphni

24 25

27

Zakynthos

PELOPONNESE

Mycenae

23

17

Pyrgos

Olympia

Nafplio

Sounio

18

Andritsena

Epidauros

Egina

Poros

21

Ydra

22

Kalamata

Sparta

Spetses

Pylos

19

Methoni

Monemvassia

20

Kythira

73

74 Hania

CRET

75

Good beaches

1 Ypsos, Corfu
2 Glyfada, Corfu
3 Messongi, Corfu
4 Agios Georgios, sw Corfu
5 Paxi, Paxi
6 Parga, Epiros
7 Preveza, Epiros
8 Lefkada, Lefkada
9 Vassiliki, Lefkada
10 Sami, Kefalonia
11 Lixouri, Kefalonia
12 Platys Gialos, Kefalonia
13 Antirio, Gulf of Corinth
14 Nafpaktos, Gulf of Corinth
15 Rio, Gulf of Corinth
16 Kylini, Peloponnese
17 Argassi, Zakynthos
18 Laganas, Zakynthos
19 Methoni, Peloponnese
20 Dyros, Peloponnese
21 Tolo, Peloponnese
22 Kosta, opposite Spetses
23 Agia Marina, Egina
24 Akti 'A' Voula, Attica
25 Akti 'B' Voula, Attica
26 Akti Vouliagmeni, Attica
27 Akti Alianthos, Attica
28 Marmari, Evia
29 Karystos, Evia
30 Koukounaries, Skiathos
31 Skopelos, Skopelos
32 Tsangarada, Mt. Pilio
33 Agios Ioannis, Mt. Pilio

0   50   100 km
0   25   50 miles

———— Railways
════ Motorways
———— Major roads
* Outstanding sights

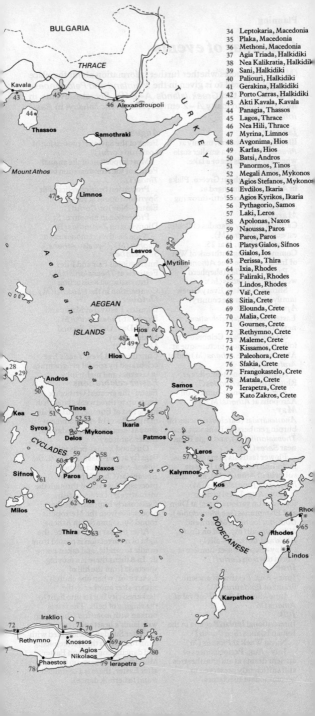

Calendar of events

(M) or (I) denotes whether further information about the place or event referred to is given in the *Mainland and Peloponnese A–Z* (M) or the *Greek Islands A–Z* (I). See also events in introduction to many *A–Z* entries, and *Public holidays* in *Basic information*.

January
Blessing of the waters, mainly at *Piraeus* (M) but on a smaller scale wherever there is sea or a lake.

February
Carnival throughout Greece. Plaka in *Athens* (M) thronged at weekends with confetti-throwing crowds.

March
Carnival Sunday. Parades of floats, especially at *Patra* (M).

National Day, Mar 25. Commemorating outbreak of War of Independence. See *Athens* (M).

Parody of a *Vlah* (shepherd wedding) at *Thebes* (M).

Shrove Monday. Every Greek family picnics in the country.

April
Easter. See *Easter celebrations*, next column.

St George's Day. Celebrated by folk-dancing; most picturesque at Aharnes outside *Athens* (M) and at *Arahova* (M).

Apr–Oct. Son-et-lumière at Rhodes town on *Rhodes* (I).

Apr–Oct. Son-et-lumière on Acropolis at *Athens* (M).

May
Anasténarides (barefoot dancing on burning embers) at Langadas near *Thessaloniki* (M). and Agia Eleni near *Seres* (M).

Flower festivals in many towns, including Kifissia and Patissia suburbs of *Athens* (M), and (late May/early June) *Edessa* (M).

May–Aug. Local artistic festivals (on various dates) at Dion and Platamonas (see *Macedonia*), *Dodona*, *Ioannina*, *Mystra* and *Nikopoli* – all (M), and on *Corfu*, *Ithaki* and *Lefkada* – all (I).

May–Sept. Son-et-lumière at Corfu town on *Corfu* (I).

June
June–Aug. Festival of ancient drama at *Epidaurus* (M).

June–Sept. Athens Festival at *Athens* (M).

July
International Ionian Regatta in the Ionian Islands. See *Corfu* (I).

Naval Week at *Piraeus* (M).

July–Aug. Performances of ancient drama at antique theatres still sufficiently preserved to accommodate spectators.

August
Feast of the Saviour (procession of boats) on *Corfu* (I).

Most important of the annual Feasts of the Annunciation on *Tinos* (I).

Procession bearing relics of St Spyridon (one of several, Easter–Nov) on *Corfu* (I).

Procession in honour of St Dionysios on *Zakynthos* (I).

Wine Festival at monastery at *Daphni* (M). (See also *Athens*.)

September
International Fair and Film Festivals at *Thessaloniki* (M).

International Sailsurfing Competition in the *Halkidiki* (M).

October
Dimitria Festival of Music and Drama at *Thessaloniki* (M).

Ohi Day, Oct 28: Second National Day.

December
Christmas and New Year's Eve celebrated by special programmes in tavernas and nightclubs.

Easter celebrations
Easter, the greatest Orthodox feast, up to three weeks later than in the rest of Europe, usually falls in Apr. Places of entertainment close at least on Good Friday and Easter Saturday.

On Good Friday bells toll and flags fly at half-mast. At 21.00, the flower-covered bier of the *Epitáphios* (Christ's funeral procession) is carried through the main streets of every parish. Particularly impressive is the procession from the Metropolis round Syntagma Sq. in Athens.

After the Sat night service, the light of resurrection is passed from candle to candle, and taken home lit. In Athens there is a moving spectacle from the hill of Lykavittos, when one church square after another in the darkened city bursts into light to the ringing of bells. The fast is broken with *magirítsa* (thick soup with lamb's heart and liver).

Easter Sunday is celebrated with lamb roasted on the spit; rejoicing and dancing continue on Easter Monday. At Megara, on the Tues after Easter, there is a costumed *tráta* (fisherfolk dance).

When and where to go

Avoid, if you can, going in Aug, when the Apr–Oct tourist season peaks in every respect, prices included. Hotels are over-full, as are all forms of transport, especially island ferries; the more accessible beaches are crowded; and food and service are inadequate due to a lack of trained staff. Greece's main cultural event, the Athens Festival, is indeed in full swing, but so too is pollution in the summer heat. Package tours are the only easy and reliable way in Aug, when only the best hotels can be trusted to honour bookings.

Things are better in early July, but as is the case everywhere around the Mediterranean, June and Sept are the best months to go. Oct, too, can be lovely and the sea will still be warm, though the weather is no longer reliable. In May the weather is even less reliable and the sea is cold.

In the height of summer, a north wind, the *meltémi*, cools the Aegean Islands and to a lesser degree the mainland east coast, while the Ionian Islands and the west coast have a heavier, more humid climate. Winter is usually mild near the sea, though it might snow once or twice, and is progressively cold to very cold from S to N in the interior. Feb is generally the coldest and wettest month, but this occasionally applies to Mar or Apr.

Insects on the whole are no problem, thanks to spraying from helicopters. This is general and necessary throughout the country, but has been known to happen in Athens in the middle of the day, when the irritation it causes to eyes and nerves makes its benefits less obvious.

Almost anywhere along the 15,020km (9,387 miles) mainland coast of Greece will make a suitable base for a holiday during the warm season. Discrimination is necessary in winter, however, when the few hotels that remain open in the larger resorts have little to offer except relaxation – not a lot of fun in the heavy rains that descend on western Greece and most of the islands.

The mountains of Greece meanwhile are a holiday virginland. There are no resorts, so mountaineering and skiing facilities are embryonic in all the major mountain ranges.

Area planners and tours

Greece divides naturally into two areas, the mainland and the islands. Within these two basic divisions fall a number of separate touring areas, any of which can be enjoyed alone, although you will probably wish to visit sights in a combination of areas. Almost all mainland sights lie within easy reach of airports and the very few that don't, such as Delphi, are visited by organized tours, so that the problem isn't how to get there, but how to get away from the thundering herd!

The maps provided relate to suggested excursions. Refer otherwise to the colour maps at the end of the book. For those with more specialized reasons for visiting the country, a brief summary of the caves, spas and casinos of Greece is given at the end of this section of the book.

Cross-references in the islands *Area planners* are to the *Islands A–Z*. Except where otherwise stated, all other cross-references will be to the *Mainland A–Z*.

Area: Attica and the southeastern mainland
Athens is an obvious must, containing as it does the country's
outstanding archaeological site and museum, as well as being
the most convenient centre for touring. From here you can
make excursions on land to *Delphi* (in summer including
Ossios Loukas) and Sounio, and by sea to the Argo-Saronic
Islands: Egina, Poros, Ydra and Spetses. Other good choices
are Amfiaraio, Daphni, Eleusis, Marathon, Perahora and
Vraona, which are included in the excursions suggested below,
and *Porto Germeno* and Mt. Parnis. See also *Attica*.

Three days for a first visit to Athens should be sufficient, plus
another four for excursions, combined with swimming at
beaches where there is unpolluted water. This region is not
particularly recommended for beach holidays, however.

Although regular buses shamble daily to the remotest
mountain villages, visits to all but the major antique
monuments in Attica require private transport. The hardy
could take a bus to the nearest village and walk, or in some
cases, ask the driver to stop the bus at the monument and hope

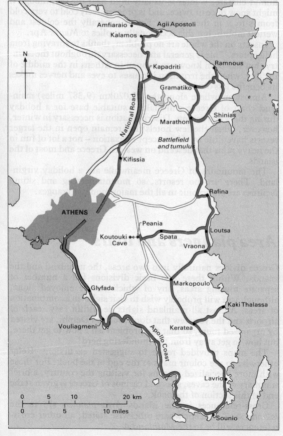

to be able to stop it also for the return, but this is tempting fate. The first two excursions suggested below therefore assume the use of a car. Places in italics are described in detail in the *Mainland A–Z*; those in bold will be found under *Attica*.

From Athens to Amfiaraio, Ramnous and Marathon

Take Vassilissis Sofias and Kifissias out of Athens to the NE garden suburb of **Kifissia**, where you join the National Road, leaving it (before paying toll) at the Kapadriti exit to the right. Take the road N via Kalamos to *Amfiaraio*, an idyllic 4thC BC sanctuary and spa. The fish tavernas of **Agii Apostoli** are invitingly near, but resist the temptation and return to Kapadriti, bearing left towards the village of Marathon. Then branch left and head past the fine and uncrowded beach of Shinias towards *Ramnous*, the most dramatic of the Attic sites, appropriately dedicated to Nemesis, goddess of vengeance.

Returning to the main road at Gramatiko, drive S through the village of Marathon to the battlefield of *Marathon*, with its Tumulus of the Plataeans, a small museum and a prehistoric graveyard. Nearby, on the left, is the Tumulus of the Athenians. The best place for a meal is a few turnings farther on the left, the string of fish restaurants at the tiny port of **Rafina**. The road to Rafina is signposted, as are all the above sites.

From Athens to Sounio and Vraona

Leave the centre of Athens going towards the SW by Amalias Ave. and Syngrou Ave., as far as the sea. Then follow the lovely Apollo Coast SE via **Glyfada** and **Vouliagmeni**, passing all its beach resorts to reach Poseidon's Temple at *Sounio* at the tip of the peninsula. It is always crowded with coach tours but they generally turn back here.

Continue N along the coast to **Lavrio**, unattractive with slagheaps since the 5thC BC working of its silver mines, then turn inland NW through the wine villages of Attica to Keratea. Here you might turn right to a good beach at **Kaki Thalassa**, below a convent that would suit the scenery of a Russian ballet.

Alternatively, continue inland, to **Markopoulo** where several pleasant tavernas serve the local *rétsina*, then branch right NE, towards the sanctuary of *Vraona*. Then, either follow the coast N via the beach of Loutsa to Rafina, to combine excursions *1* and *2*, or strike W inland from Loutsa to **Peania**, birthplace of the 4thC BC orator Demosthenes, and continue 5km (3 miles) up **Mt. Ymitos** to the **Koutouki Cave**.

The Saronic Gulf

There are organized one-day cruises of the *Argo-Saronic Islands* (see *Islands A–Z*), as well as a wide choice of hydrofoils from Zea Harbour, Piraeus, or hourly ferries from the main harbour to *Egina*, *Poros*, *Spetses* and *Ydra* (see *Islands A–Z*). Except for Egina, they are all connected to the mainland by road, and can, for example, be easily combined with excursions from Athens to *Nafplio* and *Monemvassia* on the Peloponnese.

Salamis, historically the best known of these islands, is now impossibly polluted. So too is *Eleusis*, N on the mainland, across the once-lovely bay in which dozens of rusting hulks have been laid up, while shipyards, petrol refineries, iron works and cement factories surround the antique ruins and contribute the main ingredients of the notorious 'chemical cloud' that hangs over Athens.

Area: The Peloponnese

This region offers the best of everything: antique Bassae, Corinth, Epidaurus, Isthmia, Ithomi, Megalopoli, Messini, Mycenae, Nemea, Olympia, Pylos, Sparta, Tirynth; medieval Karitena, Kastel Tornese, Methoni, Mystra, Monemvassia; Venetian Nafplio; a good choice of beaches; and splendidly varied scenery.

The region is well served by one- to five-day organized tours from Athens; and although the multitude of places to visit justifies using a car, you can travel also by plane, train or bus, taking a taxi from the bus-stop to Bassae or ancient Messini. By car, the itinerary suggested below will take a minimum of four days, but motoring conditions vary considerably and the recommended times given are nominal. It is far better to allow as much time as possible.

Day 1 Leave Athens NW by Kavalas Ave., passing the monastery at *Daphni*, first stop of many organized tours, before skirting the Bay of *Eleusis*. Though the motorway bypasses the town, it is best, before paying a toll, to take this chance to visit the important ruins, however unfortunately located.

80km (50 miles) W is the *Corinth* Canal, which since 1893 has separated the Peloponnese from the mainland. Just before the road and rail bridges cross the canal there is a right turn N to *Loutraki*, Greece's foremost spa, and the nearby Heraion of Perahora. Beyond the canal, turn left to Isthmia and *Epidaurus*, the great sanctuary of Asklipios, 59km (37 miles) distant.

For the first night there is a wide choice of hotels at *Nafplio*, 25km (16 miles) SW, but first it is also worth making the lovely circuit of the coast facing the islands of *Poros*, *Ydra* and *Spetses* (see *Islands A–Z*), which can all be reached by ferry.

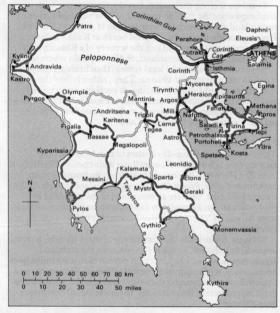

This is a journey of about 160km (100 miles), depending whether short diversions to Methana, Trizina, Kosta and *Portoheli* are included. The view from the heights at Fanari, where there is a convenient roadside cafe, is one of the finest in the Mediterranean. You will pass large hotel complexes on the beaches of Plepi, Petrothalassa, *Portoheli* and Saladi.

Your sightseeing in *Nafplio* should be done on arrival, as the next day has a crowded schedule.

Day 2   *Tirynth*, the Heraion of *Argos*, *Mycenae* and *Argos*, all clearly signposted, demand a certain amount of backtracking, but they are all nearby; the Heraion is least important. Those who simply must see the minor ruins of Mantinia and Tegea will go on to climb the main road to Tripoli.

The scenery, however, is much more beautiful on the coastal road s to Leonidio, via Mili, ancient Lerna (see *Argos*), where Herakles slew the nine-headed Hydra, and Astro. The road continues inland sw via the Monastery of Elona to Geraki, then right, heading w to *Sparta*, a mere 183km (115 miles) total for the day. The intrepid traveller, additionally, can brave the very variable and lonely 170km (106 miles) circuit of the largely uninhabited s coast, from Geraki to *Monemvassia* and back via *Gythio* to Sparta.

Day 3   Visit *Mystra*, which will involve some walking. Then, if the weather permits the road to be open, a spectacular 60km (37 mile) drive w over the Taygetos takes you through the fir forest at 1,000m (3,300ft) to *Kalamata*. The shorter inland road N continues for 114km (71 miles) via *Megalopoli* and Karitena to *Andritsena* and the nearby Temple of Bassae.

Much more rewarding is to turn left heading w via Messini (see *Kalamata*) – possibly visiting ancient Messini and Ithomi – to *Pylos*, and then N along the enchanting w coast via Kyparissia to Phigaleia (see *Andritsena*) then inland along a narrow road to the Temple of Bassae, a total of 199km (125 miles). A further 70km (44 miles) takes you abruptly from the stark Arkadian mountains to the idyllic hills round *Olympia*.

Day 4   The new motorway to *Patra* on the N coast might open any time between 1983–85. But although neither Pyrgos, about half-way up the w coast, nor the remains at Andravida of a very modest Gothic cathedral are of much interest, *Kastel Tornese* is Greece's finest example of a medieval castle, so estimate 152km (94 miles) for a journey which can include a rest at Kylini beach.

The 139km (87 miles) toll motorway E to Corinth skirts the Corinthian Gulf through vineyards and orchards; the great chain of the Parnassos, snow-covered most of the year, can be seen across the blue sea. Return to Athens on the motorway.

Other mainland areas

After even a long excursion like the four-day tour of the Peloponnese suggested above, the exhausted visitor will still hardly have begun to explore the mainland. The essential approach for a fulfilling visit to Greece is to be selective, and the most renowned and widely scattered sights outside Attica and the Peloponnese are better seen as part of an organized tour. A good example are the Meteora monasteries, often included with Delphi in a three-day tour. A brief outline of the three other mainland regions of Greece is provided here, and full descriptions of the main sights can be found in the *Mainland A–Z*.

Planning

Epiros and the western mainland

Though interesting – with antique *Dodoni, Nikopoli*, Stratos, Thermo (see *Agrinio*); Byzantine *Arta*; the mosques of *Ioanina* and the nearby Perama stalactite cave (see *Ioanina*); *Metsovo* in its alpine setting; Venetian *Parga*; and uncrowded beaches – this region tends to be visited mainly en route to the ferry at Igoumenitsa or on the way to Corfu.

Thessaly

The outstanding religious as well as scenic site in Greece is the group of rock-needles crowned by the Meteora monasteries (see *Kalambaka*). The region has a magnificent landscape, with Mt. Pilio (see *Volos*) and the *Vale of Tempe*, but is sparse in antiquities, although it does have Pagasae (see *Volos*).

Macedonia and Thrace

Thessaloniki, the capital of northern Greece, has the largest number of remarkable Byzantine churches in Greece, and also has the Archaeological Museum that contains the Hellenistic treasures from **Derveni** and **Vergina**. The tombs at the latter certainly deserve a visit, as do the excavations at **Dion** and **Pella**. The waterfall at *Edessa* irrigates the vast orchards of the plain below, which bloom in April. **Mt. Olympos** can be climbed, but very few avail themselves of the opportunity. (For places printed in bold see under *Macedonia*.)

The *Halkidiki*, Macedonia's playground, has innumerable hotels. The strictly regulated visits to the monasteries of **Mt. Athos** are best made from a cruise ship, but only men may land. *Kavala*, redolent of tobacco, has a Roman aqueduct with Byzantine fortifications and the 18thC mansion of Mohammed Ali, founder of the royal dynasty that ruled Egypt until 1952. Nearby are the impressive Roman ruins of *Philippi*.

The attractive islands of *Thassos* and *Samothraki* (see *Islands A–Z*), both endowed with important ruins, are usually visited from Kavala or Alexandroupoli. Those in search of the Orient in Europe will appreciate the mosques of Thrace, which has a Moslem minority. The main antique site is Messemvria (see *Alexandroupoli*). The 70 tiny Byzantine churches of *Kastoria*, on a picturesque but polluted lake in the west, are of interest only to connoisseurs. The town is the capital of the fur industry, which holds its annual fair in Thessaloniki in May.

One day is sufficient for Thessaloniki, four for a tour of the region's major sites. In the warm seasons, allow ample time for a restful stay in the Halkidiki.

The Ionian Islands

Because they are strung out along an extended N–S axis with ferry links mainly to the mainland, island-hopping within the Ionian group (see *Islands A–Z*) is not practised with the same ease as in the Aegean, although some excursions between them are possible. *Corfu* is an ideal holiday island, offering comfortable hotels from which a perfect mixture of town and country can be visited. The best beaches are on the west coast, although the water is colder. *Zakynthos* is an excellent choice, less developed and quieter, with equally lush vegetation.

The Aegean Islands

The islands of the Aegean are the answer to a holiday prayer, offering everything from sun and sea to ruins and scenery. Delos, Kos, Lesvos, Naxos, Paros, Patmos, Rhodes and Samos are outstanding for antique and medieval sites. The leaders for natural scenery are spectacular Thira, with its town built on the rim of an active volcano, and Evia, Hios and the Sporades. If on the other hand your idea of a good holiday is to find the best modern beach resorts and all that goes with them, Mykonos and Rhodes are ideal. In fact, Rhodes, the largest island after Crete (which is treated separately later), offers something of everything.

Nearly 100 islands have accommodation, sometimes only in private houses, and between them one can experience the summers of a lifetime. You should resist the temptation to try to see too many islands in one summer, however, so stick to one of the main groups, the Cyclades, Dodecanese or Sporades, perhaps combined with one of the larger islands off the coast of Asia Minor, such as Hios, Lesvos or Samos. Some recommendations are given below.

Countless cruises, from three days to a fortnight, pack in the largest number of islands in greatest comfort at maximum price, but one of the real joys, the opportunity to experience the individuality of each island, is lost. This quality is much more pronounced on the smaller islands, where boats call only once or twice weekly and even the smallest aircraft can't or won't land. Singling out any of these dreamy places would obviously spell its end, as the tourist cannot help destroying what he likes best. Most of the islands that have already been discovered boast an airport and are well served by ferry boats and hydrofoils.

It is not a bad idea to take the car to the islands off Asia Minor, and to Kos and Rhodes, from which excursions can be made into Turkey. Island hopping within one group is easy, less so from one group to another. The remoter the island, the older the boat, and berths have been known to be sold twice on all of them.

Yachting is ideal for the experienced, not only for seeing but also for absorbing the Aegean world all the year round, except perhaps in Aug when the *meltémi* demands particularly efficient seamanship. Zea Harbour in Piraeus has the largest and best equipped of the 100 yacht supply stations in Greece. There is a wide range of craft for hire, from the humble caique (fishing boat) to luxury yachts. Except for the former, boats are definitely a rich man's toy; moreover, complaints about delays, breakdowns and outright neglect are not infrequent. It is therefore essential to choose a reliable yacht broker.

The Cyclades
Mykonos is a must, though the jet set moved away when everyone else moved in. It has replaced nearby *Delos*, to which it sends boatloads of visitors even in a bad *meltémi*, as the centre of the archipelago, and is served by daily flights and numerous ships. Ermoupoli, capital of *Syros* and of the Cyclades, is the port of trans-shipment for the Aegean Islands, but warrants a visit for its own sake, as do *Naxos*, *Paros* and, above all, *Thira*. Either *Samos*, or *Hios* and *Lesvos*, might be added to this cruise of the Cyclades, but not all of them, and only if there is plenty of time – sweeping through the islands should be left to the *meltémi*. . . .

The Dodecanese
Planes and ships go to *Rhodes* and most go to *Kos*. These islands are the ultimate for tourism, even too much so in the

43

case of Rhodes, which has the largest hotel capacity in the Aegean, although Lindos, the island's highlight, has only one large hotel, and is overcrowded only by daytrippers. Daily boats make it easy to visit the Monastery of St John on *Patmos*, but accommodation there is inadequate both in quality and quantity. There are two flights daily to the one hotel on *Karpathos*, but rooms in private houses on this unspoilt island are clean, if basic. The other islands in the group are reserved for the adventurous.

The Sporades

The 'Scattered Isles' are often described as pebbles flung by the gods over the northwestern Aegean after the Creation. Luckily the hotels on lovely *Skiathos* are also rather scattered, except at Koukounaries, where the main beach is fringed by stone pines. There are two or three planes daily for the numerous foreign (especially English) residents. Daily ferries sail from mainland Agios Konstantinos which is on the toll motorway, as well as from Volos, and continue to much quieter Skopelos and four times weekly to green, unspoilt Alonissos. Skyros, the largest island, on its own in the SE, is reached in about 5hr by bus from Athens, then ferry from *Evia*. See also *Sporades*.

Crete

Greece's southernmost and largest island, *Crete*, requires all the time available in an ordinary holiday. Iraklio Airport is served from several European towns, mostly by charter flights, and both it and Hania Airport also have frequent flights from Athens. Ferry boats from Piraeus call daily at both towns; there is a service from Rhodes, and another from Gythio in the Peloponnese to Kissamos.

Cretan ruins date back 4,000yr. Knossos and Phaestos, the Roman remains at Gortys, and the Venetian fortifications of Hania, Iraklio and Spinalonga should not be missed. The great natural site is the Samaria gorge in the White Mountains, open Apr–Oct. The N coast is more developed than the S, but a circular road takes in most of the island, so it is worth bringing or hiring a car.

Any of the large hotels studding the entire N coast of the island arranges tours to the main historic sites. For the individual sightseer without a car Iraklio is the most convenient centre with numerous buses in all directions. Agios Nikolaos offers the brightest nightlife, but Elounda has the best hotels. Matala is ideal for beach holidays, and the island's coastline is studded with fine beaches.

Casinos in Greece

The only casinos are at Mt. Parnis near *Athens*, Porto Carras in the *Halkidiki*, and on *Corfu* and *Rhodes* (see *Islands A–Z*).

The caves of Greece

Only a fraction of the country's 6,600 caves are open to the public, but quality makes up for the small quantity. Outstanding among those that provided shelter to primitive man is the Petralona Cave in the *Halkidiki*. Alepotrypa (Foxhole) near Pyrgos Dirou in the *Mani* is of both natural and archaeological interest, but is not yet open. The nearby Glyfada Cave (see *Mani*) is possibly the world's largest sea cave. The Perama stalactite cave near *Ioanina* and the Koutouki Cave near Peania (see *Attica/The plains*) can be explored on foot.

The spas of Greece

The oldest thermal stations in Europe began as religious
sanctuaries but developed later into popular watering places,
especially during the Roman Empire. They are greatly
appreciated by modern Greeks but remain little visited so far by
foreigners, mostly because of the lack of medical supervision.
Only those with adequate hotel accommodation are listed here.

For liver and kidney disorders: *Loutraki*, the largest spa,
bottled water from which is available throughout Greece.

For arthritic ailments: Edipsos on *Evia* (see *Islands A–Z*)
and, across the narrow sea, *Kammena Vourla*, both very
comfortable; Methana in the Peloponnese opposite the island
of Poros, has fewer hotels; Thermae on *Ikaria* (see *Islands
A–Z*); Ypati near Lamia (see *Karpenissi*).

For respiratory troubles: Loutra Kylinis in the NW
Peloponnese (see *Kastel Tornese*).

Accommodation

In c.400BC the historian Xenophon published a treatise ad-
vocating the state's establishment of *xenodohía* – literally 'receptacles for strangers', the word still used for hotels. Nowadays
these concrete receptacles are not as grim as they sound, for
Greek hotels conform very much to the standards of design and
comfort prevailing all round the Mediterranean. Modernism
reigns, however, in dreary uniformity, whether in the towns, by
the sea or in the mountains.

Almost all of the approximately 4,500 hotels, with their total
capacity of close to 300,000 beds, and certainly all those listed in
this book, have been built or modernized since 1960. The five
official categories – L, A, B, C, D – correspond to our very
expensive (▦), expensive (▦), moderately priced (▦), inexpensive (▢), and cheap (▢). There are also some 500
category-E hotels, recommended only for emergencies in the
remotest areas, and about 40,000 mostly clean but very basic
rooms in private houses in the main tourist regions. Many
hotels close Nov–Mar inclusive.

Most L-, A- and B-hotels are air-conditioned. Virtually all
rooms have baths (or at least showers with WC in C- and
D-hotels), lifts and room telephones. Rooms have radios down
to B-, and TVs (transmitting in Greek only) can be hired in
L-hotels. Hotels generally provide bed and breakfast, while
those additionally offering residential terms have a ▱ symbol.

The best choice is often a small, family-run D-hotel, especially in minor beach resorts, though any specific recommendations would tend to defeat the purpose, their main attraction
being their absence of popularity. But seek and you shall find,
along the coast and on the islands.

Because strict uniformity in each of the various categories
makes choice somewhat arbitrary, descriptions of hotels outside Athens will be kept to a minimum, though a selection will
be listed.

Since 1981 only minimum prices have been legally set in each
hotel category, so make sure of the price when you book, and do
so long in advance for the tourist season, preferably through a
travel agent. If you must make your own booking, write in

45

English, which will be understood by any hotel likely to answer; attempts at Greek are considered eccentric.

Except in the luxury and chain hotels, quality of service can change as suddenly as management, usually on a descending scale. Efficient managers are rare; housekeepers to inspect the rooms are practically unknown, so dripping taps and burnt-out bedlights are not uncommon; and there are insufficient trained staff, especially cooks. Service can be indifferent, and the best advice in larger, impersonal establishments is to adopt a politely formal approach, giving tips but insisting on your rights. In small, family-run hotels it can be quite different, and a personal touch by guests is likely to be appreciated.

Besides hotels, there are over 100 holiday camps and organized camping sites on or near the coast, those of the GNTO being the best. Renting a villa is relatively expensive for what you get; plumbing in particular is often deficient. Small apartments however can be economical for a longer stay.

Food and drink

Restaurants in Greece are classified on the same scale as hotels (see *Accommodation*), corresponding in exactly the same way to our five categories. Sadly, not one deserves its luxury status, at least by western standards, and though prices, relatively, are lower than in the rest of Europe, restaurants are not cheap for what they actually offer; food is usually limited in variety and imagination, and though there may be a breathtaking view from the table, you can't eat the view. . . .

Greek restaurants in London or New York serve better food than the unimaginative international dishes on offer in most hotels in Greece. With most resort hotels insisting on half-board residential terms, only occasionally are local specialities introduced to vary the cheap fixed-menu meals.

Hotel dining-rooms are almost the only places in Greece where you will find fixed menus. Continental-style breakfast can be served in your room for a reasonable extra charge, though perhaps not in high season from category B-hotels downwards, and hardly ever on package tours. Few C- and hardly any D-hotels serve any meals other than breakfast.

Your best bet therefore is probably one of the innumerable fish restaurants and tavernas lining the coast in or near all ports and beach resorts. There is a good chance that the seafood will have been caught the same morning, though perversely local delicacies such as crayfish may often be unobtainable, having been bought up by Athenian wholesalers. They are frequently classified A or B and charge accordingly, and legally the category must be prominently displayed. Their often unsmart appearance should not necessarily be taken to mean that they are cheap.

Fish should always be chosen personally, being expensive enough to warrant meticulous attention. In class-A restaurants it will be brought out on a tray for inspection, but in most places you investigate the fridge and have your choice weighed and priced. Though specializing in seafood, tavernas usually serve meat but offer desserts only rarely. For these you must adjourn to a *zaharoplastío*, which can be found even in the smallest village, for Greeks have a very sweet tooth.

There is no lack of adequate restaurants in Athens and the bigger towns, and around Macedonia. But in the villages of the Peloponnese and Crete, and sometimes even in the smaller towns, the menu might be limited to the standard *souvláki* or *katsíki* and the eternal tomato salad. Incidentally, as it is impossible to reserve tables in restaurants in smaller towns and villages, many restaurants included in this book have provided no telephone number.

Menus
Handwritten menus in tavernas are practically illegible and the waiter will almost certainly ask you to choose straight from the pots in the kitchen, or from the fridge. Printed restaurant menus are nearly always bilingual, but the English is often an unintelligible repetition of the Greek in roman characters. Reference to *Food and drink* in *Words and phrases* will prove helpful.

Meal times
Lunch in Greek restaurants is served from 12.30 until 15.00 or 15.30, followed from 14.30 until 16.30 or 17.00 by that widespread Mediterranean custom, the *siesta*. Dinner begins in winter at 19.30, in summer at 20.30, continuing until 1.00 in Athens, 24.00 outside.

Food
Little is known about Greek cooking in antiquity, though the widespread employment of Greek chefs in imperial Rome seems to indicate high standards. Nowadays, nobody comes to Greece for its food and drink or stays away because of it. Most cooking is done in olive oil, usually well-refined but used far too liberally. Food is rarely served hot, a regrettable hangover from the days when lack of firewood meant meals were cooked communally, and were at best lukewarm on reaching home.

Yet food in Greece can be very tasty, whenever sufficient trouble has been taken over its preparation. Local ingredients are generally excellent, particularly vegetables, at least before they are drenched in oil and tomato sauce. Seafood is good but expensive, although sauces are practically unknown. On more remote islands, fish, usually fried, sometimes boiled in a soup or much more rarely grilled, will be the only alternative main course to *katsíki* (goat), which can be exceedingly tough even as *katsikáki* (baby goat).

Drink
Oúzo, a colourless aniseed spirit, is the nationwide aperitif, sometimes served with *mezés*, which are tasty appetizers. *Cinzáno* and *Bótrys* are adequate local vermouths. *Digestifs* you are likely to be served in cafes include sweet *konyák*, apparently based on rosewater, or *Metaxá* brandy, which is good but highly individual. The various synthetic fruit-syrup liqueurs that are available are sickly sweet.

Rétsina, mostly from Attica, served from barrels in tavernas and in bottles in restaurants, is Greece's very own invention and should be served ice-cold. Its distinctive turpentine flavour derives from the time when wine was kept in goatskins sealed with pine resin, and the taste has lingered. A good bottled variety is *Kourtákis*. Less resinated but rarely served adequately chilled is the rosé *kokkinéli*.

Though some orthodox wines can be located by a place name

or the producer's name, few indicate the grape variety or vintage. Very drinkable white wines include *Rómbola* from Kefalonia, *Verdéa* from Zakynthos and *Theotókis* from Corfu. Passable red wines from the Ionian Islands include *Rópa* from Corfu and the rough *Santa Maura* from Lefkada. *Pórto Carrás* from the Halkidiki, in white, rosé and red, is outstanding and available in all good establishments. *Mirabéllo* from Crete and *Cellar* and *Hyméttus* from Attica are all worth trying. And if the general standby, *Deméstica*, is unremarkable, the red *Petit Château* is delicate, and the semi-sweet, dark-yellow *Nihtéri* from Thira has considerable character.

All beers (*býres*) served in Greece are in fact lagers, though that term is never used. The local brand is *Fix*, and several Dutch and German brands are brewed under licence in Greece, all served well-iced.

The best still and fizzy mineral waters come from the thermal sources of Loutraki, Nigrita and Sariza.

Shopping

As a rule, shops open Mon, Wed, Sat 8.00–14.30; Tues, Thurs, Fri 8.00–13.30 and 17.00–20.00. See also *Shopping and business hours* in *Basic information*.

What to look for

Among several reputed jewellers marketing original designs at competitive prices, the two leaders, **Lalaounis** and **Zolotas**, with designs based largely on ancient motifs, have branches throughout Greece retailing at prices considerably lower than, say, in Paris or Switzerland. Gold articles, on the other hand, are more expensive.

Furs are very much in a class of their own, for no animals ever wore such coats. Yet it's the real stuff – scraps and snippets left over from cutting, sent from all over the world to the town of Kastoria in Macedonia where they are pieced together, with a skill perfected over centuries, into rolls of somewhat heavy skins. They are sold by the metre like any textile, and eventually end up as mink coats, leopard jackets or beaver hats, though much cheaper than the orthodox article. Leather goods, from bags to shoes, are another good buy.

Traditional handicrafts still flourish in some regional centres. The most original are the vividly dyed sheepskin *flokáti* rugs, and *tagária*, the shopping bags made from coarse woollen fabric with colourful designs, both from Arahova, and sold as well in nearby Delphi. Also pleasing is the handwoven woollen material found in Crete, at Metsovo in Epiros and on Mykonos. The latter also produces handwoven cotton in brilliant colours for blouses, shirts, skirts and towels.

Ioanina still produces silverware and filigree, often adorned with turquoises. Corfu offers embroidery, as do Crete and Ouranoupoli in the Halkidiki, the latter in surprising Aboriginal patterns introduced by a resident Australian.

Rhodes continues its traditional ceramics, with ashtrays, tiles and some very fancy vases, the latter also being produced in Crete. Attractive, though fragile, brightly-coloured glazed dishes, pots, cups and saucers are made and sold along the main road to Kifissia, a suburb of Athens.

Woodcarving is practised in the mountain villages of the Peloponnese where there are still some forests left.

All these traditional handicrafts are obtainable in Athens and major tourist centres. But beware of machine-made imitations: the genuine article is displayed and sometimes sold by the **National Organization of Greek Handicrafts** in Athens and provincial capitals, and sold also in specialized shops owned by cooperative and welfare organizations in Athens and luxury hotels throughout the country.

Chemists are plentiful; when closed, a sign is posted in the shop window indicating the nearest chemist on duty. But if you need nothing more than an aspirin, soap or razor blades, a *períptero* (street kiosk) will supply them, as well as newspapers and magazines (foreign editions are available only in town centres and near large hotels), cigarettes, matches, batteries and sweets.

Antiques and Byzantine ikons require an export permit which is never given if they are any good, so if you want to avoid either bureaucratic frustration, or acquaintance with a Greek jail if caught by Customs, you would do best to forget about them. Consolation prizes however include the more common ancient coins; weapons, jewellery and other objects from the Turkish occupation; and ikons of the last two centuries. A visit to the Benaki Museum in Athens can be a great help before deciding on any more costly purchase, and professional advice is even better.

The **Greek National Tourist Organization** card offers some degree of guarantee of quality and price. You should pay in the national currency, but dollars are accepted almost anywhere, although often at an unfavourable rate. There is no black market for goods.

See also *Shopping* in *Athens*, *Patra* and *Thessaloniki* in *Mainland A–Z*, and *Corfu* and *Rhodes* in *Islands A–Z*.

Clothing sizes

When shops give clothing sizes in inches or centimetres, use the following conversion scale to determine the correct size

12 *in*	16	20	24	28	32	36	40	44	48
30 *cm*	40	50	60	70	80	90	100	110	120

When standardized codes are used, although these may be found to vary considerably, the following provides a useful guide.

Women's clothing sizes

UK/US sizes	8/6	10/8	12/10	14/12	16/14	18/16
Greek sizes	42	44	46	48	50	52
Bust *in/cm*	31/80	32/81	34/86	36/91	38/97	40/102

Men's clothing sizes

European code (suits)	44	46	48	50	52	54	56
Chest *in/cm*	34/86	36/91	38/97	40/102	42/107	44/112	46/117
Collar *in/cm*	13½/34	14/36	14½/37	15/38	15½/39	16/41	16½/42
Waist *in/cm*	28/71	30/76	32/81	34/86	36/91	38/97	40/102
Inside leg *in/cm*	28/71	29/74	30/76	31/79	32/81	33/84	34/86

Men's and women's shoe sizes

UK/US sizes	3/4½	4/5½	5/6½	6/7½	7/8½	8/9½	9/10½	10/11½	11/12½
European	36	37	38	39	40	41	42	43	44

Sports, leisure, ideas for children

Numerous sports and activities can be enjoyed whilst in Greece; for a full list, and for details of what is available in particular parts of Greece, contact the **GNTO**. The following are a few suggestions.

Camping
Unauthorized camping is forbidden. Contact the GNTO for a list of authorized sites, or ask the local Tourist Police.

Fishing
Summer and autumn are ideal for angling and underwater fishing, and boats and fishing tackle may be widely hired along the coast.

Golf
There are 18-hole courses at: **Glyfada**, 18km (11 miles) s of Athens (☎89–46–820); **Livadi Ropa**, near Ermones, on Corfu (☎94–220); **Afandou**, on Rhodes (☎51–129).

Riding
There are several riding clubs in Attica, Thessaloniki and on Corfu. The nearest to Athens are the **Athens Riding Club** (*Gerakas, Agia Paraskevi* ☎66–11–088), and the **Hellenic Riding Club** (*Paradissos 18, Maroussi* ☎68–26–128).

Sailing
Information on training schools, regattas and general sailing facilities is available from the **Hellenic Sailing Federation** (*Xenofondos 15a, Athens* ☎32–35–560).

Skiing and mountain sports
Information on ski centres and mountain refuge huts is available from the **Greek Skiing and Alpine Federation** (*Karakeorgi Servias 7, Athens* ☎32–34–555).

Sub-aqua
The **Hellenic Federation of Submarine Activities** (*Agios Kosmas Sports Centre* ☎98–19–961) provides training facilities and general information.

Swimming
Most GNTO beaches and swimming pools have facilities that include changing rooms, children's playgrounds, cafes and restaurants, shops, tennis courts and provision for other field sports, and boats and wind-surfing equipment may be hired. Understandably, they tend to be crowded, and not all the beaches are clean enough for swimming. Eighty good beaches (some are GNTO) are identified on the *Orientation map* in *Planning*.

Tennis
For information on public tennis courts, contact the GNTO. Information on tournaments can be obtained from the **EFOA** (*Patissiou 89, Athens* ☎82–10–478).

Water-skiing
For general information, apply to the **Water-Skiing Federation** (*Stournara 32, Athens* ☎52–31–875).

Wind-surfing
For information on training and hire, contact the **Hellenic Wind-Surfing Association** (*Filellinon 7, Athens* ☎32–30–068).

Mainland and Peloponnese A – Z

Most visitors to Greece will select either the mainland or the islands for their holiday, and for convenience the alphabetical description is divided into the *Mainland and Peloponnese A–Z* and the *Greek Islands A–Z*.

In the *Mainland A–Z*, peninsulas such as *Attica* and regions such as *Macedonia* which are distinctive entities, both geographically and historically, have their own entries, in which various towns, resorts and sights are usually included. In addition, major sights and places in each region deserving particular attention are listed separately.

Unless otherwise stated, hotels stay open all year in the main towns and Apr–Oct in the beach resorts, with price reductions in the off-season.

Further advice on visiting the Mainland and Peloponnese can be found in the *Planning* section of the book, where there is a *Calendar of events*, recommendations for *When and where to go*, suggested geographical groupings in *Area planners and tours*, and information on *Accommodation, Food and drink* and *Shopping*.

Museums and archaeological sites
Standard opening times
These are almost everywhere subject to local variations, but nevertheless provide a useful general guideline. Where available, telephone numbers have been given in the text to enable you to check in advance.

Spring (Apr 1–May 15)
Weekdays 9.00–13.30, 16.00–18.00.
Sun and hols 10.00–16.30.
Summer (May 16–Aug 31)
Weekdays 8.30–12.30, 16.00–18.00.
Sun and hols 9.00–15.00.
Autumn (Sept 1–Oct 15)
Weekdays 9.00–13.00, 15.00–17.00.
Sun and hols 10.00–16.00.
Winter (Oct 16–Mar 31)
Weekdays 9.00–15.30.
Sun and hols 10.00–16.30.
Closed Jan 1, Mar 25, Good Friday till 12.00, Easter Sunday, Dec 25 and every Tues, except where otherwise stated.

Admission free on Sun for individual visitors, and for groups of up to five persons unaccompanied by a guide.

Actium   See *Aktio.*

Aegósthena   See *Porto Germeno.*

Agía Lávra, Monastery of   See *Kalavryta.*

Agíi Apostóli   See *Attica/Euboean Gulf.*

Agrínio
Map 7G4. 277km (173 miles) NW of Athens. Getting there: By bus, from Athens via ferry at Rio, and from all towns in W mainland; by air, to Aktio Airport, then bus. Car-hire facilities available. Population: 35,000.
Agrinio is the largest town in the SW mainland, and is surrounded by tobacco plantations. It is an important local

crossroads, and a convenient centre for excursions to the neighbouring ruins of antique Aetolia-Akarnania.

The road NE leads along the flanks of Mt. Panetoliko towards *Karpenissi*, 112km (70 miles).

Sights and places of interest
The nearby major ruins are those at Stratos, Thermo and Oeniadae. **Stratos**, 13km (8 miles) N, was once a city of some importance on the banks of the river Aheloos. **Thermo**, 35km (22 miles) SE, was the capital of ancient Aetolia, and is reached by a drive through romantic olive and cypress groves past the Myrtia monastery along the N shore of **Lake Trihonis** (and it is worth coming back in a round trip along the S shore). **Oeniadae** (The Vines), 32km (20 miles) SW, is hardly worth the difficulty of the last inadequate stretch of road, although it offers extensive ramparts, arched gates and a buttressed quay. It was once a strategic port at the mouth of the Aheloos, and much fought-over.

H **Alice** 🏠 (*Papastratou 2* ☎ 23–056 💵 ▭ 34 🚗); **Galaxias** ✿ (*Kazatzi 19* ☎ 23–551/3 ☎ 0342136 💵 ▭ 36 AE ◑ ◓); **Soumelis Hotel** (*1.6km (1 mile)* N *of Agrinio on the national road* ☎ 23–473 💵 ▭ 20 🚗 ◑ VISA)

Akro-Corinth   See *Corinth*.

Áktio (*Actium*)
*Map **6**F3. On the coast, 54km (34 miles) W of Amfilohia. Getting there: By twice-hourly (7.00–24.00) car ferry across the strait from Preveza; by air, from Athens.*

Aktio is best known as the site of the decisive battle in 31 BC between the victorious heirs of murdered Caesar, Octavian and Mark Antony. Mark Antony's 120,000 infantry and 12,000 cavalry were camped round the **Temple of Apollo** (of which there are a few remains on the promontory), while his 500 large ships, far outnumbering Octavian's galleys, lay in the shallow cove now dominated by the **Chapel of Agii Apostoli** †

Plutarch dramatically recounts how Antony's naval attack seemed to be succeeding when Cleopatra's 60 ships fled unexpectedly. Antony abandoned the battle to follow her and Octavian won a famous victory.

Antony's army surrendered to Octavian, and the new master of the world, subsequently known as Augustus, commemorated his victory by the foundation of **Nikopoli** (see *Preveza*) across the strait on the site of his camp.

Alexandróupoli
*Map **5**C10. 175km (109 miles) E of Kavala. Getting there: By bus, from all parts of Thrace; by train, on the Thessaloniki–Edirne (in Turkey) line; by air, from Athens. Port: Ferries to Samothraki and Limnos. Car-hire facilities available. Population: 28,000.*

The only port in Thrace (Thraki) and the last stop on the road to Turkey. The up-and-coming beach resort of **Nea Hili** is 3km (2 miles) W.

Sights and places of interest
Mákri
A further 3km (2 miles) W on the national road beyond Nea Hili is the **Cyclopean cave** at Makri, supposedly the scene of Odysseus' most daring exploit.
Messemvría
Just after the main road E to *Komotini* turns inland, there is a branch to **Messemvria**, where excavations are in full swing. This was a Hellenistic town belonging to the kingdom of *Samothraki* (see *Islands A–Z*), with

3km-long (2 miles) ramparts climbing from the sea up to the acropolis and back again in a half-circle, enclosing notably the **Sanctuary of Dimitra**. Rich finds were made in its vast cemetery.

Ⓗ **Astir Motel** (*Komotinis 280* ☎ *26–448* ||||| 🛏 *27* 🚗 ⇌ 🅰🅴 🅲🅱 ⓓ ⓒⓓ 𝘝𝘐𝘚𝘈 ⚑ 🏋); **Dionyssos** ▬ (*Makris Ave., Nea Hili* ☎ *26–845* ||▬ 🛏 *33* 🚗 ⇌ *10% price reduction Oct–Feb*); **Egnatia Motel** ❦ (*Makris Ave.* ☎ *28–661/3* ||▯ 🛏 *96* 🖭 ⇌ ⓒⓓ ⚑ ≫).

Amfiáraio

*Map **8**G7. 38km (24 miles) N of Athens. Getting there: By bus to Agii Apostoli, 5km (3 miles) SW, or by tour bus.*

The prophet-warrior Amphiaraos was one of the "Seven against Thebes", and he perished when his chariot was swallowed up by the earth. His cult became centred near a curative spring in this idyllic ravine on the N coast of Attica above the Euboean Gulf, and became popular from the 4thC BC onwards. Pilgrims sacrificed a ram, wrapped themselves in its fleece for the night, and their dreams, interpreted by priests, advised them on how to achieve a cure. The waters of the spring, emerging in a fountain into which the suppliants threw coins, were also thought to be efficacious.

The **Doric temple** still has its **monumental altar** in front. Further on is the **Enkoimeterion**, or Dormitory, a long stoa of 44 exterior Doric and 17 interior Ionic columns where the patients waited for their revelatory dreams. Across the brook was the **hospital**, 14 rooms round a court with 13 Doric columns. In Hellenistic times additions were made to it, *ex-votos* and statues of benefactors were erected by the altar, and a small **theatre** was added behind the Enkoimeterion. The Romans built an **aqueduct** to serve their baths.

Fresh seafood is available on the sea-front at **Agii Apostoli**, 5km (3 miles) SW. See *Attica/Euboean Gulf* for nearby hotels.

Amfilohía

*Map **6**F3. 48km (30 miles) NW of Agrinio. Population: 5,500.*

In a lovely position at the head of the Ambrakian Gulf, the little town founded by Ali Pasha in the early 19thC is a good stop for seafood, on the main N–S road of the W mainland. A fine drive along the gulf brings you to *Aktio*, 54km (34 miles) further W.

Ⓗ **Mistral** (*Stratou 37* ☎ *22–287* ||▯ 🛏 *40* 🖭 ⇌ ❦ *on roof*).

Amfípoli (*Amphipolis*)

*Map **3**C7. 60km (37 miles) SW of Kavala.*

Founded during Perikles' highly successful expedition to the Hellespont in 436BC, this colony, on a spur of gold-bearing Mt. Pangeo at the mouth of the Strymonas valley, was intended to safeguard Athenian interests in the N Aegean. Instead it became a thorn in the mother city's flesh, and deserted in 423BC, a mere 13yr later. The Athenian general Thoukydides was sent too late, and succeeded only in relieving its port. His superbly impartial *History of the Peloponnesian War*, conceived "as a thing to last for ever rather than as a piece of journalism", was written in exile following his failure.

The stubborn refusal of Amphipolis to return to the fold contributed in 420BC to the breakdown of the Peace of Nikias that had briefly suspended the Peloponnesian War. The town continued to defy the Athenians and the urgings of Demosthenes in the 4thC BC, falling to Philip II in 358BC.

Subsequently under the Romans it became the capital of one of the four administrative areas of Macedonia. From its port Pompey sailed after his defeat at Pharsala in 48BC to Alexandria, where he was murdered. St Paul was a later visitor.

Sights and places of interest

Tremendously strong **ramparts** surrounded the town, where new finds continue to come to light. The more important, such as jewellery and the pieces of a fine equestrian statue, have been sent to the museum in *Kavala*; the rest are exhibited in the nearby **museum** (■■ *standard opening times*). Some 1,200 tree trunks and stakes buried in the sand of the river supported a wooden bridge mentioned by Thoukydides; it was used for 1,000yr and guarded later by Byzantine towers. There are also **remains of an Early Christian basilica**. The huge **stone lion** now standing near the modern bridge was found in the river bed.

Ámfissa

*Map **7**G5. 140km (88 miles) NW of Athens. Getting there: By bus, from Athens, Itea and Nafpaktos. Population: 5,000.*
Above the olive groves of the Sacred Plain of *Delphi*, this pleasant town climbs a spur of Mt. Parnassos beneath the ruins of a **castle** built by the Franks and Catalans in the early 18thC. Its quadrangular and polygonal ramparts with two watchtowers and gates enclose a circular dungeon, a cistern, a Byzantine and a Frankish church. It partly incorporates an old **acropolis**. Amfissa is justifiably famous for big, purple olives.

Amphipolis See *Amfipoli*.

Andrítsena

*Map **10**I4. 44km (27 miles) NW of Megalopoli. Population: 1,000.*
The pretty village of Andritsena – with an interesting local **library** in an Othonian building – spreads over a mountain slope on the Megalopoli–Pyrgos road. From it, a paved road leads to the second best preserved temple in Greece at **Bassae**, high up in the forbidding grandeur of the barren Arkadian mountains.

Sights and places of interest

Bassae (*Vásses*) ■■■ ☆
12km (7.5 miles) S of Andritsena. Getting there. By tour bus.
The temple, the second best preserved in Greece after the **Hephaesteion**, or **Thission**, in the **Agora** in Athens (see *Athens/Sights*), is situated on a mountain ridge between two ravines (hence its name: *vássa* means 'ravine'), 1,128m (3,700ft) above sea-level. It was raised by the inhabitants of nearby Phigaleia in thanks to Apollo *Epikoúrios* (Succourer) for delivery from the plague of 430BC. It was designed, according to Pausanias in his 2ndC AD *Guide to Greece*, by Iktinos, the architect of the Parthenon in Athens (see **Acropolis** in *Athens/Sights*). But it impresses more by its location than its intrinsic beauty, since it lacks the refinements of the Parthenon, though it has nearly as many peculiarities. The best time for a visit is early morning or late afternoon, when the mountains are bathed in deep pink or violet hues, and the temple's majestic isolation is undisturbed by coach parties.

The emplacement dictated the temple's unusual N–S axis, but the rear of the *naos*, the *adyton*, could be entered from the traditional E by an additional door to the side, opposite the cult statue. The adyton was marked off by a central column with a Corinthian capital – the oldest known specimen, now destroyed, but faithfully recorded in a 19thC architect's drawing. The *naos* proper is flanked on each side by a row of Ionic columns terminating five spur-walls jutting in obliquely from the outer masonry – another oddity. These carried a frieze, representing the ever-popular combats between Lapiths and Centaurs, Greeks and

Amazons, which is now in the British Museum – as are a hand and a foot from the statue, the clothed part of which was in wood, while the visible flesh was in marble. Outside, there was also once a colossal bronze statue of Apollo, but this was carried off to **Megalopoli** in 371 BC and replaced by a marble copy.

Nearby sights

The road to Bassae leads on down the coast past the 5km (3 miles) **ramparts of ancient Phigaleia** (Ano Figalia), with a medieval **fortress** on the acropolis. There is a c.1000 three-aisled Byzantine **basilica** with fine decorative brickwork at **Kato Figalia**.

H Theoxenia (☎ 22–219 ▮▯ ▭ 46 ⟵ ⇌ AE ⊕ ⊚ VISA ⌂).

Apollo Coast   See *Attica/Saronic Gulf*.

Aráhova

Map 7G5. 8km (5 miles) E of Delphi. Getting there: By bus, from Athens and Livadia. Population: 3,000.

The road to Delphi narrows dangerously as it passes through this picturesque village clinging precariously to the flank of **Mt. Parnassos** above the Plistos gorge. It is obstructed moreover by numerous coaches, parked in front of the souvenir shops selling sheepskin and handwoven rugs, and woollen handicrafts for which the region is famous. The local cheese and honey are also very good. Ski-hire facilities are available.

At the E end of the village a road branches off and climbs to a beautiful hidden highland. Through fir forests it passes between the main ski centres in Greece, **Fterolaka** and **Gerontovrahos**. As yet there are no hotels and, despite their ski-lifts and refuges near the summit, 2,450m (8,040ft), they are not in the international winter-sports league. The road crosses Parnassos to the village of Eptalofos to join the Livadia–Lamia road at **Amfiklia**, 42km (26 miles).

H Anemolia ♣ (*at the turn-off from the Delphi road to the ski centres* ☎ 31–640/4 ▮▮▮ ▭ 42 ▦ ⌂ ⇌ AE CB ⊕ ⊚ ◀€).

Árgos

Map 11I5. 56km (35 miles) SW of Corinth. Getting there: By bus, from Nafplio and from all parts of the Argolis; by train, on the Athens–Tripoli–Kalamata line. Population: 20,000.

Argos is the oldest continuously inhabited town in Europe. Here Danaos fled with his 50 daughters from the wrath of his twin brother, Aegyptos. But the latter's 50 sons followed and, after forcibly marrying their cousins, were murdered by their brides on their wedding night. One, however, helped her husband, Lynkeos, to escape, and he returned and slew Danaos. All but one of the murderous Danaïds were thrown into Tartaros (see *Mythology* in *Culture, history and background*) and eternally condemned to fill a bottomless cask with water carried in sieves. The remaining Danaïd escaped this fate by giving herself to Poseidon, by whom she bore Nauplios, founder of *Nafplio*.

The founding of towns seemed to run in the family: of Lynkeos' two sons, Proetos founded *Tirynth* and Akrisios became king of Argos. Akrisios was warned by the Delphic oracle that he would be killed by his own grandson, and secluded his only child, Danaë, in a tower of brass to protect her from the advances of men. But all in vain, for Zeus, in the form

55

of a shower of gold, visited and seduced her. Akrisios then cast both mother and the infant Perseus into the sea; they were washed ashore on the island of Serifos, where Perseus grew into an outstanding mythological hero. After accidentally killing his grandfather with a discus – so fulfilling the prophecy – he felt loath to succeed his victim as king of Argos and instead founded *Mycenae* and a new royal line.

Classical Argos, in continual rivalry with Sparta for the control of Lakonia and Arkadia, was decisively defeated in 546BC. Reviving in the 5thC BC, Argos succeeded in capturing and destroying both Mycenae and Tirynth, but was a loser in the Peloponnesian War. In Roman times the town was relatively prosperous, and there are some impressive remains.

The nearest beach is at **Nea Kios**, 7km (4.5 miles) s, where fish tavernas line the sea-front, but there is better bathing at **Mili**, 12km (7.5 miles) sw and at *Nafplio*, 12km (7.5 miles) SE.

Sights and places of interest
The ruins
The most striking Roman remains are large **baths** and an **odeon**, next to the ancient **theatre** seating some 20,000 spectators in 90 tiers cut into the steep hill. Other remains lie scattered nearby but below street-level. Mycenaean pottery, a rare example of 8thC BC bronze armour and some interesting 5thC AD mosaics are in the **museum** (▨ *standard opening times*).

The hill is crowned by a 13thC Frankish **castle** 🏰 which was enlarged by the Venetians and repaired by the Turks.

The Heraion of Argos (*Iréo*)
11km (6 miles) NE of Argos.

At the Argive Heraion, Agamemnon of Mycenae was chosen to lead the Achaeans against Troy. It was once the ancient shrine of the Great Goddess which the conquering Dorians transferred to the worship of Hera. The foundations of the 8thC BC temple, which stood on a **terrace** supported by **Cyclopean walls** made up of 5 by 2m (17 by 7ft) blocks, are the oldest identifiable ones in Greece. The first temple was burnt down in 423BC through the carelessness of a priestess, and the second temple, of which also only foundations remain, was reached by a large **stoa** and a monumental **stairway**.

Lérna
Near Mili, 12km (7.5 miles) sw of Argos.

Continuing excavations of ancient Lerna have brought to light a large building called 'the House of the Tiles', dated to about 2800BC. Here also Herakles slew the nine-headed Hydra.

Ⓗ Mycenae 🏨 (*Agiou Petrou Sq. 12* ☎ *28– 569* ▯ ▭ *24* 🚗).

Árta
*Map **6**F3. 75km (47 miles) s of Ioanina. Getting there: By bus, from Athens and all parts of Epiros. Population: 21,000.*

The southernmost town of Epiros is heralded as you approach it by orange and lemon groves, a special delight in spring when the fragrance of their blossom pervades the entire plain. Founded by the Corinthians in 636BC, ancient Ambrakia soon achieved independence. In 294BC Pyrrhos, king of Epiros, made it his capital, after he had gained the kingdom for the third time during the struggle for territory following the death of Alexander the Great, to whom Pyrrhos was related.

The last king of Epiros, Ptolemy, was murdered by a mob in 231BC. At that time strong ramparts enclosed the royal palace, several temples and two theatres; all were destroyed by the Romans in 189BC.

In 1214 the Angeli despots, the former Byzantine imperial family expelled by the Latin conquest of Constantinople in

1204, renamed the town Arta as their new capital, and built a
fortress on the acropolis, strategically sited beside the Arahthos
river. The Angeli despotate extended from Corfu to
Thessaloniki and during its brief flowering developed a
distinctive church architecture.

The city surrendered to the Turks in 1449, on terms stating
that the governor should be the only Moslem allowed to reside
within the walls. In 1794 a flood of the Arahthos devastated the
town, but spared the graceful 18thC bridge. The story goes that
the bridge proved impossible to complete until a bird revealed
to the master-builder that he must immure his wife in the
foundations of the raised middle span. The arches were then at
last joined, but the builder committed suicide. Popular ballads
on this Freudian theme are sung about several bridges in the
Balkans and even inspired Ivo Andric's Nobel Prize-winning
novel *Bridge over the Drina*.

Sights and places of interest
Panagía Parigorítissa (*Our Lady of Consolation*) 🏛 †

Despot Michael I and his consort built this expertly restored 13thC
church above a wide square. It is a high rectangular brick-and-stone
construction, built in a Byzantine style uniquely modified by
Romanesque features gleaned from the Latin Angevin court of the
nearby island of Kefalonia. The notable cupola, with a fine mosaic
Christ, is supported on pendentives rising above engaged marble
columns. The refectory houses a **museum** (🔲 *standard opening times*) of
local finds, including minor archaic sculptures, Tanagra figurines,
helmets, a rare bronze sepulchral urn, coins and ikons.
Other sights
Recent excavations below the strategic hill beside the Arahthos river
have uncovered scattered remains extending over 1.5 hectares (4 acres).
They include remains of the **ramparts** destroyed by the Romans, the
Temple of Apollo, a small **theatre** and **Hellenistic buildings**.

The **Church of Agia Theodora** † was dedicated to Despot Michael
II's wife, who became Arta's patron saint because of her impeccable
behaviour during her husband's quarrels with his family. The painted
exterior of **Agios Vassilios** † is quite well preserved and so are its
low-reliefs in varnished terra cotta. Some mosaics survive in **Agios
Nikolaos** † The oldest church is the 12thC **Agios Katsounis** †

Among the orange groves, outside the crenellated **medieval walls**, are
the **Convent of Kato Panagia** (*Our Lady Below*) and the **Monasteries of
Petra and Vlahernae**, the latter containing the **tomb of Michael II**. The
walls, which once protected the Despot's palace, now enclose the
romantically situated **Xenia** hotel.

🇭 **Kronos** (*Kilkis Sq.* ☎22–211/3 ▮▮▯ 🛏 55 ⬛ ➡ 🔵 💳); **Xenia**
♣ (*in the fortress* ☎27–413 ▮▮▯ 🛏 22 ⬛ ➡ 🆎 💠 🔵 💳 ⌂ ◁
🏊), excellently located (see above) – book well in advance in summer.

Athens (*Athína*) ★
*Map **14–15**, **16**D2&**8**H7. Area: 414sq. km (160sq. miles).
Airport: Elleniko, 11km (7 miles) from the city centre; for
Elleniko East ☎97–99–466 (all airlines except Olympic
Airways), buses depart every 20min, 6.20–0.20, from
Amalias Ave. 4; for Elleniko West ☎98–14–093 (Olympic
Airways only), buses depart every 20min, 6.20–0.20, from
Olympic Airways terminal, Syngrou Ave. 96 ☎92–92–251;
taxis to airport ▨ For ferries, see Piraeus in Athens/Sights.
Railway stations: Stathmos Athinon (Athens station)
☎82–13–882, for international services and destinations in
N Greece; Stathmos Peloponnissou (Peloponnisos station)
☎51–31–601, for the Peloponnese narrow-gauge line;
both stations are together in the NE of Athens; central ticket*

Athens

*office (English spoken), Sina 6 ☎36–24–402/6; stations for
Kifissia–Piraeus electric railway at Monastiraki Sq., Thission
and Victoria Omonia. Buses: For Europabus international
buses, Karolou 1 ☎52–40–519; for Peloponnese and N
Greece, main terminal at Kifissou 100 ☎51–24–910,
except bus 62, bus-stop at corner of Villara and Menandrou
(near Omonia Sq.); for Evia (Euboea) and E Central Greece,
Liossion 260, except buses 63 and 64, bus-stop at Amalias
Ave. (by National Gardens near Syntagma Sq.); for Elleniko
Airport, see above; for Piraeus, green buses from Filellinon
or Omonia Sq.; for suburbs of Athens, yellow trolley buses or
new diesel buses, 5.00–1.00; for Attica, ask at hotel or GNTO
office. For consulates, emergency and medical services, main
post offices, places of worship, tourist information and
tour operators, see Useful addresses in Basic information.
Population of Greater Athens: 4,000,000 (estimated).*

Since the beginning of time, men have fought for possession of
the world's great cities. Athens alone was contended for by the
gods. When Poseidon struck the **Acropolis** with his trident, his
gift, a fiery war horse, emerged; but Athena, goddess of
wisdom, caused an olive tree to grow as a symbol of peace and
prosperity, and the council of gods appointed her patron of the
city which has borne her name ever since.

The legendary Phoenician Kekrops founded the first
settlement at least 4,000yr ago, on the mighty rock near the
excellent ports of the Saronic Gulf protected by a semi-circle of
mountains. But the Athenians, characteristically prone to
wanting things not just both ways but three, or preferably four,
proudly proclaimed themselves to be the indigenous founders
of the city. In fact the Pelasgians, who may or may not have
been Greek, built the original Cyclopean walls on the rock in
about 1700BC. Yet classical Athens claimed to be the mother
city of the Ionian inhabitants of the islands and Asia Minor,
over whom she extended her empire.

In the 14thC BC the legendary Theseus united the village
communities of **Attica** under the leadership of Athens. The
Athenians soon started their seminal experiments in democratic
government, the first attempt ending in civil war, and
subsequent increasingly radical reforms paving the way only for
the rise of demagogues, chaos and the return of authoritarian
government. Advocate of the value of compromise, the
statesman Solon warned "Nothing in excess", but his advice
went unheeded.

Though the 5thC BC Athenian Empire was short-lived,
Athens remained culturally predominant throughout antiquity.
Despite resisting first Macedonian, and then Roman, rule – in
both cases to no avail – and backing the losing side in the three
great Roman civil wars of the 1stC BC, its cultural prestige kept
it safe from virtually all retribution. Successfully trading liberty
for prosperity, Athens not only became the foremost university
town of the Roman Empire, but remained an important
commercial centre in her own right. The Emperor Hadrian
built a large new quarter, later embellished by his Antonine
successors, and by the banker Herodes Atticus, the model for
those private benefactors who have endowed modern Athens
with public buildings. But although, during the long stability of
the *Pax Romana*, its fortunes waxed as never before or since, the
creative impulse of the city's youth had gone for ever.

The sack of Athens by Alaric's Visigoths in the 4thC AD was a
taste of evil days to come, and the closure of the Academy by

58

Justinian in 529 put an end to its intellectual pre-eminence. The paucity of monuments from the Byzantine Period shows how rapid was its decline, with frequent plunderings and occupations by every invader of any note who terrorized the eastern Mediterranean. After an incongruous, inconsequential interlude as a Frankish duchy from 1206–1455, at the end of which it was sold by its warlike conquerors to Florentine bankers, the Acciaiuoli, it became, under Turkish misrule, nearly extinct. When in 1834 king and government moved back to Athens, only some 6,000 wretched refugees huddled round the Acropolis, which had survived many sieges, while a few thousand more made a precarious living in Piraeus and the outlying villages.

By the time of the Treaty of Lausanne, 1923, Athens had grown into a typical Balkan capital, distinguished by its Neo-Classical public buildings, mostly erected by rich emigrant Greeks, and the Othonian architecture of its private houses. The port of **Piraeus** was still separated from Athens by extensive vegetable gardens, on which the first wave of refugees from Asia Minor settled in wooden shanties, the remaining green space being wholly occupied by the next wave of refugees from the civil war of 1946–49.

Athens, the eye of Greece, mother of arts
And eloquence, native to famous wits. . . . .

Milton, *The Passion*

The 1960s saw the start of rapid industrialization, adding each year about 100,000 inhabitants to an unplanned urban sprawl. Even today, the city is still divided at local government level into two towns and more than a dozen municipalities, carved up between the two administrative districts of Attica.

As the city spreads ever further out across the plain, engulfing the villages along the coast and in the foothills, and in the absence of any official definition of Greater Athens, calculations of size and population are a matter of intelligent estimation. A rough arbitrary estimate would be that some 4,000,000 people live in about 414sq. km (160sq. miles) – a space containing fewer parks than any city of comparable size in the western world. This estimate does not include **Eleusis** in the west – behind barren **Mt. Egaleo**, probably still wooded when Xerxes sat on his throne to watch the battle of Salamis in 480BC – whose dense concentration of heavy industry adds noxious fumes to the notorious 'chemical cloud' that pollutes Athens, except on days when a strong northerly wind restores to Attica the luminous clarity for which it was once famous.

Events: Blessing of the waters, Jan 6, port of Piraeus: youths dive for a cross thrown ceremonially into the water by the Bishop of Piraeus with great public celebration.

Carnival, Feb, especially on weekend evenings in the Plaka.

National Day, Mar 25: a military parade salutes the President before the Tomb of the Unknown Soldier.

Easter, Apr: see *Calendar of Events* in *Planning*.

St George's Day, Apr: folk-dancing at village of Aharnes, 6km (3.75 miles) N.

Son-et-lumière, Apr–Oct, Acropolis.

Flower festivals, May, at suburbs of Kifissia and Patissia.

Athens Festival, June–Sept.

Naval Week, July, Piraeus.

Wine Festival, Aug, at Daphni Monastery.

Sights and places of interest

Acrópolis ▥ ★

Map 14E3 ▨ ◱ *on Sun ✗ Open May–Oct 8.00–20.00, at
night during full moon; Nov–Apr 9.00–17.30, Sun and hols
10.00–16.00. Entrance off Dionysiou Areopagitou.*

A precipitous limestone cliff rising over 60m (200ft) above a
small, arid plain, not far from three safe ports and only slightly
further from four protective mountains, the Acropolis has been
a centre of attraction for settlers, conquerors, or just travellers,
for more than 5,000yr. Each of the monuments on its roughly
oblong top – 270m (886ft) at its longest, 156m (512ft) at its
widest – merits a separate entry but, because they so
triumphantly achieve the intended harmonious whole, it seems
wrong to divide where for once human genius succeeded in
uniting; each monument, however, is fully described below.

The Acropolis was founded in legend by the Phoenician
Kekrops and enlarged by Erechtheos, at the sight of whose
serpent tail the royal attendants leapt to their death from the
rock, and who lies buried in the **Erechtheion**. King Aegeus also
hurled himself into the sea (see *Islands A–Z/Aegean Islands*
and *Crete*) as his son Theseus' ship sailed into view. Theseus,
becoming king, united the villages of Attica, providing Athens
with the security to spread on to the plain, while the Acropolis,
the Upper City, remained a place of refuge round the fortified
royal palace.

The Acropolis was an outstandingly good citadel, being not
only a sheer impregnable rock but also having its own water
supply. In Mycenaean times it was the residence of the ruler,
and throughout its history it was liable to be recalled to its
defensive function: for the Florentine dukes against the Turks,
for the Turks against the Venetians, even for the British against
the Communists in 1944. It remained purely a fortress until the
6thC BC, when the tyrant Pisistratos built the first Propylaea
(monumental gate); the building of the first Temple of Athena
began the transformation of the fortress into a shrine where
beauty held precedence over the gods.

Following total destruction by the Persians in 480BC, the
combination of Themistokles' political genius and Kimon's
military prowess brought Athens to the peak of her wealth and
power. This allowed Perikles, marvellously misusing the
Delian League's funds transferred in 454BC from *Delos* (see
Islands A–Z), to finance the building of the most perfect
architectural complex of antiquity in Europe. It is worth
remembering that the whole glorious expanse of buildings on
the Acropolis was painted, as was customary, in vivid reds,
blues and golds, which would perhaps have seemed a little
barbaric to our taste. However, all that gleaming white Pentelic
marble might have produced a cold, monotonous, even
sepulchral effect, judging by modern imitations. Instead, time
and neglect have added a delicate golden patina, one that is now
being steadily eaten away by the sulphuric acid 20thC pollution
has put into the rain. The marble has not been so white for
centuries, but also never so frail. Despite an international
campaign mounted under the auspices of UNESCO, no
effective protection has yet been found, and the buildings can
now only be walked round and not entered, being no longer
strong enough to take the vibration of so many visitors' feet over
their floors.

Once past the pedlars plying their objectionable souvenirs at

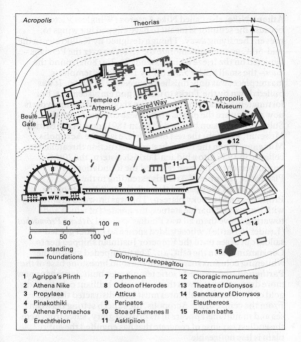

1 Agrippa's Plinth
2 Athena Nike
3 Propylaea
4 Pinakothiki
5 Athena Promachos
6 Erechtheion
7 Parthenon
8 Odeon of Herodes Atticus
9 Peripatos
10 Stoa of Eumenes II
11 Asklipiion
12 Choragic monuments
13 Theatre of Dionysos
14 Sanctuary of Dionysos Eleuthereos
15 Roman baths

the coach park, one ascends in a zig-zag up the ramp which every 4yr the Panathenaea procession also once climbed, carrying a new robe for Athena, in the most solemn event in the city's calendar. On the 8.2m-high (27ft) **plinth** on the left, the pragmatic Athenians replaced an earlier statue of some Hellenistic benefactor with that of the Roman general Agrippa.

Between 437–432BC, the architect Mnesikles brilliantly executed his commission to build the **Propylaea**, which Perikles intended should "crown the citadel of the gods with a radiant diadem". Across the 46m (150ft) western front of the Acropolis, the portico, with six fluted Doric columns on the outside, doubled by slender Ionic on the inside, stood over the five splendidly-worked gates.

The N wing, the **Pinakothiki**, housing a picture gallery in which the 5thC BC paintings of Polygnotos dominated, was the residence first of the Orthodox archbishops, then of the Acciaiuoli dukes. The latter added a square keep, completing the transformation into a fortress – an excrescence demolished in 1875 at the archaeologist Schliemann's own expense.

As if to add insult to injury, the Turkish commander used the central portico as a powder magazine, which in 1645 was struck by lightning. Guns were placed in the shattered walls and the building suffered further in the siege of 1827, during the War of Independence. Fortunately, reconstruction (including the marble beams and parts of the decorated coffers of the roof) has been sufficiently successful to recall the former splendour of this superb entrance.

The S wing is greatly shortened, to allow easy access to the western bastion of the Acropolis, where stands the **Temple of**

Athena Nike, also called **Nike Apteros** (Wingless Victory) because the sculptor is meant to have clipped her wings to prevent her flying away. Though designed by Kallikrates in the mid-5thC BC to commemorate the victories over the Persians – depicted on the frieze which extends 26.2m (86ft) round the *naos* – the small 8.2 by 5.5m (27 by 18ft) Ionic temple, a masterpiece, was only finished between 427–424BC. It was pulled down by the Turks to make a gun emplacement, but fortunately they left the pieces lying about, and the main parts now missing are the panels of the frieze collected with the Sultan's permission by Lord Elgin in 1801, now in the British Museum, London; the rest of the frieze is in the **Acropolis Museum**. When the 19thC first reconstruction threatened to collapse in 1936 into a hidden Turkish cistern, the 20thC reinforcement of the base revealed the foundations of the E. Pisistratos' **Temple of Artemis** extending to the E.

The **Sacred Way** passed through the middle gate of the Propylaea on to a rocky plateau. This was crowded in antiquity with bronze and marble statues, the greatest of which and towering above them all was Phidias' colossal *Athena Prómachos* (Leader in Battle), whose gilded spear and helmet guided sailors out at sea until the Emperor Justinian shipped her to Constantinople in the 6thC AD. The unimpeded view of the whitening columns soaring from the solid limestone base of the **Parthenon**, the greatest Doric temple ever built, is perhaps now more dramatic that it was then, when the brilliant colours and gold of the massed sculptures must have distracted the eye. From the centre of the Acropolis, the superb setting between sea and mountains appears in its pristine glory, since from here the endless expanse of concrete that has engulfed the entire plain is less noticeable.

The Parthenon was built between 447–432BC on the foundations of earlier temples. Its architect was Iktinos and the master builder Kallikrates, with Phidias as master sculptor. Of traditional rectangular layout and surrounded by respectively 17 and eight fluted columns, the temple is laid out not in straight lines but in very subtle curves. The floor is slightly convex; the columns bulge just below the middle, incline inwards, and are closer and thicker in the corners; the cornices of the pediments are oblique; and the entablature rises in the middle.

This subtle sophistication was complemented by Phidias' 92 sculptured metopes depicting mythological battles, 44 statues in the pediments (*Athena's Contest with Poseidon* in the W, *The Birth of Athena* in the E) and the 160m (524ft) frieze depicting the Panathenaea procession. Most of the surviving fragments were taken away by Lord Elgin, and are now in the British Museum, London; the rest of the sculpture, with the exception of a few bits in the Louvre than a French ambassador managed to conjure from the Turks before Elgin arrived, is in the **Acropolis Museum**, including parts of the frieze until recently *in situ*, very damaged by pollution.

The name Parthenon, meaning the **Hall of the Virgin**, originally applied to one room in the temple, but eventually the whole building came to be called by that name. Here, in the *naos* proper, two storeys of Doric columns surrounded the chryselephantine statue of *Athena*. The Parthenon was both a place of worship and the national treasury, and the statue had a detachable robe of solid gold.

The Parthenon's later history included the installation of

Dimitrios Poliorkitis (the Besieger) with his mistress in the Hall of the Virgin in the 4thC BC. In Christian times it was dedicated at first to Holy Wisdom and then, with virginity coming again to the fore, to Our Lady. In 1460 the Parthenon was converted into a mosque, and a minaret (since removed) was added. Then, in 1687, the Venetian artillery commanded by Admiral Morosini scored a direct hit on the gunpowder the Turks had stored there, and blew out the *naos* and 28 columns. A plan to use parts of the building for the royal palace and to demolish what was not needed was rejected by King Ludwig I of Bavaria in 1834, and Ludwig paid for more suitable accommodation for his son Otho in Syntagma Sq.

The **Erechtheion**, most sacred of the shrines on the Acropolis, has just emerged from its 1980–82 restoration, not quite as good as new, since it had suffered too much, but it is now possible once again to observe its multiple sacred roles. Athena's sacred olive tree was just outside this superbly graceful Ionic jumble, built on different levels with three irregular porticos. But the fountain that welled up when Poseidon's trident struck the rock was inside, next to the tombs of Kekrops and Erechtheos.

Each one seemed venerable when it was born, and at the same time a youthful vigour makes them appear today as if they were newly built.

> Plutarch, *Life of Perikles*, 1stC AD, on the
> buildings of the Acropolis

Another portion was reserved for Athena *Pólias* (Patroness of the Town), whose ancient wooden idol, believed to have fallen from heaven, was kept here. It was to this artless carving, and not to Phidias' splendid statue in the Parthenon, that the Panathenaea procession brought a new robe every 4yr. The temple also sheltered a golden lamp that was always kept burning and a bronze palm tree. The main entrance was by the E portico, much less impressive than the larger and lower N portico dedicated to Zeus *Hýpatos* (The Highest). This Ionic masterpiece preceded the door, famous for its rich ornamentation, to the chamber of Erechtheos. Most famous of all, however, are the six caryatids of the S portico; one was taken by Elgin, the others, much the worse for pollution, are in the **Acropolis Museum**. They have been replaced by glass-fibre copies in the recent reconstruction, which removed some of the Roman, Byzantine and Turkish adjuncts.

The Erechtheion, designed by Mnesikles, was begun during the brief interval of peace in 421BC, and completed in 405BC, just before Athens' final defeat in the Peloponnesian War. Its caryatids are outstanding examples of the late, enriched classical style, and the Emperor Hadrian even had copies of them made for his villa at Tivoli; remains of the frieze, of dark grey Eleusinian marble decorated with white Pentelic marble sculptures, are also in the **Acropolis Museum**. Like the Parthenon, the Erechtheion was used as a church in Byzantine times, but then became the harem of the Turkish commander, at a suitable distance from his own residence in the Propylaea, while the sacred trident mark was used as a WC.

Along the N side of the Acropolis are the foundations of older temples and even of the Mycenaean fortress-palace.

The **Acropolis Museum** is listed separately in *Athens/Sights*.

The south slope of the Acropolis

The S slope of the Acropolis was given over in classical times to recreation and health care. Its main monuments are the **Theatre of Dionysos** and the **Odeon of Herodes Atticus** to the W (the locale of the annual Athens Festival, June–Sept) with the **Sanctuary of Asklipios**, the god of healing, between them. The entrance from Dionysiou Areopagitou leads directly into the **Sanctuary of Dionysos Eleuthereos**, to whom the tyrant Pisistratos built a temple and in whose name he instituted in 534BC the Festival of the Greater Dionysia, held in early spring. Pisistratos' temple was destroyed by the Persians, and the new one constructed in 420BC by the general, Nikias, the 2ndC BC **altar** in front of it, and the **Roman baths** to the left are all now equally ruined.

During the annual Greater Dionysia competition, dramas by three tragic and five comic poets were staged each day, for several days. In the 5thC BC the winners usually were Aeschylos, Sophokles or Euripides, or in the comedy section, Aristophanes. The production of the plays was financed by wealthy citizens who often commemorated their victorious protégés by setting up a monument, either here or on the other side of the rock, in the Street of the Tripods (see **Lysikrates Monument**). Two **Corinthian columns** which supported choragic bronze tripods can still be seen.

The **Theatre of Dionysos** with a proper stage facing the 67 tiers of seats, rising against the slope of the Acropolis and accommodating some 17,000, was not built until the 4thC BC. It was easily able to accommodate the People's Assembly (see opposite), which had moved over from the Pnyx at the W of the Acropolis.

The stage was then enlarged by the Romans and decorated with bas-reliefs – including a nice crouching *Silenus* – in Nero's time. The finely-carved front seats, inscribed with the office of the priests and dignitaries for whom they were reserved, are Hellenistic; the most elaborate of them all, dead centre, was for the priest of Dionysos. The marble railing was put up when the Romans introduced gladiatorial contests.

Linking the Theatre of Dionysos to the Odeon of Herodes Atticus ran the **Stoa of Eumenes II**, ruler of the Hellenistic kingdom of Pergamon in Asia Minor. Its two storeys, each with 64 Doric columns, 164m (179yd) long, ran parallel to the **Peripatos**, or Promenade, behind. This was a favourite walking place for philosophers teaching their students on the move rather than in classrooms, a habit developed by Sokrates and taken up by Aristotle – hence the 'Peripatetic' school.

The **Odeon of Herodes Atticus** at the W end, erected by the famous 2ndC AD banker in memory of his wife, had 32 tiers seating 5,000. The **Odeon of Perikles**, to the right of the Sanctuary of Dionysos, was considered the finest ancient concert hall; it was burnt down, possibly by Sulla, and though it was rebuilt, very little remains. Like all odeons, both were roofed over for year-round musical and dramatic performances.

The **Sanctuary of Asklipios** extends over most of the upper terrace beyond the Peripatos. The worship of the god of healing was introduced during the terrible plague of 429BC. The **old Asklipiion**, a one-storey, 83m-long (91yd) stoa opened in 420BC, was so successful that the **new Asklipiion**, a two-storey, 49m-long (54yd) stoa, was added in the 4thC BC. The sister of Asklipios, Hygia, who was also connected with healing, was associated with the latter.

The hills to the west of the Acropolis
From the junction of Dionysiou Areopagitou and Apostolou
Pavlou, a road and footpaths lead into three hills within sight of
the Propylaea: the Hill of the Muses, the Pnyx and the
Areopagos. The **Hill of the Muses**, first and highest, 147m
(482ft), is always called **Philopappos**, after the Roman consul
and last descendant of the Hellenistic Kommagene kings,
Philopappos, whose **monumental tomb** was erected in it in
AD116. He stands in the garb of an Athenian citizen in the
middle niche of the 12m-high (39ft) edifice; on the left is a
statue of *Antiochos IV*, his grandfather. Nearby are the remains
of the fortifications erected by Dimitrios Poliorkitis in 294BC,
from which the Venetians blew the Parthenon apart in 1687.

All the hills are honeycombed with caves, which in the
overcrowding of the city during the Peloponnesian War formed
a troglodyte quarter, but which were otherwise empty or were
used as tombs by the Romans. Near the **Chapel of Agios
Dimitrios Lombardaris †** three rooms hewn out of the rock are
known as, but not proved to be, the **Prison of Sokrates**, who in
a dreadful miscarriage of justice was tried and induced to
commit suicide by drinking hemlock in 399BC.

The **Pnyx**, across a ravine, was the site of the People's
Assembly from the time of Klisthenes in the late 6thC BC until it
was moved to the more convenient Theatre of Dionysos on the S
slope of the Acropolis, nearly 200yr later. The name means
'tightly crowded together', although of the 18,000 citizens in
the Golden Age hardly more than 5,000, the quorum, would
usually attend, despite the indemnity paid after the identity
check at the single entrance. Naturally it was the poorer citizens
who took advantage of the ever-increasing attendance
payments, which largely accounts for the success of
irresponsible demagogues and the rapid decline of democracy.
Most of the ancient retaining wall has disappeared, and
spectators can watch the *son-et-lumière* performance from the
unfenced natural slope below the rectangular rock where
orators stood to harangue the citizens.

Close to the **Observatory**, built in 1842 by the Greco-
Austrian Baron Sina, is the **Barathron**, an antique quarry into
which criminals originally were thrown alive, though in later
times they were executed first. Less rough-and-ready justice
was dispensed on the rocky knoll across Apostolou Pavlou and
to the left of the Propylaea ramp, the **Areopagos** (Hill of Ares).
Here the god of war was brought to trial before the Olympians
for the killing of Poseidon's son – thus replacing private
vengeance with formal justice and setting a precedent for all
future homicide trials. Several millennia later the name was
revived for the Supreme Court of modern Greece.

Below the rock of the Areopagos is a cave, traditionally the
Sanctuary of the Eumenides, the infernal goddesses, avengers
of murder – known euphemistically as *The Kindly Ones*,
supposedly to appease them. From the rock, St Paul preached
his *Sermon to the Athenians* and converted the senator
Dionysios, who was canonized with the epithet 'the Areopagite'
and became patron saint of Athens.

Acropolis Museum ★
Map 14E3. At the SE corner of the Acropolis ☎ *32–36–665*
▣ *Standard opening times.*
When Themistokles ordered the hasty rebuilding of the
ramparts in 479BC, while he led an embassy to keep the Spartans

talking till it was done, broken columns and statues from the temples just sacked by the Persians were used for the revetment. To this we owe the preservation of the hoard of archaic sculpture now in the Acropolis Museum. Outstanding are the 6thC BC *Korae*, draped maidens dedicated as offerings. Most of them were sculpted by Ionian artists during the rule of Pisistratos and Hippias, but the one signed by the Athenian Antenor and dating from the end of the tyranny is perhaps the finest. Also noteworthy are the **coloured fragments of figures from the pediments of 6thC BC temples**, such as those of *Herakles Battling with a Triton* from the 'Hekatompedon', the Pisistratan forerunner of the Parthenon, the *Shepherd carrying a Calf across his Shoulders*, and the *Lion devouring a Bull*.

Several terra cottas show the transition to the classical style. Its developed perfection is displayed in the 20-odd slabs of the Parthenon frieze, showing the Panathenaea procession in chariots or on horseback, punctuated by marshals giving directions, with standing or walking attendants carrying sacred implements and, on one slab, three of the Olympians who witnessed the climax, the robing of Athena's statue. The friezes from the Temple of Athena *Nike* and the Erechtheion show the more exuberant, freer late classical style.

The museum has such an embarrassment of riches that the construction of a larger building, at the foot of the Acropolis, has become imperative.

Agíi Apostóli   See **Byzantine churches**.

Agíi Theodóri   See **Byzantine churches**.

Ágios Nikódimos   See **Byzantine churches**.

Agora ☆ and sights nearby
*Map **14**D2. Thission Sq.* ☎ *32 – 10 – 185* 🚇 *Standard opening times.*

The **Agora**, the centre of ancient Athenian public life, is dominated by the best preserved temple in Greece, the Thission, on the left of the present entrance, which faces the reconstructed Stoa of Attalos II, now the Agora Museum. In between, the civic institutions, shops and stoas, through and around which ancient life revolved, lie utterly ruined. Although it was excavated and mapped by the American School of Classical Studies at the expense of the Rockefeller Foundation in the 1950s, this ancient market place inevitably causes considerable confusion to the visitor.

The **Thission** (Theseion) 🏛 so called since the Middle Ages because its mutilated frieze depicts the exploits of Theseus, was in fact the Ifestion (Hephaesteion), or Temple of Hephaestos, god of smiths and potters, whose forges and workshops for centuries occupied this quarter. Designed by Iktinos, the architect of the Parthenon, it lacks the touch of genius that makes the Parthenon unique. Its full complement of 34 Doric columns has been knocked slightly awry by earthquakes, though they still support the roof. The entrance was changed from the usual E to the W when Justinian dedicated the temple to St George in the 6thC. Inevitably it later became a Turkish mosque, and was a burial ground for British Protestants in the 19thC.

The huge quadrangle of the Agora was reconstructed on a grander scale after its destruction by the Persians in 480BC. It was mostly surrounded by long stoas or porticoes, in whose shade and shelter business could be transacted in all weather; here Sokrates discussed with Plato, and Zeno explained the principles of Stoicism (the name is in fact derived from 'stoa').

The corner below the Ifestion was taken up by the three most important governmental buildings: the **Bouleuterion**, meeting place of the 500 magistrates who supervised the Assembly; the circular **Tholos** where, in rotation through the ten-month Attic year, 50 of them slept and took their meals during their month of vigilance; and the 2ndC BC **Metroon** (with a layout rivalling in peculiarity the Erechtheion on the **Acropolis**), which was both the state archive and a temple for the Mother of the gods. From the 2ndC BC, temples to Ares, Apollo and the Twelve Gods were added between the Thission and the present electric railway; indeed, the Twelve Gods are now partly under the railway. Stoas, altars and an odeon were also added at this time to the **gymnasium**, the site of which is marked by three gigantic statues.

The 2ndC BC **Stoa of Attalos II** 🏛 was built by the King of Pergamon in recognition of the education he had received at Athens. He was brother and successor to Eumenes II, who erected a stoa on the S slope of the **Acropolis**. Here, in two superimposed colonnades of 134 columns, Doric below, Ionic above, lavishly decorated with statues, were the most fashionable shops. The Stoa was meticulously reconstructed by the Americans in the 1950s at a cost of $1.5 million, but its present vast expanse of gleaming white marble perhaps justifies the antique practice of applying vivid colours. It now serves as the **Agora Museum** (📷 *standard opening times*), and contains mainly vases and a great number of headless or limbless sculptures. On slightly higher ground is the 11thC **Agii Apostoli** ✝ (see **Byzantine churches**).

Leaving the Agora by nearby Polygnotou, one comes to four columns surmounted by a pediment: this is the entrance to the **Agora of Augustus**, built between 10BC and AD2 with funds from the Emperor. In Roman times the centre of civic life moved here, and the Emperor Hadrian surrounded it with marble colonnades. The remains of the **Library of Hadrian**, to the N, once a huge rectangle enclosing a court of 100 columns, give some idea of its original magnificence.

On the other side of the Roman Agora stands the **Tower of the Winds**, so called after its reliefs depicting the eight winds. In fact it was a 1stC BC hydraulic clock with a sundial and a weather vane, the practical gift of Andronikos Kyrrestes to the business community. Under Turkish rule it was occupied by dervishes of the Bektashi order, who preserved it as the tomb of the two local prophets, Sakhratis and Aflatun (Sokrates and Plato).

Arch of Hadrian See **Olympion**.

Areópagos (*Hill of Ares*) See **Acropolis**.

Benáki Museum ☆
Map **15**D5. *Vassilissis Sofias Ave. 17* ☎*36–11–617* 📷 🅾 *on Sun. Open Wed–Mon 8.30–14.00.*
Really too many collections of ceramics, ikons, jade, jewellery and textiles of Byzantine, Islamic, Coptic and Chinese origin are shown in overcrowded rooms. However, there are also good displays of Greek national costume in all its colourful variety.

Byzantine churches

The unity of period and style of Athens' Byzantine churches
makes it easier to treat them as a group and, although they are
scattered, they are all within easy walking distance of Syntagma
Sq. Of minute proportions, these 11th or 12thC shrines were
constructed in the eastern cross-in-square plan under one or
more cupolas supported by octagonal drums (see *Art and
architecture* in *Culture, history and background*). More
interesting than beautiful, they stand out in the tide of
modernity that has all but engulfed them. But although their
original interior decorations have been lost through the ravages
of time, despoliation and restoration, all the buildings are still in
religious use.

Agii Apostóli (*Holy Apostles*) †

Map 14D2. Agion Apostolon, above the Agora.

The church of the Holy Apostles, above the **Agora**, which
commemorates St Paul's preaching there, was expertly restored
by the American School of Classical Studies during excavations
in the Agora. It is 11thC, and typical in plan and exterior.

Agii Theodóri (*Sts Theodores*) †

Map 14D3. Klafthmonos Sq.

The alternating stone and brick of the oldest of the Byzantine
churches in Athens date from the reconstruction of 1409,
though it was an 11thC foundation. Also 15thC are the cupola
and three apses, the terra cotta frieze and the handsome door,
but the bell-tower and the interior decorations are 19thC.

Ágios Nikódimos †

Map 15E4. Fillelinon.

The largest of the Byzantine churches in Athens, the building
dates from the 11thC and was raised over the foundations of a
Roman bath-house – substituting godliness for cleanliness. It
was appropriated by the Russian colony in 1847 and somewhat
over-restored at the expense of the Tsars by a Bavarian
architect. The bell-tower is 19thC.

Kapnikaréa (*Our Lady of the Robe*) †

Map 14D3. Ermou.

The narthex and the cruciform nave, under a dome supported
on four tall re-used Roman columns, are 11thC; the pillared
side-porch (*exonarthex*) and an additional, smaller nave
(*parecclesion*) with a second cupola are 13thC. The tiny church,
belonging to Athens University, is utterly incongruous amidst
the surrounding drapers' shops, but quite possibly their
medieval predecessors were responsible for the church's name,
meaning Our Lady 'of the Robe' – given the remarkable
continuity, even in modern Athens, of traditional locations of
the various commercial activities.

Old Mitrópolis ▥ †

Map 14D3. Mitropoleos Sq.

The tiny, elegant late-12thC edifice, 7.3 by 11m (24 by 36ft) in
plan, is of old, golden Pentelic marble in which classical
fragments were incorporated. When the Franks ousted them
from their previous residence in the Parthenon, the Orthodox
archbishops made this their cathedral. It was replaced in the
19thC by the adjoining **Mitropolis**, a monstrosity constructed
from the remains of 70 ruined churches in a style that can never
have been classifiable.

Panagía (*Our Lady*) †

Map 14D3. Monastiraki Sq.

Though pure of style, with a rare elliptical cupola, this remnant
of an 11thC monastery is not very inspiring.

Byzantine Museum 🏛 ☆
*Map **15**D5. Vassilissis Sofias Ave. ☎ 72–11–027 🚗*
Standard opening times, but closed on Mon not Tues.

The lack of medieval sacred art and furnishings inside Athens' churches is amply compensated for by the wealth of the collection housed in the 19thC residence of the Duchess of Piacenza, an American-born daughter-in-law of one of Napoleon's marshals, and a leading spirit in the court of King Otho. It includes sculpture, frescoes, illuminated books, embroideries and, above all, ikons. Its most famous exhibit is the **Epitaphios of Thessaloniki** ☆ – a 14thC embroidery *Lamentation over Christ*. Extensions had to be made in 1981–82 for pre- and post-Byzantine religious objects.

Epigraphic Museum   See **National Archaeological Museum**.

Eréchtheion   See **Acropolis**.

Évzones Barracks   See **Parliament**.

Hill of the Muses (*Philopáppos*)   See **Acropolis**.

Kaisariani Monastery ☆
*Map **16**D2. 6.5km (4 miles) E of central Athens. Getting there: By bus from the University, Venizelou.*

The groves round the spring on the lower slopes of **Mt. Ymitos** (ancient Hymettus) command an extensive view over Athens down to the sea and are so natural a setting for a sanctuary that a former shrine of Aphrodite on this site inevitably continued in use, as a Christian church, after the 5thC AD. Some 600yr later, monks in search of peace and contemplation rebuilt the Church of the Panagia (Holy Virgin) ✝ in the diminutive proportions characteristic of late-Byzantine architecture.

The cross-in-square plan is crowned by a dome with a projecting roof above an octagonal drum pierced with windows, supported by four columns with Ionic capitals from the pagan temple. An altar of porphyry stands in the middle of the three semi-hexagonal apses of the E end, and several antique bas-reliefs have been inserted into the exterior walls, which are decoratively coursed by squared stones alternating with bricks. The 16thC **frescoes of the Cretan School** illustrate biblical stories in colourful, uplifting serenity round the walls, while *Christ Pantokrátor* (Almighty) blesses from the dome; just beneath are the *Vision of Ezekiel* and the *Preparation of the Throne*, separated by a circle of angels and another of prophets. In the conch of the apse the *Virgin with the Holy Infant* presides over the *Divine Liturgy* and the *Communion of the Apostles*.

The **narthex** was added about 1690, and although the inferior workmanship bears witness to the hard times, there are fine paintings by the Peloponnesian Ioannis Ypatios, with a new animation displayed in the *Scenes from the Life of Christ*, the *Holy Trinity*, *Angels* and *Saints*.

The bath is in a domed trefoil building in which the arch of the furnace is still visible. Fronting the living quarters and the cloister was an arched **loggia** for meditation. The late 16thC **refectory** was divided by a storeroom from the **kitchen**, where the stone benches on which sat the monks still surround the fireplace, with its 9m-high (30ft) brick cupola from which cooking vessels were hung.

Perhaps the most striking feature of Kaisariani is the harmony between architecture and surroundings. Well, but not over-restored, it is the most attractive and evocative of Athens' Byzantine remains.

Kanelópoulos Museum ☆

Map 14D3. In the Plaka, at the junction of Panos and Theorias ☎*32–12–313* ◫ *Standard opening times.*

This typical 19thC *Pláka* house contains a small but representative collection of Byzantine jewellery and ikons, and traditional and folk art.

Kapnikaréa   See **Byzantine churches**.

Keramikos Cemetery and Museum ☆

Map 14D2. Ermou 148. Museum ☎*34–63–552* ◫ *Open Mon, Wed–Sat, except hols, 9.00–15.15.*

The Keramikos cemetery is an important archaeological site in rather depressing surroundings, although the nearby gas-works, which for the past century have polluted the cemetery's monuments with foul black smoke, are at last to be replaced by a park. It was usual in the ancient world to be buried beside the road just outside the city walls, and the Keramikos, or Potters' Field, was located at the point where the roads from **Piraeus**, Boeotia and *Eleusis* converged before the **Iera Pyli** (Sacred Gate) and the adjacent **Dipylon** (Double Gate). The Iera Pyli received the Sacred Way along which the Panathenaea processions en route to the Parthenon would come, pausing at the Pompeion just inside, where ritual equipment was kept, and where Hipparchos was murdered in 514BC. The Dipylon was the main entrance and exit to the city.

Our love of the things of the mind does not make us soft.
                                                    Perikles' funeral oration, 429BC

One layer of tombs was superimposed upon another until in 1861 the earlier graves came to light during the construction of modern Pireos, the main road down to the port. The funerary *stelae* of wealthy Athenians line the **Street of the Tombs**, notably that of Dexileos, 4thC BC. The theme is mostly departure, often showing horsemen off to war, but on one tomb there is a magnificent charging bull. Many other *stelae*, as well as vases (since ceramics were often used for monuments), are in the **Keramikos Museum** to the s, but the most important pieces have been taken to the **National Archaeological Museum**. Perhaps, however, the most lasting memorial of the Keramikos was the famous funeral speech over the first victims of the fateful Peloponnesian War, delivered here by Perikles in 429BC.

A visit, inclusive of the small museum, takes at the most 1hr, unless you have a thing about cemeteries, and is therefore usually combined with sightseeing on the **Agora**, with which it is connected by Apostolou Pavlou Ave.

Lykavittos (*Mt. Lykabettus*) ★

Map 15C5. Funicular ◫ *every 15min, 8.00–24.00 from Aristipou; steep path from Loukianou. Road to open-air theatre from Sarandapihou.*

The view from the 731m (2,400ft) crag which rises precipitously from the elegant Kolonaki residential district is both stunning and frightening – for the entire plain, from the mountains to the sea, has been filled by cement, leaving hardly any green spaces. Egina and the mountains of the Peloponnese form a splendid backdrop on a clear day, and sometimes a northerly wind lifts the pollution sufficiently to restore to Mt. Ymitos its fabled violet hue. At the summit, reached by the funicular, are the **Dionyssos** (see *Athens/Restaurants*), the **Chapel of Agios Georgios †** and an open-air theatre used for performances during the Athens Festival.

Lysikrátes Monument ▥
Map 14E3. Corner of Tripodon and Lysikratous.

To the E of the Acropolis, modern Tripodon retraces roughly the ancient **Street of the Tripods**, where the bronze prizes of the winners in the drama competitions of the Dionysia (see **Acropolis**) were displayed. The round monument of Lysikrates at its s end supported one of these; six Corinthian half-columns support the architrave of this elegant choragic monument, whose **frieze** depicts Dionysos transforming into dolphins the pirates who had captured him. An **inscription** identifies the members of the winning choir, Lysikrates, who paid for the performance, and the date, 334BC.

Museum of Greek Popular Art
Map 14E3. Kydathineon 17, in the Plaka ☎ 32-13-018 🖼
Open Tues – Sun, 9.00 – 14.00.

The collection has much in common with those of the **Benaki** and **Kanelopoulos** museums, though with a stronger emphasis on folk art. It includes a fine collection of **Rhodian pottery** and of clerical robes.

National Archaeological Museum ▥ ★
Map 15B4. Tossitsa 1 ☎ 82-17-717 🖼 🖾 *on Sun and some hols. Standard opening times, but closed on Mon not Tues. Numismatic and epigraphic collections only: open 7.30 – 13.30.*

Housed in an appropriately Neo-Classical building, this is the principal museum of Greece, its permanent collections being constantly enriched by new finds from all over the country. However, many of these, such as the **Minoan frescoes from Thira ★** – recovered from beneath the pumice and lava at Akrotiri (see *Islands/Thira*) – will stay here only until a local museum has been constructed. The same is true of the **ceramics and clay figurines from Thessaly**, which are of the prehistoric period till 1100BC, **marble figurines and vases from the Cyclades**, and the **treasure from the royal tombs of Homeric Mycenae ★** discovered by Schliemann.

There is an incredible wealth of **ceramics** on the first floor, from Protogeometric, Geometric and Orientalizing pottery to Corinthian and Attic vases, and black-figured, red-figured and Polychromatic ware. But the historical period is dominated by **sculpture**, starting with Daedalic statues and archaic *kouroi* (young men). The climax reached in the classical period includes bronzes of gods, heroes and even mortals. The magnificent bronze **Poseidon ★** is outstanding, and the charming bronze *Jockey* and marble *Head of the Goddess Hygia* are both noteworthy. There is also much fine Hellenistic and Roman sculpture. The numerous reliefs, either architectural from the pediments of temples or bas-reliefs from funerary *stelae*, also deserve attention.

Metalwork is mostly bronze, with examples of figurines, armour, tripods, mirrors and decorative articles. Most striking is the **Stathatos collection** ☆ of gold jewellery and funeral wreaths.

In the same building are the **Numismatic Museum** with a collection of 250,000 coins and the **Epigraphic Museum**, a collection of historical inscriptions.

National Historical Museum of Modern Greece

Map **15***D4. Palea Vouli (Old Parliament), Stadiou*
☎ *32–37–617* 🖼 *Open Wed–Mon 9.00–13.00.*
Formerly the Parliament building, the museum contains mainly relics and pictures from the War of Independence, including some souvenirs of Byron's command at *Messolongi.*

National Picture Gallery (*Pinakothíki*)

Map **15***D5. Vassileos Konstantinou 50, opposite the Hilton*
☎ *72–11–010* 🖼 *Standard opening times.*
The El Grecos are hopeful but unlikely, the large number of 19thC Romantic paintings fairly hopeless. Not worth visiting except for its special exhibitions.

National and Zápion Gardens ☆

Map **15***E4. Entrances from Amalias, Vassilissis Sofias Ave. and Irodou* 🖼 *Open sunrise to sunset.*
Most of this oasis in the centre of Athens was designed as the Palace garden by a German landscape gardener for Queen Amalia, wife of King Otho, in the mid-19thC. The rare wild goats of Crete, *kri-kri*, are the only noteworthy inmates of a tiny zoo. The **Zapion**, a Neo-Classical exhibition hall with a formal garden below, is named after its donor; nearby is a cafe, where an orchestra plays on summer evenings, and an open-air cinema.

Numismatic Museum See **National Archaeological Museum**.

Old Mitrópolis See **Byzantine churches**.

Olympíon ☆ 🏛

Map **15***E4. Corner of Amalias Ave. and Olgas Ave.*
The 2ndC AD **Arch of Hadrian** 🏛 is a Roman archway topped by Corinthian pillars, architrave and pediment. It bears on one side the inscription 'This is the city of Theseus', on the other 'This is the city of Hadrian'.

The Olympion, behind the Arch, was also built by Hadrian, reviving the original colossal scheme of the 6thC BC tyrant Pisistratos, whose immense Doric columns, 2.5m (nearly 8ft) in diameter were first raised here. The Ionic columns of a Hellenistic temple subsequently built on the site were then removed by Sulla in the 1stC BC for re-use in the temple of Jupiter Capitolinus in Rome. Hadrian employed columns of the Corinthian order, which, though some one-third smaller in diameter than those of Pisistratos, were still the largest in Europe, as indeed was the whole temple, measuring 108 by 41m (354 by 135ft). Hadrian's friend and rival in the embellishment of Greece, the banker Herodes Atticus, was appointed the first high priest of this grandiose temple to Olympian Zeus.

Its 104 Corinthian columns were subsequently shipped away by the Genoese and Venetians. In 1759 the Athenian-born

Turkish governor burnt one of them for lime for the mosque in
Monastiraki Sq. The last of a long line of *stylites* (hermits living
on top of pillars) built himself a hut on one of them in the early
19thC. **Sixteen columns** still remain, of which 13, in the SE
corner, retain their **architrave**.

Panagía   See **Byzantine churches**.

Panepistimíou   See **Venizelou**.

Parliament (*Vóuli*)
*Map **15**D4. Syntagma Sq.*
After deciding not to incorporate the Parthenon into a new royal
residence on the Acropolis, Ludwig I of Bavaria built this
austere palace for his son Otho, first king of modern Greece. It
was finished by 1843, when Otho reluctantly granted the nation
its first constitution. In 1923 it was used to shelter refugees from
the Treaty of Lausanne, and since 1933 as the debating
chamber of the various régimes Greece has experienced.

The retaining wall of the palace ramp holds the bronze and
marble bas-reliefs of the **Tomb of the Unknown Soldier**. Here
the guard of tall, colourful, kilted *Évzones* is changed at 11.00
on Sun – a major tourist attraction. You can have your
photograph taken with the guards outside their **barracks** at the
back of the Palace, in Irodou Attikou.

Better still, try the guards who stand opposite, in front of the
Presidential Palace, which was built by the German architect
Ziller in the Neo-Renaissance style current in the 1890s. After
the restoration of the monarchy in 1935 it became the royal
residence, and is now used for the President's official functions.

Parthenon   See **Acropolis**.

Philopáppos   See **Hill of the Muses** in **Acropolis**.

Pinakothíki   See **National Picture Gallery**.

Piraeus (*Piréas*)
*Map **16**D1&**8**H7. To the sw of Athens. Terminus of the
Kifissia–Athens–Piraeus electric railway. Buses from
Athens. Port: Ferries from the main harbour to the Argo-
Saronic Islands and the Peloponnese, and the Cyclades,
Dodecanese and numerous other Aegean Islands; hydrofoils
from Zea Harbour for the Argo-Saronic Islands and the
Peloponnese.*
Under Perikles, ancient Piraeus, the port of Athens, was laid
out on a grid system round a central agora by the architect
Hippodamos of Myletos. It was destroyed by Sulla in 86BC and
did not really regain its importance as a national commercial
centre until the mid-19thC. It has since merged in practice, if
not administratively, with Greater Athens, and has become one
of the main ports in the eastern Mediterranean.

Opposite the breakwater of **Zea Harbour**, crowded with
luxurious yachts, the **Naval Museum** (■ *standard opening
times*) displays ship models covering a period of 4,000yr. Along
the waterfront are remains of the 4thC BC **wall**, and above it a
ruined **Hellenistic theatre**, next to the **Archaeological
Museum** (*Harilaou Trikoupi* ■ *standard opening times*) which
was reopened in 1981, but whose contents are of comparatively
minor interest. On the opposite side of Zea Harbour, the traces

of the **Asklipiion**, behind one of the few tasteful Neo-Byzantine churches, are both hard to find and insignificant.

There is another, larger **theatre** of the 5thC BC on Profiti Ilia hill, next to the modern, comfortable open-air **Veakio theatre**, where ballets, concerts and plays are performed in summer against the splendid backdrop of the Saronic Gulf. Next door is a bowling alley and below it **Mikrolimano** (Small Harbour), famed for its seafood and brimming with small boats.

Pláka
Map 14D−E3

The old town, between Syntagma Sq. and the Acropolis. Now a pedestrianized zone and the centre of tourist entertainment. See *Athens/Nightlife*.

Pnyx   See **Acropolis**.

Presidential Palace   See **Parliament**.

Queen Sophia Ave.   See **Vassilissis Sofias Ave.**

Stádio (*Stadium*)
Map 15E4. Beyond Zapion Gardens, opposite corner of Irodou Attikou and Vassileos Konstantinou.

The white marble of the reconstructed ancient Stadium once again shines out, almost blindingly. The site of the athletic competitions of the four-yearly Panathenaea Festival, it was covered in stone by Lykurgos in 330BC and in marble by Herodes Atticus in about AD140. In post-classical times it served as a convenient quarry until excavations were begun by Ziller, which continued under King George I. A modern benefactor, George Averof, built this exact replica of Herodes Atticus' stadium, which was used for the first modern Olympic Games held in 1896.

The ancient stadium was laid out in a fold of the pine-clad Arditos hill above the stream of the Ilissos, where Racine's Phèdre walked and Plato's Sokrates conversed. Since the 1960s the stream has been covered over by wide avenues reaching down to the sea at Nea Faliro. To the NW is the 19thC **First Cemetery**, with sculptures including Chalepas' *Sleeping Maiden* and Vitsaris' *Weeping Angel*.

Street of the Tombs   See **Keramikos Cemetery and Museum**.

Street of the Tripods   See **Lysikrates Monument**.

Thissíon (*Theseion*)   See **Agora**.

Tomb of the Unknown Soldier   See **Parliament**.

Tower of the Winds   See **Agora**.

Town of Athens Museum
Map 14D3. Klafthmonos Sq. 🔲 *Open Mon, Wed, Fri 9.00−13.30.*

The first residence in Athens of King Otho, the museum still contains original furniture and prints.

University   See **Venizelou.**

Vassilíssis Sofías Ave. (*Queen Sophia Ave.*)
Map **15***D4–5.*
Lined with expensive hotels, residences, state buildings,
embassies and museums, 'millionaires' row' leads from
Syntagma Sq. out to the northern garden suburbs of Psihiko,
Filotheï and Kifissia below **Mt. Penteli's** marble quarries.

Venizélou (*also known as Panepistímiou,*
University St.)
Map **14***C3–***15***D4.*
This principal thoroughfare, between elegant Syntagma Sq.
and popular Omonia Sq. above the underground electric
railway station, is lined with elegant hotels, shops and
important public buildings. The Neo-Classical **Palace of Ilion**,
once the residence of Heinrich Schliemann, archaeologist of
Troy and Mycenae, used to house the *Areópagos*, the modern
Greek supreme court. Next door is the vaguely Italianate
Catholic **Cathedral of Agios Dionysios Areopagitos †**
dedicated to the patron saint of Athens.

The marble **Academy**, a gift of the Austrian-Greek Baron
Sina, is a smaller replica of the Parliament in Vienna, down to
the tall Ionic columns with statues of *Apollo* and *Athena*. The
University (*Panepistimion*), fronted by a painted colonnade, is
now used only for ceremonies, and teaching goes on in the
Panepistimioupoli (University City) out beyond the Hilton,
although the Doric **National Library** is still here. All these
19thC Neo-Classical buildings were designed by the Danish
Hansen brothers.

The **Theatre Museum ▥** behind the National Library,
though of purely local interest, is a pleasingly restored
Othonian mansion.

Vóuli   See **Parliament**.

War Museum
Map **15***D5. Corner of Vassilíssis Sofías Ave. and Rizari*
☎ *72–39–560* **▦** *Standard opening times.*
Containing flags, uniforms, weapons and plaster models of
ancient battles, this expensive and hideous modern building is
regarded by some as the worst mistake of the Colonels who
governed Greece from 1967–74.

Zápion   See **National and Zapion Gardens**.

Zéa Harbour   See **Piraeus**.

Where to stay
Despite the very large number of hotels in Athens (most of them
built since 1960), it is essential to book well in advance for
June–Sept, and for Easter and Christmas; in May and Oct some
of the larger hotels are occupied by congresses, but there will be
no difficulty finding accommodation next door. Hotels in
Athens are open all the year round.

The three main concentrations of hotels in inner Athens are
round Syntagma Sq. (categories L–C), round Omonia Sq., the
noisier and shoddier centre (categories A–D), and near the US
Embassy, elegant, less crowded, but not really within walking
distance of the main sights and shops (categories L–B). For an
explanation of these categories, see *Accommodation* in *Planning*.

Visitors who do not mind the expense of taxis or the discomfort of overcrowded buses might consider the 'Apollo Coast' (see *Attica/Saronic Gulf*), but prices are higher there than elsewhere on the Greek coast, planes roar over day and night to Elleniko Airport, and the sea is polluted, at least by other countries' standards, as far as Vouliagmeni. Nearest to Athens is Neo Faliro (categories B–C), but it is a long way from the centre and faces both pollution in the sea and dust from apparently never-ending public works (see *Attica/Saronic Gulf*). Nor is Piraeus particularly attractive, but for those changing boats two tolerable establishments will be listed. Kifissia (see *Attica/The mountains*) is quiet, cool, and on the electric railway.

A short description of the outstanding hotels follows, and then merely a listing of a few in each category. Avoid category D in Athens (none is listed here), unless you are really hard up, since the decline in quality is out of all proportion to the saving in price. The few pensions, merely cheaper hotels usually without private showers, are not worth mentioning. For a longer stay, an air-conditioned service flat can be pleasant.

Hotels in Athens

Aphrodite ✿
Apollonos 21, Athens 118
☎ *32–34–357/9. Map* **14D3** ▥
▱ *84* ▤ ▱ CB ✦ ◉ VISA
Location: Well placed between Syntagma Sq. and the Plaka. Outstandingly good value among Athens' many inexpensive hotels. Matches dearer hotels both in location and facilities.
❧ *on roof.*

Ariane Hotel Apartments ⌂ ✿
Timoleontos Vassou 22, Athens 602 ☎ *64–86–361/2. Map* **16D2** ▱ *to* ▱ ▱ *26* ▤
▱ AE CB ✦ ◉ VISA
Location: In the quiet residential area near the US Embassy, a short taxi or bus ride from the centre. One of the best of Athens' luxury furnished-apartment accommodations. Breakfast and drinks served.

Astor
Karageorgi Servias 16, Athens 125 ☎ *32–55–555/60*
☎ *214018. Map* **15D4** ▥ ▱ *133* ▤ ▱ ▱ AE CB ✦ ◉ VISA
Location: Just off Syntagma Sq. Conveniently central, and better value than its neighbours. Front rooms rather noisy, but good views from the roof-terrace restaurant.
◃€

Athenian Inn ✿
Haritos 22, Athens 139
☎ *72–38–097* ☎ *215735. Map* **15D4** ▱ ▱ *28* AE CB ✦ ◉ VISA
Location: 100m (110yd) from

Kolonaki Sq. Near to the most elegant district of central Athens, busy with restaurants and cafes, and to the station for the Mt. Lykavittos cable cars. No restaurant, though breakfast is served, and no air-conditioning, but otherwise rooms are adequate.
◠

Athens Gate
Syngrou Ave. 10, Athens 403
☎ *92–38–302/9* ☎ *219660. Map* **14E3** ▥ ▱ *106* ▤ ▱
▱ AE CB ✦ ◉ VISA
Location: Opposite the Olympion within easy walking distance of the Acropolis and of the bus terminal for the sea. Modernistic decor with air-conditioned lounge-cum-bar. Indifferent food served in a clean, clinical dining-room.
♿ ◃€

Divani Zafolia Alexandras ✿
Alexandras Ave. 87, Athens 702 ☎ *69–25–111/4* ☎ *214468. Map* **15B5** ▥ ▱ *200* ▱ ▱ ▱
AE CB ✦ ◉ VISA
Location: On a busy main road, far from the centre, halfway between the new law courts and the park. Commodious open-plan public rooms. Roof-terrace with swimming pool.
♿ ≈ ◨

Dorian Inn
Pireos 15, Athens 112
☎ *52–39–782* ☎ *214779. Map* **16D1** ▥ ▱ *146* ▤ ▱ ▱ ▱
AE CB ✦ ◉ VISA

Location: On a busy main road, in central Athens though at the wrong end of it. One of the large concentration of middle-priced hotels round Omonia Sq. The public rooms are small, but the air-conditioned private rooms are ample. Above-average service in the restaurant.
≈

Electra Palace ✿
Nikodimou 18, Athens 118
☎ 32–41–401/10 🕾216896.
Map **14E3** ⅢⅢ ⬜ 106 ⬛ ⇋ *AE*
CB ⬤ *CD* *VISA*

Location: In a fairly quiet side-street in the centre, on the fringe of the Plaka. The public rooms are rather dark. One of the few hotels in its category to have a secure garage.
& ⬜ ⬇ on roof ≈

El Greco ✿
Athinas 65, Athens 112
☎ 32–44–553/7 🕾219682.
Map **14D3** ⅢⅢ ⬜ 92 ⬛ ⇋
AE *CB* ⬤ *CD* *VISA*

Location: Set back slightly from noisy Athinas, running from Omonia Sq. to Monastiraki and the Plaka. This is one of the cheapest of the many perfectly adequate hotels in the neighbourhood. Only the public rooms are air-conditioned, but the bedrooms are comfortable, and the service is willing, and the restaurant is at least as good as the more expensive examples in this category.

Grande Bretagne 🏨 ✿
Syntagma Sq., Athens 133
☎ 32–30–251/9 🕾219615.
Map **15D4** ⅢⅢ ⬜ 425 ⬛
⇋ *AE* *CB* ⬤ *CD* *VISA*

Location: In the very centre, opposite Parliament, within easy walking distance of the museums, shopping streets and, at a pinch, the Acropolis. The hotel began life in 1862 as a guest house for the former Royal Palace, now Parliament, but has since been rebuilt and expanded to its present capacity of 400 rooms and 25 suites. Parades and public ceremonies, which usually culminate at the Tomb of the Unknown Soldier, are visible from the front rooms, but for those preferring quiet (and Syntagma Sq. can be noisy) there is a choice of cheaper interior rooms. The range of prices and variety of accommodation should be sufficient to satisfy everyone requiring the luxury category. See also *Athens/Restaurants*.
⌂ & ⬜ ◁€

Hilton 🏨 ✿
Vassilissis Sofias Ave. 46,
Athens 612 ☎ 72–20–201
🕾215808. Map **15D6** ⅢⅢ ⬜ 480
⬛ ⬛ ⬛ ⬛ ⬛ ⇋ *AE* *CB* ⬤ *CD* *VISA*

Location: A 10min walk from the centre along Vassilissis Sofias Ave. The architecture and layout are pleasantly functional, and though the green space is smaller than usual, the swimming pool is large and well-equipped. The choice of restaurants caters to all tastes, from the Galaxy roof-garden with its splendid view over the Acropolis and the sea and its dinner-dances, to the surprisingly cheap Byzantine Cafe. The Hilton still ranks first for comfort, service and price among the US chains represented in Athens.
⌂ & ⬜ ⬇ on roof ◁€ ≈ ⛱
🚶

Holiday Inn ✿
Mihalakopoulou 50, Athens
612 ☎ 72–48–322 🕾218870.
Map **15D5** ⅢⅢ ⬜ 198 ⬛ ⬛
⬛ ⇋ *AE* *CB* ⬤ *CD* *VISA*

Location: Near the US Embassy. The latest hotel to open in this area. A typical, comfortable example of the chain, with eight suites.
⌂ & ⬜

Lycabette ✿
Valaoritou 6, Athens 134
☎ 36–33–514/8 🕾215077.
Map **15D4** ⅢⅢ ⬜ 40 ⬛ *AE* *CB*
⬤ *CD* *VISA*

Location: Well located in the small pedestrianized section of central Athens, among the concentration of middle-priced modern hotels round Omonia Sq. and close to the shopping streets. Functionally modern bedrooms; rather dark public rooms. No restaurant, but breakfast is brought to your room; service is friendly. Good views from the upper terrace.
⌂ ◁€

N.J.V. Meridien 🏨 ✿
Syntagma Sq., Athens 133
☎ 32–55–301/9 🕾210568/9.
Map **15D4** ⅢⅢ ⬜ 171 ⬛
⇋ *AE* *CB* ⬤ *CD* *VISA*

Location: The latest addition to the group of smart central hotels round Parliament, within easy walking distance of the museums, shopping streets and, rather further, the Acropolis. A new member of the French-managed chain. There are 14 suites; the Brasserie des Arts is a valiant attempt at Parisian atmosphere.
& ⬜ ◁€

77

Sirene
Lagoumitzi 15, Athens 404
☎92–29–310/6 ▥ ▭ 109 ▤
🚗 � ⌗ AE CB ◑ ◒ VISA
Location: On a busy but not too noisy road, not quite in the centre but within walking distance of the Acropolis. Modern layout and furnishings, air-conditioned public rooms, roof-terrace with swimming pool and a moderate view. But wear and tear from package tours is showing.
≈

Stanley ✿
Odysseos 1, Athens 107
☎52–41–611/8 ☎216550.
Map **14C2** ▥ ▭ 400 ▤ 🚗 🏠
🚆 ⌗ AE CB ◑ ◒ VISA
Location: On Kareskaki Sq., not in the centre and within walking distance only of Omonia Sq. and its underground station. The public rooms are modern open-plan, the bedrooms strictly utilitarian. These are air-conditioned, but the swimming pool on the roof is often too polluted for comfort. Package tours are efficiently handled, but the individual traveller may feel he is in the way.

Titania
Venizelou 52, Athens 142
☎36–09–611/9 ☎214673.
Map **15D4** ▥ ▭ 39 ▤ 🚗
🚆 ⌗ AE ◒ VISA
Location: Nearer the Omonia Sq. end of Venizelou. The front rooms are noisy, but the interior rooms are quiet enough. There is a roof bar overlooking the Acropolis, and a useful 24hr snack-bar. There is also a shopping arcade; the garage is underground. This, one of the more comfortable hotels in its category, also caters for the handicapped.

Other recommended hotels in Athens

Comfortable hotels, all having ▤ AE CB ◑ ◒ VISA **Divani Zafolia Palace** ✿ (*Parthenonos 19, Athens 402* ☎92–22–945/9 ☎218306, map **14E3** ▥ ▭ 193 🚗 ≈ *within easy walking distance of the Acropolis and the Plaka; same management as the Divani Zafolia Alexandras* ▭ ≈); **Electra** ✿

(*Ermou 5, Athens 132* ☎32–23–222/7 ☎216896, map **14D3** ▥ ▭ 110 🚗 🚆 *almost in Syntagma Sq.; same management as Electra Palace*); **President** ✿ (*Kifissias Ave. 43, Athens 613* ☎69–24–600 ☎218585 ▥ ▭ 513 🚗 ☘ *out beyond the US Embassy* ▭ ☘ *on roof* ≈ ◑); **Riva** ✿ (*Mihalakopoulou 114, Athens 610* ☎77–06–611/5 ☎214736, map **15D5** ▭ 59 🚗 🚆 *near US Embassy; furnished flats, 50 suites; see also Athens/Restaurants* ▭).

Moderately priced hotels, all having ▤ AE CB ◑ ◒ VISA **Alexandros** ✿ (*Timoleontos Vassou 8, Athens 601* ☎64–30–464 ☎216013 ▥ ▭ 96 🚆 *near US Embassy* ✉); **Athens Center** ✿ (*Sofokleous 26, Athens 112* ☎52–26–110/9 ☎214483, map **14C3** ▥ ▭ 136 🚆 *near Omonia Sq.* ☘ *on roof*); **Candia** ✿ (*Deligianni 40, Athens 108* ☎52–46–112/7, map **14C2** ▥ ▭ 142 🚗 🚆 *near Omonia Sq.* ≈); **Eretria** ✿ (*Halkokondyli 12, Athens 141* ☎36–35–311/9 ☎215474, map **14C3** ▥ ▭ 63 🚗 *near Omonia Sq.*); **Galaxy** ✿ (*Akadimias 22, Athens 134* ☎36–32–831/9 ☎215077, map **15D4** ▥ ▭ 102 🚆 *halfway between Syntagma Sq. and Kolonaki Sq.*); **Grand** ✿ (*Veranzerou 10, Athens 102* ☎52–22–011/4, map **14C2** ▥ ▭ 99 🚗 🚆 *near Omonia Sq.*); **Ilissia** ✿ (*Mihalakopoulou 25, Athens 612* ☎74–40–051/5 ☎214924, map **15D5** ▥ ▭ 69 🚗 🚆).

Inexpensive hotels, both having ▤ AE CB ◑ ◒ VISA **Iniohos** ✿ (*Veranzerou 26, Athens 102* ☎52–30–811/5, map **14C3** ▥ ▭ 134 ▤ 🚆 *near Omonia Sq.*); **Omonia** ✿ (*Omonia Sq. 4, Athens 101* ☎52–37–210/9, map **14C3** ▥ ▭ 260 🚗 🚆).

Hotels in Piraeus

Both having ▤ 🚗 🏠 ☘ *on roof* ◑ **Cava d'Oro** (*Vassileos Pavlou 19* ☎41–13–744/5 ▥ ▭ 74, *overlooking Mikrolimano*); **Park** (*Kolokotroni 103* ☎45–24–611/5 ☎212228 ▥ ▭ 80, *in a quiet street close to the main harbour*).

Where to eat, drink and shop for food

Restaurants, offering Greek, international and the better-known national cuisines – mostly French and Italian, but also Lebanese, Chinese and Japanese – are to be found in the same areas as hotels, round Syntagma Sq., Omonia Sq., and near the

US Embassy. For seafood, picturesque **Mikrolimano** in **Piraeus** is closest, although a larger but equally expensive choice is available on the 'Apollo coast' (see *Attica/Saronic Gulf*). For general information on Greek restaurants and tavernas, see *Food and drink* in *Planning*.

The Greek tavernas should, however, be sampled in the Plaka, although this, once the essence of 19thC Athens, has now become the entertainment district, bright with neon lights and resounding with *bouzóuki* and pop music. In general, the louder the noise, the worse the food, but it should be experienced once, and people have been known to come back for more. Greeks will gladly take their foreign friends there but, left to themselves, they will seek out the smaller, quieter tavernas, away from the hurly-burly of the Plaka.

Cafes/patisseries are everywhere. Most are *zaharoplastía* (patisseries), frequented in their expensive versions by ladies of a certain age, and in their basic neighbourhood form by the local youth; they have almost entirely superseded the old-fashioned *kafenía*, which survive only round Omonia Sq., still the exclusive preserve of men sipping their coffee or their *óuzo* for hours. *Kafenía* are the real victims of westernization, since they have been replaced neither by the equivalent of pubs or beer cellars, which can be counted on the fingers of one hand, nor by hotel bars, frequented only by the sophisticated few. *Zaharoplastía* are not, however, tea-shops; if you want tea, it is obtainable in hotels or the smarter cafes, though generally Greeks regard tea as medicinal.

Fruit sold from street vendors' barrows is often more expensive than from greengrocers, and their *tyrópittes* (cheese pies) and *koulóuria* (pretzel with sesame seeds) are not reliably hygienic. Good greengrocers abound round Kolonaki Sq., and opposite the University on Venizelou, while those round Omonia Sq. are cheaper but generally of a high standard. Specialized shops selling dried fruits and nuts – the most interesting local products – are gathered round Omonia Sq.; two of the best are **Danopoulos** (*Venizelou 44, map 15D4*) and **Nafpliotis** (*Eolou 102 and 103, map 14C–D3; Veranzerou 5, map 14C3*). But, except for the Greek olives, fruit and tomato juices, and goat and sheep cheeses, in which they take proper pride, most grocers seem to have more care for imported goods than for local produce.

Galaktopolía (dairies) sell not only milk and butter but honey, excellent yoghurt, and all kinds of sticky sweets, and are the only shops that stay open uninterruptedly from early morning to late at night. They also sell alcohol (though mostly sweet local liqueurs), ices and iced drinks (not, however, fresh fruit or juices). The fish and meat market is in Athinas, between Omonia Sq. and Monastiraki.

Restaurants in Athens

L'Abreuvoir ⌂
Xenokratous 51
☎ 72–29–061. Map **15D5** ▮▮▮
to ▮▮▮ ⌷ ⇌ AE CB ◉ ◎ VISA
Outstanding among the quite plentiful French restaurants, though with a rather restricted menu.

Located in the Kolonaki district, it is frequented more by the resident foreign colony than by visitors. French wines – at a price. *Specialities: Steak au poivre.*

American Coffee Shop ☕
Nikis 1 ☎ 32–46–873. Map **15D4** ⌷ ⌷ ▮ ◎ *Closed Sun.*
Just off Syntagma Sq., this is good for substantial breakfasts, or for a snack until 22.00.

Balthasar ✿
Tsoha 27 ☎ *64–41–215* ▮▮▮▮ ▭
▱ ◢ AE ⊕ ⊚ *Closed for
lunch and on Sun.*
Pleasant setting in an old house,
beyond the US Embassy, with a
small garden. Good curries.

Corfu ✿
Kriezotou 6 ☎ *36–13–011.
Map* **15**D4 ▮▮▯ ▭ AE CB ⊕ ⊚
VISA
Just off Syntagma Sq., in the
arcades of the King's Palace Hotel,
this is excellent for business
lunches or a quick dinner, but is
rather busy in season. Service is
polite and efficient; the wine is
properly chilled, but though the
menu is extensive with several *plats
du jour*, there are no specialities –
not even Corfiote ones. . . .

Delphi ✿
Nikis 15 ☎ *32–34–869. Map*
15D4 ▮▯ ▭ AE CB ⊕ ⊚ VISA
Very 'touristy' but not pretentious:
it provides an adequate meal in
close proximity to Syntagma Sq. in
the shortest possible time. Not
grande cuisine, but there is
sufficient variety to satisfy all
tastes, though the quick turnover
can mean there are people waiting a
bit too close for comfort to take
your place.

Dionyssos *(Acropolis)* ⌂
Robertou Galli 43
☎ *92–33–182. Map* **14**E2–3
▮▮▮▮ AE CB ⊕ ⊚ VISA
The Zonar chain's finest
restaurant. Opposite the Acropolis
with a view that can only enhance
its reliable and varied fare
(especially dinner during summer,
when there are *son-et-lumière*
performances). It is naturally
much favoured by visitors, while
being too expensive to be swamped
by coach parties. It is advisable
however to reserve a table,
especially for dinner. *Specialities:
Hors-d'oeuvres, excellent cakes.*

Dionyssos *(Lykavittos)*
*Mt. Lykavittos, by the upper
cable-car terminal*
☎ *72–26–374. Map* **15**C5 ▮▯
▭ ◢ AE CB ⊕ ⊚ VISA
Restaurant closed for lunch.
This member of the Zonar chain
offers an even better view than the
Acropolis Dionyssos, from the top
of Mt. Lykavittos over all Athens
and Piraeus and down to the sea.
Neither the food nor the prices,
however, match the location. It is
easily reached by cable-car from

Kolonaki Sq., and the cafeteria and
patisserie are open from the earliest
to the last cable-car.

G.B. Corner ✿
*Hotel Grande Bretagne,
Syntagma Sq.* ☎ *32–30–251.
Map* **15**D4 ▮▮▯ ▭ ◢ AE CB ⊕
⊚ VISA
Ideally central, with a civilized,
quiet atmosphere, its quick, polite
service is of the sort achieved only
by long tradition, while the prices,
furthermore, are very reasonable.
Either come early or book a table.
   The menu is not very large, but
offers a representative selection of
both French and Greek dishes, and
everything on it, including the *plats
du jour*, is good. In particular the
sherbets are delicious every day,
and it is one of the rare places
where you can get very drinkable,
non-resinated Greek wines, even
by the glass. See also
Athens/Hotels.

Maxim ✿
Milioni 4 ☎ *36–15–803. Map*
15D4 ▮▯ ▭ AE CB ⊕ ⊚ ⊚ VISA
Closed for lunch.
A handy and pleasant restaurant
off Kolonaki Sq. Unrelated to the
Parisian restaurant of the same
name. Besides the Greek and
international dishes there are a few
Turkish specialities well worth
trying. *Specialities: Hot meat
dishes with yoghurt, swordfish kebab.*

Papakia ⌂
Iridanou 5 ☎ *72–12–421. Map*
15D6 ▮▮▮ ▭ ◢ AE CB ⊕ ⊚
VISA *Closed for lunch, on Sun in
Aug.*
In one of the few 19thC houses –
rather than mansions or palaces –
left in Athens, this restaurant
offers genuine atmosphere and
personal service, with a pleasant
patio for outdoor dining in
summer. *Specialities: Duckling
(papáki is Greek for duckling) à
l'orange, duckling aux olives.*

Le Quartier
Kolonaki Sq. ☎ *36–04–765.
Map* **15**D4 ▮▮▯ ▭ ◢ AE CB ⊕
⊚ VISA
A cafe/restaurant specializing in
light meals and snacks, served
almost all year round (at least in the
middle of the day) out of doors,
where you can see all Athens go by.
It has so far not succumbed to the
persistent craze for pizzas, but
offers a tasty selection.
*Specialities: Traditional macaroni
dishes.*

Stagecoach ☖
Loukianou 6 ☎ *72–43–955.*
Map **15**D5 ▥ ☐ AE CB ⊕ ⓒ
Closed for lunch.
Situated next to the British
Embassy, in the Kolonaki district,
the Stagecoach sports the
appropriate decor, boasts a long
bar, is better on hard liquor than on
wine, and serves good steak – but
has very little of the Wild West
about it. ***Specialities:*** *American
dishes, steak.*

Theofilos
Vakhou 1 ☎ *32–23–901* ▥
Closed for lunch. In the Plaka.
A taverna opened in 1899,
decorated with drawings and
graffiti. *Kokkinéli* (rosé *rétzina*)
from Crete.

Vasilis ✿
Voukourestiou 14a
☎ *12–12–801. Map* **15**D4 ☐
☐ AE CB ⊕ ⓒ VISA
The oldest of the cheaper tourist
restaurants in the centre (just off
Syntagma Sq.), it has the right
formula and has deservedly
outlived its competitors. Adequate
food, with good vegetables, in
plain surroundings at low prices.

Xynou ✿
Angelou Geronta 4
☎ *32–21–065. Map* **14**E3 ▥
☐ ☖ ♪ *Closed for lunch and on
Sun.*
The largest and most comfortable
of the Plaka tavernas that have food
worth mentioning. The authentic
Greek dishes are well prepared,
though the choice is not large.

Zonar's ☖
Venizelou 9 ☎ *32–30–336.*
Map **15**D4 ▥ to ▥ ☐ ☖ AE
CB ⊕ ⓒ
The mother-house of the Zonar
Dionyssos chain. It started as a
zaharoplastía and its strength still
lies in its cakes and ices, though the
bar is popular and there is nothing
wrong with the food. However,
both choice and space are
restricted. ***Specialities:*** *Cakes.*

Other restaurants and cafes in Athens

Athens Cellar ✿
Anagnostopoulou 1
☎ *36–11–707. Map* **15**D4 ▥
☐ ■ *lunch only* AE CB ⊕ ⓒ
VISA
Situated on the corner of Kolonaki
Sq., this restaurant serves Greek
and international dishes.

China ✿
Efroniou 72 ☎ *72–45–746.*
Map **15**D6 ▥ ☐ ■ ⊕ ⓒ VISA
Closed Sun lunch.
In the Ilissia district, near the
Hilton; serves Chinese dishes.

Escargot ✿
Ventiri 9 ☎ *72–30–349. Map*
15D6 ▥ ☐ AE ⊕ ⓒ *Closed Sun.*
In the Ilissia district, near the
Hilton. French food.

Gerofinikas
Pindarou 10 ☎ *36–22–719.*
Map **15**D4 ▥ ☐ AE CB ⊕ ⓒ
VISA *Closed for lunch.*
In the Kolonaki district, the
restaurant serves Turkish
specialities.

Ideal ✿
Venizelou 46 ☎ *36–14–604.*
Map **15**D4 ☐ ☐ AE CB ⊕ ⓒ
Open 10.00–24.30.
Very large choice.

Maralinas
Vrassida 11 ☎ *72–35–425.*
Map **15**D6 ▥ ☐ ☖ AE CB ⊕
ⓒ
Near the **Hilton**, the restaurant
serves Lebanese specialities.

Michiko
Kydathineon 27
☎ *32–20–980. Map* **14**E3 ▥
☐ ⊕ ⓒ VISA *Closed Sun.*
In the Plaka, the restaurant serves
Japanese dishes.

Prunier ✿
Ipsilantou 63 ☎ *72–23–379.*
Map **15**D4 ▥ ☐ CB ⊕ ⓒ
Closed for lunch and on Sun.
In the Kolonaki district. French
specialities, but no connection with
Prunier of Paris or London.

Riva ✿
Mihalakopoulou 114
☎ *77–06–611* ▥ ☐ AE CB
⊕ ⓒ VISA
Near US Embassy. See also
Athens/Hotels.

Steak Room ✿
Eginitou 6 ☎ *72–17–445* ▥
☐ AE CB ⊕ ⓒ *Closed for
lunch.*
Between **Hilton** and US Embassy.
Specialities: *Steaks.*

Ta Nissia ✿
Vassilissis Sofias Ave.
☎ *72–24–900. Map* **15**D5 ▥
☐ ■ AE CB ⊕ ⓒ VISA
Ta Nissia means Island Tavern.
Specialities: *Seafood.*

Templar's Grill ✿
*In the Royal Olympic Hotel,
Athanassiou Diakou 28*
☎ 92–30–315. Map **14E3** ▯▯▯
▭ *AE* *CB* ⊕ ⊚ *VISA* *Closed for
lunch.*
Live piano music. *Specialities:
Charcoal grills.*

Restaurants in Piraeus

Aglamair ✿
*Akti Koumoundourou 54,
Mikrolimano* ☎ 41–15–511.
Map **8H7** ▯▯▯ ▭ *AE* *CB* ⊕ ⊚
VISA
Aglamair is the best and dearest of

the fish restaurants lining the
picturesque Mikrolimano harbour.
A commendably large repertoire
even includes some sauces – a rarity
in Greece. Reservations are needed
for summer evenings only.
Specialities: Lobster, prawns.

Miaoulis
*Akti Koumoundourou 22,
Mikrolimano* ☎ 41–11–401.
Map **8H7** ▯▯▯ ▭ 🍴 *AE* *CB* ⊕
⊚ *VISA*
Named after a naval hero in the
Greek War of Independence; a
good representative of the dozen or
so fish restaurants on the seashore.

Nightlife and cultural entertainment

In summer, Apr–Oct, you can watch *son-et-lumière* on the
Acropolis from the Pnyx nightly in English at 21.15 (liable to
changes). This is the curtain-raiser to the **Athens Festival**, July
to mid-Sept, a worthy revival of the Dionysia instituted by
Pisistratos in the 6thC BC. In the superb golden marble theatre
of the **Odeon of Herodes Atticus**, on the S slope of the
Acropolis, there are not only presentations of ancient tragedies
and, to a lesser extent, comedies (all in modern Greek
translation), but also operas, ballets and concerts performed by
both Greek and foreign companies. The drama is sufficiently
impressive not to require a knowledge of Greek, but it is worth
reading up your Sophokles beforehand. Bring a backrest, for
cushions only are provided for the marble seats.

Plays ancient *and* modern are performed during the Festival
at the **Lykavittos Theatre**, and folk dancing is the speciality of
the **Philopappos Theatre**. Prices for all performances are very
reasonable in comparison with other international festivals. Do,
however, book well in advance (*ticket office in the passage at
Stadiou 4*).

Another aspect of the Dionysiac tradition comes tippling in
Aug–Sept, at the **Daphni Wine Festival**. For a very moderate
price, and even less for a carafe to take home, any number of
local wines can be sampled to your heart's content. Self-service
food at cheap to moderate prices can be bought in the monastery
grounds, as Greeks rarely drink without eating; the drink is
free, and not everybody can hold it. . . . Also, in Athens itself,
the **National and Zapion Gardens** are enlivened in summer by
cafés chantants, reminiscent of the inter-war period.

Athens' only casino is at the **Mt. Parnis Hotel**, at the top of
the funicular. The hub of Athenian nightlife however is the
Plaka, though it spills elsewhere into the centre and along the
seashore.

The Plaka's attractions include restaurants, discotheques,
nightclubs, live music, dancing, revues and 'adults only' clubs.
The scene is so changeable that it is very difficult to make
specific recommendations about what to find where in the
throng of clubs (where anyone walking in with the price of a
modest drink is a 'member'), tavernas and *boîtes*. Live music
may range from pop or *bouzóuki* orchestras, to a doleful guitarist
strumming verses by Greek Nobel Prize-winners set to music
by Theodorakis; or it may turn out to be a jukebox. The revues,
usually heavy-handed in their humour and heavy-footed in

their dancing, are always liable to fold up, not only in the Plaka or the more elegant parts of the centre, but even in the luxury hotel nightclubs. (These last are not to be confused with the staid dinner-dances available at the **Hilton** or the **St George Lykabettus**.) In summer, the more lasting revues move to the Attic seaside, to add to the unpredictability. For the most part it is all good clean fun, but outrageously priced 'nightclubs open all day' can be found below Syntagma Sq.

The *bouzóuki*, a clanging oriental version of the mandolin, brought to the mainland by refugees from Asia Minor, is distinctively Greek and immensely popular. It was taken up by the smart set and intellectuals and thereafter became exploited commercially. There are huge establishments purveying *bouzóuki* in the town centre and along the Faliro seashore of Attica, all catering for tourists and serving obligatory food and drink. Though contrived and expensive, they are probably the closest most visitors will come to the real thing. More genuine, but equally noisy, are smaller *bouzóuki* orchestras, often with lady singers of astounding girth, performing all over the working-class suburbs. Food and drink, though again obligatory, will be no worse and certainly cheaper than in the big tourist establishments. But these neighbourhood entertainments are best kept out of travel guides, lest they lose the very reason for visiting them, so go with Greek friends.

In winter, the cultural scene for the non-Greek speaker is bleaker than the weather. The numerous small theatres, closed all summer, present revues newly returned from the seaside. They also stage plays; unfortunately no sooner do Greek actors or actresses achieve a name than they set up by themselves (Greek politicians tend to do the same thing), which makes for strong leads with poor supporting casts. From Oct–May the **Opera** manages some creditable performances with the help of guest stars and an excellent chorus; but the **Ballet** seems to be still in search of a choreographer. During the winter the **Opera orchestra** also performs on its own, responding well to a good conductor, though its impressive new home near the US Embassy remains unfinished – the donor, a former Minister of Finance who transformed his family mansion into the Athens Museum, has since fallen out with officialdom.

Nightclubs

Given here are representatives of the various categories that have proved their staying power over several seasons, though that is no guarantee for the future, and some other places that are currently popular at the time of writing.

Apotsos

In the passage of Venizelou 10 ☎ 36–37–046. Map ***15****D4 🍸 Open 11.00–23.00.*

Athens' oldest *óuzeri* in pleasant, sober, traditional decor, much frequented by foreign residents.

Autokinissis

Kifissias 12 ☎ 68–21–024 ● ☰ Open 22.00–2.00.

A highly popular newcomer, crowded on weekends. Lots of plants and clever use of spotlights. Dine on the second-floor circle.

Neraida

Vassileos Georgiou II (in Kalamaki) ☎ 98–12–004. Map ***16****D2 ▮▮▮▮ ☽ ♫ ☰ AE CB ⊕ ● VISA Open 22.00–2.00. Closed Sun.*

For many years a leader among the numerous nightclubs along the Apollo Coast. Food, drink, singing and dancing plus a moderately good show create a lively atmosphere – sometimes excessively so.

9 Muses (*Enéa Móusae*)
Oct–May: Akadimias 43 ☎ *36–01–877. Map* **15***C4. June–Sept:
Astir Palace Hotel, Vouliagmeni* ☎ *89–62–030. Map* **14***F3* ◫◫ ●
≈ *Open 22.00–2.00.*
A favourite with the younger set, it moves in summer to the grounds of
the **Astir Palace Hotel**, where food and drinks improve.

9+9 (*Enéa sýn Enéa*)
Agras 5 (by Stadiou Sq.) ☎ *72–22–258. Map* **15***E5* ⏜ ● ≈ *Open
22.00–2.00.*
So sure of its leadership among Athenian discos that the name isn't even
displayed. A bar shares the fairly small room with the disco; few seats.
Good but expensive restaurant. Pleasing decor with a lot of mirrors.

Stork
Agios Kosmas ☎ *98–29–865. Map* **16***D2* ◫◫◫ ⏶ ▨ AE CB ⊕ CD
VISA *Open 22.00–2.00.*
Well-known Greek and occasionally European showbiz names.

Studio 4
Kifissias 4 (at Paradisos Marousiou) ☎ *68–23–326* ◫◫◫ ● ≈
Open 22.00–2.00.
Reasonable food and drink, but fancy and expensive.

Athens by night

The organized *Athens by Night* tours, representing what the
visitor is supposed to think Athenian nightlife is all about,
sample a number of clubs, among which the following are
included. **Palia Athena** is the most genuine, but also the most
expensive. All are in the heart of the Plaka.
Athens by Night (*Mnisikleous 15* ☎ *32–30–727, map* **14***D–E3*);
Mostrou (*Mnisikleous 22* ☎ *32–25–558, map* **14***D–E3*); **Palia Athena**
(*Flessa 4* ☎ *32–22–000, map* **14***E3*). All ⏶ ▨ ≈ AE CB ⊕ CD VISA
and open 22.00–2.00.

Bouzóukia

As *bouzóukia* feature in most tourist programmes they might as
well be tried in the easily accessible Plaka, where the following
are among the better establishments, rather than in the larger,
even noisier (and equally expensive) *bouzóukia* farther out.
Aigokeros (*Lisiou 15* ☎ *32–19–895, map* **14***D–E3*); **Napoleon** (*Lisiou
20* ☎ *32–47–906, map* **14***D–E3*), both ⏜ ≈ *and open 22.00–2.00.*

Floor-show and striptease

The following are both at the side of Syntagma Sq.; **Maxim's** is
superior, and more expensive, but is still very reasonable by
European standards.
Copa Cabana (*Othonos 10* ☎ *32–32–061, map* **15***D4*); **Maxim** (*Othonos
6* ☎ *32–34–831, map* **15***D4*). Both ▨ AE CB ⊕ CD VISA
and open 23.00–3.00.

Shopping in Athens

Stadiou and Venizelou, running parallel NW from Syntagma
Sq., start off with souvenir shops. At the beginning of
Venizelou are two international jewellers, **Lalaounis** and **La
Chrysothèque Zolotas**, and there are others in Voukourestiou,
on the right leading off Venizelou. Smart boutiques abound
along the right side of Venizelou and down Voukourestiou and
Amerikis, and they extend through to Kolonaki Sq., with their
heaviest concentration in Skoufa and Tsakalof. Also in
Voukourestiou are arts and crafts, and excellent shops for
candied fruit and chocolates.

South of Monastiraki Sq., Pandrossou alternates shoeshops,
where cheapness rather than elegance prevails, with a choice of

slightly suspect, expensive antiques and genuine objects of the not-too-distant past. To the N, Ermou, appropriately named after Hermes, god of commerce, abounds in shops selling local and imported textiles, all the way up to Syntagma Sq., where the Kastoria furriers are mostly concentrated.

Though the capital naturally prides itself on its bigger and better shops, as far as department stores are concerned it does badly; the largest is **Lambropoulos**.

The **flea market** in Ifestou, off Monastiraki Sq., on Sun morning, offers second-hand clothes, new clothes which also manage to look second-hand, spare parts of all kinds, and old furniture. The likelihood of discovering something of unrecognized value however is nil, and the fun of the experience is really the milling crowd. Ifestou is perhaps more interesting on a weekday, when copper- and blacksmiths ply their trade in the street of their patron god, Hephaestos, as they have done for some 2,600yr.

For folk art it is worth applying to the **National Organization of Handicrafts** (*Mitropoleos 9, the other side of Ermou, map 14D3*). This has a large, priced display and will provide a list of shops where purchases at these set prices can be made.

The best variety of shops – from jewellery to fashion and shoes, food stores, electrical and photographic equipment, coins and stamps, and flowers – is along Stadiou. Flowers just as lovely, and somewhat cheaper, can also be bought in the ten shops in the Parliament ramp at the beginning of Vassilissis Sofias Ave. English bookshops are to be found in Amerikis and Nikis.

There is always a pharmacy within easy walking distance, with someone available who speaks English or French, and all shops in the centre have at least one English and French speaker.

Any major complaints should be addressed to the **Consumer Protection Institute** (*Venizelou 43* ☎ *32–42–626*), a member of the International Organization of Consumer Unions.

Several shops mentioned below have branches at the **Tower of Athens**, a suburban highrise development at the far end of Vassilissis Sofias Ave. For food shops, see *Athens/Restaurants*. See also *Shopping* in *Planning*.

Bookshops
American News Stand ♣ (*Amerikis 23, map 15D4; Hilton, map 15D6, President, and Royal Olympic, map 14E3, hotels*); **Eleftheroudakis** ♣ (*Nikis 4, map 15D4, and Tower of Athens*); **Pandelidis** ♣ (*Amerikis 11, map 15D4*). All take ⒶⒺ ⒸⒷ Ⓓ

At all these three chains, a good selection of books on Greece and bestseller paperbacks are available. Hotel branches also stock newspapers and periodicals.

Boutiques
Christian Dior (*Kriezotou 7, map 15D4*); **Contessina** (*Venizelou 4, map 15D4*); **Elle** (*Stadiou 4, map 15D4*); **Lanvin** (*Anagnostopoulou 3, map 15D4*); **Marie Manot** (*Voukourestiou 2, map 15D4*); **Nikos & Takis** (*Venizelou 10, map 15D4*); **Sinanis** (*Voukourestiou 2 and 23, map 15D4*); **Travassaros** (*at the Hilton, map 15D6*); **Tsantilis** (*Stadiou 4, map 15D4*); **Yves St Laurent** (*Kriezotou 10, map 15D4*). All take ⒶⒺ ⒸⒷ Ⓓ Ⓓ ⓋⒾⓈⒶ

These are the best boutiques between Stadiou and Kolonaki Sq.

Crafts
Attalos/Greek Art Gift Shop ♣ (*Stadiou 3, map 15D4*); as **Coin d'Art** (*Venizelou 6, map 15D4*); as **Kalokerinos** (*Venizelou 3, map 15D4, and Voukourestiou 8, map 15D4*); as **La Greca** (*Karageorgi Servias 14, map 15D4*); as **Martin** (*Karageorgi Servias 6, map 15D4*). All take ⒶⒺ ⒸⒷ Ⓓ Ⓓ ⓋⒾⓈⒶ

All these shops are just by Syntagma Sq. Large selection of Greek 'gifts': outstanding among them the embroidered linen, leather-, silver-, and copperwork after traditional models. In all respects more reliable, if a little more expensive, than the similar shops round Omonia Sq. Shipment to all parts of the world.

National Welfare Organization ✿

*At the Hilton. Map **15D6**. Voukourestiou 24. Map **15D4**. Also at Vassilissis Sofias Ave. 135 (near the Tower of Athens). All take* AE CB
CD CD VISA

The best shops (founded by the late Queen Frederika) for embroidery, needlepoint, tapestries, handwoven rugs, handknotted carpets, wooden and beaded articles, ceramics.

YWCA Gift Shop ✿

*Amerikis 11, off Venizelou. Map **15D4**.*
Some worthwhile, handmade souvenirs can be found here; self-service cafeteria.

Department store

Lambropoulos

*Eolou and Lykourgou. Map **14C3*** AE CB CD CD VISA *At the Omonia end of Stadiou.*
Useful for beachwear and equipment, and for international cosmetics at slightly cheaper prices than in the pharmacies.

Furs

Sistovaris ✿

*Ermou 4. Map **15D4**. Venizelou 9. Map **15D4***
Sistovaris is the leading establishment for Kastoria furs, sold by the metre or in every kind of clothing.

Hydra, Mitsakou, Naoum, Samaras and **Voula**, all in Mitropoleos, the main furrier street (*map **14D3***), are also good, as are **Fur House**, **Mary's Furs Salon** and **Toronto Furs** (*at Filellinon 7, 4 and 1, map **15D4**, respectively*). All take AE CB CD CD VISA

Haute-coiffure and hairdressers

Costi-Taki ✿

*At the Hilton. Map **15D6*** AE CB CD CD VISA
Hairdressing for men and women.

George ✿

*Kanari 2, between Syntagma Sq. and Kolonaki Sq. Map **15D4**. Tower of Athens. Grande Bretagne. Map **15D4**. Also at King's Palace. Map **15D4*** AE CD VISA
Haute-coiffure for ladies. Foreign-trained stylists. Also in Glyfada, Lagonissi and Vouliagmeni.

Jewellers

La Chrysothèque Zolotas ✿

*Venizelou 10. Map **15D4**. Athens (Elleniko) Airport. Map **16D2*** AE
CB CD VISA

A rival to **Lalaounis** next door, as in the Rue St-Honoré in Paris. Holds exclusive Greek rights to museum reproductions.

Lalaounis ✿

*Venizelou 6. Map **15D4**. Hilton. Map **15D6**. Grande Bretagne. Map **15D4**. Tower of Athens. At Mesogeion 2. As Tresor at Stadiou 4. Map **15D4*** AE CB CD CD VISA
Particularly following antique and Byzantine models: cheaper here than in the French and Swiss branches. For a good choice of less expensive trinkets try the Tresor branch.

Leather goods
Eleni ✿ (*Kriezotou 14, map 15D4*); **Skourletis ✿** (*Ermou 28, map 14D3, and Venizelou 6, map 15D4*); **Viennezikon ✿** (*Stadiou 9, map 15D4*). All take [AE] [◯]

Handbags and leather goods of good quality at reasonable prices.

Shoes
Petridis ✿ (*Venizelou 9 and 51, map 15D4, Kolonaki Sq., map 15D4*); as **Charles Jourdan** (*Ermou 10, map 15D4*); as **Studio** (*Amerikis 19, map 15D4, and Tower of Athens; also at Iakovou Dragatsi 4, Piraeus*). All take [AE] [CB] [◯] [◉] [VISA]

With Sevastikis the leading shoe-chain: good-quality aniline-tanned leather.
Sevastikis ✿ (*Venizelou 55, map 15D4. Stadiou 3 and 44, map 15D4, Ermou 36, map 14D3; also at Vassileos Georgiou 19, Piraeus*). All take [AE] [CB] [◯] [◉] [VISA]

Similar to Petridis, both in quality and products.

Walks

Though Greater Athens is vast, the antique and Byzantine monuments are conveniently close together – although what looks like easy walking distance may seem exhaustingly extended by heat, dirt and holes in the pavement.

Antique walk
Allow at least 4hr, including an absolute minimum of 1hr on the **Acropolis**. Information about the individual monuments, several of which will repay a separate visit, is given in *Athens/Sights* under the headings cross-referenced in bold.

Start at Syntagma Sq., the very heart of Athens, where the dignified **Tomb of the Unknown Soldier**, of classical inspiration, stands below the Neo-Classical **Parliament**.

Take Amalias Ave., bordering the **National Gardens**, to the corner of Olgas Ave., unless you particularly want to see the **Stadio** (Stadium), in which case you should cut through the National Gardens; the stadium is an 1896 reconstruction on the ancient site. From the Stadio you will need to walk back up along Olgas Ave. to reach the Roman **Olympion** and **Arch of Hadrian**, otherwise reached by Amalias Ave.

Across from these, Lysikratous leads to the delicate 4thC BC **Lysikrates Monument**, later incorporated into the French Capuchin monastery and the lodging of the poet and champion of Greek independence, Lord Byron, in 1809. So it is fitting to take Vyronos (Greek for Byron) down to its junction with Dionysiou Areopagitou. Turn right, and on your right, opposite the new Acropolis Museum under construction, is the entrance to the 6thC BC Theatre of Dionysos and the ruined monuments of the S slope of the **Acropolis**. A romantic but strenuous climb winds round the Asklipiion to the ramp just beneath the Propylaea; the usual approach is up Dionysiou Areopagitou, along the Stoa of Eumenes II culminating in the Odeon of Herodes Atticus, and then right to the ticket office at the beginning of the ramp.

After visiting the temples of the Acropolis proper, the Dionyssos restaurant, at the foot of the Pnyx, is in exactly the right spot for lunch, or at least some refreshment in its cafeteria. No need to ascend **Philopappos**, the southernmost of the hills to the W of the Acropolis, but the **Pnyx** is low enough to warrant a look at the semi-circular terrace on top, where the orators of antiquity addressed the people. The descent by Apostolou Pavlou between the Pnyx and the **Areopagos** affords a particularly fine view of the Acropolis. Then, to the right, is the

— Antique walk
--- Byzantine walk

Agora, dominated at the near end by the 5thC BC so-called
Thission (Theseion), really the Ifestion (Hephaesteion), and at
the far end by the reconstructed Hellenistic Stoa of Attalos II;
remains of the governmental and commercial buildings of
ancient Athens, which once lined the Sacred Way taken by the
Panathenaea processions up to the Acropolis, lie in between.

There is an exit from the Agora by the 11thC **Agii Apostoli**,
which looks somewhat incongruous in this setting, along
Polygnotou towards the Roman Agora to get back to Syntagma
Sq. (see below). But if you still have stamina, you can follow the
electric railway, which cuts through the E end of the Agora,
back to the entrance and up to the Thission station. Then cross
Ermou to the **Keramikos**, the unprepossessing site of the main
gates into the ancient city and of the cemetery outside them.
Proceed back along Ermou and then right at Monastiraki Sq.,
where the mosque lends an oriental touch (it now houses some
folkloric items), down Areos, past the few remaining columns
evoking the imperial splendour of Hadrian's Library, and back
to the Roman Agora.

The quickest way from the Roman Agora to Syntagma Sq. is
to make for Ermou by heading N up Eolou. But before doing so
do not miss the **Tower of the Winds**, really a 1stC BC hydraulic
clock, which is just by the Roman Agora to the E.

Byzantine walk
This walk takes in all the Byzantine churches dating from
c.12thC within the medieval town. They hardly deserve
separate visits, but are rewardingly seen as a group, if only to
study the decline from perfection to mere quaintness. Several
are further described under **Byzantine churches** in
Athens/Sights. Allow 2hr.

Start at the lower end of Syntagma Sq., and walk S along
Filellinon. On the left is **Agios Nikodimos †** which, despite an

over generous 19thC restoration, still compares favourably with the Neo-Norman Anglican St Paul's ✝ higher up, at the intersection with Amalias Ave. Turn right and wander through the Plaka, blissfully quiet in the daytime since it is mostly a pedestrian zone, and therefore an attractive setting for several chapels. Do not fret if churches such **Agios Simeon** ✝ and **Agios Sotir** ✝ are closed, since there are others with as many mosaics, frescoes and ikons.

If **Agii Apostoli** has not been seen while visiting the **Agora**, have a look at it down Agion Apostolon and also at the sad Gothic remains of 13thC **Ypapanti** ✝ – Athens' only Frankish church, in Vouleftiriou. By this or another route go round the Agora to Thission Sq., to find **Agii Assomati** ✝ Then turn back along Ifestou, the street of copper- and blacksmiths since antiquity, to Monastiraki Sq., where only the **Panagia** (Our Lady 'All-Holy') remains of the former monastery. Panagia is notable chiefly for its rare elliptical cupola. Then follow Mitropoleos to the 19thC **Mitropolis** ✝ which dwarfs the exquisite 12thC **Old Mitropolis**.

Kapnikarea is also dwarfed, this time by the tall commercial buildings on Ermou; reach it from Mitropoleos by Evangelistrias. Then continue N on Evangelistrias until it becomes Agiou Markou through the warren of the commercial district, to reach Evripidou. (Or you can go past Kapnikarea and turn right on Eolou as far as Evripidou.)

Looking left down Evripidou, note the single-naved **Agios Ioannis Kolonna** ✝ which is remarkable only because it is built round a Roman column to which requests to the saint are still tied in what was originally a pagan custom. Going right towards Klafthmonos Sq. (Square of Weeping) – the weepers were dismissed civil servants who were subsequently reinstated – one sees the oldest church, **Agii Theodori**, restored in the very early 15thC. Cross the square and go down Stadiou to return to Syntagma Sq.

Attica (Attikí) ★

Map 16&8H7. Population of region: 4,250,000.

Attica, whose name is derived from the Greek for 'promontory', is a mountainous peninsula which forms a natural geographical unit. In antiquity its inhabitants shared a common racial background, and both factors proved favourable to the evolution of a cultural and political union.

The earliest organized Neolithic settlement has been found near **Nea Makri**, dating from about 4000BC. During the early Bronze Age Indo-Europeans settled in natural defensive positions along the coast, such as **Rafina** and **Agios Kosmas**. These settlers (Pelasgian, according to Athenian tradition) had close cultural and trading links with the Cyclades and were active in the development of the Helladic civilization. Gradually they moved into the interior and established most of the prehistoric settlements of which, after the Ionian occupation in the second millennium BC, the 12 states of historical Attica consisted. When the semi-mythological Theseus achieved the unification of these petty rival kingdoms, the history of Attica merged with that of Athens, despite a certain autonomy in purely local matters.

Nature conveniently divided Attica into five parts for tourist purposes: the three distinctive coasts, the plains and the mountains, each being generally described here. All but one are then followed by an alphabetical selection of centres where the visitor may find accommodation, restaurants, or nightlife. Additional information may also be found on several major villages, towns or sights in the region under their entry in the *Mainland A–Z*, and for these clear cross-references are given.

As elsewhere in Greece, most seaside hotels close Nov–Mar. There are usually 20% price reductions for Apr–May and Sept 15–Oct 31, and up to 40% for those remaining open in winter. All distances given are from the centre of Athens.

Saronic Gulf *(Saronikós Kolpós)*

The SE coast from Piraeus to Sounio has for some unfathomable reason acquired the name of the 'Apollo Coast' (Akti Apollonos) in the brochures. The quickest approach from Athens is down Syngrou Ave. to the **Faliro Delta**, which they have been filling in for more than 10yr at great expense but with disproportionately small results – eventually all kinds of attractions, such as marinas, gardens and a stadium, are promised. Possidonos Ave. (appropriately enough) turns left along the sea through **Paleo Faliro**, and continues through **Kalamaki** and **Alymos**, then past Elleniko Airport and the **Agios Kosmas** Sports Centre, to **Glyfada**. This part of the coast can be reached directly from Athens by Vouliagmenis Ave.

Villas, blocks of flats and hotels have blurred the boundaries between the seaside villages. Past **Voula** are the pine-clad headlands of **Kavouri** and **Vouliagmeni**. Unbuilt-upon, rugged nature comes to the fore as the road winds between cliffs and coves to **Lagonissi**, **Saronida**, the salt mountains of **Anavyssos**, and finally, at the head of the peninsula, the ancient ruins and bathing resort of **Sounio**.

Bathing on this coast is not to be recommended until Glyfada (just). The sea becomes cleaner at Voula and improves thereafter.

Most of the w coast of the Saronic Gulf belongs administratively to the Megarid, but touristically to Attica. The toll-motorway, by-passing *Eleusis*, affords an unimpeded view over the gulf but has only one exit to it, at **Megara**, so for the coastal resorts it is necessary to take the winding corniche road from Eleusis, following in reverse the route taken by Theseus as he came from **Trizina**, ancient Troezen (see *Islands/Poros*), to claim Athens from his father, King Aegeus. From **Nea Peramos** a ferry plies to the **Monastery of the Faneromeni** (Appearance of Our Lady), the main attraction of the nearby island of **Salamis** (see *Argo-Saronic Islands* in *Islands A–Z*), separated only by a thin strip of sea.

From afar the town of **Megara** looks picturesque enough on the twin hills it has occupied for 4,000yr, but only the terra cotta piping of an aqueduct leading to a monumental fountain near the church, and a few fragments built into the medieval towers and chapels on the w hill, remain from its days of glory in the 7thC BC, when it was a leading colonizing city. Bathing is possible at **Pahi**, near the ancient port of Nisaea, linked to Megara in 459BC by walls 3km (2 miles) long.

The **Gerania mountains**, 1,351m (4,432ft), descend sheer into the sea at the **Skironian rocks**. Here Theseus performed one of his road-clearing feats by flinging the giant bandit Skiron into the sea, where a monstrous man-eating turtle lurked. **Kineta**, 55m (34 miles), and **Agii Theodori**, 65km (41 miles), are popular beaches, but then the coast is once again spoiled by the refineries beside the Corinth canal.

For hotels in *Sounio*, see entry in *Mainland A–Z*.

Agii Theódori
Map 8H6. On the w Saronic coast, 65km (41 miles).
A popular beach resort.

H **Hanikian Beach** ♣ (☎ *67–151/60* ▥ ▭ *221* ▦ ☕ 🏠 ⇌ ⊙ ⛷ ⛵ ♒); **Siagas Beach** (☎ *67–501/3* ⏱ *232132* ▥ ▭ *101* 🏠 ⇌ ♒ ⊙), opposite the beach.

Ágios Kosmas
Map 16D2. On the se Saronic coast, 13km (8 miles).
The **Agios Kosmas Sports Centre** (☎ *98–15–572*) offers instruction in swimming, diving and underwater fishing, as well as tennis and other ball games.

Nightlife

Annabella (☎ *98–11–124* ⊙); **Storke** (☎ *98–29–865* ♫ ♪ ☺ ▨).

Alíanthos (*Varkiza*)
Map 16E2. On the se Saronic coast, 31km (19 miles).
A huge bathing establishment on the longest stretch of fine sand along this coast.

H **Glaros** (*Xeniou Dios 1* ☎ *89–71–217/8* ▥ ▭ *48* 🏠 ☕ ⇌ AE CB ⏺ ⊙ VISA *on roof* ♒), opposite the beach.

Álymos
Map 16D2. On the se Saronic coast, 12km (7.5 miles).
With a GNTO beach, but bathing cannot be recommended.

H **Albatross** (*Georgiou Ave. 77* ☎ *98–24–981/4* ▥ ▭ *80* ▦ 🏠 ☕ ⇌ AE CB ⏺ ⊙ VISA ♒), opposite the beach.

R **Bosporos** (*Georgiou Ave. 85* ☎ *98–12–873* ▥ ⬚ 🏠 ⇌ AE ⏺ ⊙ VISA *closed Sun evening*), Turkish and international cuisine, live music in the evening.

Anávyssos
Map 16E3. On the se Saronic coast, 50km (31 miles).
Surrounded by salt pans and glittering mountains of sand.

H **Alexander Beach** (☎ *53–461/3* ⏱ *219840* ▥ ▭ *105* ▦ 🏠 ⇌ AE CB ⏺ ⊙ VISA ⛷ ≈ ♒ ⊙), opposite the beach, nautical sports; **Eden Beach** (☎ *52–761/5* ⏱ *214533* ▥ ▭ *350* 🏠 ☕ ⇌ ⏺ ⊙ ⛷ ≈ ♒ ⊙), nautical sports.

Glyfáda
Map 16D2. On the se Saronic coast, 18km (11 miles).
Though bathing is only just possible here, Glyfáda has some of the best hotels and entertainment on this coast, and an 18-hole golf course. Easily reached from Athens by Vouliagmenis Ave.

Hotels

Beau Rivage (*Georgiou Ave. 87* ☎ *89–49–292* ▥ ▭ *82* ▦ 🏠 ☕ ⇌ CB ⏺ VISA ⛷ *on roof* ♒ ♒ ✓), opposite the beach; **Emmantina** ♣ (*Georgiou Ave. 33* ☎ *89–32–111/5* ▥ ▭ *80* ▦ 🏠 ⇌ AE CB ⏺ ⊙ ⊙ VISA ⛷ *on roof* ♒ ♒ ✓), opposite the beach; **Golden Sun** (*Metaxa 72* ☎ *89–55–218/9* ▥ ▭ *65* ▦ 🏠 ☕ ⇌ AE CB ⏺ ⊙ VISA ♒ ✓); **Palace** (*Georgiou Ave. 4* ☎ *89–41–611/4* ▥ ▭ *80* ▦ 🏠 ☕ ⇌ AE CB ⏺ ⊙ VISA ♒ ✓), opposite the beach.

Restaurants

Outstanding among several fish restaurants on the harbour:
Antonopoulos (*Diadohou Pavlou 55* ☎ 89–45–677 ▥ ▭ 🍴 🚗);
Psaropoulos (*Diadohou Pavlou 28* ☎ 89–46–242 ▥ ▭ 🍴 🚗).
Other restaurants: **Asteria** 🍴 (*on Astir beach* ☎ 89–45–675 ▥ ▭
AE CB ⊙ ⊚ VISA 🍸, *in evening, closed for lunch*); **Nefeli** (*Georgiou Ave. 71* ☎ 89–32–119 ▥ ▭ 🍴 🚗 *closed for lunch*), Chinese, French and Italian cuisine.

Nightlife

Deilina (*Georgiou Ave.* ☎ 89–47–321 🎵 ♫ 🍷), live *bouzóuki* music.

Kalamáki
Map **16***D2. On the* SE *Saronic coast, 11km (7 miles).*

Ⓗ **Marina Alymos** (*Georgiou Ave. 15* ☎ 98–28–911/8 ▥ 🛏 28 ▦
🏠 AE CB ⊙ ⊙ ⊚ VISA), furnished apartments, no meals; **Nefeli**
(*Fan Vaik 5* ☎ 98–27–049 ▥ 🛏 40 ▦ 🏠 🚗 🌱 *on roof* 🐕),
opposite the beach.

Ⓡ **Sta Kavourakia** (*Georgiou Ave. 17* ☎ 98–10–093 ▥ ▭ 🍴 🚗
closed for lunch; specialities: fish, grilled crab, octopus).

Nightlife

Neraida (*Georgiou Ave. 3* ☎ 98–12–004 🎵 ♫), *bouzóuki* orchestra.

Kavouri
Map **16***E2. On the* SE *Saronic coast, 21km (13 miles).*
On a pine-clad headland.

Ⓗ **Apollon Palace** 🏨 (☎ 89–51–401/10 ⓣ214250 ▥ 🛏 286 ▦
🏠 🚗 ⇌ AE CB ⊙ ⊙ VISA 🔥 ▭ 🌱 🏊 ⇌ 🐕 ♪ 🎿 🎵),
nautical sports; **Cavouri** (*Terpsihoris 7* ☎ 89–58–461/9 ⓣ215334 ▥
🛏 114 ▦ 🏠 🚗 ⇌ AE CB ⊙ ⊙ VISA ▭ ⇌ 🐕).

Kinéta
Map **8***H6. On the* W *Saronic coast, 55km (34 miles).*
A popular beach resort.

Ⓗ **Kineta Beach** (☎ 62–512/4 ▥ 🛏 192 ▦ 🚗 🏠 ⇌ ⊙ 🌱
🐕), bungalows, nautical sports.

Lagonissi
Map **16***E2. On the* SE *Saronic coast, 41km (26 miles).*

Ⓗ **Xenia Lagonissi** 🏨 (☎ 83–911/25 ⓣ215661 ▥ 🛏 357 🚗 🏠
⇌ AE CB ⊙ ⊙ VISA ▭ 🌱 ⇌ 🐕 ♪ 🎿 🎵), hotel and
bungalows, nautical sports.

Legrena
Map **16***F3. On the* SE *Saronic coast, 64km (40 miles).*

Ⓗ **Minos** (☎ 39–321/3 ▥ 🛏 38 🚗 🏠 ⇌ 🐕).

Paléo Faliro
Map **16***D2. On the* SE *Saronic coast, 8km (5 miles).*
A garden suburb overwhelmed by concrete, though
conveniently near to Athens.

H **Possidon** (*Possidonos Ave. 72* ☎ *98–22–086* ▥ ☐ *90* ▦ ☐ ☐
▭ AE CB ⊕ ⊙ VISA ✔ *on roof* ⇌ 🐾), opposite the beach.

Saronida
Map 16E3. On the SE Saronic coast, 47km (29 miles).

H **Saronic Gate** (☎ *53–711/5* ⊙ *216722* ▥ ☐ *105* ▦ ☐ ▭ ☐
⊙ ⊙ ✔ 🎿 ⇌ 🐾 ⤳).

Vóula
Map 16E2. On the SE Saronic coast, 22km (14 miles).
Reasonable bathing.

H **Rondo** (*Dodekanissou 6* ☎ *89–58–605* ▥ ☐ *44* ☐ ▭ 🐾),
opposite the beach.

Vouliagméni
Map 16E2. On the SE Saronic coast, 24km (15 miles).
Vouliagmeni is in many ways the pick of the SE coast resorts,
though like all the others it lies in the flight-path to the very
busy Elleniko Airport. It has two beaches, one popular but
quite adequate, the other chic to the point of possessing its own
6thC BC **temple ruins**, a yacht harbour and the coast's most
luxurious hotel. It also has a small sulphurous lake with
dramatically overhanging rocks, where the last spurs of **Mt.
Ymitos** come right down to the sea, and where rheumatism and
skin complaints are treated.

Hotels

Astir Palace ▥ (☎ *89–60–211/9* ⊙ *215013* ▥ ☐ *404* ▦ ☐ ▭
▭ AE CB ⊕ ⊙ VISA ⚓ ☐ ✔ 🎿 ⇌ 🐾 ⤳ ☂ ⊙), hotel and
bungalows, three restaurants (see also *Restaurants*), nautical sports;
Greek Coast (*Panos 8* ☎ *89–60–401* ▥ ☐ *55* ▦ ☐ ☐ ▭ AE CB
⊕ ⊙ VISA *on roof* ⇌ 🐾), opposite the beach; **Strand** (*Litous 14*
☎ *89–60–705/7* ▥ ☐ *72* ▦ ☐ ☐ ▭ 🐾 ⊙).

Restaurants

Club House (*Astir Palace hotel* ☎ *89–60–211* ▥ ☐ ☐ ▭ AE CB
⊕ ⊙ VISA), lovely setting above the sea (see also *Hotels*); **Lambros**
(*opposite the lake* ☎ *89–60–144* ▥ ☐ ☐ 🐾), good choice of seafood
and *mezés* (appetizers); **Mooring's** ⊖ (*Vouliagmeni Marina*
☎ *89–61–310* ▥ ☐ 🐾 AE CB ⊕ ⊙ VISA), international
cuisine and seafood; **To Limanaki** (*Vakhou* ☎ *89–60–405* ▥ ☐ 🐾
🐾), excellent fresh fish and seafood of every kind; **Toscana** (*Theseos 16*
☎ *89–62–497* ▥ ☐ 🐾 🐾 *closed for lunch*), Italian specialities of
many different regions.

Corinthian Gulf *(Korinthiakós Kólpos)*
The outstanding site on the Attic coast of the gulf is *Porto
Germeno*. From this a secondary road leads to *Psatha* and the
good beach of **Alepohori**, 61km (38 miles), connected to
Megara by a direct 22km (14 miles) branch. The coast road
continues to **Skhinos** before turning inland to *Loutraki* and
Perahora. For hotels see town entries in *Mainland A–Z*.

Euboean Gulf *(Evoïkos Kólpos)*
The quickest way from Athens is through the suburb of **Agia
Paraskevi**, continuing straight on at the **Stavros** fly-over to the
middle of the NE coast, where most of its beaches are situated.

At **Palini**, which produces one of the better white wines, branch right through gently undulating hills, covered mostly with vineyards, to **Spata**, where Athens International Airport is due to open in 1985. Continue past Spata to **Loutsa**, 30km (19 miles), which has the longest sand beach in Attica, so far without cabins or showers.

A delightfully scenic coast road leads s past *Vraona* (ancient Brauron) to **Porto Rafti**, 38km (24 miles), popular with Athenians but without much of a beach. Alternatively, you can take the road N to Rafina, then past **Mati** to **Agios Andreas**, 31km (19 miles), and **Nea Makri**. Then the coast road goes past the village of **Marathon** and the *Marathon* tumulus to regain the sea at **Shinias**, 44km (28 miles), with an undeveloped beach under pine trees. Another road passes close by the temples at *Ramnous* to **Agia Marina**, 47km (29 miles), which offers the shortest ferry crossing to **Styra** on **Evia** (Euboea).

Further N, **Agii Apostoli** is best reached from Athens by branching off the motorway for the N at **Kapadriti**. The drive past the remains at *Amfiaraio* to **Skala Oropou** is particularly recommended, although there is also a later turning off the motorway direct to Skala Oropou.

For hotels in *Marathon* and *Vraona*, see *Mainland A–Z*.

Agíi Apostóli
*Map **16**B3. On the NE coast, 47km (29 miles).*
Best reached from Athens by branching off the motorway for the N at Kapadriti. Several inviting fish tavernas.

[H] Dolphins (☎ 81–202 Ⅰ□ ▦ 138 ▬ ⌂ ⇄ ⚓ on roof ≈ ●), opposite the beach; **Kalamos Beach** (☎ 81–465/7 ⅠⅠ□ ▦ 204 ⌂ ⇄ ⌂ ≈ ◔ ∽ ●).

Máti
*Map **16**C3. On the E coast, 29km (18 miles).*

[H] **Mati** (*Possidonos 33* ☎ 71–511/5 ▦▦▦ ▦ 70 ▬ ⌂ ⇄ ⚓ ⋖⋶ ≈ ◔ ●).

Néa Mákri
*Map **16**C3. On the E coast, 35km (22 miles).*

[H] **Marathon Beach** (☎ 91–255 ⅠⅠ□ ▦ 166 ▬ ⌂ ⇄ ⋖⋶ ≈ ◔ ●); **Nirefs** (☎ 91–214 ⅠⅠ□ ▦ 127 ⌂ ⌂ ⇄), opposite the beach.

Rafína
*Map **16**D3. On the E coast, 28km (17.5 miles).*
A small port for ferries to southern Evia (Euboea) and the N Cyclades, with several excellent seafood tavernas.

[H] **Avra** (☎ 22–781/3 ⅠⅠ□ ▦ 96 ▬ ⌂ ⇄ ⋖⋶ ●), opposite a rather poor beach.

Skála Oropóu
*Map **16**B2. On the NE coast, 51km (32 miles).*
A fishing village and ferry port to Eretria on Evia (Euboea).

[H] **Alkyonis** (☎ 32–490/4 ⅠⅠ□ ▦ 91 ▬ ⌂ ⇄ ⋖⋶), opposite a rather poor beach.

The plains (*The Messógia*)
Messogia, or mid-earth, is the interior of Attica, comprising the

smaller plain now filled from sea to mountains by Greater Athens and the larger plain and its hills between Mt. Ymitos and the NE coast. This latter part is given over to olive groves and vineyards specializing in *rétsina*, which can be drunk in numerous tavernas in a string of prosperous local villages. The first on turning right at the **Stavros** fly-over is **Peania**, from which the **Koutouki Cave** (**☎** *open 10.00–17.30*) is 5km (3 miles) away up the slope of **Mt. Ymitos**.

From **Koropí** and **Markopoulo**, in the middle of this rich agricultural region, roads radiate to the NE and SW coasts. Off from **Keratea** to the S, 7km (4.5 miles) E, is a convent of the *Palaioïmerologitae* (or followers of the Julian calendar), which is curiously reminiscent of a stage-set for the Ballet Russes. Below the convent is the beach of **Kaki Thalassa**, or Bad Sea, which indeed it is under the prevailing N wind. The S road continues from Keratea to join the coast just before **Lavrio**, source of the silver which financed the fleet built by Themistokles to defeat the Persians at Salamis; the unsightly slag-heaps are evidence of mining resumed in modern times. The road continues a further 10km (6 miles) to *Sounio*.

Koropí
*Map **16**D2. 25km (15.5 miles)* SE.
A lively village, surrounded by vineyards.

Ⓡ **Old Stables Barbecue**
2km (1.25 miles) past Koropi on the Markopoulo road
☎ 66–43–220 ▥ ⌷ ➤ ➘ ➟ ¥ ✺ *Not open before 21.00.
Closed Mon.*
An old stable transformed into a bar, taverna and nightclub. Good
rétsina.

Peanía
*Map **16**D2. 18km (11 miles)* E.
Birthplace of the orator Demosthenes; the **church** has Neo-Byzantine murals by the contemporary painter, Kontoglou.

Ⓡ **Kanakis** (*Very Nice*)
Lavriou 76 **☎** 66–42–385 ▥ ⌷ ➤ ➘ ➟ *On the main road from
Athens.*
The charcoal grills and good *mezés* (appetizers) can be washed down with
excellent *kokkinéli* (a rosé *rétsina*), in a pretty garden.

The mountains

A horseshoe of mountains rings Athens from sea to sea, with a long spur trailing off NE. To the W, towards *Eleusis*, barren, low **Mt. Egaleo** is considered a mountain mainly by romantic tradition – the rocky brow, in Byron's poem, "which looks o'er sea-borne Salamis". On the landward side of it lies *Daphni*, in the narrow gap that is the only exit W before you come to the foothills of **Parnitha** (Mt. Parnis), rising gradually to its highest peak, 1,413m (4,636ft).

Parnitha is accessible either by 13km (8 miles) of hairpin bends rising up from the village of **Aharnes** or by the funicular from **Metohi**, which takes 4min to reach the hotel and casino on its broad central ridge. Here, where fir trees first begin to replace the Attic pines, skiing is just possible.

Slightly W, through the suburb of **Liossia** and the village of **Fili**, a road ascends past the **Monastery of Panagia Kliston** (Our Lady of the Defile – an apt name in this maze of gorges and ravines) to **Phyle**, where one round and two square towers

remain of the 4thC BC **fortifications** which guarded the
Athenian border with Boeotia. The older **ramparts** nearby were
occupied by Athenian exiles coming from Thebes to overthrow
the Thirty Tyrants, puppets of the victorious Spartans, in
403BC. A third road penetrates this formidable range to the NE,
passing the military airport and the lovely woods round the
former royal estate of **Dekelia**, where the Spartans built a
fortress during the Peloponnesian War.

The usual exit by road to the N from Athens is along
Vassilissis Sofias Ave. and Kifissias Ave., through the garden
suburb of **Psyhiko**, past the hotels and restaurants of Kifissia,
to the motorway, 3km (2 miles) to the W of Kifissia. It is also
possible to join the motorway in the western suburbs.

Kifissia is in the foothills of **Penteli**, ancient Mt. Pentelicon,
1,109m (3,638ft). Turning E, one can cross the pine forest
below the disused marble quarries to the vaguely Gothic marble
palace of the Duchess of Piacenza, a 19thC eccentric. The
building was not finished until 1960, when it was the residence
of the then Crown Prince Constantine. Concerts are
occasionally held in the courtyard. The shortest way from here
back to Psyhiko passes the white-washed buildings and arcaded
cloister of the large new **Monastery of Moni Penteli**; there are
oleander and laurel round the clock tower and the church, built
to house the jewelled skull of the 16thC founder.

To the N of Kifissia, the villages of **Kastri**, **Ekali** and **Drossia**
blend into each other. A road branching to the right crosses the
thickly wooded northern foothills of Mt. Penteli to **Nea Makri**,
via the tavernas of Dionysos and the insignificant ruins of
ancient **Ikaria**, where the god of wine revealed the blessings of
the grape to his host, Ikarios. The next branch to the right leads
to the artificial **lake of Marathon**, 48km (30 miles), fed by
pipelines from Lake Ilaki and the river Mornos more than
160km (100 miles) northwest.

The road continues 8km (5 miles) down to *Marathon*,
crossing the 72m (236ft) high, 281m (923ft) wide dam, the only
one in the world to be faced with marble. Below the dam, the
American firm in charge of its construction in the 1920s built a
very attractive **reproduction of the Athenian Treasury** at
Delphi.

From Athens again, a road winds towards Ymitos past the
Kaisariani Monastery (see *Athens/Sights*). It continues
through fragrant oregano and thyme bushes to the **Byzantine
chapel †** at **Asteri**, then to the Greek Air Force installations on
the bleak summit of Ymitos, ancient Mt. Hymettus, 1,025m
(3,365ft). In the evening, when the north wind blows the
pollution away, this barren grey mountain turns a deep purple
which earned Athens the epithet of 'violet-crowned'. From the
summit, the view extends over the two plains and the
surrounding sea.

Kifíssia

Map **16**C2. 14km (9 miles) NE.
A northern garden suburb of Athens.

Hotels

Kostis Dimitrakopolous (*Deligianni 65, Kefalari* ☎ 80–12–546 ▮▮▮▮
▭ 27 ▭ ▭ ≈ ▭), smallest but most modern of the seven top hotels
in Kifissia; **Nafsika** (*Pellis 6* ☎ 80–13–255 ▮▮ ▭ 17 ▭ ▭ ▭),
good location; **Roussos** (*Tsaldari 18* ☎ 80–14–624 ▮▮ ▭ 39 ▭ ▭
≈ ≋ ✍).

Restaurants

Belle Hélène ♣ (*Politias Sq.* ☎ 80–14–776 ▮▮▮ ☐ ⌂ ⇔ ▭ AE CB Ⓓ Ⓒ VISA), French cuisine; **Blue Pine** ♣ (*Tsaldari 27* ☎ 80–12–969 ▮▮▮ ☐ ⇔ ⇔ AE CB Ⓓ Ⓒ VISA *open 20.30–1.00, closed Sun*), country-club atmosphere, with background music; **Ponderosa** (*Amalias 8* ☎ 80–12–356 ▮▮▮ ☐ ⇔ ⇔ AE CB Ⓓ Ⓒ VISA *open 20.30–1.00, closed Sun*), Greek specialities; **Red Dragon** (*Zirini 12* ☎ 80–17–034 ▮▮▮ ☐ ⇔ ⇔ AE CB Ⓓ Ⓒ VISA), Cantonese cuisine; **Strofili** (*Tsaldari 18* ☎ 80–83–330 ▮▮▮ ☐ AE CB Ⓓ Ⓒ VISA), Greek cooking.

Párnitha
*Map **16**C2. 26km (16 miles) NW.*

Ⓗ **Mont Parnis** ▦ (☎ 24–69–111/5 ⓣ 215366 ▮▮▮ ⌂ 106 ⇔ ⌂ ⇔ AE CB Ⓓ Ⓒ VISA ⌕ ⇔ ≋ ♪ ♫ ❀), altitude 1,050m (3,444ft) – reached by funicular or car.

Bassae (*Vásses*)   See *Andritsena*.

Brauron   See *Vraona*.

Corinth (*Kórinthos*)
*Map **8**H6, **11**H6. 82km (51 miles) w of Athens. Getting there: By bus, from Athens and all parts of the Peloponnese; by train, on the Athens–Peloponnese line. Population: 22,000.*
Corinth controls the only road from central Greece to the Peloponnese and its two ports link two seas. Naturally, as an old settlement it has numerous sights, described below in the order in which they are approached from Athens and central Greece.

The modern town is 8km (5 miles) sw of the road and rail bridges across the canal. It replaced the town which had risen over the antique site, which in 1858 was totally destroyed in an earthquake. Similarly destroyed itself in 1928, it was rebuilt and escaped relatively lightly in the earthquake of 1981.

Sights and places of interest
The Corinth Canal
The canal was completed by a French company in 1892, but was not a new idea: Periander, tyrant of Corinth, one of the Seven Sages of antiquity, attempted to construct one about 600BC. Defeated by technical obstacles, he created instead a paved road, on which light craft were hauled over wooden rollers until the 12thC AD. Alexander the Great, Julius Caesar and Caligula toyed with the project, and finally Nero inaugurated work with a golden pick-axe. It was continued by 6,000 prisoners from newly-conquered Jerusalem, who dug several sections, until civil war in AD68 caused the work to be abandoned until 1882. The modern canal, 6.3km (nearly 4 miles) long and 23m (75ft) wide, runs at its centre through a cutting 87m (285ft) deep.

The isthmus
In the 12thC BC the Achaeans built a **wall** in defence against the Dorians, across the narrow neck of the isthmus. It was reinforced by the Spartans against the Persians in 480BC, fortified by the Emperor Justinian against the Avars in the 6thC and rebuilt by the Emperor Manuel II Palaeologos in 1415. Despite all this effort it never kept out a determined invader.

Little remains of the **Temple of Poseidon**, near the Aegean end of the wall, nor of the **theatre** and the **stadium** in which were held the biennial Isthmian Games – the most important in Greece after those at Olympia – since all these provided building material for the last two restorations of the wall. The small **museum** (🖾 *standard opening times*) houses some local finds, including a set of **glass mosaics** from Egypt, retrieved intact from a ship that sank in the harbour on the Saronic Gulf.

The isthmus is historically famous as the place where, in 481BC, 31

Daphni

Greek states swore union in the Panhellenic League against Persia. In 338 and 336BC, first Philip and then Alexander the Great of Macedonia were here acclaimed leaders of the Greeks against the Persians, and in 196BC the Roman general Flaminius proclaimed here the liberation of Greece from Macedonia.

Old Corinth ★

In the 7thC BC, under the enlightened rule of tyrants, Corinth became the leading commercial and colonial power in Greece. In the 5thC BC, however, it was eclipsed by Athens, and Thoukydides attributed the outbreak of the Peloponnesian War between Athens and Sparta largely to fomentation motivated by Corinthian envy. During Hellenistic times Corinth made a comeback, becoming the capital city of the Achaean League, as a result of which it was razed in 146BC by the Roman general Mummius. Its famous statues were despatched to Rome, and only seven squat monolithic columns of the 6thC BC Doric **Temple of Apollo** remain of the ancient Greek city. But the site was too advantageous to remain deserted, and the colony founded by Julius Caesar in 44BC soon grew into the richest and, by reputation, most frivolous town in Greece. St Paul fulminated against its morals in AD51 which led to a riot, but though arrested he was released by the Roman proconsul.

The **Roman Agora** of Old Corinth (🏛 *standard opening times*) was extensive. It was adorned by marble **stoas** with Corinthian columns, six **temples**, **propylaea** and the **Julian Basilica**. The **Peirene Fountain** on the N of the Agora was decorated by the banker Herodes Atticus. The **Lechaion Road**, the main thoroughfare, lined with colonnades, which led N out of the Agora, descended to the artificial port of Lechaion on the Corinthian Gulf. To the NW of the Agora lay the **Glauke Fountain**, of which only sockets now remain of the pillars that rose above it. The **Odeon**, in front of the large **theatre** behind the fountain, was also embellished by Herodes Atticus.

The **museum** (🏛 *standard opening times*) contains pottery, small bronzes, some large Roman statues and mosaics excavated by the American School of Classical Studies.

Akro-Corinth ★

The heights of Akro-Corinth, 575m (1,885ft), were inhabited by the surviving citizens of Corinth after an earthquake in AD375 was followed by a raid by Alaric the Goth in 395. It was famous in antiquity for its **Temple of Aphrodite**, where 1,000 sacred prostitutes served her until they had earned a dowry. It says a lot for the vigour of ancient men that after the steep climb they were still eager to satisfy the carnal and financial exigencies of the priestesses. The old Latin tag, *non cuivis homini contingit adire Corinthum* (it is not everyone that can get to Corinth) is thought to imply such delights.

The road ascends from the museum of Old Corinth to the tourist pavilion (🍴) at the first of the **gates** through the **triple wall**. This first gate, with a drawbridge, is Turkish, the second Venetian, the third, with **flanking towers**, 4thC BC, when a Macedonian fortress here constituted one of "the three fetters of Greece". Within the 3.2km (2 miles) of **crenellated walls** are a medieval **keep**, a brick **underground cistern** and the **ruins of the Turkish quarter**, topped by a crumbling minaret. Best of all, there is a marvellous view over the Saronic and Corinthian Gulfs.

⊞ **Ephira** (*Vassileos Konstantinou 52* ☎ 22–434 ▯▯ ▱ 45 🚗);
Isthmia Motel (*4km (2.5 miles) from Corinth* ☎ 23–454/5 ▯▯ ▱ 76 🚗
🚗 ⇌ ⟨€ ≈), good but noisy location; **King Saron** (*in Isthmia, 6km (3.75 miles) SE of Corinth* ☎ 37–201/4 🆔232139 ▮▮▮ ▱ 161 ▦ 🚗 🚗
⇌ AE CB ① ⑥ VISA ⟨€ ≈ 🐟 💭), off-season reductions.

Daphni (*Dafní*) ★

Map 16D1. 11km (7 miles) NW of Athens. Getting there: By bus, from Athens.

On what was originally the site of the Temple of Apollo *Daphneios* on the Sacred Way from Athens to *Eleusis*, the Emperor Justinian in the 6thC AD built a fortified monastery. But the present **Church of the Dormition of the Virgin †** and **refectory** belong to the 11thC, a Golden Age in Byzantine art, as the splendid **mosaics** provide eloquent proof. From the central dome, Christ *Pantokrátor* (Almighty), his thin-lipped mouth turned down at the side, his index finger crooked over the *Book of Judgement*, looks down reprovingly over venerable prophets, saints and angels. The fierceness of the Messiah's eyes was not diminished by the crossbolts fired by Frankish crusaders at the 'Christ of the heretics' when they sacked the monastery in 1205. The surrounding biblical scenes are both colourful and show a masterly attention to detail. There is a floor-plan and key to the mosaics in *Art and architecture* (see *Culture, history and background*).

The Frankish dukes installed Cistercian monks from Burgundy in the 13thC, who added antique Ionic columns to the Gothic cloister where many of the dukes are buried. The last Acciaiuoli duke strangled his usurping aunt before the altar, giving Sultan Mohammed II the justification he needed to occupy Athens. The duke was executed and the Cistercians expelled, and Orthodox monks returned to the monastery.

During the War of Independence Daphni again became a fortress, but was later abandoned, restored, and is now one of Greece's outstanding national monuments.

Event: There is a wine festival held at the end of the summer (Aug–Sept) in the grove nearby, where unlimited quantities of wine can be consumed for a modest entrance fee. (See *Athens/Nightlife*.)

Delphi (*Delfí*) ★

Map 7G5. 176km (110 miles) NW of Athens. Getting there: By bus, from Athens, Amfissa and Livadia; by ferry, from Egio to Agios Nikolaos, near Eratini, to the SW. Population of village: 1,500.

Delphi's majestic combination of legend, history, architecture and landscape inspires awe, even in modern tourists transported by the bus-load along the Sacred Way to the shrine. These arrive in such numbers that it is possible only in the early morning or late evening to enjoy the overwhelming vastness and silence of the site, over which great eagles glide and gyre.

The sanctuary lies in a natural amphitheatre formed by the **Phaedriades** (Shining Rocks), two immense grey cliffs towering above the steep Plistos gorge. Dense groves of olive trees cascade over the gorge as it expands into the **Sacred Plain**, the wide breach in the mountain barrier formed by the bay of Itea; across the water rises the sheer wall of **Mt. Kirfis**.

The rise of Delphi dates from an earthquake, which opened up a fissure from which strange fumes emanated. When a shepherd boy investigated why his goats were jumping about madly, he, too, was seized by a frenzy. The news spread to the neighbouring pastoral tribes, and by the 14thC BC Mother Earth (Gaea) was worshipped here together with her son, the eponymous serpent Python (see *Mythology* in *Culture, history and background*).

But, as at Dodona, the Great Goddess was supplanted by a male Dorian god. According to legend, the Delphic cult of Apollo was introduced by Cretan sailors. A dolphin guided their ship to Kirra, where, turning into a beautiful youth, Apollo *Delphínios*, he hastened to the sanctuary, dethroned Gaea and slew Python. A 7thC BC Homeric hymn offers an Ionic version of the story, in which Python pursued Apollo's mother, Leto, and for this was killed by her avenging son (see *Mythology* in *Culture, history and background*, and *Islands/Delos*). The

Pythian Games were dedicated to the victorious Apollo *Pýthias*, who spoke through his priestess Pythia. Though Apollo was always the god of the oracle, concessions were made to rivals: there was accommodation for Hermes, Herakles (with whom, in another myth, Apollo contended for possession of the oracular tripod), Poseidon, and Dionysos, who presided in Apollo's absence during the winter.

Two conical stones, belonging to an age before the art of stone sculpture had been mastered, were annointed daily and adorned with flowers in Apollo's temple. One, now a prize exhibit in the museum, was the **Omphalos** (Navel of the Earth), located by two golden eagles released simultaneously by Zeus from the ends of the earth, which met here midway. The other was the stone given by Rea to Kronos as a substitute for their sixth child (see *Mythology* in *Culture, history and background*), which was eventually disgorged with the other five children and kept here by grandmother Gaea as a souvenir in her favourite sanctuary.

For centuries the oracle was consulted on important matters of politics, religion and commerce. Its pronouncements were not only crucial to the plot of numerous myths, but also played a part in historical or semi-historical events. Lykurgos and Solon sought the oracle's advice about their constitutions for Sparta and Athens respectively. Colonies were never founded until it had been consulted. "Inadequate consultation" was a favourite loophole for complaints. But while ambiguity was an effective means of avoiding being caught out, and so of maintaining its prestige, the oracle also influenced events positively by acting as an arbitrator and peacemaker. The priesthood developed in effect into an international diplomatic institution, fed by the intelligence brought by so many visitors from different lands.

Despite the venal motives of many of its political pronouncements, the oracle continued to be revered, and after one outstanding vindication Aristotle declared: "It's hard to believe and harder still to deny". One of its best predictions was the assassination of Philip II of Macedonia in 336BC, just before his planned invasion of Persia; whether the Delphic oracle knew of the plot, and how, is a matter for speculation.

In the Roman era Delphi was plundered by Sulla and Nero. Although Domitian restored the temple, and Hadrian and the Antonine emperors contrived a brief revival in the 2ndC AD, the crowds came less as pilgrims than as tourists, to view the masterpieces which had been amassed over a millennium. Constantine the Great stole some of these to embellish his new capital on the Hellespont, among them the gilded serpent column that still stands in the Hippodrome in Istanbul.

At the end of the 4thC, Theodosius closed the temple, and his son Arcadius pulled it down. The remains of a 5thC Christian church show that another god had finally claimed the Delphians' allegiance.

For the next 1,000yr villagers used the marble to build their houses, and the shrine of Athena (see over) became known as *Marmária*, the marble quarry. The site of Apollo's sanctuary was buried beneath land- and rock-falls, its location forgotten and its very name changed to Kastri. However, an entire village built of ancient marble and inscribed stones could not remain entirely unnoticed and in 1675 two travellers published their conclusion that this was indeed Delphi.

Preliminary surveys were made in 1830 and in the 1860s the French School of Archaeology started excavations which very

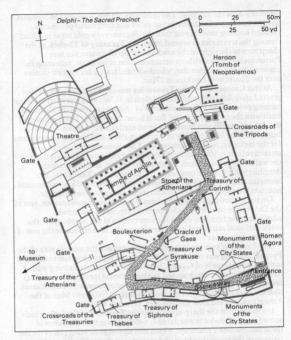

Delphi – The Sacred Precinct

N

0   25   50m
0   25   50yd

Heroon (Tomb of Neoptolemos)

Gate

Theatre

Gate

Crossroads of the Tripods

Temple of Apollo

Stoa of the Athenians

Treasury of Corinth

Gate

Gate

Bouleuterion

Oracle of Gaea

Treasury of Syracuse

Monuments of the City States

Roman Agora

to Museum

Gate

Gate

Gate

Sacred Way

Entrance

Treasury of the Athenians

Gate

Crossroads of the Treasuries

Treasury of Thebes

Treasury of Siphnos

Monuments of the City States

soon brought to light the *Naxian Sphinx*, now in the museum.
The discovery of the **Stoa of the Athenians** in 1880 persuaded
the French government to vote one million francs to fund the
transfer of Kastri to a new position, 1.6km (1 mile) W, where
today a flourishing village, once again bearing the ancient
name, is entirely occupied with the tourist industry. Systematic
diggings started in 1892, and, though the main buildings were
swiftly unearthed, they are still continuing, while the site has
been restored with both patience and consistency.

A good road winds downhill from the site (with a branch right
to *Amfissa*) leading to the **Sacred Plain** and the **ruins of Kirra**.
This is now almost completely covered by centuries-old olive
trees, though the remains of the ancient pier are visible at the
bottom of the sea. The road leads on to the beach and harbour of
Itea, where cruise-ships anchor.

The sanctuary
The Sacred Precinct
Standard opening times.

Apollo's precinct forms a rough square above the Arahova road and
below the temple. The paved square in front of the main gate was the
Roman Agora, where pious offerings could be bought in the shops of the
stoa, of which several Ionic columns have been re-erected. Other **Roman
buildings** outside the enclosure, mainly baths, are easily recognizable by
the use of brick.

Five steps prevented chariots entering the **Sacred Way**, winding in a
zigzag uphill to the entrance to the temple, and lined with the treasuries
and monuments of the city states; the **bases** of the monumental statues
can still be seen. All the ruined splendour, jostling for attention in
sometimes unedifying competition, commemorates the ridiculous as

101

Delphi

often as it does the sublime. The luxurious marble **Treasury of Siphnos**, with its two caryatids, frieze in bas-relief and sculptured pediments, recalled nothing more heroic than the discovery of a gold mine in 530BC. Among the treasuries of several cities, the **Treasury of Thebes**, at the sharp turn to the right of the road, is a model of austerity in grey Parnassos limestone without ornamentation or columns, reflecting the personality of Epaminondas, who dedicated it after his historic victory over the Spartans at Leuktra in 371BC.

At this **Crossroads of the Treasuries** was the **Treasury of Syrakuse**, erected after Athens' humiliating defeat in 413BC, which proved to be the turning point of the Peloponnesian War. Adjoining it was the Doric one built with the spoils of Athens' finest hour, Marathon. The **Treasury of the Athenians 🏛** was destroyed by an earthquake; it was rebuilt with funds from the Municipality of Athens in 1906, substituting plaster-casts for the metopes, now in the museum. The reconstruction of this attractive little edifice was facilitated by the rich array of inscriptions on the walls – Delphic decrees, edicts of the Senate, enactments of the Amphictyonic Council (see below), a dedication by Xenophon, the historian and friend of Sokrates, and (a unique record of ancient musical notation) two hymns to Apollo with their musical accompaniment.

On the left are the rectangular foundations of the **Bouleuterion**, seat of the Delphic Senate, whose 15 members exercised a restricted administrative function under the supervision of the *Amphictyóni*, the council of local states and major Greek powers; later it became the seat of the Roman governor.

The Sacred Way gives into a round space where the miracle play of the Python's slaying was performed. Behind the empty pedestals to the right is the original **Oracle of Gaea**. Closer to the polygonal retaining wall of the temple terrace (which served as a noticeboard for official decisions) are scattered the drums of an Ionic column once crowned by the *Naxian Sphinx*. Against this wall backs the 30m-long (33yd) Ionic **Stoa of the Athenians**, erected after the defeat of Xerxes in 479BC.

On the right at the sharp upturn was the **Treasury of Corinth**, which according to Herodotos was dated c. 640BC. It was thus the oldest of these temple-like Treasuries, which also served as meeting places for the citizens of the states that built and maintained them. The Sacred Way ends at the **Crossroads of the Tripods**, opposite the temple's front; its flagstones, lying underneath the main street of the medieval village, were not laid bare until the 1930s. A wealth of gold, ivory, iron and terra cotta objects, now in the museum, came to light.

Here the most valuable offerings were displayed, including Kroesos' 2.4m (8ft) bowl of silver, and a gold tripod on a serpent column with the names of the 31 states that participated in the battle of Plataea in 479BC, erected by the Spartan general Pausanias and removed by Constantine in the 4thC AD to the Hippodrome at Constantinople. Several items of this glittering array of precious metal were melted down by the Phokians, who temporarily gained control of the region between 353 and 347BC.

The Temple of Apollo

The **Heroon**, or Tomb of Neoptolemos, son of Achilles, who was killed and buried at Delphi, stood in the N corner of the area in front of the temple, and probably marks the spot of the oldest shrine at Delphi. Before the temple proper, the sixth built on the site, was the silver altar – an offering, according to the inscription on top of the black and white marble steps, from Chios (Hios); the same island paid for the unsilvered reconstruction of 1920. The ramp, parts of the wall and several columns of the **Temple of Apollo** are also reconstructions.

The legendary first temple was a hut of laurel and a shrine of beeswax and feathers. The Brazen House mentioned by Homer, though ascribed to the god Hephaestos, is more realistic, however, since in historical times there was a wooden temple plated with bronze at *Sparta*. In the 7thC BC a stone temple with a tiled roof was built, accidentally burnt down in 548BC. The Athenian family of the Alkmaeonids, exiled by the tyrant Pisistratos, undertook the rebuilding of the temple with the help of international subscriptions, notably from Kroesos of Lydia and Amasis of Egypt, while the Alkmaeonids themselves paid for the E pediment. This was in Parian marble, reputedly the first on the mainland to be built in such a costly material (see *Islands/Paros*). Naturally the oracle persistently urged the Alkmaeonids to overthrow the Pisistratids.

An earthquake in 373BC destroyed the much admired archaic temple (of which some sculpture fragments are preserved in the museum). Another subscription, collected from Marseille to Trebizond, raised most of the 700 talents needed for rebuilding. A significant part of the expense was the carting of the enormous bluish limestone blocks from distant quarries; in the mysterious ways of Greek logic, the limestone of Parnassos was thought unsuitable. The new edifice, completed in 330BC by the architects Agathon and Xenodoros, was a peripteral Doric building measuring 60 by 24m (66 by 26yd), with 15 by six columns.

Those seeking the counsel of the oracle had to come to the temple. Although the exhalations that were Delphi's *raison d'être* had ceased, probably after an earthquake, in historical times, the Pythia still took her seat on the sacred tripod over the deep fissure, inducing a trance now by chewing the poisonous leaves of the laurel. At first the Pythia was a young maiden, but after a scandal it was decided she should be over 50, to ensure her chastity. Originally she uttered her mysterious gibberings only once a year, on Apollo's birthday, and her frenzy was occasionally so violent that she died. With increasing popularity she took to pronouncing on the seventh day of every month, and finally every day, though not during winter, when Apollo was absent. Her ravings were interpreted by an attendant priest, the prophet; given of old in verse, mere slipshod prose had to do for *hoi polloi*, or even prepared answers picked out by the prophet from an amphora the Pythia had shaken. There was also a staff of exegetists, or interpreters, who could help with ambiguous answers. During the oracle's heyday the rank and file had to cast lots for admission, but princes and embassies were given precedence.

The theatre and stadium

The theatre, behind the temple in the NW (upper left) corner, was built in the 4thC BC in local limestone. It aligns perfectly with the gigantic crescent of the surrounding cliffs, so that the Plistos gorge and precipices of Mt. Kirfis form a superb backdrop for the plays that are still occasionally performed. The small arena holds 5,000 spectators in 35 tiers, and is well-preserved, although the imperial box, the stage with its frieze of sculpture (now in the museum) and the apparatus for the *deus ex machina* are all ruined, as is the **stoa** that sheltered the audience.

A steep path winds up to the stadium, 645m (2,116ft) above sea-level, the only space where it was possible to level out the 177 by 27m (194 by 30yd) area required for athletic events. Twelve tiers cut into the mountain on the N and six in an artificial embankment on the S accommodated 7,000, with some room for overflow on the higher slopes. Herodes Atticus, the great 2ndC AD benefactor of Athens, provided stone seating, including a marble **rostrum** for the president and judges; he also built the **triumphal arch** through which the contestants entered. On the ridge behind are the ramparts and towers of the **Phokian fortress** that guarded a gap in the escarpment.

The Kastalian Spring and Marmária

Nearby, to the w along the Arahova road, the icy clear water of the Kastalian Spring wells up once more in the deep cleft between the two towering cliffs of the Phaedriades, an earthquake having restored in the 19thC the flow that had ceased during the Middle Ages. Here, under the shady trees, the Pythia and her suppliants underwent purification before approaching the oracle; the two basins survive. The Romans also used the water to fill the swimming pool and hot baths of the *palaestra*. This was the square where athletes exercised, surrounded by colonnades, rest rooms and dressing-rooms, where they were annointed and massaged. In the conglomeration of ruins below, the **Gymnasium** can be made out on a slightly raised terrace; it consisted of an open track and a 4thC BC stoa parallel to it, 160m (525ft) long by 7m (23ft) wide, in which athletes could continue to train in bad weather.

On a third, artificial terrace to the left among olive groves, the shrines of Marmaria consist of two temples, two treasuries and a **rotunda**, or *tholós*. Nearest, on the E, is the early 5thC BC **Old Temple of Athena Pronáia** (Guardian of the Temple) or **Prónoia** (Providence). Here in 480BC a landslide killed raiding Persians, though it also damaged the temple. When, in 373BC, an earthquake damaged it still further, the **New Temple of Athena**, smaller but again Doric, was built at the w end of the terrace. In 1905, when 15 columns of the Old Temple had just been excavated, a further rockfall crushed 12 of them.

The *tholós*, built in the 4thC BC by the Athenian architect Theodoros, is of supreme elegance in its simplicity. Three of its original 20 Doric columns, with their entablature, have been re-erected, and the mystery of its purpose only adds to its aesthetic delightfulness.

The museum

🖼 *Standard opening times.*

At the opposite end of the sanctuary is the incongruous concrete modernity of the museum. Its oldest exhibit is the **Omphalos** or Navel of the Earth ★ From the 7thC BC come numerous tripods, cauldrons, vases, tools and weapons. The earliest stone sculpture is 6thC BC, beginning with the colossal early archaic statues of *Kleobis* and *Biton*, whose broad faces, wide-open eyes and naked bodies are fixed in an almost Egyptian rigidity.

Also worth a visit are the sculptures from the Siphnian Treasury, the *Sphinx* of the Naxians, the metopes of the Athenian Treasury and the pediments of the Temple of Apollo. The E pediment, of Parian marble, the gift of the Alkmaeonids, was sculpted by Antenor: it shows *Apollo* in a chariot surrounded by attendants. More lively is the w pediment, in stuccoed tufa, depicting the *Battle of the Giants*. A room is set aside for the finds of the 1930s, notably the heads of a chryselephantine *Apollo* and an *Artemis* also in gold and ivory, and a lifesize *Bull*, consisting of 50 sheets of silver attached with nails of silver over wood, all 6thC BC. The bronze *Charioteer* ★ is one of the great surviving masterpieces of antiquity.

The metopes of the Athenian Treasury, some of which were used as tombstones in the Middle Ages, depict the *Labours of Herakles* and *Theseus* and are of about the same date. From the 4thC BC, the friezes of the Marmaria *tholós*, and a capital in the form of three graceful dancing girls, are outstanding. A worthy contribution from Rome is the statue of Hadrian's deified favourite *Antinous*.

Hotels

Delphi

Amalia (*Apollonos* ☎ 82–101/5 ⓥ 215161 ▮▮▮ ▭ 185 ▦ ⇔ ▭ ⇌ ⒶⒺ ⒸⒷ ⊙ ⒸⒹ 𝗩𝗜𝗦𝗔 ⌂ ◁€), good views; **King Iniohos** (*Ossiou Louka* ☎ 82–701/3 ▮▮▮ ▭ 40 ⇔ ⇌ ↯ *on roof* ◁€); **Parnassos** (*Vassileos Pavlou* ☎ 82–321 ▮▮ ▭ 23 ⇔ ▭ ⇌ ◁€), good views. Itea (*13km (8 miles) sw*)

Panorama (*Paralia* ☎ 33–161/2 ▮▮▮ ▭ 27 ⇔ ◁€ ⒶⒷ).

Dion See *Macedonia*.

Dodona (*Dodóni*) ☆

*Map **6**E3. 21km (13 miles) sw of Ioanina, where sightseeing tours start.*

In a secluded valley below Mt. Tamaros, the Great Goddess' most ancient oracle passed under the protection of Zeus after the 13thC BC Dorian invasion of Greece. The new master gave his response through the rustling in the foliage of the sacred oak tree or in the sound of a metal whip blown by the wind against a brass basin. These noises were interpreted by the priests, the *Selloi* or *Helloi*, whom Homer called *aniptópodas*, dirty-footed, because they went barefoot so as to keep contact with Mother Earth. From *Helloi* comes the word *Hellene* (Greek).

The Dodona oracle could not compete with *Delphi* in the art of ambiguity, and lost prestige in particular after encouraging the Athenians in their disastrous expedition against Syrakuse in the Peloponnesian War. It was thereafter consulted on rather more petty matters, as the questions submitted on inscribed lead tablets and so preserved for eternity show: 'Agis asks whether the blankets and pillows have been lost or stolen', runs one; 'Lyssanias asks whether the child in Nyla's womb is his', runs another. From this decline into domesticity the oracle was rescued by the munificence of the Macedonian kings – who thought it as well to keep a check on divine pronouncements.

The sacred buildings were destroyed by the Aetolians in 221BC, rebuilt, then pillaged by the Roman consul Aemilius Paulus in 168BC and by the Thracians in 88BC. The oracle nevertheless continued to function until the sanctuary was converted to Christian use in the 4thC AD. A Gothic raid in the 6thC AD obliterated all traces.

Event: Epirotika Festival in Aug.

The ruins

In 1876 the amateur archaeologist Karapanos discovered beneath 9m (30ft) of rubble and earth the **foundations of a temple** built in granite, the **Sacred House** where Zeus' priests gave out his pronouncements, smaller temples, the **priests' dwellings** and an Early Christian **basilica**. On the s slope of the fortified acropolis the Macedonians built in the 3rdC BC an exceptionally large **theatre**, used by the Romans as an arena for the slaughter of wild beasts and today for performances of ancient drama during the Epirotika Festival.

Dráma

*Map **4**B8. 36km (22 miles) NW of Kavala. Getting there: By train, on the Thessaloniki–Alexandroupoli line; by bus, from E Macedonia and Thrace. Population: 32,000.*

Situated in what the Turks called the 'Golden Plain' – not only for its fertility but also for the radiant light of its summer evenings – Drama is a prosperous modern town, and a convenient stop on the inland route through E *Macedonia*.

H **Xenia** (*Ethnikis Amynis 10* ☎ 23–195/6 ▮▯ ▭ 24 ▤ ◄ ◢ ▣) CB ⊕ ⊚ VISA ●), good location, on the river.

R **Nissaki** (*on an island in the Agia Varvara springs* ▮▯ ▭ ▱ ◢ ◂).

Édessa ☆

*Map **2**C5. 89km (56 miles) NW of Thessaloniki. Getting there: By bus, from Thessaloniki and W Macedonia. Population: 15,000.*

Edessa was always believed to be ancient Aegae, capital of Macedonia until the move to Pella at the end of the 5thC BC. But the recent discovery of Philip II's tomb at **Vergina** (see *Macedonia*), down to the s on the other side of Veria, makes it more likely that Aegae, like Pella, was situated on the plain; for Philip II was murdered at Aegae.

And yet, at 320m (1,050ft) on the steep NE slope of Mt. Vermio high above the orchards of the widening valley over which there is a superb view, this seems a fine site from which to rule a turbulent kingdom. The town, which was renamed Edessa by the Romans, is very attractive, being crossed by many small brooks which unite into spectacular waterfalls hiding a small stalactite cave.

Event: There is a flower festival in late May/early June.

H **Alfa** (*Egnatia 36* ☎ 22–221/2 ▮▯ ▭ 30 � ⊕ ⊚ ◄€); **Katarraktes** (*Karanou 4* ☎ 22–300/2 ▮▯ ▭ 44 ◢ � AE CB ⊕ ⊚ VISA ⚓ *on roof*), by the waterfall.

Égio

*Map **7**G5&**11**G5. 35km (21 miles) E of Patra. Getting there: By train, on the Athens–Patra line; by bus, from most of the N Peloponnese; by ferry, across the gulf from Agios Nikolaos, 8km (5 miles) from Eratini. Population: 20,000.*

Attractively situated on the s shore of the Corinthian Gulf, Egio has some fine Othonian buildings and a 19thC **cathedral** designed by the German architect, Ziller. The **Church of Zoödohos Pygi** (Our Lady, Fountain of Life), partly built, partly hewn out of the cliff face about 1650, contains a 14thC ikon of *Agios Georgios*.

H **Eliki** (*in Valimitika, 5km (3 miles)* E *of Egio* ☎ *91– 301/4* ⫿⫾ ⯐ ⯐ *144* ⯐ ⯐ ⯐ *◁〒 ≋ ⯐ ●*); **Poseidon Beach** (*in Nikoleika, 6km (4 miles)* E *of Egio* ☎ *81– 400/2* ⫿⫾ ⯐ *90* ⯐ ⯐ ⯐ *◁〒 ≋ ⯐ ℅*).

Eleusis (*Elefsína*)

*Map **8**H7. 26km (16 miles)* nw *of Áthens. Getting there: By bus, every 30min from Athens. Population: 30,000.*

Once magnificent, the site of the most venerable mysteries of the ancient world, Eleusis is now singularly unattractive, surrounded by factories whose pollution has caused greater destruction than invading Goths or the passage of time.

From *Daphni* onwards, the modern road follows the **Sacred Way** along whose 16km (10 miles) the candidates for initiation once walked each autumn. It passes on the right the ruins of the **Sanctuary of Aphrodite**, on the left the Bay of Eleusis, filled with laid-up rusting ships. The bay is blocked by the island of **Salamis**, separated from the mainland only by narrow straits: it was here that the smaller, more manoeuvrable Greek triremes defeated the vastly superior number of larger Persian ships in 480BC. Heavy industry is ruining not only the natural beauty of the bay, but also the marble monuments of the ancient site.

Passing on the right two salt lakes, sacred to Demeter and her daughter Persephone, the road crosses the Thriasian Plain, where corn, Demeter's gift, first grew. On the left are the remains of the **antique bridge** that carried the Sacred Way to Eleusis. What exactly happened at the initiation into its Mysteries is one of the best-kept secrets of antiquity, though Aristophanes alludes to it:

> To us alone, initiated men,
> Who act aright by stranger and by friend,
> The sun shines out, to light us after death.

It seems that at the fertility rites of the pre-Hellenic matriarchies the spring king was sacrificed and his organs and limbs scattered over the fields. In Mycenaean times animal sacrifices replaced human ones, and king-priests superseded the queen-priestesses. The original orgiastic celebrations and fertility rites evolved into a cult of The Beyond, in which the endurance of ordeal might enable the soul to gain release from human bondage.

The mythological link is made through Triptolemos, Prince of Eleusis, who saw Hades' chariot re-enter the earth and thus helped Demeter in her search for her daughter Persephone, who had been abducted by the god of the Underworld. As his reward, the goddess instructed Triptolemos in her mysteries and gave him an ear of corn and a wooden plough to teach mankind agriculture, an occasion depicted in a bas-relief in the **National Archaeological Museum** in *Athens*.

Although Athens had annexed Eleusis by the end of the 7thC BC, the priesthood remained hereditary to the family of the former kings, and the sanctuary always retained its autonomy. In Hellenistic times and later, not only Athenians but the elite of Greece and Rome sought initiation, and eight emperors successfully passed the trials.

The ruins
🔲 *Standard opening times.*

The ancient Sacred Enclosure (to which entry was forbidden on pain of death to the uninitiated) was first enlarged by Pisistratos, and was restored munificently during the 5thC BC after the incursion of the Persians. It reached its full splendour in the 2ndC AD.

The Sacred Way passed through a large Roman courtyard, bordered E and W by long stoas, with two triumphal arches, exact replicas of **Hadrian's Arch** in Athens (see *Athens/Sights*), at the SE and SW. In the middle was the Doric Temple of Artemis *Propyláea* and Poseidon *Páter*. The **Greater Propylaea** to the S, a copy of the central section of Mnesikles' Propylaea on the **Acropolis** (see *Athens/Sights*), were also Roman. They were built by Marcus Aurelius, one of the initiated emperors, with six **Doric columns** crowned by a **pediment** with his **relief bust in a heraldic shield**. This has been pieced together and now lies in the courtyard. In the extensive complex to the W was the Roman **Prytaneion**, the large **'House of the Heralds'** with Roman frescoes and, at a deeper level, the **silo** built by Pisistratos for offerings of first fruits.

The inner, **Lesser Propylaea** were built, according to an inscription on the architrave, by the Roman consul Appius Claudius Pulcher in 54BC. Their roof was supported by two columns with Corinthian capitals, now in the museum. Three doors opened into the inner portico, which had two caryatids, round which peasants, mistaking them presumably for Demeter, were still frolicking in 1802, when one caryatid was removed by the London Society of Dilettanti to Cambridge, England, where it now reposes in the Fitzwilliam Museum; the other is here in the museum. On the right is the triangular **wall of the Ploutoneion**, the 4thC BC sanctuary of Pluto-Hades, which is built against the rock fissure from which Pluto emerged from the Underworld (see *Mythology* in *Culture, history and background*). The theatrical layout of the broad **flight of steps leading to a terrace** suggests that part of the nocturnal ritual may have taken place here.

The centre of the complex was the **Telesterion**, an immense hypostyle hall built by Iktinos, architect of the Parthenon, under the initiative of Kimon and Perikles. It had seats for 3,000 initiates round its four sides (one of which was hewn from the rock), and six colonnades, each of two tiers of seven columns, supported the wooden roof, with a lantern-shaped aperture in the centre. Beyond the Telesterion another stairway served as a grandstand for the ceremonies round the open-air altar. The temple on the terrace above – partly obscured by the **Church of Panagia** (Our Lady All-Holy) ✝ – may have been dedicated to the wife of Antoninus Pius, the Empress Faustina, who was deified as the new Demeter. A fortified acropolis crowned the top of the hill, and beyond it lay the ancient city.

The **museum** (🔲 *standard opening times*) contains various discoveries from the site as well as the pieces referred to above.

Epidaurus (*Epídavros*) ★
*Map **8**|6&**11**|6. 28km (18 miles) E of Nafplio. Getting there: By bus, to Lygourio, 3km (2 miles) NW; Epidaurus is included in all Peloponnesian sightseeing tours.*

The tranquil atmosphere of this sanctuary of Asklipios, god of healing, is provided by the peaceful remoteness of the surrounding pine-clad hills. To preserve it, the god forbade the extremes of birth or death within his precinct.

For healing, Asklipios (see *Mythology* in *Culture, history and background*) relied not only on medicinal herbs but also on his sacred snakes, which licked the patient. He was always portrayed flanked by reptiles, with a snake encircling his staff, and in 293BC, when the Romans were ravaged by an epidemic, they sent for a serpent from Epidaurus. Later, herbs and the thyme-fragrant air were supplemented by dieting and even by surgery; according to recommendations given by the god to patients in their dreams. Other facilities were libraries, a stadium and a theatre, one of the best preserved in Greece.

Event: Festival of ancient drama, June–Aug.

Epiros

The ruins
🔊 *Standard opening times.*

The 4thC BC **theatre** 🎭 was designed by Polyklitos, and possesses superb acoustics, which can be enjoyed in summer during the annual festival, June–Aug. The theatre holds up to 14,000 spectators in 55 tiers. The remnants of the **stadium**, the **Doric temple** (dated 380–375BC), the elegant and luxurious **stoas** and the **baths** are of less interest.

But the ***tholós***, or rotunda, of about 360–330BC, recalls the one in *Delphi*, though it is less well preserved. Its function is similarly uncertain, being connected with worship of the Underworld, probably requiring initiation. The splendour of its original 26 exterior Doric and 14 interior Corinthian columns is best appreciated by studying the marbles in the **museum** (🔊 *standard opening times*), which has architectural and sculptural elements from both this and other buildings, and numbers of *stelae* inscribed with accounts of miraculous cures. It also has a plaster model of the sanctuary, a great help in visualizing it during its heyday.

The ruins of the ancient town of some 70,000 inhabitants are visible beneath the transparent sea at **Palea (old) Epidavros**, 16km (10 miles) E.

🏨 **Paola Beach** (*Palea Epidavros* ☎ 41–397 ▯▯ 🛏 27 ⬅ 🍴 ≋ 🐟), on the sea, among several other inexpensive hotels; **Xenia Bungalows** (*near the ruins at Epidaurus* ☎ 22–003 ▮▮▯ 🐟 24, most with baths ⬅ 🍴 ≋ ⒜Ⓔ Ⓒ🅱 Ⓓ 🆔 Ⓥ🅸🆂🅰 ✉), good location.

Epiros (*Ípiros*) ☆
Map 6. Airports: Aktio and Ioanina. Ports: Igoumenitsa, Parga and Preveza. Population of region: 350,000.

Epiros, the Greek for continent or mainland, originally extended even further N into the Balkan landmass, but the muddled peace treaty terminating the Balkan Wars of 1913 awarded northern Epiros to the newly created state of Albania. It is a mountainous country of subtle hues, familiar to many from the watercolours of Edward Lear, which culminates in the great Pindos chain to the E. In this harsh terrain, its people for long remained unruly and independent. Through its almost inaccessible northern uplands the Dorians penetrated into Bronze Age Greece, upon which they forced their rule and religion from 1200BC. With the rising power of Macedonia, Epiros intermittently came under its larger neighbour's control. It was devastated by the Roman general Aemilius Paulus in 167BC, but thereafter enjoyed the *Pax Romana*, being hardly disturbed, for example, by the battle of *Actium*.

After centuries of ruinous invasions during the Middle Ages, stability returned from 1204, when the imperial Angeli dynasty, exiled from Constantinople, established the Despotate of Epiros with their capital at *Arta*; and in 1263, when the Byzantine Empire was reconstituted, Epiros was incorporated into it. From 1358 it suffered the harsh rule of the Serbs; the Turks, from the mid-15thC, were not much of an improvement.

The second half of the 18thC saw the meteoric rise to power of an Albanian adventurer, Ali Pasha, who aimed at the formation of an independent Greek-Albanian state; he was tolerant in matters of religion, but otherwise was as ruthless as his predecessors. Following his final defeat by the Turks and assassination in 1822, Turkish suzerainty was restored for a further 90yr. Liberation was achieved by a Greek army in 1912–13 under Crown-Prince Constantine.

Sights and places of interest
A recommended tour by car through the region is from Ali Pasha's stronghold, *Ioanina*, to *Kastoria*, centre of the distinctive Greek fur industry, 197km (123 miles) on a good,

uncrowded road through the wild mountains on the Albanian border. Ancient sites in Epiros include *Aktio*, *Dodona* and *Nikopoli*; for beaches see *Parga*, an 18thC village dominated by three castles, and *Preveza*, near Nikopoli. Inland from the latter is *Arta*, capital of the Angeli despots from 1214, while the attractive mountain village of *Metsovo* is on the Ioanina–Kalambaka road.

Igoumenítsa

Map 6E2. 37km (23 miles) sw of Ioanina. Port: Ferries to Bari, Brindisi and other Italian ports, and hourly 6.30–20.00 to Corfu i GNTO office at ferry terminal.

The major port of present-day Epiros, Igoumenitsa is the starting point of the reconstructed Roman *Via Egnatia*, from the Ionian Sea to Thessaloniki and Turkey. Though probably no one would visit Igoumenitsa for its own sake today, it may prove convenient to stay there on your way elsewhere and two reasonable hotels are therefore recommended below.

H **Jolly** (*Vassileos Pavlou 2* ☎ 23–970/4 ▯▯▭ 27 ◆═◄), on waterfront, within easy walking distance of beach; **Xenia** (*Vassileos Pavlou 20* ☎ 22–282 ▯▯▭ 36 ◆◻═ AE CB ✦ ◉ VISA ▱), good location at entry to village, and within easy walking distance of beach.

Nekromantéion

Map 6F2–3. 22km (14 miles) SE of Parga.

On the lower Aheron (Acheron, one of the rivers of the Underworld), the Nekromanteion, or Oracle of the Dead, stands on the summit of a hill. It was considered to be one of the entrances to Hades. At the w foot of the hill lay Ephyra, mentioned by Homer, now the village of **Mesopotamo**. Its 3rdC BC maze, destroyed in 167BC, was visited by those wishing to communicate with the souls of the dead.

Ermióni

Map 8I6&11I6. 195km (122 miles) sw of Athens; 53km (33 miles) SE of Nafplio. Getting there: By hydrofoil, from Zea Harbour, Piraeus; by bus, from Nafplio. Population: 2,500.

Ermioni is a pleasant Peloponnesian fishing village on the s end of the Argolis, opposite the island of *Ydra* (see *Islands A–Z*), reached by motorboat. It is the centre of a group of beach holiday complexes, all grouped round a central hotel.

Hotels

Ermioni
Costa Perla (☎ 31–111/4 ▯▯▭ 191 ◆◻═ AE CB ✦ ◉ ◉ VISA ▱ ◆ ℘ ◉).

Petrothalassa (*7km (4 miles) SW*)
Aquarius (☎ 31–430/4 ▯▯▭ 415 ◆◻═ AE CB ✦ ◉ ◉ VISA ▱ ◆ ℘ ◉); **Lena-Mary** (☎ 31–450/1 ▯▯▭ 120 ▤▤ ◆◻═ AE CB ✦ ◉ ◉ VISA ▱ ◆ ℘ ◉).

Plepi (*E of Ermioni*)
Kappa Club (*8km (5 miles) E of Ermioni* ☎ 41–206 ▯▯▭ 272 ▤▤ ◆◻═ AE CB ✦ ◉ ◉ VISA ▱ ◆ ℘ ◉); **Porto Hydra** (*11km (7 miles) E of Ermioni* ☎ 41–270/4 ▯▯▭ 271 ▤▤ ◆◻═ AE CB ✦ ◉ ◉ VISA ▱ ◆ ℘ ◉).

Saladi (*21km (13 miles) w on the Argolic Gulf*)
Saladi Beach (☎ 71–391/2 ▯▯▭ 404 ◆◻═ AE CB ✦ ◉ ◉ VISA ▱ ◆ ℘ ◉).

Etolikó

Map 7G4. 26km (16 miles) sw of Agrinio. Getting there: By bus, from Agrinio and Messolongi. Population: 5,000.

On a small island in the narrow straits between the two vast lagoons of Etoliko and Messolongi; the 15thC Byzantine

Basilica of the Panagia (Our Lady) † has interesting frescoes and ikons. Handwoven rugs, bedspreads and so on are good bargains. Across the river Aheloos, 12km (7.5 miles) w, are the ruins of **Oeniadae** (see *Agrinio*).

Filípi   See *Philippi*.

Flórina

Map 2C4. 160km (100 miles) w of Thessaloniki. 34km (22 miles) NE of Kastoria. Getting there: By train, from Thessaloniki; by bus, from Thessaloniki and all w Macedonia. Population: 11,000.

A prosperous modern town; recently unearthed archaic statues seem to confirm that this was the capital of *Macedonia* until about 800BC, though little of archaeological interest remains. **Great Prespa Lake**, to its N, scenically an interesting detour, is shared with Albania to the w and Yugoslavia to the NE.

   Event: Florina holds a strawberry festival in July.

🏨 **Lyngos** (*Tagmatarhou Naoum 3* ☎ 28–322/3 ▮▯▮ 🛏 40 ⇐ ⇌ 🖐).

Glyfáda   See *Attica/Saronic Gulf*.

Gýthio

Map 11J5. 46km (29 miles) s of Sparta. Getting there: By bus, from Sparta and the E Peloponnese. Port: Ferries to Kythira and Crete. Population: 5,000.

When Paris eloped with Helen, they sailed from Gythio (ancient Gytheion), the port of *Sparta*, and took refuge at Aphrodite's sanctuary on the islet of **Kranae** in the bay before sailing on to Troy. Gythio is also the port of embarkation for the island of **Kythira**. It is an attractive town, with its Othonian houses climbing steeply from the sea towards the ruined castle, and there are magnificent views over the Laconic Gulf.

Sights and places of interest

The **museum** (🏛 *standard opening times*) houses finds from antique Gytheion. The **theatre**, hollowed out from the hill of the acropolis, the foundations of a **temple to Augustus and Tiberius**, and the remains of an aqueduct survive. On the beach, just beyond the brook to the N is the half-submerged ruin of an ancient building with mosaics.

🏨 **Lakonis** (*on the N beach* ☎ 22–666/7 ▮▯▮ 🛏 74 ⇐ 🍴 ▭ AE CB 🖐 🖐 VISA ⌂ ⇌ 🐟), bungalows; **Laryssion** (*in town* ☎ 22–021/6 ▮▯ 🛏 78 🍴 ⇌ ☇ *on roof*).

The Halkidikí (*Chalcidice*) ☆

Map 3C–D6–8. 70–147km (44–92 miles) SE of Thessaloniki. Getting there: By hotel bus, from Thessaloniki Airport; by local bus, to all villages. Car-hire facilities available at Thessaloniki. Population: 65,000 in winter, double in summer.

Romantics see in the peninsula a three-fingered hand grasping the Aegean Sea between the **Thermaic Gulf** to the w and the **Gulf of the Strymon** to the E. The wrist is formed by the elongated lakes of **Koronia** and **Volvi** in the depression to the N of the knuckles, the mountainous chain crossing E–W; the fingers are the promontories of **Kassandra**, **Sithonia** and **Athos**.

   Each promontory is described later, with the route leading to it across the Halkidiki, and a list of recommended hotels. The monasteries of **Mt. Athos** are described at the end.

All hotels have ⛵ 🏠 ⇌ AE CB ⊕ ⊙ VISA ≪ ⇌ 🐾 ⊷, and, except for those in **Porto Carras**, all close Oct–April.

Event: International Sail-Surfing Competition, Sept.

Kassándra and the Thermaic Gulf

The road s from Thessaloniki passes the airport at **Mikra** and branches left into the mountains to **Polygyros** and eventually Athos. The right branch continues mostly along the Thermaic Gulf towards the Kassandra promontory, with enormous hotel and bungalow complexes, nightclubs and handicraft shops.

On the Kassandra road the first branch to the w leads to **Agia Triada**. The road continues via **Eleohoria**, where there is a branch left, 8km (5 miles) N, to the **Petralona Cave** (🖼 *standard opening times*), in which bones and tools dating back 500,000yr have been found. Further on are the negligible remains of ancient **Potidea**, near the bridge which crosses the canal at the narrow neck of the Kassandra promontory. Potidea once contributed to the outbreak of the Peloponnesian War.

The road travels down the E coast of the promontory, with lovely views over the Kassandran Gulf to Sithonia opposite and the peak of Athos visible behind it. The first branch to the right ends at **Sani** on the w coast. The E coast road continues to **Kalithea**, **Kryopigi** and **Haniotis**, crossing after **Paliouri** through idyllic hills to the w coast, and looping past **Kalandra** to finally rejoin the E road at Kalithea.

Hotels

Agia Triada (*Map 3C6. On the Thermaic Gulf, 13km (8 miles) sw of Thessaloniki*)
Sun Beach (☎ *51–221/4* ⊙*219216* ▥ ▭ *120* ▦).
Haniotis (*Map 3D7. On the E coast of Kassandra*)
Dionyssos (☎ *51–402* ▥), 32 furnished flats.
Kalandra (*Map 3D7. On the w of Kassandra*)
Mendi (☎ *41–323/7* ▥ ▭ *172*).
Kalithea (*Map 3D7. On the E coast of Kassandra*)
Ammon Zeus (☎ *22–356/7* ⊙*416009* ▥ ▭ *112* ▦); **Athos Palace** (☎ *22–100/10* ⊙*412488* ▥ ▭ *600* ▦), hotel and bungalows; **Pallini Beach** (☎ *22–480* ⊙*412418* ▥ ▭ *495* ▦), hotel and bungalows.
Kryopigi (*Map 3D7. On the E of Kassandra*)
Alexander Beach (☎ *22–433* ▥ ▭ *90*); **Kassandra Palace** (☎ *51–471/5* ⊙*418331* ▥ ▭ *192* ▦).
Paliouri (*Map 3D–E7. In the hills, near the southern tip of Kassandra*)
Xenia (☎ *92–277* ▥), 72 bungalows.
Sani (*Map 3D6. On the w coast of Kassandra*)
Robinson Club Phocea (☎ *31–225/8* ⊙*412415* ▥ ▭ *218*), bungalows in wooded grounds.

Sithonía and the north Kassandran Gulf

The road leaving Kassandra forks above Potidea and, taking the right branch, skirts the N coast of the Kassandran Gulf. 3km (1.9 miles) N is a huge mound, now all that remains of ancient **Olynthos**, once capital of the local federation but completely destroyed by Philip II in 348BC.

Rejoining the coast at **Gerakina**, the road then branches NE to **Ormylia**, or continues along the w coast of the Sithonia promontory to the prestigious resort complex known popularly as **Porto Carras**, but officially named Neos Marmaras. The complex extends for 10km (6 miles) among coves and beaches, and includes among its attractions a golf course, riding and conference facilities, a casino, a yachting marina, an indoor and an outdoor theatre and a wide range of restaurants and nightclubs. The whole spacious layout is set amidst olive groves and vineyards which produce excellent *Pórto Carrás* wine.

The road runs in a loop round the coast of the promontory touching the marinas at **Koufos**, near its pine-clad tip, and **Ormos Panagias**, at the top edge of the E coast.

Hotels

Gerakina (*Map 3D7. On the N coast of the Kassandran Gulf*)
Gerakina Beach (☎ 22–474 ✆ 412487 ▮▮ ▭ 503), hotel and bungalows.
Ormylia (*Map 3D7. Inland from the N coast of the Kassandran Gulf*)
Sermili (☎ 51–308/11 ▮▮ ▭ 123).
Porto Carras (*Map 3D7. On the w coast of Sithonia*)
Both ☎ 71–381/4 ✆ 412496 ▮▮▮ ⛵ ⛷ ▭ ✿: **Meliton Beach** (▭ 445) and **Sithonia Beach** (▭ 456); **Village Inn** (☎ 71–221 ▮▮ ▭ 85).

Athos and the west Gulf of the Strymon

Usually the approach to the Athos promontory from Thessaloniki is by the main road across the Halkidiki, turning left before **Polygyros**. This allows a glance at the hideous statue of *Aristotle* and the remains of his birthplace, **Stagyra**. The road continues to **Ierissos**, where a small medieval **castle** and some ancient walls stand above the excellent beach. It then crosses the depression left by the **canal** dug by Xerxes in 478BC to preserve his fleet from storms raging round the cape of Athos, like those which wrecked the fleet of his predecessor, Darios, in 492BC. It is a further 15km (9 miles) to **Ouranoupoli**, on the w coast of the Gulf of the Strymon; this is the last village before Athos where women and children are permitted.

Hotels

Ierissos (*Map 3D7. On the Strymon Gulf*)
Mount Athos (☎ 22–225 ▮▮ ▭ 42).
Ouranoupoli (*Map 3D7. On the NW coast of Athos*)
Eagles' Palace (☎ 71–230 ✆ 412208 ▮▮▮ ▭ 162 ▦); **Xenia** (☎ 71–202 ▮▮ ▭ 42).

Mount Athos: The Monasteries (*Ágion Óros, Sacred Mountain*) ★
Map 4D8.

No women or children are permitted to set foot on the Sacred Mountain beyond **Ouranoupoli** and, since 1977, non-Orthodox laymen have been allowed to stay on it overnight, for a maximum of four days, only if they have religious or scientific business. To visit, individual foreigners need a letter from their consulates addressed to either the Greek Ministry of Foreign Affairs in Athens or the Ministry of Northern Greece in Thessaloniki; these ministries then instruct the port authorities of **Ierissos** and Ouranoupoli, which will issue no more than ten permits per day. These regulations are strictly enforced. Additionally, however, guided groups are permitted to land from cruise ships (which are forbidden to approach closer than 500m to the shore when there are women on board) at a few monasteries, or at the port of **Dafni** for a quick drive inland to **Karyes**, the capital, on the only road, constructed for the millennial celebration in 1963.

According to local belief, the Virgin, while sailing to visit

Lazarus in Cyprus, was blown off course to Athos, and when she landed the pagan idols broke of their own accord. Pleased with this tribute, she declared the mountain her own garden, and forbade it to all other women. Most monasteries naturally claim foundation during the Virgin's visit, but historically hermits first began to settle in this almost impenetrable 518sq. km (200sq. miles) of wilderness in the 9thC. An edict issued in 1060 by Emperor Constantine IX forbade access to "any woman, female animal, child, eunuch or smooth visaged (person)". Nowadays beards are optional and even hens are tolerated, but otherwise the old rules are strictly preserved.

It is known that there were already numbers of monks on the Holy Mountain when the hermit St Peter the Athonite died in about 890. He had lived for 50yr in a cave – a practice still followed with antique fervour amid the sheer cliffs on the southernmost cape – but in the late 10thC St Athanasios organized the hermit settlers into the first communal ('coenobitic') monastery, the **Megistis Lavras** (Greatest Lavra, or Cell), directed by an abbot elected for life. Its foundation dates from 963, after the Byzantine general Nikephoros Phokas, who had promised to take vows in return for the monks' blessing for his expedition against Crete, realized that his success brought the imperial sceptre within his grasp. He therefore bought himself off his promise by supplying building funds to the monastery, and also a piece of the True Cross and a splendidly illuminated Bible – the greatest treasure of this rich house.

Athanasios established not only the rules that are still in force today but also the standard monastic layout. The monastery is built in the form of a spacious quadrangle, composed of buildings three or four storeys high in stone or wood, with cells and guest rooms opening on to galleries or corridors. In the centre of the courtyard, in which stand several churches and chapels, is the main church or *katholikón*, flanked by a basin for blessing the holy water and a keep in case of any need to take refuge. The kitchens, workshops and storerooms are on the ground floor, with no windows looking out.

A gradual decline was successfully reversed for a while both by the introduction of the idiorhythmic rule, or individual discipline, which is sometimes stricter than coenobitic, and by a relaxation of the rules in the richer houses.

Lack of novices is the main problem now facing the Holy Community, the representatives of the 20 autonomous monasteries who, since 1920, have ruled under the supervision of a Greek governor and several celibate gendarmes. Although the number of monks has recently increased slightly to almost 1,000, they are hardly enough to keep up the maintenance of the huge buildings. Furthermore, many of them live outside the monasteries in *skítes*, communities of semi-independent fathers, or in chapels, churches and hermitages scattered throughout the magnificent forest. Some of these communities are also found in the attractive capital, **Karyes**, and the village of **Kapsokalivia**, where woodcarving and other handicrafts sustain the few inhabitants.

Quite as serious a threat are the fires that increasingly devastate whole wings, caused by a combination of wooden structures, overheating stoves, overturning candles and lack of manpower. But at least all the treasures, manuscripts and books have now been catalogued, so that the illegal sale of priceless valuables has been brought under control.

113

All the monasteries are shown on the main colour map (*4D8*) at the end of the book. Each is well worth a visit, since even if the art and architecture are of minor importance, the sites are truly spectacular. Shortage of space however (and the strictly limited number of (male only) visitors allowed) prevents their individual description here.

Hymettus (*Mount Ymitós*)   See *Attica/The mountains*.

Igoumenítsa   See *Epiros*.

Ioanina (*Yannina*) ☆
Map **6***E3. 75km (47 miles)* N *of Arta. Getting there: By air, from Athens; by bus, from all of Epiros, and from Agrinio, Trikala and Athens. Car-hire facilities available. Population: 42,000* **i** *GNTO, Nap. Zerva 2* ☎ *25–086.*

Above the ramparts of a promontory jutting out into a large grey lake surrounded by bare and often snow-covered mountains rise mosques and minarets, but Ioanina, once the headquarters of the Albanian adventurer, Ali Pasha (see *Epiros*), today is generally a town of undistinguished modernity. Only the often repaired walls of the pentagonal citadel recall the early 19thC, when Ioanina was the centre of the Hellenic revival and the most prosperous town in Greece. Even the traditional silver- and coppersmiths' industry has lost its originality.

Event: Ioanina is the centre of the Epirotika Festival in Aug.

Sights and places of interest

Ali's splendid wooden palace, together with most of the rest of the town, was burnt at the end of the epic siege of 1820–22, when an army under no less a person than a former Grand Vizier re-established Turkish control. But his **harem**, on the height nearest the lake, has been reconstructed and is now used for cultural events. Nearby is the graceful, but badly neglected **Fethye Mosque**, of 1430. The larger rectangular **Mosque of Aslan Pasha** (1619) on the second eminence houses the **Museum of Popular Art** (▩ *standard opening times*), containing Epirotic miscellanies.

The delapidated *medressé* (Islamic school) has a refectory, library and baths, and is next to the weed-grown cemetery where Ali, headless, was buried next to his favourite wife (his head was taken to decorate the walls of Constantinople). Ali's tombstone with its wrought-iron canopy disappeared during World War II. Above the main square is the partly rebuilt **fortress-palace of Ali's son, Muhtar Pasha**, who betrayed him to the Turks and hastened his fall. In the small garden on top of the palace is the **Archaeological Museum** (▩ *standard opening times*), with some unexciting ancient finds and a collection of 19thC paintings.

More attractive is the view over the lake and the mountains from the nearby cafe. There are more cafes under the plane trees near the landing-stage where motorboats (▩) leave for the island, which has six tiny monasteries. The oldest of them is the 11thC **Agios Nikolaos Dilios** (St Nicholas the Hairless), but the most interesting is the 17thC **Agios Panteleimon**, where the 82yr-old Ali Pasha, despite the promise of the Sultan's pardon, was shot dead through the wooden floor. It contains interesting engravings of the period.

Swimming in the lake is definitely not recommended, even if the corpses of the ladies whom Ali had thrown in by the dozen have long since been cleaned up by the eels and water snakes that flourish in its muddy bottom.

Nearby sights
Monastery of Panagía Dourakhán
10km (6 miles) E *along the shore of the lake.*
With its Turkish name, this is the only monastery ever built by an unconverted Turk. Dourakhan Pasha marched his army in the darkness of the winter of 1434 over the frozen lake without realizing the danger,

and in gratitude for his safe arrival at the other shore built the monastery
to the Virgin, near the spot where he had set off.

Perama Cave ★

5km (3 miles) NE along the Metsovo road 🚫 *Standard opening times.*
A well-lit concrete path meanders for more than 900m (over 1,000yd)
through a varied succession of lofty halls and weird stalactite chambers.

H **Alexios** (*Poukevil 14* ☎ *24–003* 🛏 🖵 *92* 🍴); **Xenia** (*Vassileos
Georgiou, on outskirts of town* ☎ *25–087/9* 🛏 🖵 *60* 🍴 🚗 AE CB ⊕
CD VISA ✉).

Ípiros   See *Epiros*.

Kaisariani Monastery   See *Athens/Sights*.

Kakí Thálassa   See *Attica/The plains*.

Kalamáta

*Map 11J5. 145km (91 miles) SW of Argos. Getting there: By
air, from Athens; by train, from Corinth and Patra; by bus,
from Athens and all towns in the Peloponnese. Population:
40,000.*

This modern capital of fertile Messenia was laid out by French
military engineers in 1829 after the total destruction of the town
in the War of Independence. A string of hotels, restaurants and
cafes lines the long, sandy beach, 3km (2 miles) S.

Sights and places of interest

Nothing remains of Homeric Pherae and little of classical Kalamae,
except for the over-restored **theatre** which accommodates performances
of ancient drama during the summer. Above it is the very ruined
Frankish castle, once the possession of Geoffroy de Villehardouin, and
nearby is a convent, where the nuns sell handmade silks. But Kalamata is
better known for its fine black olives. Near the fruit and vegetable
market, tiny 10thC **Agii Apostoli †** was cunningly incorporated into a
slightly larger 17thC church.

There are beautiful drives along the Messinian Gulf E into the *Mani* or
W and round the coast to the Venetian **fortress of Koroni**, 56km (35
miles) from the town.

A worthwhile excursion is to the impressive 4thC BC ramparts of
ancient **Messini**, built by the Theban general Epaminondas on the slopes
of Mt. Ithomi, 798m (2,618ft) high. The best approach to it is along a
well-marked turn-off left from the Kalamata–Tripoli road, rather than
by dreary modern Messini. The road leads past the village of Arsinoë
right into the fortifications, but it is a steep climb down among the olive
groves to the ruined agora, theatre, stadium and temples.

H **Elite** (*Paralia* ☎ *25–015* 🛏 🖵 *60* 🍴 🚗 🏊 ●), with the beach
across the road; **Filoxenia** (*Paralia* ☎ *23–166/7* 🛏 🖵 *118* 🍴 🏠 🚗
AE CB ⊕ CD VISA ◁ 🏊 ♨ ●), at the far end of the beach, somewhat
isolated – 20% reduction, Nov–Mar 14.

Kalambáka

*Map 2E4. 92km (58 miles) W of Larissa. Getting there: By
train, on the line from Paleofarsalos, Karditsa and Trikala; by
bus, from towns in Central Greece and Epiros, and Athens.
Population: 6,000.*

Kalambaka is on the W confine of the Thessalian plain, its
orchards rising gently between the peaks of the **Pindos** range
and a sheer cliff, which reaches 555m (1,820ft) above sea-level.
Its 14thC **Old Mitropolis †** – a basilica with frescoes inside and
outside – has a rare marble pulpit in the centre of the nave. But
this is only a preface to the unique wonder of the **Meteora**,
reached by a road that winds towards the village of Kastraki.

Kalambáka

Sights and places of interest
The Meteóra 𝕀𝕀𝕀 ★
3km (2 miles) from Kalambaka. Included in organized tours of Central Greece.

The Meteora are an unearthly forest of 24 perpendicular rock needles, upon which the spirit of the 14thC found expression in stone and brick. A circular road twists among these gigantic pillars, popularly believed to be meteors but in fact split and eroded into their incredible shape by the inland sea that once covered the plain.

Hermits seem first to have taken refuge in the shallow caves in the rocks during the turbulence of the 11thC, and soon formed a community of ascetics. By the even more turbulent 14thC, when the Byzantine emperors were defending the fertile valley against the Serbian rulers of Trikala, each of the impregnable pinnacles was crowned by a monastery. The monks adopted the strict coenobitic rules of their counterparts on **Mt. Athos** (see *Halkidiki*) excluding all women and female animals; the initiator of these rules was another Athanasios, the founder of the **Monastery of the Transfiguration** on the **Great Meteoron**.

After his death, his disciple, the Serbian hermit-king Joasaph, and his successor as abbot, the exiled Byzantine Emperor Ioannes Kantakousinos, both claimed the authority of Superior, and a dispute over arable land further aggravated their struggle. This violation of the founding Christian precepts caused a rapid decline, so that many of the proud buildings on the towering summits became empty, wind and weather bared again the black rocks, and today only six monasteries remain to witness a way of life that has virtually vanished.

Gone are the days when visitors were hauled up in outsize string bags on a rope that, by tradition, was replaced only after it had broken. The rusty windlasses are still used for supplies, but in the 1920s galleries were hollowed out of the cliffs, which are easily accessible by road. The restricted space on top determined the irregular shape of the vaulted buildings, built mostly in the traditional alternating brick and stone, with rotting wooden balconies overhanging breathtaking precipices.

Great Meteóron 𝕀𝕀𝕀
After a steep climb up the rock gallery, the massive gate of the Great Meteoron opens on a large courtyard built on different levels. The cloisters, refectory and chapels have been barred to the ceaseless stream of tourists in an attempt to retain some monastic discipline among the few remaining old men, but the **Church of the Transfiguration** † can still be visited. The 16thC frescoes in the large dodecagonal dome are fairly well preserved, but the wall-paintings have suffered. Though some Byzantine manuscripts survive in the library, more have been eaten by worms, sold or stolen. But the spectacular view remains, at its best in spring when the Pindos and the distant Olympos mountains are still snow-covered, the almond and peach trees are in bloom, and the green sea of wheat is bordered by the blue sea – but that is for sharp eyes only.

Monastery of the Manuscripts
The highest rock-needle is topped by the ruins of the Monastery of the Manuscripts, which specialized in the illumination of scrolls and books. The legend that the first hermit climbed up on a rope fastened to an eagle's leg seems hardly more incredible than the fact that the shallow niches high up in the sheer cliff were used as prisons for disobedient monks, who were exposed there to the rigours of the climate without any visible means of support.

Óssios Varlaám 𝕀𝕀𝕀
Ossios Varlaam, founded in 1517 in honour of a local anchorite, possesses the most remarkable frescoes in its **Church of all Saints** † These were painted by Frankos Kastellanos, a member of the Cretan school, in about 1566, and expertly restored in 1870.

Other monasteries
At **Agia Triada** (Holy Trinity), the **Church of St John the Baptist** † has an attractive arcaded facade and an outstandingly precarious position. **Agia Rosani**, founded in 1369, underwent conversion, once unthinkable, into a nunnery, and was followed in 1963 by **Agios Stefanos**, where the sisters have opened an orphanage. A single bridge spans Agios Stefanos' grim abysses, which have been instrumental in preserving at least some of the treasures bestowed on it by Emperor Andronikos III Palaeologos. The three-domed **Church of Agios Haralambos** † (1798) contains an exquisitely carved **ikonostasis** and

abbot's throne. **Agios Nikolaos**, on the lowest rock, recently restored, has so far remained empty.

H **Motel Divani** (☎ 22 – 583/4 ▥▥ ▯ □ 111 ▦ ▬ ⇌ AE CB ◎ ⓒ VISA ⇌); **Odyssion** (☎ 22 – 320 ▯▯ □ 21 ▬).

Kalávryta

Map 7H5&11H5. 75km (47 miles) SE of Patra. Getting there: By rack-and-pinion railway, up from the port of Diakofto, SE along the coast from Egio; by bus, from Patra and Tripoli. Population: 2,200.

The present name derives from *kalés vrýsses* (good springs) for which the town, 750m (2,300ft) above sea-level up the slopes of Mt. Helmos, is famous.

The ancient town, Kynaetha, was destroyed by the Aetolians in 220BC. The ruined castle, built on the site of the ancient acropolis, was erected by the Frankish barons of Kalovrate in 1205. It underwent the usual fortunes of a Peloponnesian town, but with one notable variation from 1440 – occupation by the Knights of St John for 4yr after they had purchased the town. On Dec 13, 1943, Kalavryta was burnt to the ground and more than a thousand of its inhabitants massacred by the Nazis.

Nearby places of interest
Monastery of Agía Lávra
6km (4 miles) SW of Kalavryta.

The monastery of Agia Lavra, where Bishop Germanos of *Patra* is believed to have raised the banner of revolt against the Turks on Mar 21, 1821, was also burnt down in 1943, but has been reconstructed on the same site, on a hill overlooking the upland. In the **museum** (▧ *standard opening times*) are the historic banner and ikons.

Monastery of Méga Spíleo
12km (7.5 miles) NE of Kalavryta, on the road to Diakofto on the coast.

The eight-storey monastery of Mega Spileo clings to a bare cliff, screening the large cave which gave the monastery its name. Two monks discovered in the cave one of the miraculous ikons of the *Virgin* painted by St Luke, which has survived the repeated fires that necessitated constant rebuilding of the monastery, most recently in 1934. The small number of monks now barely fills one wing of the huge building; guests are lodged in a second wing. In the **church**, on the third storey, and opening into the cave, are some 17thC frescoes, while in the **museum** in the sacristy are illuminated Gospels, silver plate and some showy jewellery donated by Catherine the Great of Russia.

H **Helmos** (☎ 22 – 217 ▥▯ □ ✿ 27, *some with baths* ▬ ⇌ ▭).

Kamména Vóurla

Map 8G6. 175km (109 miles) NW of Athens. Getting there: By bus, from Athens and Lamia. Population: 2,200.

This rapidly developing spa (opposite the more old-fashioned spa at Edipsos on the island of *Evia* – see *Islands A–Z*) has numerous modern hotels strung along the attractive N entrance to the Euboean Gulf. The sulphur springs are popular with rheumatics but bathing beaches are crowded.

Sights and places of interest
Thermopýles (*Thermopylae*)
11km (7 miles) NW of Kamména Vourla.

Thermopyles (Hot Gates) is also a spa, not yet modernized, but known primarily for the 300 Spartans' battle in 480BC against Xerxes' 180,000-strong army. Opposite the spa is the **memorial to the Spartan King Leonidas**, with its inscription 'Stranger, tell the Lacedaemonians that we lie here, obedient to their command'.

[H] **Acropole** (☎ *22–502* 📟 🛏️ *27* 🍴 ⚓); **Galini** (☎ *22–247/8* 📶 *131* 🍴 🛏️ 🍴 [AE] [CB] ⊙ ⊙ [VISA] ⚓ ⇌ 🏊 ⊙), large reductions in off-seasons, public beach across road; **Poseidon** (☎ *22–721/5* 📶 🛏️ *93* 🍴 🛏️ ⇌ [CB] ⊙ ⋖⋗ ⇌ ⚓); **Sissy** (☎ *22–190/1* 📶 🛏️ *102* 🍴 🛏️ ⇌ ⋖⋗ ⇌ 🍴 🎯 ⊙), good location at town entrance.

Karpeníssi

*Map **7**F4. 78km (49 miles) w of Lamia. Getting there: By bus, from Lamia and Agrinio. Population: 5,000.*

The drive to Karpenissi is perhaps more worthwhile than the town itself, although Karpenissi is one of the very few mountain resorts in Greece combining skiing possibilities with decent accommodation. It is also a good excursion centre for the mountainous heart of Central Greece.

The 78km (49 miles) road w from Lamia follows the fast-flowing Sperhios upstream, past a branch first left to **Ypati**, a popular spa for rheumatic diseases, 25km (16 miles) from Lamia; after Makrakomi, it crosses the fir forests of Mt. Tymfristos at the Rahi ridge, 1,000m (3,281ft) high, and then descends to Karpenissi.

To the sw, the road leads on to *Agrinio*, 112km (70 miles), and is kept open all the year round, although snow-chains may be needed. On its way it crosses the **Tatarna bridge**, over Lake Kremasta, formed by the damming of the Afrifotis, Aheloos and Tavropos rivers. A branch right before the bridge leads to a 160m-high (525ft) dam over the gorge of the Aheloos.

[H] **Anessis** (☎ *22–840* 📟 🛏️ *25* ⇌ ✉️); **Lecadin** (☎ *22–131/5* 📶 🛏️ *104* 🍴 🛏️ ⇌ ✉️ ⋖⋗).

Kastel Tornese

*Map **10**H3. 86km (54 miles) sw of Patra. Getting there: By train, to stations on separate Kylini and Loutra Kylini branches from the main Patra–Pyrgos line; by bus, from the NW Peloponnese. Port: At Kylini, for ferries to Zakynthos. Population of Kylini: 600.*

Only an expert can unravel the difference between the neighbouring villages of **Kastro** and **Kylini**, both dominated by the great fortress of Kastel Tornese. Maps, GNTO handouts and official hotel lists contradict themselves as to the location of the main holiday accommodation at this westernmost point of the Peloponnese, the four-block **Kyllini Golden Beach** (the spelling also of course differs. . . .) which lies about half-way between Kylini and Loutra Kylinis at the village of Kastro, below the castle. There is a fine beach at Kylini, and the waters of **Loutra Kylinis** are recommended for respiratory ailments.

Sights and places of interest
The castle 🏰 ☆
📷 *Standard opening times.*

Known also as the Castle of Hlemoutsi, the excellently preserved hexagonal castle was built in 1220 by Geoffroy II Villehardouin to defend the town and important commercial centre of Glarentza. Once the port of antique Elis and today, as Kylini, terminal for the Zakynthos ferry, it was at that time the port of the medieval Principality of Achaia. The town was razed in 1427 by the last Byzantine emperor, Constantine Palaeologos, for which a curse was laid on him, and only scattered foundations remain.

The castle was originally named Clairmont but became Kastel Tornese when the Frankish mint of the *tornesi* (coins) was moved up from the port to the keep on its steep hill.

Convent of Vlahérnes
5km (3 miles) sw.

The convent stands in an idyllic landscape of verdant hills, and has a late-12thC, three-aisled basilica 🏛 ✝ containing interesting Byzantine and Gothic elements.

🅗 **Kyllini Golden Beach** (☎ 95–205 🕿 372104 ▥ 🖵 *332* 🍴 🚗 🚘 ⇌ 🄰🄴 🄲🄱 💷 🄾 🄾 💳 🛥 ✈ ❂), see introductory text earlier.

Confusingly, there are two Xenia hotels, both in a pine grove 150m (165yd) from the beach at Loutra Kylini: **Xenia (1)** (☎ 96–270/3 ▥ 🖵 *80* 🍴 🚗 🚘 ⇌ 🄰🄴 🄲🄱 🄾 🄾 💳 🛥 ✈ ❂); **Xenia (2)** (☎ 96–275/7 🎬 🖵 *75* 🚗 🚘 ⇌ ❂).

Kastoriá ☆

*Map **2**C4. 216km (135 miles) w of Thessaloniki. Getting there: By air, from Athens; by bus, from w Macedonia, Athens and Ioanina. Population: 17,000.*

Straddling the narrow isthmus of a triangular headland, prosperous fur-trading Kastoria has two fronts on to Lake Orestias, named after the town's supposed founder, Orestes.

The traditional furriers' industry flourishes as never before, and furs (see *Shopping* in *Planning*) can be bought by the metre or made up cheaper than in Athens.

Event: There is a carnival at Epiphany.

Sights and places of interest

Kastoria was a military outpost of the Byzantine Empire, and the governors constructed numbers of tiny churches; these were supplemented in the 17th and 18thC by private chapels which the rich fur traders attached to their mansions. The few remaining **patrician residences**, *arhontiká*, tasteful, comfortable, with stout beams, often decorated, supporting two or three storeys jutting over the windowless lower floors, are badly neglected, but one has been converted into a **folk museum** 🏛 (🕿 *standard opening times*) on Kapetan Lazarou.

Hidden between huge concrete blocks of flats, the churches can be found by signposts. The oldest of them is the triple-naved **Basilica of Agios Stefanos** ✝ but the most unusual is the 11thC **Panagia Koubelidiki** (Our Lady of the Cylindrical Dome) ✝ in the court of the high school. Further down Mitropoleos is 12thC **Agios Nikolaos** ✝ a miniature single-naved basilica with interesting frescoes. There are frescoes again in 14thC **Taxiarhes** (Archangels) ✝ and in **Agios Athanasios** ✝ close to the big modern **Mitropolis** (cathedral) ✝

At the furthest point of the headland is the **Monastery of Panagia Mavriotissa**, the church of which – **Agios Ioannis** ✝ – has frescoes showing *Christ stilling the Waters*, featuring the local flat-bottomed punts. The monastery is reached by a one-way, circular road, shaded by old plane trees – an idyllic drive or walk, 4km (2.5 miles).

🅗 **Orestion** (☎ 22–257/8 🎬 🖵 *20* 🚗); **Tsamis** (*on the main road 3km (2 miles) s* ☎ 43–331/5 ▥ 🖵 *153* 🚗 🚘 ⇌); **Xenia du Lac** (*on the highest point of the headland* ☎ 22–565 ▥ 🖵 *26* 🚗 🚘 ⇌ 🄰🄴 🄲🄱 🄾 🄾 💳 🛥 ❂).

Kavála ☆

*Map **4**C8. 160km (100 miles) NE of Thessaloniki. Getting there: By bus, from Thessaloniki, E Macedonia and Thrace. Port: Ferries to Lesvos, Thassos and Piraeus. Car-hire facilities available. Population: 49,000. **i** GNTO, Filelinon 2 ☎ 222–425.*

Kavala, ancient Neapolis, was a colony founded on the basin-like slopes of Mt. Symvolo opposite *Thassos* (see *Islands A–Z*). As the port of the Roman foundation of *Philippi* to the NW, it prospered until devastated by Alaric's Goths in AD396. As Christoupolis (Christ's Town) in the Byzantine Empire – so called perhaps because so many saints, including Luke, Paul, Silas and Timothy, had visited it in AD43 – it was again destroyed, this time by the Normans, in 1185. As a relay station for changing horses, it re-emerged as Kavala, the Levantine word for 'on horseback'. In modern times, as a centre of the tobacco trade, it developed into the fifth-largest town of Greece.

In 1769 Mohammed Ali, son of a wealthy tobacco merchant, was born in Kavala. He succeeded where Ali Pasha of *Ioanina* failed, founding the royal dynasty of Egypt, conquering Syria and being prevented from ascending the throne of the Turkish Empire only by the intervention of the great powers.

Sight
Mohammed Ali's birthplace
◻ *On the E promontory.*

The house where Mohammed Ali was born stands preserved amidst decaying Byzantine fortifications. It is laid out in typical Islamic style, with lattice wooden screens in the **harem**, from which a lift brought food to the male gatherings on the first floor. The only pieces of furniture were the cupboards in which the men's rugs and cushions were daily put away, as if in preparation for a journey – the result of deep-seated nomadic instincts. The **equestrian statue of Mohammed Ali** in front of the house is considered the finest modern bronze in Greece.

Other sights

Mohammed Ali never forgot his birthplace: he repaired the **Roman aqueduct** that still spans the lower parts of the town, and established a **religious school** ▥ – Greece's most distinguished Moslem building.

The **museum** (*on the seafront* ▨ *standard opening times*) contains finds from all over E Macedonia, notably from *Amfipoli*.

Hotels

In town

Esperia (*Erythrou Stavrou Ave. 42* ☎ 229–621/5 ✆ 452164 ▯ ▭ 105 ▦ ▬ ▭ ▭ on roof); **Oceanis** (*Erythrou Stavrou Ave. 32* ☎ 221–980/5 ✆ 452208 ▯ ▭ 168 ▦ ▬ ▭ AE CB ⓕ VISA ▼ on roof ≈ ●).
Kalamitsa (*1.6km (1 mile)* w)
Lucy (☎ 832–600/5 ✆ 452127 ▯ ▭ 217 ▦ ▬ ▭ AE CB ⓕ ⓓ VISA ≈ ▲ ●).

Kifíssia   See *Attica/The mountains*.

Komotiní

Map **4**B9. 113km (71 miles) NE of Kavala. Getting there: By train, on the Thessaloniki–Alexandroupoli line; by bus, from Thrace and E Macedonia. Population: 33,000.

Slim minarets lend an oriental air to the capital of Thrace, though the mosques themselves are undistinguished. The **Archaeological Museum** (*Symeomidi 4a* ☎ 22–411 ▨ *standard opening times*) houses finds from all over Thrace. Near **Lagos**, 25km (16 miles) SW, at the beginning of the long dyke which divides the lagoon from the sea, there are **prehistoric tombs**, **flagstones** from the Roman *Via Egnatia*, a small **Byzantine church** ✝ and the best beach to be found in N Greece, with 8km (5 miles) of fine sand, so far unexploited except for a camping site. The beach stretches as far S as **Fanari**.

Event: Display of Thracian folkloric customs in mid-May.

▥ **Orfeus** (*Vassileos Konstantinou Sq. 48* ☎ 26–701/5 ▯ ▭ 79 ▦ ▬ ▭ AE CB ⓕ ⓓ VISA ▼ on roof).

Kórinthos   See *Corinth*.

Koutóuki Cave See *Attica/The plains*.

Kylíni See *Kastel Tornese*.

Lárissa
Map 2E5. 355km (222 miles) NW of Athens. Airport: Just E of the town. Getting there: By air, from Athens; by train, on the Athens–Thessaloniki line; by bus, from Athens, Ioanina, Thessaloniki and all Thessaly. Car-hire facilities available. Population: 74,000 i GNTO, Koumoundourou 18
☎ *250–919.*

Lying as it does in the middle of the Thessalian plain, Larissa has played a leading part in the history of Thessaly ever since its foundation by Akrisios, the legendary king of *Argos*. The ancient city was ruled for centuries by the Aleuad family, who claimed descent from Herakles, and early on it became the chief city in a Thessalian federation. Although they spoiled their record by submitting to Xerxes in 480BC, the Aleuads still attracted celebrities to their court, notably the Theban poet Pindar and the physician Hippokrates from *Kos* (see *Islands A–Z*). In the 4thC BC, however, in a moment of difficulty, they asked for help from their powerful neighbour Philip II (see *Macedonia*), who seized the opportunity to annexe Larissa and Thessaly. The Romans made Larissa the capital of an enlarged federation, and Christianity was introduced to the town by a shadowy St Achilles – thus keeping a link with pagan tradition, for the great Homeric hero had ruled in this vicinity.

No town in Greece with such a distinguished past is so devoid of significant remains, but under the Turks Larissa was too important for building materials there to have been left unused.

Some relief from the oppressive summer heat is offered by the park on the banks of the Pinios, ancient Peneus, where there are open-air restaurants and cafes.

Event: Shrove Monday is celebrated at **Tyrnavos**, 16km (10 miles) N, where large amounts of the local *óuzo* are consumed out of gaudily painted, outsize phallic vessels.

Ⓗ **Divani Palace** (*Vassilissis Sofias 19* ☎ *252–791/4* ▦ ▭ 77 ▦ ➟ ➞ AE CB ◑ ◉ VISA); **El Greco** (*Megalou Alexandrou 35* ☎ *252–411/3* ▯ ▭ 90 ● ➞ ➞ ♉ *on roof* ◉), **Metropole** (*Roosevelt 8* ☎ *229–911* ◑ *295148* ▯ ▭ 95 ▦ ➞ ◑ VISA ♉ *on roof* ≋).

Lavrio See *Attica/The plains*.

Lerna (*Míli*) See *Argos*.

Litóhoro See *Macedonia* for hotels.

Livadiá
Map 8G6. 45km (28 miles) NW of Thebes. Getting there: By train, on the Athens–Thessaloniki line; by bus, from Athens, Delphi, Lamia and Thebes. Population: 17,000.

Livadia is a town of white houses with balconies overhanging the river, attractively situated in the foothills of **Mt. Elikonas** (Helicon), two of which rise steeply above the gorge of the Erkyna. In Roman times, Livadia replaced Thebes as the most important town in Boeotia, a position it retained throughout the Middle Ages, when the Catalans built the **fortress**, the ruins of which still dominate the town. Under the Turks, Livadia was for a time second only to Athens.

Sights and places of interest

Gorge of Erkýna (*Hercyna*)

Here the oracle of Trophonios (The Food Provider) attracted large numbers of pilgrims from the 6thC BC onwards. The oracle, halfway between *Delphi* and *Thebes*, could be consulted as a kind of double check, after the petitioner had drunk from the fountain of Lethe (Oblivion) and Mnemosyne (Remembrance) (see *Mythology* in *Culture, history and background*), usually located in Hades but here identified as being in the Erkyna gorge.

[H] **Levadia** (*Katsoni Sq. 4* ☎ *23–611/7* 51).

Loutráki

*Map **8**H6&**11**H6. 86km (54 miles) W of Athens; 8km (5 miles) NE of Corinth. Getting there: By bus, from Athens and Corinth. Population: 8,000.*

The largest spa in Greece, 5km (3 miles) N of the isthmus of *Corinth*, Loutraki has retained its popularity with affluent elderly Greeks despite the collapse of several of its hotels during the earthquake of Feb 1981, which had its epicentre in the Halcyon Gulf. Numbers of hotels, restaurants and thermal establishments still line the shore, and both sparkling and still Loutraki water, recommended for liver and kidney disorders, are bottled and are obtainable throughout the country.

Sights and places of interest

The Heraion (*Iréo*)

13km (8 miles) NW of Loutraki.

Beyond the idyllic lagoon of **Perahora**, a rocky promontory divides the Corinthian and Halcyon Gulfs. From the tiny ancient harbour a path climbs to the foundations of the Heraion, which, though of little architectural interest, offers superb views over the gulf.

[H] **Mitzithra** (*Venizelou 25* ☎ *42–316* 43 *on roof*); **Paolo** (*Korinthou 16* ☎ *48–742/3* 80 AE CB VISA *on roof*); **Pappas** (*1.6km (1 mile) from town at Pezoulia–Pefkaki* ☎ *43–936/8* 84 AE CB VISA).

Loutrá Kylínis

See *Kastel Tornese.*

Macedonia (*Makedonía*) ★

*Map **2–3**. Airports: Kastoria, Kavala and Thessaloniki. Ports: Kavala and Thessaloniki. Main railway stations: Drama, Edessa, Florina, Seres, Thessaloniki. Population of region: 2,000,000.*

Macedonia has never been a stable geographical unit and still means different – though not necessarily exclusive – areas to different nations. It roughly comprises the area bordering the Aegean between the Pindos mountains and Epiros to the W, Mt. Olympos and Thessaly to the S, and Thrace, beyond Kavala, to the E. It has always been coveted by its northern neighbours, seeking to control its fertile river valleys and its outlets to the Aegean, and it was exposed to invasions some 2,000yr earlier than the country to the S of the mighty Olympos chain. Its climate is harsher than in the S, with bitterly cold winters inland and icy winds which blow down the Axios river to the Thermaic Gulf. The orchards and forest-clad mountains of the W are divided by the Axios from the granary plains of the E.

Macedonia sometimes has been part of and sometimes separate from the rest of Greece. Macedonians fought on the Trojan side against the Achaeans in the Trojan War, and as late as the 5thC BC the Greek cities were still implanting colonies there among people they regarded as barbarians. Like Epiros, Macedonia remained an unruly feudal monarchy throughout the early classical period, until the kings adopted the military techniques of southern Greece which enabled their yeoman infantry to unhorse the nobles' cavalry.

In the early 5thC BC, Alexander I united the kingdom, then, after betraying to the Greeks his overlord Xerxes' plan to outflank their army, placed a guard on the *Vale of Tempe*. The Greeks, prudently, had already retreated to *Thermopylae*, and for this action Alexander was honoured by being admitted to the Olympic Games.

The court of Archelaos, Alexander I's grandson, at *Pella*, became an intellectual centre. Here the 80yr-old Euripides wrote his last tragedies, *Archelaos* and the *Bacchae*. Archelaos was murdered in 399BC, and 7yr of successive coronations and assassinations followed, until Amyntas III finally subjugated the highland chiefs. His widow murdered their eldest son, then with her son-in-law and lover, Ptolemy, ruled in the name of her second son, Perdikas. Meanwhile, the third son, Philip, was held hostage in *Thebes*. When, after several more assassinations and dethronements, Philip was crowned as Philip II, he put to good use what he had seen in Thebes of the generalship of the great Epaminondas. At the battle of Chaeronea in 338BC he defeated Athens, Sparta and Thebes, made himself master of all Greece, and the history of Macedonia and Greece became united.

After the death of Alexander III the Great in 323BC, Macedonia was fought over ruthlessly for 50yr, until in 276BC Antigonas Gonatas (of the Big Knee) established a new dynasty. The union of Macedonia and southern Greece remained essentially intact, even after the defeat of the last king of Macedonia, Perseus, by the Romans in 168BC. Subsequently, however, southern Greece was detached from Macedonia as the separate province of Achaea. Macedonia was the main possession of the Byzantine Empire, despite repeated Slav incursions, until just before the Empire's final dissolution at the hands of the Turks. The latter remained in Macedonia until 1913, when the region became once more united with Greece.

See also individual entries on *Amfipoli*, *Drama*, *Edessa*, *Florina*, *Halkidiki*, *Kastoria*, *Kavala*, *Philippi*, *Seres*, *Siatista*, *Thessaloniki* and *Veria* for further information about these towns and sights.

Event: Olympos Festival, Dion and Platamonas, July–Aug.

Important sites

In Greece, hardly a week passes by without an important archaeological discovery, but the discoveries at **Vergina** in 1977 were a worldwide sensation, and the antiquities of Macedonia have been revealed in increasing splendour since 1958. An exhibition of its choicest items which recently toured the USA attracted large crowds. The finds are now mostly to be seen in the **Archaeological Museum** in *Thessaloniki*.

Dion
Map 2D5. Between Katerini and Litohoro, 5km (3 miles) w of the Thessaloniki–Larissa motorway.
This was a sanctuary of Zeus, embellished by Archelaos with a temple to the guardian deity, a theatre and a stadium, and surrounded by a wall with defensive towers. The Temple of Artemis-Isis is also being exhumed from a swamp. The Romans added two large baths and, in

The Máni

375AD, a Christian basilica with fine mosaics. A museum is under construction. The **theatre** at Dion, rebuilt in Hellenistic times, shares with the well-preserved 14thC Catalan **Castle of Platamonas** ▥ a little further s on the motorway, performances during the Olympos Festival.

Mount Olympos

Dion's greatest attraction is its superb site, at the foot of majestic Mt. Olympos, the well-chosen home of the gods. Guides for the ascent are at **Litohoro**, 5km (3 miles) s, on the next branch w from the motorway.

Pella *(Pela)*

Map 2 C5. Halfway between Edessa and Thessaloniki.

The ancient capital of Macedonia seems to have been at *Florina*. At the end of the 5thC BC Archelaos transferred the capital to Pella, protected by swamps and the island fortress of Phakos at the edge of the plain. Here, so far, some public buildings with colonnades and fine pebble mosaics, depicting notably *Alexander the Great being saved by Krateros at a Lion Hunt, Helen of Troy*, and *Dionysos riding a Panther*, have been unearthed, and some entire streets of the huge ancient town have also been found. But there is no sign as yet of the royal palace, where the frescoes of the famous 4thC BC painter Zeuxis drew sharp criticism from the nobility for their un-Macedonian extravagance. The small **museum** by the site (☎ *standard opening times*) contains large marble and clay roof tiles, terra cotta vessels and figurines, coins, a beautiful bronze statuette of *Poseidon* and a vase portraying a *Battle between Greeks and Amazons*.

Vergína ☆

Map 2 C5. 21km (13 miles) SE of Veria. The site may be closed for excavations.

At Vergina, on the banks of the Aliakmon, a large mound had fallen prey to looters and excavators for centuries. The 19th grave to be opened there by modern excavators had already revealed an *Abduction of Persephone*, the first complete ancient wall-painting in Greece, when, in 1977, Professor Andronikos of Thessaloniki University discovered 5.2m (17ft) below ground a large Doric grave monument, decorated with a painted frieze of a lion hunt. It also contained intact in its two chambers all its treasures and, above all, five small ivory heads, believed to represent those of Philip II's family. These convinced Andronikos that he had found the tomb of Philip and his seventh wife, Kleopatra.

Since then, seven more royal grave monuments have been uncovered, including perhaps those of Philip's two brothers, and what has been hailed as the greatest archaeological find of the century has also started a considerable archaeological dispute. For Philip was murdered at his daughter's wedding feast at Aegae in 336BC, and by long tradition *Edessa* has been identified with that ancient capital. It seems hardly likely that the royal tombs should be at neither of the two capitals, and exposed on an open plain. Or was Aegae at Vergina? Or were these the tombs not of the Temerid but of the Antigonid dynasty, whose **ruined palace** still crowns a hill at nearby **Palatitsia**?

Hotels

As well as individual entries for major towns and sights (see introductory text earlier), other places to stay in Macedonia include the following.

Litohoro *(Map 2D5. 20km (12.5 miles s of Katerini)*

Aphroditi *(Eleftherias Sq.* ☎ 21 – 415 ▮▮ ▱ ◨ 24 ☜); **Olympios Zeus** *(across the motorway from Litohoro, on the seafront* ☎ 71 – 215/7 ▮▮ ▱ 100 ◢◣ ▱ ☴ closed mid-Oct to Easter ◁▷ ☀ ☞), bungalows, camping.

Platamonas *(Map 3D6. Halfway between Katerini and Larissa)*

Maxim *(next to the castle* ☎ 41 – 305 ▮▮ ▱ ◨ 73 ◢◣ ☴ ◁▷); **Platamon Beach** *(on the seafront* ☎ 41 – 485/6 ▮▮ ▱ ◨ 170 ◢◣ ▱ ☴ AE CB ◉ ● VISA closed mid-Oct to Easter ◁▷ ≈ ☀ ☞).

The Máni ☆

Map 11 J– K5. 82km (51 miles) SE of Kalamata; 26km (16 miles) sw of Gythio. Getting there: By bus, from Kalamata and Gythio to all villages. Population: 2,000.

The region takes its name from one of its several Frankish and Venetian castles, **Maina**, or Le Grand Maigne, built by

Guillaume de Villehardouin in the 13thC on the tip of the middle prong of the s Peloponnese, at **Cape Tenaro**. It encloses the area roughly between *Kalamata* and *Gythio*, comprising most of the **Taygetos** mountain chain. The lushness of the Outer, landward Mani, at its finest in the archetypal romantic landscape at **Kardamili**, 35km (22 miles) SE of Kalamata on the Messinian Gulf, contrasts dramatically with the stark Inner, peninsular Mani.

Blood feuds continued through the 19thC, leading to the building of tower-houses for which the Mani is famous. The main village is **Areopoli**, 82km (51 miles) SE of Kalamata.

Sights and places of interest
Glyfada Cave ☆
Near Pyrgos Dirou, 12km (7.5 miles) s of Areopoli ☎ *52–222/3*
🖾 ✗ *Standard opening times.*

The Glyfada Cave is really a subterranean river which runs in two parallel streams, connected by electrically-lit lakes and lofty galleries of stalagmites and stalactites. Thought to be possibly the world's largest sea-cave, it has been explored for about 5km (3 miles), and about one-third is accessible to visitors by comfortable motorboats. It was believed in antiquity to be one of the entrances to the Underworld.

About 180m (200yd) along the shore, the **Alepotrypa Cave** (Foxhole) has impressive vaults and corridors with stalactites and stalagmites, in which human and animal bones, tools, vessels, paintings and rock-carvings of the Palaeolithic and Neolithic eras have been found – including even a pottery workshop. But this is not yet open to the public.
The towers
The warring families of the Mani shut themselves up in the characteristic tower-houses of which nearly 800 were scattered around the countryside. Though most are now ruined, some have been restored – notably at **Vathia**, in the s, for future use as guesthouses, and at **Areopoli**, where one is already functioning in that capacity.

Hotels

Areopoli (*Map 11J5*)
Mani (☎ *51–269* 📖 🖾 *16* 🛏 ➾); the tower-house 🏛 described above has six rooms.

Marathon (*Marathónas*)
*Map **16**C3&8H7. 42km (26 miles) NE of Athens.*
In 490BC, 9,000 Athenians and 1,000 Plataeans won a momentous victory over the 30,000 Persians of the Great King Darios. The runner who brought the news of victory collapsed and died on his arrival, but the Marathon race from here to Athens was instituted in commemoration, and still provides the name and generally the distance for such races today. In modern times the ancient race is run over the original course.

Sights and places of interest
The 12m-high (39ft) **tumulus** commemorating the 192 Athenians who died in the great battle rises amid orchards on a crescent-shaped bay. The smaller **mound of the Plataeans** (*5km (3 miles) inland*) is nearer the actual battlefield. Nearby, a rarely open concrete construction protects a **Bronze-Age cemetery**, where the complete skeletons of astoundingly small men and horses can be seen in open graves.

In the adjoining **museum** (🖾 *standard opening times*), the most interesting statue is 'in the Egyptian manner' which, deliberately reminiscent of archaic sculpture, became popular in the later Roman Empire. It was found on Herodes Atticus' estate in this fertile region.

🔟 **Golden Coast** (*3km (1.9 miles) from the village* ☎ *92–102* 📖 🖾
242 🔢 🛏 🖭 ➾ ⇆ ⚲ ♨ ⚲ ●).

Megalópoli (*Megalopolis*) ☆

Map 11I5. 56km (35 miles) N of Kalamata. Getting there: By train, on the Pyrgos–Kalamata line; by bus, from central Peloponnese and Athens. Population: 3,000.

Megalopolis means 'great city', and was and remains the only town in Greece planned formally as a national capital. It was founded by Epaminondas of *Thebes* in the 4thC BC, and the inhabitants of 41 Arkadian villages were forcibly transplanted in order to man it. By 368BC its 2m-thick (7ft) walls of unbaked brick, fortified with both round and square towers, extended for almost 10km (6.25 miles). It was intended by Epaminondas to form a bulwark in the central Peloponnese against *Sparta*, but when the first flush of artificial nationhood had passed, the Arkadians returned to their several ways, and the city declined into the 'Great Wilderness'.

Sights and places of interest

Of its outsize public buildings, only the 20,000-seat **theatre** built into a wooded hill, and the **Thersilion**, the Federal Assembly where the 10,000 citizens of Megalopoli met under ancient Greece's largest covered edifice, measuring 65 by 53m (213 by 174ft), are recognisable among the monuments unearthed at the end of the last century. The foundations of the various temples and stoas round the **Agora** are hardly of more interest than the modern town.

H **Pan** (*Papanastassiou 7* ☎ 22–270 ⬜ ⌂ 17, *a few with showers,* ⬅).

Méga Spíleo, Monastery of   See *Kalavryta*.

Messemvría   See *Alexandroupoli*.

Messíni   See *Kalamata*.

Messolóngi (*Missolonghi*)

Map 7G4. 38km (24 miles) S of Agrinio. Getting there: By bus, from Athens, Patra and W Central Greece. Population: 13,000.

Situated on the edge of a wide, stagnant lagoon and undistinguished in appearance, Messolongi is famous for its heroic role in the Greek War of Independence. In 1823, as a tribute to Lord Byron's fame as a poet but even more to his generous financial support, he was appointed here as commander-in-chief of the Greek forces. His disillusionment at the rapacious struggle between the various Greek factions, which ruined his sound strategy, are shown in his *Lines on completing my Thirty-sixth Year*:

> The land of honourable death
> Is here; up to the field and give
> Away thy breath. . . .

Although his health was bad, he insisted on daily rides even in torrential rains, and caught pneumonia. Despite his protests, he was treated with blood-letting and plasters. He died on Easter Monday, 1824, during a thunderstorm of rare violence.
One year later, a Turko-Egyptian army laid siege to what was almost the last town still held by the insurgents on the mainland. Disease and hunger had reduced the original 4,000 defenders to less than half, when they partially succeeded in a desperate attempt to break out, the famous *Éxodos*, on the night of Palm Sunday, 1826. The memorial service held every year on

this day in Messolongi commemorates not only the exploits of
the warriors, but also the self-sacrifice of the women and
children who, as the enemy were entering, set fire to the powder
magazine, thereby killing more than 3,000, both friend and foe.

Sights and places of interest
The **Gate of the Exodos** is next to the **Park of the Heroes**, where a
statue of Lord Byron in the place of honour is flanked by a marble
Daughter of Greece and by a **tumulus** containing the remains of the
Philhellenes; their leaders have separate tombs. Byron's house was
destroyed by an Italian bomb in World War II, but a room in the **Town
Hall Museum** (⬛ *standard opening times*) contains memorabilia of the
most popular Briton in Greece.

A causeway extends 5km (3 miles) into the lagoon, past the **forts of
Vassiladi and Kleissoura**, which kept out the Turkish fleet, to the **islet
of Tourlis**, where the dramatic sunsets inspire painters and poets.

Ⓗ **Liberty** (*Polytehniou 41* ☎ 28–050 ▮▮ ▭ 60 ⬛ ⇌ ⌂).

The Meteóra   See *Kalambaka*.

Methóni ☆
Map **10***J4. 11km (7 miles) s of Pylos. Getting there: By bus,
from Pylos and Koroni. Population: 1,300.*
The **fortress** ▥ at Methoni, a well-preserved example of
military architecture, was Venice's strongest in the
Peloponnese. At **Koroni**, 23km (14 miles) SE on the Messinian
Gulf, the opposite shore of this western peninsula of the
Peloponnese, there is a rather less impressive **fortress**, and
together they were known as "the eyes of the Serene Republic".
Methoni's fine sandy beach tends to get overcrowded in summer.

Ⓗ **Alex** (☎ 31–219 ▮▮ ▭ 20 ▤▤ ⬛ ◁≪ ⬤), near the beach.

Métsovo ▥
Map **6–7***E3–4. 56km (35 miles) NE of Ioanina. Getting there:
By bus, from Ioanina and Kalambaka. Population: 3,000.*
Local benefactors have restored the original architecture of this
attractive village, 1,160m (3,805ft) above sea-level on the
spectacular road from *Ioanina* to *Kalambaka*. It was
established by the Romans as one of a series of fortresses in the
Pindos range. The inhabitants still speak Koutsovlach, a Latin
dialect, and they wear a distinctive dark-blue homespun
costume on feast days or for tourist occasions. Their prosperity
under the Turks was due to the hospitality once extended to a
16thC Grand Vizier, temporarily out of favour. When he was
restored, he offered his hosts a royal recompense, but was
instead asked for autonomy. This was granted in four decrees,
which are proudly displayed in the **Town Hall**.

There are beginnings of a winter-sports resort.

Sights and places of interest
The 18thC **Tositsa Mansion**, with its wooden beams, has been fittingly
and pleasingly converted into a **Museum of Popular Art** (⬛ *standard
opening times*). The Tositsa Foundation has also restored churches
throughout the district, for instance the Byzantine **Monastery of Agios
Nikolaos** near the source of the Arathos, and the 1511 **Church of Agia
Paraskevi** ✝ whose original roofing, Baroque cloisters and clock-tower
reveal Venetian influence; the modern mosaics come from Ravenna.

Ⓗ **Egnatia** (☎ 41–263 ▮▮ ▭ 36 ⬛ ⌂ ⇌ ⌂).

Míli (*Lérna*) See *Argos*.

Missolonghi See *Messolongi*.

Mistrás (*Mystra*) See *Sparta*.

Monemvassía Ⅲ ☆

Map 11J6. 60km (37 miles) SE of Gythio. Getting there: By hydrofoil, from Zea Harbour, Piraeus; by bus, from Gythio and Sparta. Population: 400.

Monemvassia, meaning 'Only Passage' because of the short causeway to its great rock, and often called the Gibraltar of the eastern Mediterranean, was an important Byzantine fortress. Famine forced its surrender to Guillaume de Villehardouin in 1248, but 14yr later it was ceded back, together with the castles of **Maina** (see *The Mani*) and **Mystra** (see *Sparta*), as ransom paid to Emperor Michael VIII Palaeologos. Thereafter, like most impregnable fortresses, it was in fact taken rather frequently.

Simple hotels and tavernas are on the mainland opposite.

Sights and places of interest

Venetian ramparts enclose the **upper town**, reached after a steep climb. There, amidst a sad jumble of Byzantine, Frankish and Turkish ruins, rises the 14thC **Agia Sofia †** on the cliff-edge, painted a very unattractive brown. The frescoes under the octagonal dome were badly damaged when it was converted into a mosque in 1540. The Turks destroyed not only frescoes but the vines for which Monemvassia, corrupted to Malvoisie or Malmsey, was famous.

The view, however, is still splendid. The walls, and most of the 40 **Byzantine churches**, are crumbling; the exceptions are those restored by the Venetians during their second occupation (1687–1715), particularly the 14thC **Basilica of Christ** *Elkoménos* (Lifted on to the Cross) **†**

Ⓗ **Minoa** (☎ 61–209 ⅡⅢ ▭ 16).

Mount Athos See *Halkidiki/Mt. Athos*.

Mount Ólympos See *Macedonia*.

Mount Pílio (*Pelion*) See *Volos*.

Mount Ymitós See *Attica/The mountains*.

Mycenae (*Mykínes*) ★

Map 8H6 & 11H6. 11km (7 miles) N of Argos. Getting there: By bus, from Argos and Corinth to the village, 1.6km (1 mile) from the ruins; included in all sightseeing tours of the Peloponnese. Population of village: 400.

Homer called Agamemnon's Mycenae, capital of a loosely-knit feudal kingdom, "rich in gold". How right he was was proved by the sensational finds of gold, electrum (gold and silver alloy) and ivory ornaments, death masks, vessels and weapons, since Heinrich Schliemann, a wealthy, self-taught, German amateur, began excavations in 1874. These treasures, and further ones uncovered by British digs in the Bronze-Age town (inhabited from about 3000BC) at the foot of the citadel, where the last, grim acts of the Atreids' family drama were played out, are now in the **National Archaeological Museum** in *Athens*.

Schliemann's discoveries, both here and, in 1871, in Troy, not only vindicated his own personal belief in the authenticity of

Homer, whose geographical indications proved amazingly accurate, but transformed legend into history.

Sights and places of interest

The tombs

Mycenae is at the end of a branch E, 3km (2 miles) long, off the Argos–Corinth main road. Before reaching the reconstructed **ramparts of the acropolis**, it passes seven monumental **beehive tombs**, the largest of which was named the 'Treasury of Atreus' by Schliemann and is called the **'Tomb of Agamemnon'**. It is neither, dating in fact from about 1550BC, three centuries before the Trojan War, and, like the shaft-graves within the ramparts, does not correspond with Homer's description of Mycenaean cremation. It is entered along a 37m-long (40yd) passage cut into the hill, lined with huge, finely fitted ashlar blocks, ending in two enormous monoliths supporting a 122-tonne (120 tons) lintel; there were once green pilasters on either side, now in the British Museum. The passage opens into a circular chamber vaulted in very impressive masonry, and dug out of the hill through a vertical shaft, while the smaller beehive tombs were cut into the rock from the horizontal passage.

The **'Tomb of Klytemnaestra'** is a smaller version of the 'Tomb of Agamemnon'; so is the less well-preserved **'Tomb of Aegisthos'**, her lover.

The acropolis

Entrance to the **acropolis** is by the famous **Lion Gate**, its massive lintel supporting a triangular slab with a bas-relief of two rampant lionesses. These originally had metal heads, turning outwards threateningly. Near the gate are the six **shaft-graves** in which Schliemann found gold masks and scales that covered the dead kings of the dynasty founded by Perseus (see *Argos*). A second circle of graves later yielded similar treasures.

The palace

The palace, which is based in design and decoration on Minoan precedent, extended over two terraces connected by an exterior stair. The supports for four wooden pillars that supported the roof of the main hall, entered through a portico from a colonnaded court, are still visible; the roof had an opening above the sacred hearth. The top part of the palace is obliterated by the **foundations of a temple** built in the 6thC BC and rebuilt in Hellenistic times, but the smaller **women's quarters** on the lower terraces are still discernible. A large **cistern**, hewn out of the rock, is near the postern gate from which Orestes, Agamemnon's son, is said to have escaped after taking his revenge on Aegisthos and his mother.

H **La Petite Planète** *(2km (1 mile) from the ruins in the village, Mykines* ☎ 66–240 ▯□ ➡ 13 ➡ ➡); **Xenia** *(close to the ruins* ☎ 66–223 ▯□ ➡ 4 ➡), handy for refreshments after sightseeing.

Mystra *(Mistrás)* See *Sparta/Mystra.*

Náfpaktos *(Naupactus)* ☆

Map 7G4 & 10G4. 21km (13 miles) NE of Patra. Getting there: By ferry (20min), every 20min from Rio-Antirio, 10km (6 miles) SW; by hydrofoil, from Patra; by bus, from Agrinio, Amfissa, Athens, Messolongi, Patra. Population: 9,000.

Náfpaktos, on the coastal strip at the mouth of the river Mornos, was first settled in about 1500BC. Its most distinguished citizen was the poet Hesiod (8thC BC), who lived here for many years in exile. The town first rose to importance in 455BC, when it was taken by the Athenians, and, remaining loyal throughout the Peloponnesian War, was a thorn in the flesh both of the Spartans and of the Corinthians, because of its strategic position at the entrance to the Corinthian Gulf.

The usefulness of its harbour was apparent also to the Venetians, who occupied the town in 1407, renaming it Lepanto. It subsequently passed to the Turks, who, on Oct 7, 1571, set sail from it with 300 ships under the personal command of Sultan Bayazid II, to engage the 200 ships of the Holy League under Don Juan of Austria. The ensuing battle at last decided possession of the eastern Mediterranean, and was a triumph for Venice and for Pope Pius V, who had summoned the League.

The fairytale **castle** on the thickly wooded hill, the tiny **fortified port**, the **Castle of the Roumeli** and **Castle of the Morea**, guarding the straits between **Rio** and **Antirio**, all belong to the last period of Venetian occupation, from 1687–1700. The beaches are adequate, and there is a splendid view across the straits to **Mt. Panahaïko** on the Peloponnese.

Ⓗ **Akti** (*at Gribovo, near the beach* ☎ 28–464/5 ▮▯ 🖵 60 🛥 ⇌ ◁€ 🐟€); **Lido** (*at Psani, near the beach* ☎ 22–501 ▮▯ 🖵 15 ▦ 🛥 🛋 ⇌ ◁€ 🐟€ ●).

Náfplio (*Nauplia*) 🏛 ★

Map 11|6. 12km (7.5 miles) SE of Argos. Getting there: By hydrofoil (Apr 14–Oct 31), from Zea Harbour, Piraeus; by train, from Athens via Corinth and Argos; by bus, from Athens, and every 30min from Argos; included in all sightseeing tours of the Peloponnese. Population: 10,000. Tourist police ☎ 27–776.

The town's eponymous founder was Nauplios, son of Poseidon and a Danaïd (one of the 50 daughters of Danaos; see *Argos*). The crenellated curtain wall of the Palamidi fortress, on a formidable cliff, takes its name from Palamedes, the son of Nauplios, who was credited with a variety of inventions, including dice, backgammon, the alphabet, arithmetic, navigation and even the lighthouse.

The town

Náfplio has been the port of the fertile Argolis, the eastern peninsula of the Peloponnese, since the Bronze Age. In 1247 it was occupied by Guy de la Roche, who styled himself Duke of Athens, Lord of Argos and Nauplia. The town was then held by the Turks or by the Venetians (1388–1540, 1686–1715). During their short second stay the Venetians made it unusually attractive, with high colour-washed houses, their green shutters opening on iron balconies, the crenellated **fortress** on **Bourdzi islet**, once the residence of the hangman and now a tourist pavilion (🛥) reached by boat (🛥), and the much larger fortifications of Akro-Náfplio.

Towering above all is the **Palamidi fortress** 🏛 reconstructed near the end of their final stay by the Venetians, and military architecture at its most elegant. Within its mighty walls stood until recently the modest house of King Otho's court from 1833–34, during Nauplia's brief period as capital of the new Greek state from 1829–34, when it was transferred to Athens. It is no longer necessary to climb the 857 steps Otho's sweating Bavarian courtiers once had to negotiate, for today a road winds discreetly to the back gate, preserving the illusion of inaccessibility.

The restored ramparts of lower **Akro-Náfplio**, which now enclose the bungalows of a luxury hotel, the **Xenia Palace**, prominently display the Lion of St Mark. The **lion** carved in a rock of the Pronia suburb, however, is not Venetian, and commemorates the Bavarians who died in the plague of 1833–34.

Much else in the town has associations with the early days of the new Greek state. In the larger of the two **mosques** on the main square the National Assembly confirmed Otho's election as King in 1832. The revolt that overthrew Otho 30yr later started next door, at the officers' club in the **Venetian naval arsenal**. In the same building is a **museum** (🖾 *standard opening times*) housing Mycenaean finds, from *Tirynth* and Assini (see right) in particular. Back to back with it stands the church of a local **Agios Anastasios** ✝ the town's patron saint, who was crucified by the Turks in 1655; the nails used are still embedded in a nearby olive tree. At **Agios Georgios** ✝ King Otho and Count John Capodistrias took the oath of allegiance. Capodistrias was murdered at **Agios Spyridon** ✝ by the Mavromichalis clan in 1831.

The **Peloponnesias Folkloric Foundation** ☆ (*Vassileos Alexandrou 1* ☎ *28–379* 🖂 *standard opening times*) has fine exhibitions of Peloponnesian weaving, costumes and jewellery.

Nearby sights

Beyond Pronia, the 12thC **Church of Agia Moni** † is dedicated to Panagia Zöodohos Pigi (Our Lady Source of Life). In its pretty garden is the **Kanathos spring**, in which Hera, to the envy of mortals and immortals, annually renewed her virginity.

To the SE, past the insignificant prehistoric **acropolis**, a **Mycenaean cemetery** and the Hellenistic **Temple of Assini**, is the fine sandy beach of **Tolo**, 11km (7 miles), lined by a string of hotels and fish tavernas. On the Argos road to the N are the impressive ruins of *Tirynth*, 4km (2.5 miles).

Hotels

In Nafplio
Agamemnon (*Akti Miaouli* ☎ *28–021/2* 🖂 40 🚗 🏠 ⚓ ♿ on roof ◁€); **Park** (*Dervenakion 1* ☎ *27–428* 🖂 70 🖂 🚗 🏠 ⚓); **Xenia** (*Akro-Nafplio* ☎ *28–991/3* 🖂 58 🚗 🏠 ⚓ AE CB ◉ ◉ VISA ◁€ ≈ ♿), within walking distance of the beach; **Xenia Palace** 🏨 (*Akro-Nafplio* ☎ *28–981/3* ☎*0298154* 🖂 52 🖂 🚗 🏠 ⚓ AE CB ◉ ◉ VISA 🖂 □ ◁€ ≈ ♿), also 54 bungalows, and a small beach within walking distance.
Tolo (*11km (7 miles) SE*)
Sofia (☎ *59–567/8* 🖂 52 🚗 🏠 ⚓ ♿); **Tolo** (☎ *59–248* 🖂 39 🚗 🏠 ⚓ ♿).

Ⓡ **Savouras** (*Akti Miaouli* 🖂), best among the several fish restaurants in this area.

Naupactus See *Nafpaktos*.

Nauplia See *Nafplio*.

Navarino See *Pylos*.

Nekromantéion See *Epiros*.

Néos Marmarás (*Pórto Carrás*) See *Halkidiki/Sithonia*.

Nikopóli (*Nikopolis*) See *Preveza*.

Olýmpia ★
*Map **10**H4. 119km (74 miles) SW of Patra; 16km (10 miles) SE of Pyrgos. Getting there: By train, from Athens via Corinth and Patra; by bus, from Athens, Patra and Pyrgos; included in all longer tours of the Peloponnese. Population of village: 900.*

Olympia, set amid the pastoral gentleness of Elis (Ilida), makes a striking contrast with the dramatic grandeur of the only other site to which it can be compared for importance, *Delphi*. It was nevertheless named by the Dorians, who took it over in the Dark Ages, after the home of the gods, the Mt. Olympos they had known in the N (see *Macedonia*). It had been previously dedicated to Gaea, or perhaps to Rea (see *Mythology* in *Culture, history and background*) – and even Kronos is remembered in **Mt. Kronion**, the thickly wooded hill that overlooks the site.

According to the 5thC BC poet Pindar, who wrote 16 surviving odes in honour of victors, the Olympic Games originated in the burial rites performed on the grave of Pelops, son of Tantalos, who gave his name to the Peloponnese. The first contest, according to Pindar, was instituted by Zeus, and

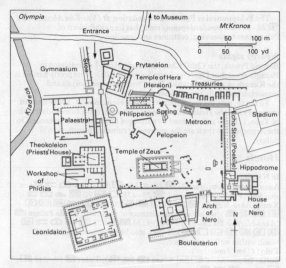

Olympia

to Museum

Mt Kronos

0   50   100 m

0   50   100 yd

Entrance

Gymnasium

Stoa

Prytaneion

Temple of Hera
(Heraion)

Treasuries

Palaestra

Philippeion

Spring

Metroon

Theokoleion
(Priests' House)

Pelopeion

Temple of Zeus

Echo Stoa (Poikile)

Stadium

Workshop
of
Phidias

Hippodrome

Leonidaion

Arch
of
Nero

House
of
Nero

Bouleuterion

Kladeos

N

was competed in by gods and heroes. However, the oldest
temple on the site was dedicated to Hera.

The Games were celebrated every 4yr, for five days during
the Aug full moon, and became the greatest athletic contest of
antiquity from 776BC, when they developed into a Panhellenic
event. The Greek calendar took its starting-point from this
date, with the quadrennial Olympiad as its unit. All
competitors had to be Greek, and, with the exception of Hera's
high priestess, they and the audience had to be male. Women
were excluded from the precinct under penalty of death,
although a Rhodian lady once gained admittance disguised as
her son's trainer, betraying herself in her maternal joy at his
victory. Her life was spared since she was both sister and
mother of victors, but thereafter trainers had to appear naked.

Like all other pagan festivals, the Olympic Games were
prohibited by Theodosius the Great in AD393, and the
sanctuary was closed. Systematic excavation by German
archaeologists began in 1875. In the intervening years the site
had been immersed under 6m (20ft) of mud and pebble, spread
by the converging rivers of the **Alfios** and the **Kladeos** when
they changed course in the Middle Ages, and there had also
been a series of landslips from Mt. Kronion. The precinct was
cleared and also replanted, though with pine instead of the
original plane and olive, by the Germans.

3km (2 miles) E, on the road to Tripoli, is the **Olympic
Games Museum** (*standard opening times*), of interest only to
enthusiasts of the history of the revived Olympiads. The
moving force behind the revival in 1896 was Baron de
Coubertin, whose bust stands at the entrance to the **Altis**. Near
the museum is the **International Olympic Academy**, where the
meetings of the Olympic Committee and of past victors are
held. The construction of a permanent Olympic Village, with
all the resulting damage to the idyllic countryside, has become a
distinct possibility following recent approval by the European
Parliament. The 2,023 hectares (5,000 acres) of the **Grove of
the Sacred Altis** have been a national park since 1976.

The sanctuary (Altis)

📷 Standard opening times.

The entrance and NW buildings

The present entrance is across the **stoa** of a 3rdC BC gymnasium, adjoined on the right by the hardly discernible Roman **Propylaea** and the restored double colonnade of the *palaestra*, or wrestling ground. Just inside the low wall of the rectangular Altis, to the left, is the **Philippeion**, an Ionic rotunda glorifying the victories of Philip II and Alexander the Great. To the N of this are the remains of the 5thC BC **Prytaneion**, which contained the sacred hearth of Hestia, the banqueting hall where the victors were entertained, and the living quarters of the representatives of Elis, the city which long remained the protecting power.

The N side: The Heraion

Behind and to the E of the Philippeion, beside the N wall of the Altis, is the 7thC BC Doric peripteral **Temple of Hera** (Heraion), which originally had wooden columns, replaced over the ages by stone ones of different patterns. Several of these still stand, together with 90cm (3ft) of the tufa wall of the *naos*; above it rose unbaked brick and a wooden roof.

The lightness of the temple's fabric preserved the **head of the statue of Hera** and the famous **statue of Hermes**, both now in the museum. This was seen inside the temple by the traveller Pausanias in the 2ndC AD, and described by him simply as *"Hermes with Dionysos*, a work by Praxiteles, in marble". The artistic quality of the full complement of votive offerings can be gauged from the fact that this comes from two chapters devoted to the Heraion in the *Guide to Greece*.

Temple of Zeus and centre of the Altis

When Pausanias visited the Altis, the accumulated ashes of the sacrifices had risen to a mound more than 6.7m (22ft) high, called the **Pelopeion**. This stood between the Heraion and the Temple of Zeus, which dominates the Altis from a central platform. Its six frontal and 13 lateral columns lie broken amid a profusion of massive drums, overturned by successive earthquakes in the 6thC AD.

In the central space was also a rough circle of stone about 3m (10ft) in diameter, where the Olympic oracle manifested itself through the crackling and twisting of the sacrificial bull's hide as it burnt. The flame was allowed to go out in spring, to be rekindled by a 'spark from heaven' – a tradition that is kept alive not only in the Olympic flame, which is lit at a modern altar and carried by runners to wherever the Games are now held, but also in the Orthodox rite of the Holy Fire, held at Easter.

The N side: Other buildings

Next to the Heraion, to its E, was a gift of the great 2ndC AD benefactor Herodes Atticus, a diversion of a brook which emptied through nine spouts into a marble basin. This was surmounted by a half-dome and flanked by two circular colonnades sheltering statues of the imperial and the Atticus families. Below Mt. Kronion, in a row, stood the **Treasuries** of the leading city states, in which they kept their ceremonial paraphernalia and offerings. In front of these stood the 5thC BC Doric **Metroon**, where rites were once held in honour of Rea, Kronos' spouse.

The stadium

The vaulted passage in the NE corner of the Altis leads to the stadium, which was excavated on Hitler's personal orders. In the embankment, repeatedly raised until it accommodated about 20,000 spectators, weathered and damaged *ex-votos* were found buried, outstanding among them the **helmet of Miltiades**, dedicated after the Athenian victory at *Marathon*, and now in the museum. Still visible in the vast empty space of the stadium are the starting and finishing lines of the foot race, the most important of the 13–15 contests. The chariot race was held in the **Hippodrome** alongside, the first site to be excavated.

Increasing honours were heaped on the victors, who had become professional athletes, supported by their city, but a portrait statue was a rarity, since it could only be erected only by a three-times victor. There were, however, numbers of statues of Zeus, put up at the orders of the umpires (*Hellanodíkae*) as a penalty for infringements of the rules, bearing the offending competitor's name in eternal shame. The majority of statues were of course trophies, of which the finest surviving example, even in its present shattered state, is Paionios' superb *Nike* (Victory), commissioned in 420BC by the Messenians.

The E side

The E side of the Altis is taken up by the **Echo Stoa** or *Poekíle* (Painted

Stoa). The first name alludes to its sevenfold echo, the second to the paintings once on the rear wall. The 98m-long (321ft) colonnade of 44 exterior Doric and 21 interior Ionic columns ended at the s at the triumphal **Arch of Nero**; who ordered an extraordinary Olympic Games during his visit to Greece in AD67. He appeared in the chariot race with a team of ten horses – everyone else had four – got entangled in the reins and fell off, but was declared winner of the races all the same, and also of the singing contest he added to the fixture list. He stayed in a house specially built for him at the SE corner of the sanctuary and helped himself, as at Delphi, to quantities of statuary.

The s side

Most of the s side of the Altis was taken up by the 6thC BC **Bouleuterion**, the meeting place of the Senate; the stoa extended to the original banks of the Alfios. At the SW corner the huge **Leonidaion**, the gift of a Naxian called Leonidas in the 4thC BC, was a guesthouse for VIPs. On the w is the **workshop** where, between 456 and 447BC, Phidias executed the colossal chryselephantine statue of *Zeus*, one of the Seven Wonders of antiquity. It was eventually removed by Theodosius II to Constantinople, after an earlier attempt by Caligula when "the cranes broke and the statue smiled at his impotent efforts". Pausanias, who saw it still in its original position in the Temple of Zeus, confessed that mere noting of its measurements could give no idea of its awe-inspiring scale, and the Roman writer Quintilian reported that to gaze upon it enhanced men's understanding of religion.

The workshop, in which fragments of moulds and tools have been found, was later transformed into a church, adorned with fragments of marble filched at random from the decaying temples, and incorporated into a fortified monastery by Justinian in the 6thC AD. Beside it, the 4thC BC **Theokoleion** was the residence of the three priests of Zeus.

The museum

Across the road from the entrance 🖼 *Standard opening times.*
Most of the sculptures mentioned, together with smaller finds, are in the museum. The E **pediment from Zeus' Temple** ★ depicts *Zeus watching the Preparations for the Chariot Race*. The w **pediment** ★ shows *Apollo stopping the Fight between the Lapiths and Centaurs*, in one of the noblest classical representations of this common subject. The fine terra cottas include *Zeus abducting Ganymede* ★ and a charming *Head of Antinous* is among the several large imperial Roman statues.

Hotels in the village

Antonios (☎ 22–348/9 ▮▮▯ ▭ 65 ⚓ ⇌ ⚘ *on roof*); Ilis (☎ 22–547 ▮▮ ▭ 57 ⚓ ⇌ ⚘ *on roof*); Olympic Village (☎ 22–811/2 ▮▮▯ ▭ 51 ▦ ⚓ ⇌ ▰); SPAP (☎ 22–514 ▮▮▮ ▭ 51 ⚓ ⚏ ⇌ ⚘ *on roof*).

Óssios Loukás † ☆

*Map **8**G6. 35km (22 miles) SW of Livadia. Included in most sightseeing tours to Delphi.*
Halfway between *Livadia* and *Delphi*, at the Triple Way where Oedipos slew his father, a road branches left through the village of **Distomo** – ancient Ambryssos, known for its strong walls – to **Mt. Helicon** (Elikonas). These western slopes of the Mountain of the Muses are still as lonely as they were in AD950, when Luke the Stiriote built a hermitage that was later transformed into a church, Ossios Loukás. He had attracted pilgrims and disciples by his cures and his prophecies, including one that Byzantines would reconquer Crete. When they did, the Empress Theophano supplied architects and masons, although the work was not completed until after 1019.

The church

Now a **museum** (🖼), the church was constructed on the traditional cross-in-square plan, round a central dome, resting on an octagonal drum supported over the square by spherical niches. The drum is pierced by 16 arched windows, between which stand 16 mosaic *Prophets*.

Equally well-preserved are superb **mosaics** of *Angels* and *Saints* which stand over the arches, and of *Nations* and *Languages* in the pendentives, while round the walls are the *Annunciation*, *Nativity*, *Baptism* and *Resurrection*, resplendent in gold, and in the great apse a moving *Virgin and Child*. In the communicating **Church of the Theotokos**, with four finely carved **columns** supporting the dome, the few remaining monks still perform the long services of Orthodoxy.

The setting befits the sanctuary – the partly ruined **cells**, the **charnel-house** with skulls and bones spilling out of boxes, and the broad terrace, shady with plane trees, on which refreshments are served above the patchwork of fields in the valley.

Párga 🏛 ☆

Map 6E2. 49km (31 miles) s of Igoumenitsa. Getting there: By bus, from Igoumenitsa and Preveza. Port: Ferries to Paxi. Population: 2,000.

Magnificent olive groves tumble down from Mt. Pezebolos to Parga, an 18thC village which bears the unmistakable stamp of Venetian occupation. It is framed by two sandy beaches, each with its bungalow complex, but accommodation within the village itself is inadequate, both in quantity and quality, and its tavernas are more remarkable for their setting than their food.

Sights and places of interest

There are three **castles**, the largest on the rock dominating the coast, built in the 13thC by the Normans and restored by the Venetians; the next a small French fort on the romantic **Islet of the Panagia**; the third a fortress on the hill. None of these were of any avail when Parga was ceded by Sir Thomas Maitland, High Commissioner of the Ionian Islands, to Ali Pasha for £150,000 in 1818. The Parghiots disinterred the bones of their ancestors, collected their movables and set sail for Corfu on Good Friday the same year. When Ali's troops entered, "all was solitude and silence . . . . the nation was extinct". In 1831 some hundred families returned and restored the miraculous **ikon** of *The Virgin* and the silver candlesticks to their home, **Agii Apostoli †** on the village square.

[H] *Avra* (☎ 31–205 ▯▯ ▭ 18 ⊂⊐ ⟐ ⟨⟩); **Lichnos Beach** *(3km (2 miles) from village* ☎ 31–257 ▯▯ ▭ 84 ⊂⊐ ⟐ ⟨⟩); **Parga Beach** *(2km (1 mile) from village* ☎ 31–410 ▯▯ ▭ 80 ⊂⊐ ⟐ ⟨⟩ ▣ ◨ ⟨⟩).

Párnitha *(Mount Parnis)* See *Attica/The mountains.*

Pátra *(Patras)*

Map 7G4 & 10G4. 136km (85 miles) NW of Corinth. Getting there: By train, on the Athens–Corinth–Olympia line; by bus, from Athens, all towns in the w and Central Peloponnese, and s Epiros. Port: Terminal for most ferries from Italy, Corfu, Ithaki and Kefalonia; hydrofoil to Nafpaktos and Zakynthos. Car-hire (Avis, Hertz and Hellas) available. Population: 115,000. Tourist police: Symahon Sq. ☎ 220–903 i GNTO, Iröon Politehniou, Glyfada ☎ 420–304.

Patra is the largest town in the Peloponnese, the third largest in Greece, and the main port for the Ionian Islands and Italy, and for the export of currants, raisins and fruit. It was almost totally destroyed during the War of Independence, and rebuilt with wide arcaded streets and squares, the outstanding Neo-Classical building being Ziller's **Municipal Theatre** 🏛

Amidst vineyards 8km (5 miles) inland is the **Achaïa Klaus wine factory**, producing some popular wines which may be sampled there. Along the motorway 4km (2.5 miles) w, at **Agia**, is a large GNTO camping-site, adjoining a GNTO beach.

Event: One of the chief attractions of Patra is its carnival, the best in Greece, with a procession of floats and dancing in fancy dress in the streets on the last Sun of Epiphany week.

Sights and places of interest

The foundations of a Roman **odeon** are below the Frankish-Venetian-Turkish **citadel**. Exhibits in the **Archaeological Museum** (*Olgas Sq.* ⚫ *standard opening times*) range from Mycenaean to Roman. **Agios Andreas** ✝ – dedicated to the patron saint of the town, St Andrew, who was crucified here – is the largest church in Greece.

Hotels

In Patra
Astir (*Agiou Andrea 16* ☎ 276–311 ☎ 312167 ||||| ⬜ 120 ▤ ➡️ 🏠 ⇌ Æ CB Φ ⓒ VISA ⬇ on roof ≋); **Delfini** (*Iröon Polytehniou 102* ☎ 421–001/5 ||◻ ⬜ 71 ➡️ 🏠 ⇌ ≋), well situated on the seafront but on the E outskirts; **Galaxy** (*Agiou Nikolaou 9* ☎ 275–981/3 ||◻ ⬜ 53 ▤ ➡️ 🏠 Æ CB Φ ⓒ VISA); **Mediterranée** (*Agiou Nikolaou 18* ☎ 279–602 ||◻ ⬜ 96 ▤ ➡️ 🏠 ⇌); **Moreas** (*Iröon Polytehniou* ☎ 424–541/5 ||||| ⬜ 105 ➡️ 🏠 ⇌ Æ CB Φ ⓒ VISA ⇌).

Arahovitika (10km (6 miles) NE of Patra)
Alexander Beach (☎ 931–262/3 ||◻ ⬜ 114 ➡️ 🏠 ⇌ Æ CB Φ ⓒ VISA ⬇ on roof ⇌ ≋ 🎾 ●).

Lakopetra (10km (6 miles) sw of Patra)
Ionian Beach (☎ 51–300/1 ||◻ ⬜ 79 ➡️ 🏠 ⇌ Æ CB Φ ⇌ ≋ 🎾 ✏ ●).

Metohi (34km (21 miles) sw of Patra)
Kalogria Beach (☎ 31–380/1 ☎ 215781 ||◻ ⬜ 96 ➡️ 🏠 ⇌ 🎾 ✏ ●), hotel and bungalows.

Paralia Proastiou (3km (2 miles) sw of Patra)
Achaia Beach (☎ 991–801/4 ☎ 312233 ||◻ ⬜ 87 ➡️ 🏠 ⇌ Æ CB Φ ⓒ VISA ⬇ on roof ⇌ ≋ 🎾 ✏ ●).

Rio (8km (5 miles) NE of Patra)
Averof Grand Hotel (☎ 922–212 ☎ 312207 ||||| ⬜ 267 ▤ ➡️ 🏠 ⇌ Æ CB Φ ⓒ VISA ⇌ ≋ 🎾 ✏ ●), hotel and bungalows;
Rion Beach (☎ 991–421/2 ||◻ ⬜ 85 ➡️ 🏠 ⇌ ⇌ 🎾 ●).

R **Evangelatos** (*Agiou Nikolaou 7* ☎ 277–772 ||◻ ⬜ Φ ⓒ). The inexpensive restaurants on the water-front have a fine view.

Shopping

E.E.E. (*Mezonos 90*) is the only department store; **Sevastakis** (*Agiou Nikolaou 49* Φ ⓒ), a branch of the Athenian shoe shop.

Peanía See *Attica/The plains.*

Pelion (*Mount Pílio*) See *Volos.*

Pella (*Pela*) See *Macedonia.*

The Peloponnese (*Pelopónnisos*) ★

Map 10&11. Area: 21,463sq. km (8,287sq. miles). Airports: Kalamata and Sparta. Major railway stations: Argos, Corinth, Kalamata, Megalopoli, Olympia, Patra and Tripoli. Population: About 600,000.

The Peloponnese, or Isle of Pelops, hangs like a four-pronged leaf from the thin stem of the Corinthian Isthmus, hence the medieval name for it, the Morea, or mulberry leaf. It offers 4,000yr of history in a spectacular setting – a large variety of Bronze-Age citadels, palaces and tombs; archaic and classical temples; Roman towns; Byzantine and Latin churches; Frankish and Venetian castles; and the occasional Turkish mosque. Its climate and landscape also show considerable variety, from the lush Ionian coast to the w through the oak,

pine and fir forests of the formidable mountain ranges to the
barrenness of the Aegean shore to the E. The highest peak is Mt.
Ziria, 2,376m (7,795ft) above sea-level, and there are fertile
valleys and plains between the mountains.

For a suggested tour of the Peloponnese – taking in all its
towns and sights having separate entries in the *Mainland A–Z*,
to which you can cross-refer – see *Area planners and tours* in
Planning. This will also provide numerous ideas for shorter
visits and one-day excursions.

Perama Cave   See *Ioanina*.

Petrálona Cave   See *Halkidiki/Kassandra*.

Philippi (*Filípi*) ☆
*Map 4C8. 14km (9 miles) NW of Kavala. Getting there: By bus,
from Kavala and Drama.*
In 358BC Philip II annexed Krenides, a colony of *Thassos* (see
Islands A–Z) which controlled the gold mines of Mt. Pangeo,
and renamed it after himself. In Roman times it was a
prosperous staging-post on the *Via Egnatia*, the imperial
highway connecting the Ionian Sea to Byzantium, until it
became the battlefield in 42BC of the armies of Julius Caesar's
assassins, Brutus and Cassius, and his avengers Octavian and
Mark Antony. After their victory, Mark Antony established
here a colony of veterans, to which Octavian exiled Antonian
partisans after his victory over Antony 11yr later at *Actium*.

Enlarged and embellished, Julia Augusta Philippensium
was, like *Corinth* and *Nikopoli*, a Roman town on Greek soil,
and perhaps for this reason was chosen by St Paul for the first
sermon he delivered in Europe.

Event: Performances of Greek drama, July–Aug.

The ruins
Churches dominate the extensive ruins. Remaining from pagan times are
the three-aisled **Propylaea** leading into the forum, completed with
marble temples and stoas under Marcus Aurelius in the 2ndC AD. In the
3rdC two large baths were added. The first church, which is the earliest
known example of an **octagonal church**, dates from the mid-4thC. Two
imposing **brick pillars** are witness to a 5thC basilica, modelled on St
Sophia in Constantinople, but whose 27.5m (90ft) dome collapsed; for
400yr rubble filled the narthex, which was eventually sealed off to allow
worship in the greatly restricted space that sufficed in the last years
before its final destruction by unknown invaders.

The crumbling **ramparts of the acropolis**, across the road, are partly
Macedonian, partly Byzantine, with three **medieval towers** that catch
the eye. The **theatre**, with **shrines of minor deities** scooped out of the
rock around it, was built by Philip II, and was transformed into a
gladiatorial arena by the Romans, adding supplementary tiers and an
underground passage.

Piraeus (*Piréas*)   See *Athens/Sights*.

Platamónas   See *Macedonia* for hotels.

Pórto Carrás (*Néos Marmarás*)   See
Halkidiki/Sithonia.

Pórto Germenó (*Aegósthena*) ☆
Map 8H6. 71km (44 miles) NW of Athens. Population: 250.
Porto Germeno, ancient Aegosthena, an Athenian outpost
defending the borders of Attica against raids from the
Peloponnese, is best reached by way of the road from Athens to

Thebes via Eleusis. Just before the ramparts of the 4thC BC **fortress of Eleftherae**, which guarded the border with *Thebes*, a branch turns left to **Vilia**, a hill village where lamb is always being roasted on the spit in front of several tavernas. The branch continues through gently sloping pine forests to a string of fish restaurants at Porto Germeno, at the head of the Halcyon Gulf. The pebble beach, overcrowded on Sun, is pleasantly deserted the rest of the week.

Most of the 15 square towers that punctuated the walls of the impressive 4thC BC fortress of Aegosthena are intact.

H **Egosthenion** (☎ 41–226/7 ▯▯ ▭ 80 ➡ ◻ ⇌ ☂ on roof ⛰).

Portohéli

Map 8I6&11I6. 84km (52 miles) SE of Nafplio. Getting there: By hydrofoil, from Zea Harbour, Piraeus; by bus, from Athens and Nafplio. Car-hire facilities available. Population: 1,000.
This fishing village in a sheltered bay on the Argolis peninsula has become the largest beach resort in the Peloponnese. The **ruins of ancient Halieis** lie submerged in the shallow sea; in the nearby **Franhthi Cave**, bones and tools of the Mesolithic period (c.25000BC) were discovered in 1981, also chips of black volcanic glass imported from the island of Milos about 8000BC – the earliest evidence to be found so far of Greek seafaring.

Hotels in Portohéli *(all on or near the beach)*

Alcyon (*in village, 300m (320yd) from beach* ☎ 51–479 ▯▯ ▭ 89 ▦ ➡ ⇌ ☂ on roof ⛰ ●); **Apollo Beach** (☎ 51–431 ▯ 214230 ▯▯ ▭ 151 ▦ ◻ ⇌ ↝ ⛰ ℘ ●), bungalows; **Galaxy** (☎ 51–271/6 ▯▯ ▭ 171 ▦ ➡ ◻ ⇌ ☂ on roof ↝ ⛰ ℘); **Giouli** (☎ 51–217/8 ▯▯ ▭ 163 ▦ ➡ ◻ ⇌ ⛰); **Hinitsa Beach** (☎ 51–401/4 ▯ 215961 ▯▯ ▭ 206 ▦ ➡ ◻ ⇌ ▣ VISA ☂ ⇌ ↝ ℘ ●); **Kosmos** (☎ 51–327 ▯▯ ▭ 151 ▦ ➡ ◻ ⇌ ▣ VISA ☂ ⇌ ↝ ⛰ ℘ ●), basket and volley ball grounds, children's playground; **PLM Portoheli** (☎ 51–490/4 ▯ 298111 ▯▯ ▭ 151 ▦ ➡ ◻ ⇌ AE CB ◻ ● VISA ☂ on roof ↝ ⛰ ℘ ●); **Thermissia** (☎ 51–265 ▯▯ ▭ 88 ➡ ◻ ⇌ ⛰); **Ververoda** (☎ 51–343/5 ▯▯ ▭ 244 ➡ ◻ ⇌ ↝ ⛰ ℘ ●), hotel and bungalows.

R **Papadias** (*near the church* ▯▯▯), best fish taverna in the port.

Préveza

Map 6F3. 51km (32 miles) SW of Arta. Getting there: By frequent ferry (6.30–23.00) from Aktio; by bus, from Arta, Athens, Igoumenitsa and Ioanina. Port: Ferries to Lefkada. Population: 13,000.
When the Venetians occupied the strategic headland in 1204, they found the vast circumference of the ramparts of **Nikopolis** to be indefensible, and built more modest fortifications on the tip of the cape, on the site of the ancient town of Berenice, so named by Pyrrhos after his Egyptian mother-in-law. Preveza changed hands between the Venetians and the Turks more often than can have been comfortable for the inhabitants, until it fell to Ali Pasha following his sensational victory against the French in 1798, after which the population dwindled from 16,000 to 3,000. Ali built here another of his vast, gaudily-painted wooden palaces, which his son burnt during the Turkish siege of 1821. The town remained Turkish, with the rest of Epiros, until the Balkan Wars of 1912–13.

There are several good beaches on the Ionian coast.

Event: Epirotika Festival, July – performances of Greek
drama at Nikopoli.

Sights and places of interest

Nikopóli (*Nikopolis*) ☆
6km (3.25 miles) N of Preveza.
The extensive ruins of ancient Nikopolis, 'City of Victory', sprawl on
both sides of the road N from Preveza to Arta. The town was founded by
Octavian in 30BC on the site where he had camped before the decisive
battle against Mark Antony at *Actium*. The inhabitants of S Epiros were
forcibly resettled round its splendid temples and palaces, and tax
exemption swelled its population to 300,000. Nikopolis was the largest
Roman town in Greece, and when the Stoic philosopher Epiktetos
opened a school there it became an intellectual centre. St Paul preached
here for an entire winter, and in the 6thC the Emperor Justinian was still
adding churches and strengthening walls. The town was destroyed not so
much by raiding Goths and Bulgarians as by a devastating earthquake,
which submerged part of the town beneath the waters of the Ambrakian
Gulf, where columns and walls are still visible.

Sections of the ramparts, with huge **triple gates**, still surround the vast
expanse, dotted with ruins of the **Temples of Poseidon** and **Ares**, the
gymnasium, **stadium**, **aqueduct** (broken arches still carrying four water
pipes), a **large theatre** built into the hillside, and a **smaller theatre**, home
of the Epirotika Festival in July. Four **basilicas** reflect the town's
prosperity in the 5th and 6thC; the **floor mosaics** of the largest, **Agios
Doumetios** † were dedicated to a local bishop, and are well preserved.

Ⓗ **Dioni** (*Papageorgiou Sq.* ☎ 27 – 381/4 ⬛⬜ ▭ 30 🚗); **Preveza
Beach** (*15km (11 miles) N of Preveza* ☎ 51 – 483/4 🖥322103 ⬛⬜ ▭ 264
▤ 🚗 🏠 ⇌ 🅰🅴 🅲🅱 Ⓕ 🆑 🆅🆂🅰 ⇌ 🐾 ✍ ●), hotel and bungalows.

Pýlos ☆

*Map 10J4. 51km (32 miles) SW of Kalamata. Getting there:
By bus, from the W and S Peloponnese, and from Athens.
Population: 3,000.*
The attractive port on the S promontory of a large landlocked
bay on the SW Peloponnese has reverted to the name known to
Homer, after playing a decisive part in the War of
Independence under its medieval name of **Navarino**. In 1825,
Ibrahim Pasha had made the spacious **Venetian-Turkish
citadel** 🏛 his headquarters, and anchored his fleet in the secure
bay protected by the island of **Sfaktiria**. In Oct 1827, an
Anglo-Franco-Russian fleet blockaded the narrow entrance to
the bay. The Egyptians started firing and in the ensuing battle
were totally destroyed, and the freedom of Greece was won.

Sights and places of interest

The capital of Homer's "wise old Nestor", 17km (10.5 miles) N of Pylos,
is reached by a beautiful drive along the bay. The extensive **Mycenaean
palace** – known as **'Nestor's Palace'** – is architecturally the best
surviving example of its kind. It is centred on the **throne room**, which
had an open hearth. In the **bath-tub of painted clay**, one can imagine
Nestor's daughters scrubbing Telemachos, Odysseus' son, when he
came to ask for news of his overdue father, as Homer describes. But the
bones in the **sarcophagus** of a well-preserved **beehive tomb** nearby are
those of an earlier king than Nestor.

The finds in the **museum** (🖼 *standard opening times*) at **Hora**, 13km
(8 miles) N of Pylos, complement the 14thC BC **rock tombs**. On Sfaktiria
are **monuments to the victorious Allies** of Navarino.

Ⓗ **Galaxy** (*in town centre* ☎ 22 – 780 ⬛⬜ ▭ 34 🚗 🏠 ⇌ ♉ *on roof*
◀); **Kastro** (*on seafront* ☎ 22 – 264 ⬛⬜ ▭ 10 🚗 🏠 ⇌), bathing
from rocks across the road.

Ⓡ Fish restaurants are on the small harbour.

Rafína   See *Attica/Euboean Gulf*.

Ramnoús ☆

Map 16B3. 55km (34 miles) NE of Athens. Getting there: Leave the Agia Marina (see Attica/Euboean Gulf) bus, then walk 2km (1.25 miles), or take a taxi from Marathon.

When the Persians, on the eve of the battle of *Marathon*, attacked the Athenian fortress at the head of a desolate valley facing Evia (Euboea) across the channel, they destroyed the nearby archaic temple of Themis (Justice) at Ramnous. In the ensuing battle, Themis punished this sacrilege with the help of Nemesis (Vengeance), in whose honour a larger, Doric peripteral temple was built in about 430BC.

The ruins

The **marble cult-statue** by Agorakritos, favourite pupil of Phidias, is the only one to survive anywhere from the 5thC BC, although it is in an unusually large number of pieces; the head was appropriated by the Society of Dilettanti in the early 19thC and is now in the British Museum, London. The **temple** was preserved by its conversion into a church, but the pagan statues and, later, the marble columns were savagely treated, the latter being thought to contain treasures.

A path lined with tombs descends to the 4thC BC **fortified port**, on an impressive position on the straits. The foundations of a **Temple of Dionysos** and a **theatre** are not so impressive.

Salonica   See *Thessaloniki*.

Séres

Map 3B7. 95km (59 miles) NE of Thessaloniki. Getting there: By train, on the Thessaloniki–Sophia (Bulgaria) line; by bus, from Thessaloniki and E Macedonian towns. Car-hire facilities available. Population: 42,000.

Seres was a pre-Hellenic foundation on a tributary of the Strymonas, on the fringe of the Greek world. In 480BC, Xerxes rested his host of 180,000 here on his way across from Persia into Greece, while in the 10thC AD Emperor Basil II earned here his epithet 'the Bulgar Slayer', when he defeated Tsar Samuel and captured 10,000 Bulgars in the Strymonas gorge. He blinded 99 out of every 100, leaving the hundredth with one eye to lead his comrades home. Seres was occupied with the rest of the Golden Plain (see *Drama*) by the Turks (1368–1912).

Seres is also the birthplace of President Karamanlis, and has developed into a prosperous modern town.

Events: At the Feast of Agia Eleni and Agios Konstantinos, May 21–23, the *Anastenária* are celebrated in the nearby village of **Agia Eléni**, 5km (3 miles) away. They seem to have originated in Dionysiac ritual, and include the sacrifice of a bull after the service in church. Barefoot villagers, clasping the saints' ikons, dance on live charcoal embers.

Sights and places of interest

Near the modern **Mitropolis** ✝ the aisled **Basilica of Agios Theodoros** has been restored as a **museum** (🔲 *standard opening times*) of local finds, mostly Roman; it also has a large and badly damaged mosaic of the *Last Supper*, in which Christ appears twice, dispensing wine on the right, bread on the left. In the former mosque on the central square handwoven rugs are sold, while the romantic marble mosque among weeping willows on the riverbank is left to decay as an unwelcome reminder of Turkish rule. From the tourist pavilion (🍴) in the ruins of the 13thC **castle** on the ancient acropolis, the view extends to distant Bulgarian mountains.

⊞ **Galaxy** (*Tsaldari 1* ☎ 23–289 🔲 🖵 49 ➝); **Xenia** (*Agias Sofias 1* ☎ 22–931/3 🔲🔲 🖵 55 ➝ ⇌ 💷).

Siátista ☆

Map 2D4. 65km (41 miles) se of Kastoria. Getting there: By bus, from Thessaloniki and w Macedonian towns. Population: 4,000.

Among well-preserved 18thC *arhontiká* (mansions) 🏛 two are open to the public (🕮 *standard opening times*), and have attractive rustic murals. The wall-paintings both inside and outside **Agia Paraskevi †** (1611) belong to a more austere school. **Agios Dimitrios †** is an unusually tasteful modern church.

⊞ **Arhontikon** (☎ 21–298 ⫿⫾ 🛏 26 ⟵ ⇌ ❺).

Sóunio ☆

Map 16F3&8I7. 70km (44 miles) se of Athens. Getting there: By bus, from Athens; included in all Attica sightseeing tours.

Reaching out towards an arc of islands and exposed to strong winds, the southernmost cape of Attica was an obvious choice for a sanctuary to Poseidon, which was built over the remains of a Neolithic settlement. The archaic temple, the statuary of which is now in the National Archaeological Museum in Athens, was destroyed by the Persians in 480BC.

The Temple of Poseidon

🖼 ⓡ 🖻 ⟵ *Standard opening times.*

The destroyed archaic temple was replaced by a peripteral Doric one, with six by 13 columns of which 12 still stand. The gleaming white marble tempted Byron to engrave his name, a bad example followed by many other visitors. The temple presents a magnificent silhouette against the deep-blue sky, and the sunsets are particularly spectacular.

On a lower hill, 500m (550yd) NE, stood the **Temple of Athena Sóunias**, a simple rectangle with Ionic colonnades on two of its sides, built in the early stages of the Peloponnesian War, towards the end of which fortifications were added.

⊞ **Cape Sounion Beach** (☎ 39–391/4 ⓦ 215909 ⫿⫿⫿ 🛏 152 ⟵ 🏠 ⇌ 𝔸𝔼 ℂ𝔹 ⓕ ⓞ 𝕍𝕀𝕊𝔸 ⇌ ⁀⁀), bungalows; **Egeon** (☎ 39–200 ⫿⫿⫿ 🛏 44 ⟵ 🏠 ⇌ ⁀⁀), close to the temple; **Saron** (☎ 39–144 ⫿⫾ 🛏 28 ⟵ 🏠 ⇌ 𝔸𝔼 ℂ𝔹 ⓕ ⓞ 𝕍𝕀𝕊𝔸 ⇌ ⁀⁀), hotel and bungalows.

Sparta (*Spárti*)

Map 11J5. 119km (74 miles) sw of Argos. Getting there: By bus, from Athens and all towns in the Peloponnese; included, with Mystra, in all longer Peloponnesian tours; by air, from Athens. Population: 12,000. Tourist police: Hilonos 8 ☎ 28–701.

Sparta is far more celebrated than nearby **Mystra**, yet the latter is the great sight, and Sparta, as a result of its unique way of life in antiquity, has been left with no remarkable traces of its past.

Event: Palaeologia Festival, Mystra, final Sun in May.

The town

In his 5thC BC *History*, Thoukydides wrote: "The city is not continuous and compact, has no costly monuments, sacred or civil, but is divided into villages after the old fashion . . . . Posterity would find it difficult to believe that its power corresponded to its fame . . . . her ramparts are her men." Indeed the first entrenchment was raised on the acropolis as late as 295BC against Dimitrios Poliorkitis; it was reinforced against Pyrrhos, transformed into a wall, and strengthened by the tyrant Nabis, whereupon, in 192BC, Sparta was at last taken.

141

No traces remain of the Mycenaean city ruled by Menelaos, and comparatively little of the powerful military state that supplanted it, dominated Greece for centuries, and even ruled it for a brief period in the 4thC BC. Its Dorian warrior caste was characterized by its contempt for feminine charms, and the scant remains that exist of the period are of temples dedicated to two goddesses remarkable for their lack of femininity. Both temples are remembered more for acts of violence than for any architectural distinction.

Sights and places of interest
Ruins of ancient Sparta
On the Tripoli road, on the N outskirts of the modern town.

There are foundations of Athena's **Brazen House**, where in the 5thC BC the regent Pausanias was immured until through hunger he was too weak to resist being carried out, and then stoned. A second king, Agis, suffered a similar fate in the 3rdC BC.

The second famous building was the **Temple of Artemis Orthia**, which contained a wooden idol of the goddess, brought from Tauros by Iphigenia and Orestes (see *Vraona*); in front of it the semi-legendary law-giver Lykurgos, architect of the Spartan constitution, replaced human sacrifice by ritual scourging. The site of the temple is preserved: the Romans built an amphitheatre with the temple as stage and the altar in the middle of the arena.

Other remains are mostly Roman, or belong to the Byzantine city of Lakedemonia, centred on the acropolis. They include foundations of a small temple *in antis*, wrongly called the **Tomb of Leonidas**. The hero of *Thermopylae* is commemorated by an unsightly neo-archaic statue, not quite as bad as the statue of *Lykurgos*, in front of the modern cathedral.
The museum
To the E of the Plataea, in the town 🖼 *Standard opening times.*

The museum contains a less repellent, but damaged, 5thC BC sculpture of *Leonidas*, as well as a miscellany of *ex-votos*, *stelae*, sculpture and ceramics from archaic to Byzantine times. There are also elegant **mosaics** from the 2ndC AD, which prove that, under the Romans, Spartan life became less austere.
Nearby ruins

The **Menelaion**, a temple dedicated to Menelaos and, surprisingly, Helen, is still being excavated 3.5km (2 miles) to the E. Along the road to Gythio, 8km (5 miles) S, stood a shrine to Apollo, and semi-circular foundations mark the **tomb of Hyakinthos**, loved both by Apollo and by Zephiros, the west wind. In a fit of jealousy Zephiros blew a discus thrown by Apollo violently aside, so that Hyakinthos was mortally wounded; the clusters of hyacinths that grew from the drops of his blood constitute the attraction of **Amiklas**, although it also has some rather dreary ruins.

Mystra (*Mystrás*) ☆
*Map **11**J5. 5km (3 miles) w of Sparta. Getting there: By bus, every 30min from Sparta. Population: 1,000.*

Before the Slav invasion of the 9thC the inhabitants of Sparta withdrew to the fastness of Mt. Taygetos and into the *Mani*. The acropolis was repopulated by the Byzantines and renamed Lakedemonia, and in 1248 fell to Guillaume de Villehardouin. The following year he abandoned it and founded Mystra on a steep spur of Mt. Taygetos. Divided by a sheer chasm from the mountain range, Mystra (contracted from *Myzéthra*, goat cheese) was a much better site for a castle than the town in the plain of which 'the ramparts were her men'.

In the brief 10yr that Mystra housed the brilliant court of the Frankish Prince of the Morea, it served as a school for chivalry, attended by young nobles from the whole of western Christendom. Even after the capture of Guillaume by the returning Byzantines, Mystra epitomized the romantic climax of the Middle Ages, and was chosen by Goethe as the setting for his great play of the union of Faust with Helen. The character of their son Euphorion, a personification of the two fundamental traits of European civilization, the Romantic and the Classic, was based on that of Byron.

After being taken prisoner, with most of his barons, by Michael VIII Palaeologos in 1259, Guillaume decided, in the words of *The Chronicle of the Morea*, "to give to the Emperor in exchange for their liberty the castles of *Monemvassia* and Le Grand Maigne (*Mani*), and, last of all, the most beautiful, that of Myzethra itself". When fighting between the Franks and Byzantines continued, the Lakedemonians abandoned Sparta altogether and settled under the walls of the castle, where there was a Byzantine governor until 1348. Then the second son of Ioanis VI Kantakouzinos took possession, assuming the title of Despot, and Mystra remained an appanage of the imperial family until the arrival of the Turks. Constantine XI Palaeologos, who subsequently became the last Emperor, ruled as Despot from 1443–49, and, under his brother Dimitrios, the Despotate survived the fall of Constantinople (1453) by 7yr.

The Turks ruled until 1687, when Francesco Morosini installed Venetian governors. Mystra then had 40,000 inhabitants. Prosperity continued until, after the Turks had regained possession, the abortive revolt of 1770, when the Sultan's Albanian irregulars burnt and pillaged the city. It was again burnt and pillaged by Ibrahim Pasha's Egyptian army in 1825. History came full circle when most inhabitants left for Sparta, re-established by King Otho in 1834.

The city

Although it is now an empty shell, the stately facade and spacious vaulted hall of the **Despot's Palace III** still dominate the town – showing a rather uneasy compromise between the need for defence and the desire for beauty. But Mystra's finest buildings are the churches, expertly restored. The *mitropolis* (cathedral) is **Agios Dimitrios III** built about 1310 in the form of a basilica, but in the 15thC given a cruciform second storey that decapitated the earlier frescoes in the nave. The ikonostasis and the door-cases are of marble from Lakedemonia.

Hence one walks past the little **Evangelistria** and the large **Agii Theodori**, both 13thC, to the **Afendiko III** the church of the **Vrontohion Monastery**. This is architecturally the most unusual, since the early-14thC three-naved basilica rises into a cruciform centralized church topped by five cupolas, but the design is nonetheless harmonious, and the contrast between the luminous central dome and the twilight of the side aisles enhances the delicate colours of the frescoes. Amongst these are two portraits of *Theodoros II* as Despot and monk.

The colours of the **wall-paintings** of the **Pantanassa III** are even more beautiful. Strawberry-pink buildings blend into honey-coloured landscapes under a navy-blue sky – audacious hues for Byzantine religious painting. The Pantanassa is a 15thC convent, notable for its Gothic belfry and the ogival decorations of its apse. The nuns now have guardianship of all the churches of the town. The Pantanassa also has a superb view over the lower town and the orchards to Mt. Parnonas. There are again fine frescoes, notably the *Transfiguration* and a representation of the liturgy being celebrated by Christ in the vestment of a patriarch, in the 15thC **Church of the Perivleptos**, near the Marmara entrance; the church is partly hollowed out of the rock.

The Palaeologia Festival, on the final Sun in May, is combined with a requiem Mass for Constantine XI, the last Byzantine emperor.

Hotels

Sparta
Lida (*Atridon 5* ☎ *23–601/2* ▯▯▯ ⌷ *40* ⊸ ⇌ AE CB ⊕ ⬡ VISA ⚓ *on roof*); **Maniatis** (*Palaeologou 60* ☎ *22–665/9* ▯▯ ⌷ *80* ⊞ ⊸ ⇌).

Mystra

Vyzantion (☎ 93–309 ⅢⅢ ▭▬ 22 ━ ⇌ ▱).

R̄ At the entrance to the ruins of Mystra, **Marmara** (Ⅲ▭) – the food does not match the beautiful view.

Thebes (*Thíva*)
*Map 8G6. By motorway, 87km (54 miles) NW of Athens.
Getting there: By train, on the Athens–Thessaloniki line; by
bus, from Athens and all Central Greece. Population: 16,000.*
When Europa was abducted to *Crete* (see *Islands A–Z*) by Zeus
in the deceptive form of a white bull, her three brothers
dutifully searched far and wide for her. Two of them gave up
the hopeless quest, but the third, Kadmos, consulted the
Delphic oracle and was advised to follow a cow. The bovine
factor, a dominant and generally malevolent one in the family's
fortune (see *Crete*), turned out on this occasion for the better,
for the beast he pursued lay down on the slight eminence in the
centre of the Boeotian plain, where Kadmos built the Theban
acropolis, the Kadmea, and so founded the town. The ancient
Greek for heifer, *bous*, is the root of the name **Boeotia**, the
region of Central Greece between Attica and Mt. Parnassos,
over which Thebes established its leadership.

By the 7thC BC, Thebes had become the leader of a loose
Boeotian federation. Siding with the Persians in 480BC, Thebes
continued hostilities with Athens throughout the rest of the
century, but the triumph of Sparta in the Peloponnesian War
caused the two cities, traditionally enemies, to unite against the
victor.

The heyday of Thebes came in the early years of the 4thC BC,
when two soldier-statesmen of genius, Epaminondas and
Pelopidas, introduced the revolutionary infantry formation of
the phalanx, which shattered the invincibility of the hoplites of
Sparta. Thebes briefly ruled Greece from 371, the battle of
Leuktra, to 362BC, and remained one of the leading powers.
However, Philip II of Macedonia, who had been a hostage in
Thebes in the time of Epaminondas, perfected the phalanx and
at the battle of Chaeronea, 338BC, defeated the combined forces
of Sparta, Thebes and Athens. At Philip's death, the brilliant
oratory of Demosthenes of Athens talked the Thebans into
rebellion, and Thebes was razed in 336BC by Alexander the
Great, who spared only the temples and the house of the 5thC BC
poet Pindar. The city never recovered.

Event: The *Vláhikos Gámos*, a parody of a highland peasant
wedding, is held on Shrove Monday, and attracts enormous
crowds.

The ruins
Though there is a **frescoed Mycenaean tomb**, other ancient remains are
insignificant. In the N corner of the **Kadmea**, traces of whose **gates** can
be seen, stands the 13thC **tower** of the castle of the Frankish dukes of
Thebes and Athens. Among the archaic, classical and Roman objects in
the nearby **museum** (🕮 *standard opening times*) are some unique black
stelae, with 5thC BC painted bas-reliefs of Boeotian soldiers.

The Frankish castle was destroyed in 1311 by Catalan mercenaries,
who preferred to build another in *Livadia*, and this preference was
followed by the Turkish pashas. Thebes recovered from the status of a
wretched village in the early 19thC, and is now a prosperous if
uninteresting town.

Thermopýles (*Thermopylae*)   See *Kammena Voúrla*.

Thessaloníki (*Salonica*) ☆

Map 3 C6. 153km (96 miles) NE of Larissa. Getting there: By air, international flights, and from Athens; by train, from W and E Europe, N Greece and Athens; by bus, from Athens and all towns in N Greece. Port: Ferries to Lesvos and Limnos. Taxi (blue/white cabs), car-hire (all bigger agencies), bicycle/moped-hire and ample garage facilities available. UK and US consulates: Vassileos Konstantinou 15 and 59. Population: 650,000. Tourist Police: Egnatia 10 ☎522–587 i GNTO, Mitropoleos 34 ☎222–935, and at airport ☎425–011.

Thessaloníki, not by Greek standards a very old town, was founded in 315BC by Kassander, son of Antipater, the regent of Macedonia during Alexander the Great's conquest of Persia. It was named after Alexander's step-sister Thessaloniki, whom Kassander married. Situated below the Hortiatis hills at the head of the Thermaic Gulf (named after nearby ancient Thermae), it was the only port on the E–W artery of the Roman *Via Egnatia*, and the Romans made it the capital of Macedonia. It was well situated for trade up the Axios river into the Balkans.

Briefly a comfortable place of exile for Cicero in 58BC, Thessaloniki was naturally included in the peregrinations of St Paul and became an early centre of Christianity. Its moment of glory came in AD305, when the Emperor Galerius made it the eastern capital, after an important victory over the Goths nearby, commemorated by the **Triumphal Arch** just beside present-day Egnatia. This follows the route of the ancient *Via Egnatia*, still the city's main thoroughfare. Unfortunately the bas-reliefs of the arch are worn beyond recognition and the structure has been poorly restored in ungainly brick. There are a few Roman remains, such as the *exédra* (tribune) off Egnatia.

Galerius also built a splendid palace of which all that remains is the **mausoleum**, which never received his body. Though the pagan Galerius martyred the town's patron saint, Dimitrios, a Roman officer from a noble Greek family, he was outdone by the Christian Theodosius the Great, who massacred 7,000 citizens in the hippodrome (race-course) after the lynching of an officer who had arrested a popular charioteer for making improper advances to one of his guardsmen.

In the Byzantine period Thessaloniki flourished as a great commercial and spiritual centre, from which the brothers Cyril and Methodios set out in the 9thC to convert the Slavs. Of some 365 churches raised in its Byzantine heyday, 20 remain though only nine retain their original form.

With the erosion of the Empire, Thessaloniki was often plundered, but remained its second city in Europe after Constantinople. It was offered as such in 1204 to Bonifacio de Montferrat as a consolation prize, when the capital and imperial crown were given to Baldwin I after the fall of Constantinople to the Fourth Crusade. The Latin Kingdom of Salonika fell after 20yr to the Angeli Despots of *Epiros*, and was then conquered by the Palaeologi, who recovered Constantinople in 1261.

During the following century the town suffered severely from religious and social disorders, often violent. In 1430 it fell to Sultan Murad II after a siege, followed by sack and massacre. Crucial to the recovery of the town was the resettlement in it of 20,000 Jews driven from Spain in 1492. The autonomous Jewish community, who continued to speak their medieval Spanish, played a dominant part in the intellectual and economic revival, and could remain relatively unaffected by the

145

bitter struggle over Turkish possessions in the Balkans which
was eventually settled in the Balkan Wars of 1912–13. The
community was exterminated by the Nazis in World War II.

In 1909 Abdul Hamid II, the last absolute Ottoman ruler,
was confined by the Young Turks in the **Villa Alatini**, home of
the leading Jewish family, which now houses a charitable
institution. The revolution had started the previous year among
the officers of the Turkish garrison of the town. **Kemal
Ataturk's birthplace** in Apostolou Pavlou still stands, isolated
among tall blocks of flats, on a spur of the Hortiatis climbing to
the Eptapyrgio.

On Agios Dimitrios Day, Oct 26, 1912, Crown Prince
Constantine led the Greek army into the town, only hours ahead
of the Bulgarians. To confirm Greek possession, King George I
took up residence, and was murdered in 1913 while on his usual
unaccompanied morning stroll. The assassin turned out to be
neither a Bulgar nor a Turk, but a Greek lunatic, and the
murder seemingly had nothing to do with the Balkan Wars.

Among Greece's major towns Thessaloníki turns most
decidedly to the sea. The rather small port installations are
mostly situated to the SW of the curving seafront, but are
gradually extending S along the industrial zone; here, when the
foundations of the factories that pollute air and sea were being
excavated, 5thC BC gold and silver objects from ancient Sindos
came to light. Vassileos Konstantinou, the seafront, is lined with
consulates, restaurants, *zaharoplastía* and cafes. The nearest
good beach is at **Agia Triada**, 11km (7 miles) SW across the gulf.

Events: *Anastenárides*, May 21–23, at Langadas, 20km (12.5
miles) N: see *Seres* for further information.

Festival of Greek Light Song, early Sept.
International Trade Fair, early Sept.
Festivals of Greek and Foreign Films, Sept.
Dimitria Festival of Music and Drama on Byzantine Themes,
Oct.
Dimitrios Day, Oct 26: feast of patron saint.

Sights and places of interest
Agía Sofía (Holy Wisdom) † ★
Agias Sofias
The church heralds the transition from the domed basilica to the Greek
Cross plan that became predominant from the 8thC. Its splendid
mosaics, the *Ascension* with Christ seated on a rainbow surrounded by
angels and apostles in the dome and the *Madonna and Child* in the Apse,
date from the 10thC.
Agios Dimitrios ▥ † ★
On upper Dikastirion Sq.
The Church of Agios Dimitrios, built on the site of his martyrdom, was
burnt down in 1917, in a fire that destroyed much of the town, but was
rebuilt on its old foundations. An earlier church was burnt down in 538.

The church is even today still the second largest in Greece. It is of the
usual cruciform ground-plan, with a transept projecting from the five
naves, separated by four rows of 60 green, white and red marble
columns. Some of these are antique, but the multi-coloured marble
facing of the walls is entirely new. Wherever possible, however, the
modern reconstruction has re-used the original materials.

Just enough now remains of the **mosaics** that came to light in 1907
from beneath the whitewash beloved of the Turks (who converted the
church into a mosque) to show how great a loss they are. The saint was
shown with Leontius, protecting children, and with Agios Sergios and
Our Lady. Five 7thC **frescoes** survive, depicting *The Martyrdom of
Dimitrios*. His relics were returned from San Lorenzo in Italy on his
name-day in 1978, and rest once more in the **crypt**; this was originally
part of the Roman bath where Dimitrios had been imprisoned.

More of the bath can be seen beyond the basilica; outside its w entrance a *phiále*, a baptismal font, covered by a canopy, stands in the small garden that has replaced the original *atrium*, or entrance cloister. The foundations of the **Roman Agora** and **theatre** are exposed forlornly in Dikastirion Sq.

Archaeological Museum ★
Opposite the International Fair entrance ☎ *830–583* 📷 *Standard opening times.*

The museum's most important contents are the sensational discoveries from **Vergina** (see *Macedonia*) and the treasure found in the Hellenistic tombs at Derveni in 1961, including a unique 4thC BC **bronze vase** nearly 1m (1yd) high, with rich embossment that can justly be called Baroque. But the range of exhibits extends from the Geometric and archaic to all stages of the classical.

Notable among the latter are the rich finds from **Olynthos** (see *Halkidiki/Sithonia*), destroyed by Philip II in 348BC. A large collection of Roman sculpture, from the 1st to the 5thC AD, includes a rare likeness of *Emperor Alexander Severus* as a boy of 14. There are also sarcophagi, glass vases and mosaic floors unearthed in Thessaloníki.

Dódeka Apostóli *(Twelve Apostles)* † ☆
Off Agiou Dimitriou.

A shining example of what the Byzantine Empire was still able to achieve during the ephemeral revival under the Palaeologi in the 14thC, the church has fine frescoes, which had replaced costly mosaics.

Folkloric and Ethnological Museum of Macedonia
Vassilissis Olgas 98 ☎ *830–591.*

The museum, housed in the early-20thC former Governor's Palace, displays traditional articles of daily life in northern Greece, local costumes, ornaments, and ecclesiastical vessels and vestments.

Panagía Ahirópiitos *(Our Lady Not Made by the Hand of Man)* † ☆
Agias Sofias

The church, a triple-naved basilica, was built after the Third Ecumenical Council in 431, and is one of the best preserved representatives of 5thC eastern ecclesiastical architecture. Although the miraculous ikon after which it is named has disappeared, some of the original **mosaics** are preserved below the tribune and in the arches of the bay windows.

Panagía Halkéon *(Our Lady of the Coppersmiths)* ▥ † ☆
On lower Dikastirion Sq.

According to the inscription over the entrance, the church dates from 1042. The brickwork in the three apses projecting E, and in the narthex projecting W, is noteworthy for its decorative interplay. There is a lofty central dome over a fully developed Greek-cross plan. Both qualities lend the only surviving Guild church (as its name implies) great elegance.

Rotonda *(Ágios Géorgios)* ▥ ★
Egnatia.

Perhaps as penance for the massacre of the 7,000 citizens, Theodosius the Great decorated Galerius' Rotonda, newly dedicated to Agios Georgios, with superb mosaics. Most notable is the circle of saints below the dome praying in front of a marvellously detailed illustration of contemporary Roman architecture, against a lavish gold background. Restored to Christianity in 1912 after serving as a mosque since 1591, the Rotonda is now a national monument, but is closed at present because of the serious damage caused to it by the 1979 earthquake. Its Turkish minaret and the neglected tombs of the dervishes contrast sharply with the blocks of flats by which it is surrounded.

White Tower *(Lefkós Pýrgos)*
E end of Vassileos Konstantinou.

The Venetian sea wall was demolished in 1866 except for the massive White Tower. The symbol of the town, it is a circular keep that was once a prison garrisoned by Janissaries, the elite corps that had made and unmade caliphs for 200yr; they were massacred by Sultan Mahmoud II in the early 19thC. It was called the Bloody Tower until a Turkish pasha had it painted white in an attempt to erase its grim memories. Standing in a small garden, it occupies a strategic position between the seafronts of the old and new towns, near the Archaeological Museum and the **grounds of the International Fair**.

Behind the White Tower, the equestrian **statue of King Constantine** faces the Officers' Club, the **Theatre of Northern Greece** and the Society for Macedonian Studies, which accommodates the **Art Gallery** (📷 *standard opening times*).

Other Byzantine churches

Next to Agia Sofia (see before) is the **Chapel of Agios Ioannis Prodromos †** built out of one of the cisterns of a Roman *nymphaeon*, a colonnaded circular fountain, remains of which survive next door.

The declining fortunes of the late Byzantine Empire are evident in the 13thC **Agia Ekaterini †** on Sahini, and **Agios Nikolaos Orfanos**, now a museum (*off Athinas, standard opening times*). The same holds for **Ossios David †** on Vlatadon, a 14thC building, though its apse and mosaic of *Christ* date from the 6thC. Above Ossios David, on the cliff from which St Paul preached, stands the 14thC **Vlatadon Monastery**.

Hotels in Thessaloníki

Makedonia Palace 🏨

Megalou Alexandrou ☎ 837–520 ⑩ 412162 ▥▥ ▭ 302 ▦ ▭
AE CB ⑩ ⑩ VISA ⌂ ☐ on demand ☏ on roof.
Excellent location with a superb view. See also *Restaurants*.

Comfortable hotels: **Capitol** (*Monastiriou 8, near railway station* ☎ 516–221 ⑩ 412272 ▥▥ ▭ 194 ▭ ▭ ⇌ AE CB ⑩ ⑩ VISA); **Electra Palace** (*Aristotelous Sq.* ☎ 232–221 ⑩ 412590 ▥▥ ▭ 131 ▦ ⇌ AE CB ⑩ ⑩ VISA), in the heart of the town but fairly quiet.

Moderately priced hotels: **Astor** (*Tsimiski 20, central* ☎ 412655 ▥▥ ▭ 88 ▭ ⇌ ☏ on roof); **Capsis** (*Monastiriou 28, near railway station* ☎ 521–421/30 ⑩ 412206 ▥▮ ▭ 430 ▦ ▭ CB ⑩ ⑩ VISA ☏ on roof ⇌ ◉); **City** (*Komninon 11* ☎ 269–421 ⑩ 219216 ▥▮ ▭ 104 ▭ ⇌); **El Greco** (*Egnatias 23* ☎ 520–620 ▥▮ ▭ 90 ▦ ⇌ AE CB ⑩ ⑩ VISA); **Metropolitan** (*Vassilissis Olgas 65, slightly off centre in residential district* ☎ 824–221/8 ⑩ 412380 ▥▮ ▭ 118 ▭ ▭ ⇌ ⑩ ⑩ ☏ on roof); **Queen Olga** (*Vassilissis Olgas 44* ☎ 824–621/10 ▥▮ ▭ 148 ▭ ⇌ AE CB ⑩ ⑩ VISA).

Inexpensive hotels: **A.B.C.** (*Angelaki 41* ☎ 265–421/5 ▮ ▭ 112 ▭ ⑩ ⑩); **Delta** (*Egnatias 13* ☎ 516–321 ▥▮ ▭ 113 ▦ ▭ ▭ ⇌ ☏ on roof ⇌); **Esperia** (*Olympou 58* ☎ 269–321/5 ▮ ▭ 70 ▦ ▭ ▭ ⇌ ⑩ VISA); **Olympia** (*Olympou 65* ☎ 235–421/5 ⑩ 418532 ▮ ▭ 111 ▦ ▭ ⇌); **Vergina** (*Monastiriou 19, near railway station* ☎ 527–400/8 ▮ ▭ 133 ▭ ▭ AE CB ⑩ ⑩ VISA ☏ on roof).

Restaurants in Thessaloníki

These are generally better and cheaper than in Athens, except for the drearily unvarying hotel dining-rooms.

Stratis

Vassileos Konstantinou 19 ☎ 276–353 ▥▮ ▭ ⌂ AE
The place for the local speciality: *Mídia tiganitá* (fried mussels) with white Macedonian *Korona* wine; very popular, so reserve table.

Other restaurants: **The Grill House** (*Electra Palace hotel* ▥▮ ▭ ▭ AE CB ⑩ ⑩), probably the best meat in town – see also *Hotels*; **Kefallinia** (*Botsi 5* ▮ ▭ ⌂), serves rough but tangy food; **Krikelas** (*Gramou Vitsi 32* ☎ 414–690 ▥▮ ▭ ⌂ ▭ AE CB ⑩ ⑩ VISA), the big name in town among tavernas; **Roof Garden** (*Makedonia Palace hotel* ⌂ ▭ ▭ AE ⑩ ⑩ VISA), merely a luxury hotel dining-room, but with a splendid view – see also *Hotels*; **Soutzoukakia** (*Venizelou 8* ☎ 277–694 ▥▮ ▭ ⌂ ▭ ⑩), a popular taverna.

Pastry shops

Pastry shops line Vassileos Konstantinou, whose sidewalk tables in good weather are crowded until late at night. The big name is **Tottis**; another branch is on Aristotelous Sq. facing the **Salon Olympion**. Try the **Castello** and **Corfou** for creamy cakes and pastries.

Shopping

Elegant **Tsimiski** has numerous shops including branches of some found in Athens; **Agias Sofias**, **Egnatias**, **Ermou** and **Venizelou** are also main shopping streets.

Thíva See *Thebes*.

Tirynth (*Tíryntha*) ☆
Map 8I6 & 11I6. 4km (2.5 miles) N of Nafplio. Getting there: By bus, from Argos and Nafplio.

Tirynth, reputedly founded by Proetos (see *Argos*), was the birthplace of his descendant Herakles, who in his cradle strangled the two serpents sent by Hera in her unrelenting hatred for Zeus' extramarital progeny. Later, Herakles would rest here in between his Twelve Labours. Despite its impressive citadel, Tirynth seems never to have been of the first importance, and in the 5thC BC was destroyed by *Argos*.

The ruins
▨ *Standard opening times.*

A long **ramp** between the colossal blocks of Cyclopean walls, 6.1m (20ft) thick, rises to the great **Propylaea** of the mightiest Bronze-Age citadel in the Argive plain. The Propylaea give into the first of a series of vaulted galleries, the key figure of the **Royal Palace**. A staircase exits from the last to a postern gate.

Continuing excavations at the foot of the limestone crag projecting from the swamp at the head of the Gulf of Argos have brought to light a religious centre, with **Mycenaean frescoes** in some of the houses.

Vale of Tempe (*Témbi*) ☆
Map 2–3E5–6. 32km (20 miles) NE of Larissa. Getting there: Trains and buses to Macedonia pass through.

The beauty of this 9.6km-long (6 miles) passage between the towering cliffs of **Olympos** and **Ossa** has been extolled in ancient and modern poetry. Equalled in beauty by several other Greek mountain gorges, its fame relies more on the delightful contrast between the cool air along the tree-shaded banks of the river **Pinios** and the Thessalian plain, Europe's hottest, to the S. It is also almost the only thoroughfare between Central Greece and Macedonia; and it was here perhaps that the legend of Deukalion's flood (see *Mythology* in *Culture, history and background*) originated, when in a massive earthquake an outlet was forced by the inland sea that once extended as far W as the *Meteora*.

The vale
Tempe has several romantically named **fountains**, round which picnickers congregate in summer. The mountain walls are most formidable at the **Fountain of the Nymphs**, where the sea can be glimpsed between the arches of the plane trees. All along the fast-flowing river grow rhododendron and oleander, bound to the trees by ivy.

The pass has been fortified since recorded history began. It was held by troops under Spartan leadership against the army of Xerxes in 480BC, until they learnt that he was outflanking them by another pass further inland, whereupon they retreated to *Thermopylae*. It was taken most originally by the Roman general Marcius Philippus, who hauled his war elephants over the slopes and drove the last Macedonian king, Perseus, to defeat. Only the Emperor Alexios III Angelos succeeded in holding the pass, against the Normans of the First Crusade, thereby postponing the partition of Greece for another 100yr.

Vásses (*Bassae*) See *Andritsena*.

Vergína See *Macedonia*.

Véria
Map 2C5. 71km (44 miles) SW of Thessaloniki. Getting there: By train, on the Thessaloniki-Florina line; by bus, from Thessaloniki and W Macedonia. Population: 32,000.

First mentioned in the 5thC BC, Veria later became the capital of

Vólos

a Roman satellite republic that was soon absorbed into the Roman Empire. It sheltered St Paul on his flight from Thessaloniki, and he preached from a rock now occupied by a ruined mosque. Hidden from Turkish persecution but now well signposted in the backyards of the old houses of the lower town are several tiny **late-Byzantine chapels** † – **Agia Fotini**, **Agios Christos**, **Agios Georgios**, **Agios Nikolaos** and **Profitis Elias**, all interesting for their frescoes and woodcarvings.

H **Aristidis** (*Kentriki Sq.* ☎ 26–355/6 ☐ ☐ 50 ☐ ☐ ☞);
Polytimi (*Megalou Alexandrou 35* ☎ 23–007 ☐ ☐ 32 ☷ ☞); **Villa Elia** (*Elias 16* ☎ 26–800/1 ☐ ☐ 37 ☐).

Vólos
Map 3F6&8F6. 62km (39 miles) SE of Larissa. Getting there: By train, on the Kalambaka-Volos line; by bus, from Athens and Central Greece, and to all villages in the Pilio region. Port: Ferries to Tartoush (Syria) and the Sporades. Car-, boat- and bicycle/moped-hire facilities available. Population: 54,000 i GNTO, Riga Fereou Sq. ☎ 23–500.

At the N head of the Pagassitic Gulf, Volos is a major port for ferries to Syria. Behind it, the foothills of **Mt. Pilio** (Pelion), covered with olive groves and vineyards almost to the triangular summit, seem to close the huge circle of the Gulf.

Event: Folkloric performances with a mock wedding in Mt. Pilio style, Aug 15.

Sights and places of interest in and near Volos
Volos was rebuilt along strictly utilitarian lines after a devastating earthquake in 1955, but luckily the suburb of **Ano Volos** on the slope of Mt. Pilio was hardly touched. Here some 18thC **tower-houses** ⚏ rise above the orchards, and the **Kondou house** at Anakassia, which still has its period furniture, makes a pleasant **museum** (🕮 *standard opening times*) for the wall-paintings of Theophilos (1867–1934), one of the few genuine Primitive Greek artists (see *Islands/Lesvos*).

To the NW, on the road to Larissa, a small Byzantine church – the **Episkopi** † – marks the site of the wedding feast of Peleus and Thetis, where Eris threw the Apple of Discord and so started the Trojan War. Below the church on its romantic cypress-clad hill lies ancient **Iolkos**. Peleus was one of the Argonauts, that band of celebrities who sought the Golden Fleece. They included Herakles, Theseus, the sons of the North Wind, Orpheus and Asklipios as ship's doctor, and under the captainship of Jason they set sail in the *Argos*, the first sea-going vessel, from Pagasae (Pagasses), the port of Iolkos, on the headland opposite.

Pagasae, conquered by Dimitrios Poliorkitis in the 4thC BC, became a favourite residence of his successors, who ruled Greece from its powerful walls of which sections remain; the **theatre** is too ruined for staging ancient drama. The **aqueduct** was built by the Romans. Painted *stelae* from Pagasae are in the **museum** (🕮 *standard opening times*).

The pride of the museum, however, are the finds from Neolithic Sesklo and Dimini. **Sesklo** is a citadel 8km (5 miles) W, the first known fortified settlement in which mud-brick houses surround the larger dwelling of the chieftain. **Dimini**, 4km (2.5 miles) W, had six concentric rings of fortifications, interconnected by walls, protecting the ruler's residence, and here specimens of surprisingly advanced ceramics from the 4th millenium BC were found.

The villages of Mt. Pilio
From Volos the road climbs inland E to the mountain village of **Portaria**, 13km (8 miles). The most attractive of the Pilio villages, lying across a ravine, is **Makrinitsa**, where three *arhontiká* (mansions) ⚏ have been converted into small hotels. Its village square has a large terrace with a wonderful view over Volos and the gulf, framed by enormous plane trees shading a **Byzantine chapel** and a pretty fountain. The main road up from Portaria passes close to the **Cave of Cheiron**, centaur-tutor of Achilles and other heroes, to **Hania**, near the summit, 1,600m (5,252ft),

a local winter-sports centre, though not in the international league.

From Hania the road descends NE through forests and olive groves to **Zagora**, 41km (26 miles), largest of the 24 villages of Mt. Pilio and still bearing the imprint of its 18thC prosperity. **Tou Sotiros** (Of the Saviour) **†** dates from the 12thC. A branch leads to **Horefto** on the sea, while the circular road turns S along Pilio's most luxuriant flank. Another branch goes down to the sandy beach at **Agios Ioannis**, 53km (33 miles). Among the thick vegetation on a plateau, 503m (1,650ft) above sea-level, a few **tower-houses** 🏛 in **Tsangarada**, 56km (35 miles), have been restored; a road descends to an idyllic beach. After **Milies** the circular road joins the coastal road along the Pagassitic Gulf, which continues SE down to the end of the promontory past **Kala Nera**, **Afissos** and **Argalasti** to **Milina**, then crosses the headland to **Platania** on the open sea. Or the road goes back NW past **Lehonia** and **Agria**, 7km (4.5 miles), to Volos.

Hotels

In Volos
Alexandros (*Topali 3* ☎ *31–221/4* ▮▮▯ 🖿 *78* 🖃 🛏 ⇌ AE CB ◑ ◑ VISA); **Electra** (*Topali 16* ☎ *32–671/3* ▮▮▯ 🖿 *38* ⬤ 🛏 ⇌); **Galaxy** (*Agiou Nikolaou 3* ☎ *20–750/2* ▮▮▮ 🖿 *54* ⬤); **Park** (*Deligiorgi 2* ☎ *36–511/5* ▮▮▯ 🖿 *119* ▮▯ ⬤ ◑ ◑ ⌖ *on roof*); **Sandi** (*Topali 13* ☎ *33–341/3* ▮▯ 🖿 *39* ⬤); **Xenia** (*Plastira 1* ☎ *24–825* ▮▮▯ 🖿 *48* ⬤ 🛏 ⬤), the only hotel on a not very good beach.

Pagasses (*nearby on the SE coast*)
Filoxenia (☎ *38–336* ▮▯ 🖿 *17 double rooms* ⬤), near a clean beach.

Ⓡ **Metaftsis** (*Argonafton 23* ☎ *24–087* ▮▯ ◑), on the water-front.

Vouliagméni   *See Attica/Saronic Gulf.*

Vraóna (*Brauron*) ☆
Map **16***D3&***8***H7. 37km (21 miles) E of Athens. Getting there: By bus, from Athens to Markopoulo, then bus to site.*
With divine irony the cult of the local fertility nymph, Iphigenia, became identified at ancient Brauron with the determinedly virginal goddess Artemis. Another Iphigenia, sacrificed by her father Agamemnon at Aulis further up the coast but spirited away at the last moment by the goddess to Tauros in the Crimea, returned with her brother Orestes and landed at Brauron, bearing the wooden idol of Artemis; the goddess' High Priestess, she was deified after her death. Thus a curious combination involving both worship of Artemis and a cult of fertility prevailed, and for the sake of the latter the women of Athens made a pilgrimage on foot to Brauron every 4yr.

To complicate matters further, a primitive bear cult associated with the original Iphigenia persisted; to atone for the killing of a sacred bear, pre-pubertal girls from the best Athenian families served at the sanctuary for several years and were initiated in a complicated ritual bear dance.

Sights and places of interest
The **temple** (🖾 *standard opening times*) is partly reconstructed, and there are **foundations of an Early Christian basilica** at its entrance. The **supports for the tiny beds** on which the child-priestesses slept can be seen in the six cells of the 5thC BC **north stoa**. In the **museum** (🖾 *standard opening times*) are jewellery, bas-reliefs, statues and rare wooden vases, preserved in the mud of the Erasinos which swamped the site.

Ⓗ **Vraona Bay** (☎ *82–591/5* 📞 *210534* ▮▮▮ 🖿 *352* 🍴 ⬤ 🛏 ⇌ ⇶ 🌊 🏊 ⛵).

Yannina   *See Ioanina.*

Greek Islands A – Z

Although travel brochures promise a choice of 1,425 Greek islands, most are mere specks in the sea: dramatic, idyllic, romantic. They are enchanting, if admired from the air, even better seen from a cruise ship or, best of all perhaps, if explored from a yacht. But only about 100 islands are inhabited and holiday accommodation is available on even fewer.

> The isles of Greece, the isles of Greece!
> Where burning Sappho loved and sung,
> Where grew the arts of war and peace,
> Where Delos rose, and Phoebus sprung!
>
> Byron, *Don Juan*

Nature has decreed the division into *Ionian Islands* and *Aegean Islands*. Although the former are a mere seven in number, not counting various islets and rocks, they feature most prominently on the holiday scene.

See introduction to *Mainland A – Z* for standard opening times of museums and archaeological sights, and for general information on when and where hotels are open.

Advice on visiting the islands can be found in the *Planning* section of the book, where there is a *Calendar of events* for Greece, recommendations for *When and where to go*, suggested geographical groupings in *Area planners and tours*, and information on *Accommodation*, *Food and drink* and *Shopping*.

Aegean Islands

Mythology tries to stretch our credulity to its limit in the tale of King Aegeus, who threw himself from the Acropolis in Athens some 10km (6 miles) into the moodily changeable sea which was named after him.

The Aegean's innumerable islands, isles and rocks are the pinnacles of a section of the Balkans that once connected Europe with Asia Minor but subsided in a convulsion of unique violence even in this geologically tormented region. The islands sometimes form concentric circles round a well-defined centre, like the Cyclades around Delos; or are dominated by the largest in their group, as the Dodecanese are by Rhodes; or are scattered in an archipelago with no apparent link except proximity, like the Sporades; or lie close enough to the mainland to have participated in the history and culture of the continents, like Evia and Thassos. Only Crete lies in splendid isolation, with a civilization that was very much her own, though it was also influenced from overseas.

Throughout their history, in fact, Crete and all the islands of the Aegean have been stepping stones for the spread of migrations and cultures. Originating in Asia and Africa, they penetrated Europe, reversed, and continued back and forth.

For a catalogue of the three major island groups in the Aegean, see *Cyclades*, *Dodecanese* and *Sporades*. From these, you can select individual islands described in the *Greek Islands A – Z*, each entry giving information on sights, history and tourist facilities. See also *Crete*, *Evia*, *Hios*, *Lesvos*, *Limnos*, *Samos*, *Samothraki* and *Thassos*, and note that *Kythira*, although geographically at the western confines of the Aegean, is, in fact, historically grouped with the *Ionian Islands*.

Aegina   See *Egina*.

Alónissos   See *Sporades.*

Ámorgos   See *Cyclades.*

Anáfi   See *Cyclades.*

Ándros ☆
*Map **12**H9. 19km (12 miles) SE of Evia; 1.5km (0.9 mile) NW of Tinos; 111km (69 miles) E of Piraeus. 34km (21 miles) long by 13km (8 miles) wide. Getting there: By ferry, from Rafina and Tinos to Gavrio. Getting around: By bus to all villages. Taxi and garage facilities available. Population: 10,500.*

Andros, one of the Cyclades, is divided by a wide interior valley flanked by bare mountains with cultivated or wooded slopes. **Andros town** (locally the *Hóra*) is on a narrow headland on the E coast, and has a noteworthy **museum** (🖼 *standard opening times*). The 13thC **Venetian fortress** was partly destroyed by bombs in 1943. Only small vessels call at the town's port, **Emborios**, where there is a small but rather poor beach.

Andros, with its green hills and vineyards, more closely resembles the Attic mainland than the barren islands. Little visited by foreigners, but popular with Athenians for a short July–Aug season, choose June and Sept for a restful stay.

In the mountains near the *Hóra* are the **Sariza springs**, from which mineral waters are taken against liver and kidney ailments. Walls, a theatre and a stadium are all that remain of the **antique capital** on the W coast, which was abandoned in about AD1000 after repeated incursions by pirates. Also on the W coast, N of **Palaeopolis** (Old Town), is the modest beach resort of **Batsi**.

The island is second only to neighbouring *Tinos* (to which it is connected by ferry) in its great number of characteristically Cycladic **dovecots**. See also *Cyclades.*

Hotels on Ándros

Andros town
Paradise (☎ *22–187/9* ☎ *214253* 📵 🖵 *41* 🍴 🏠 ⇌ 🖼 ♥ *on roof*) is 90m (100yd) from the beach, but its name is an exaggeration.
Batsi (*On the w coast*).
Chryssi Akti (☎ *41–236* 📵 🖵 *61* 🍴 🏠 ⇌ 🏠).

Antíkythira   See *Kythira.*

Antípaxi   See *Paxi.*

Argo-Saronic Islands
The five off-shore islands extending from the Saronic into the Argive Gulf are the most readily accessible of the Greek Islands. Except for Egina and Ydra, however, their very proximity to the mainland deprives them of a truly 'island' atmosphere.

Salamis, the most universally known because of the momentous sea battle of 480BC, now faces the heaviest concentration of industry in the Bay of Eleusis, leaving air and water equally polluted.

The other four islands – *Egina, Poros, Spetses* and *Ydra* – are all easily reached from Piraeus by one-day cruises, hydrofoil and ferryboat or (in the case of all but Egina) across a narrow channel from the Peloponnese. They can be visited individually or as a group and are ideal for combining with a mostly mainland-oriented holiday.

Astypaléa See *Dodecanese*.

Cephallonía See *Kefalonia*.

Chíos See *Hios*.

Corfu (*Kérkyra*) ★

Map 6E2. Most northerly island, 3km (2 miles) from Albanian coast. 64km (40 miles) long by up to 32km (20 miles) wide. Getting there: By international ferry, from Bari, Brindisi and less frequently from other Italian and Yugoslavian ports; by local ferry, from Igoumenitsa; by air, direct flights from several European capitals and Brindisi, internal flights from Athens; airport ☎ 23–694; Olympic Airways terminal at 20 Kapodistriou ☎ 23–694. Getting around: By bus to all villages; the larger hotels run buses from airport to hotel. Car-hire available: Avis, Hertz and Hellas; also bicycle/moped – and boat-hire. Taxi and garage facilities available. United Kingdom vice-consulate: N. Zambeli 2 ☎ 30–055; open 10.00–12.00. Post Office: Diikitirio. Population: Island 95,000, town 30,000 i GNTO, The Governor's House ☎ 30–520.

It is little wonder that the loveliest of the Ionian Islands, lying in an elongated crescent before the stark backdrop of the Albanian and Epirote mountains, has been chosen as a setting by poets and writers from Homer via Shakespeare (if *The Tempest* is indeed situated there) to the Durrells. The island's N is hilly rather than mountainous, except for the craggy summit of **Mt. Pantokrator**, 914m (2,972ft) high, gradually flattening out to the S. The W coast has the best scenery, but the main tourist developments are on the E shore, where the capital and main port, **Corfu town**, are situated. As usual it bears the same name as the island, called in antiquity Korkyra from *koryfí*, The Peaks or, more familiarly, The Breasts, after the fortified twin rocks where the islanders sought refuge against raids.

Excursions to the delightful little island of *Paxi*, to the S of Corfu, can be made from the town. See also *Ionian Islands* and the other northern islands in the group: *Ithaki, Kefalonia, Lefkada* and *Zakynthos*.

Except where otherwise stated, all distances given in the text are from **Corfu town**.

Events: Easter procession around Corfu town; religious procession, Aug 14, at Mandouki (NW suburb of town); processions bearing relics of Agios Spyridon, on Greek Palm Sunday, Sat before Easter, Aug 11, first Sun in Nov, around Corfu town.

Son-et-lumière performances, May 15 – Sept 30, Old Fortress, Corfu town.

International Ionian Regatta, June.

Traditional cricket matches, July, between local clubs and visiting British and Maltese teams, on the Spianada, Corfu town.

Corfu Festival, July – Aug: a festival of music and theatre.

Feast of the Saviour, Aug 6, with procession of boats to Pontikonissi.

The town

The busy Mandouki harbour to the NW, where the ferries dock, is not particularly attractive, but the area is full of restaurants and tavernas, with *bouzoúkia* and discotheques along the

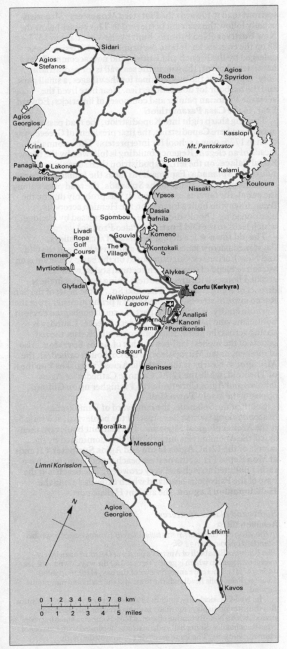

Agios
Stefanos
Sidari
Roda
Agios Spyridon

Agios
Georgios
Kassiopi
Krini
Panagia
Lakones
Mt. Pantokrator
Spartilas
Paleokastritsa
Kalami
Nissaki
Kouloura
Ypsos
Dassia
Sgombou
Dafnila
Livadi
Ropa
Golf
Course
Gouvia
Komeno
Ermones
The
Village
Kontokali
Myrtiotissa
Alykes
Glyfada
Corfu (Kerkyra)
Halikiopoulou
Lagoon
Analipsi
Vlaherna
Kanoni
Perama
Pontikonissi
Gastouri
Benitses

Moraitika
Messongi

Limni Korission

N

Agios
Georgios

Lefkimi

Kavos

0 1 2 3 4 5 6 7 8 km
0 1 2 3 4 5 miles

seafront road w towards the **Platytera Monastery**. Motorists usually follow the seafront boulevard E. This passes below the **New Fortress** (Neo Frourio) built by the Venetians in 1577–88 on the twin rocks. It bore the brunt of the 1716 siege, was enlarged by the French and British, and now accommodates a naval detachment; the gate in the sea wall is for pedestrians only. Opposite is the bus terminal for the villages, a small park and the harbour for domestic ferries. Near here lived the versatile Victorian painter and composer of limericks, Edward Lear, in the **Casa Paramythioti**.

Turning sharp right into Kapodistriou, the road passes the **mansion** where Capodistrias, the first president of Greece, was born in 1775, now a school for interpreters. The colonnaded facade of an elegant Regency building is followed by the former **Royal Palace**, on the left. Kapodistriou then runs along the w side of the **Spianada** (Esplanade) as far as the **Ionian Academy**.

On the opposite, E side of the Spianada, the road passes along the **canal**, the famous *contra fossa*. It was probably dug by the Byzantines who built a fortress on the Heraion acropolis, mentioned by Thoukydides. The canal is crossed by a bridge, which leads to the **Old Fortress** (Paleo Frourio).

The **old town ★** is a delightful maze of arched alleys, flagstoned narrow lanes and steep stairways between the Old and New Fortresses. Superimposed on the basic Venetian is an attractive blend of diverse architectural styles, with tall, arcaded houses with green shutters lining the lanes in the N district of Agios Nikolaos. Theotoki Sq., in the heart of the San Rocco maze of streets, is named after a prime minister from the Corfiote family, which forms part of a small enchanted circle of politicians who have governed modern Greece. Laundry is strung across the pedestrian zone, over which rises the red cupola of the highest bell-tower, that of **Agios Spyridon**. Also of interest, down Mitropoleos, is the Orthodox cathedral, the **Mitropolis**. Nearby is the Catholic Agios Frangiskos † on the N of Theotoki, while the 12thC Catholic Cathedral of Agios Iakovos and Agios Christophoros † is higher up on Glifford, opposite the lovely **Town Hall**.

South of the Spianada, the boulevard of Dimokratias descends along Garitsa Bay. Just off the boulevard, at Vraïla 5, is the **Archaeological Museum**. The seafront boulevard then skirts the Anemomylos suburb, which is dominated by the cupola of the 12thC **Agios Iason and Agios Sosipater** † It ends at Mon Repos Plage, the nearest beach to the town, which is a rather polluted stretch and very crowded. The beach is at the base of the Paleopolis headland which extends S along the **Halikiopoulou Lagoon**, the ancient Hyllaic port.

Sights and places of interest
Achillion 🏛 ☆
In the village of Gastouri in the hills, 9km (5.5 miles) sw of town 🚌
Standard opening times ◀
The Empress Elisabeth of Austria's palace at Gastouri has a lovely overgrown garden which is gently terraced all the way down to the sea, 145m (476ft). There are superb views of the bay, Halikioupoulou Lagoon, Paleopolis headland, the town and the mainland mountains beyond.

The Neo-Classical villa, built in 1891, is large and vaguely Florentine. But the interior displays too many revivals even for that derivative period, with a Neo-Byzantine chapel, a Neo-Pompeian smoking room, a Neo-Renaissance dining hall and a staircase decorated with frescoes of Homeric subjects. The Ionic peristyle is overcrowded with undistinguished gods, muses and philosophers. A pleasing exception is a *Dying Achilles* (1884) by the German sculptor Ernst Herter, facing away from the villa so that the empress could see only the polite parts of her favourite hero, after whom the villa is named.

After Elisabeth's assassination by an anarchist, the new owner, Kaiser Wilhelm II of Germany, introduced some sanitary but no artistic improvements. A bathroom with hot water and cold sea water was installed, an electric bell was placed next to the lavatory throne, and the Kaiser sat on an adjustable saddle while writing at his desk. He also commissioned a larger statue of *Achilles*, with the modest dedication 'To the greatest Greek from the greatest German'.

The historic vulgarities housed in the palace were faithfully preserved when the Achillion was turned into a casino in 1962 (see *Entertainment and nightlife* in *Corfu/The town*).

Agios Spyridon ✝ ☆
In the old town.

The church was built in 1589 to house the mummified body of the island's patron saint, which lies in a silver Renaissance reliquary, often paraded upright in a solemn procession through the town (see events in introduction to *Corfu*). Agios Spyridon, Bishop of Cyprus and a member of the Council of Nicaea in AD325, was not a local saint. His embalmed remains were smuggled out of Constantinople in a sack of straw after the Turkish conquest. He saved the Corfiotes from the plague in 1630 and the Turks in 1716, and an unexploded bomb in World War II further enhanced the saint's prestige, so that most males of the post-war generation bear his name.

The early 18thC paintings by Panagiotis Doxaras on the ceiling were over-restored in 1830, but there is a fine ikonostasis.

Archaeological Museum ☆
Vraïla 5 🔲 *Standard opening times.*

The museum contains interesting local finds, including sculptures from archaic to Roman, funerary *stelae*, pottery, figurines and coins. The colossal **Gorgon pediment** ☆ from the Temple of Artemis, depicting the serpent-haired Medusa flanked by Pegasos and Chrysaor, who sprang from her blood when Perseus cut off her head, is a major exhibit. So too is the ferocious **lion** ☆ which once stood on the tumulus of the 7thC Consul Menekrates.

Ionian Academy
Opposite statue of Capodistrias at upper end of the Spianada.

The Ionian Academy was built by the philhellene Lord Guilford – a man Sir Charles Napier considered "a queer fish, but very pleasant . . . . he goes about dressed up like Plato, with a gold band round his mad pate and flowing drapery of a purple hue". Another contemporary described "the pretty dress of the students, consisting of a tunic and *chlamys* (cloak), with buskins of red leather reaching to mid-leg". In spite or perhaps because of the fancy dress, the embryo university attracted scholars from all over Greece and became the nucleus of a literary revival round the poets Solomos and Mavilis. It later became a public library but was bombed by the Italians in World War II.

Mitropolis ✝
Mitropoleos.

The Orthodox cathedral in 1577 became the final resting place of Agia Theodora, a Byzantine empress canonized in the 9thC whose headless body accompanied that of Agios Spyridon on his adventurous journey from Constantinople to Corfu. Like him, she is an imported saint; the island's relaxed atmosphere has been no more successful in encouraging local female sanctity than it has male.

Old Fortress (Paleo Frourio) Ⅲ ☆
On the E side of the Spianada, beyond the canal 🔲 *Open 17.00–19.00.*

The Venetians, having barely withstood a protracted Turkish siege in 1537, transformed this strategic site into a fortress, 1553–58. It is built on a promontory with two fortified heights, one of which is reached by a 65m-long (213ft) tunnel, while a longer passage descends below the canal and town to the New Fortress.

The elegant Doric **Chapel of St George** Ⅲ ✝ now Orthodox, was built by Colonel Whitmore as the British garrison church. The fortress, against a backdrop of mountains, provides a superb setting for son-et-lumière performances in English (*weekdays 21.00–21.45*). (See events in introduction to *Corfu*.)

Platytera Monastery
Beyond Mandouki Harbour, at s of Mandouki suburb.

Buried here are Count Ioannis Capodistrias, first president of Greece, who was assassinated in Nafplio in 1831, and the revolutionary hero Photis Tsavellas. Note also the **collection of 17thC ikons** ☆ by Kantounis, Poulakis and Tzanes.

Royal Palace ⬚ ★
In Kapodistriou ▨ Standard opening times. Entrance from the Spianada.

Built in 1818–23 in Maltese limestone and designed by Sir George Whitmore, who was a colonel in the Royal Engineers, this splendid Georgian residence of the High Commissioners was known as the Palace of St Michael and St George, being also the seat of that newly founded order. After 1864, considered by many to be the finest edifice built in Greece since antiquity, it became a favourite residence of George I of Greece.

The **Chamber of the Ionian Senate**, still adorned with portraits of the British High Commissioners, is open to the public. Next to it is the **Municipal Library**. Upstairs is the **Museum of Asiatic Art** ☆ with a remarkable collection of some 8,000 Sino-Japanese objects dating back 3,000yr, donated by a former Greek ambassador to those countries. Across the hall is a smaller collection from the Far East, and ikons and frescoes of the post-Byzantine period.

A **bronze statue of the second High Commissioner**, *Sir Frederick Adam*, stands in front of a graceful colonnade, and is fittingly sited in a pool – for it was he who constructed the aqueducts, which are still in use, to ensure an adequate water supply.

Spianada (*Esplanade*) ★

This is the largest and finest of Greece's public squares, and separates the citadel of the Old Fortress from the old town, having once served as a parade and exercise ground for the Venetians. It is a vast, tree-shaded lawn, albeit a little scrubby in one part where cricket is still played (see events in introduction to *Corfu*). You can watch the games in comfort from the numerous sidewalk cafes in the **Liston** – the stately arcaded row of houses designed during the French occupation 1807–14 and inspired by the Rue de Rivoli in Paris.

The Ionian **Rotunda** commemorates Sir Thomas Maitland, first High Commissioner, known as 'King Tom' for his autocratic ways. He was considered rude but dourly efficient, and particularly disliked those bearing letters of introduction. To one of these, on a well-documented occasion, he bared his hindparts to show his scorn. Nearby is an old-fashioned green bandstand from which concerts are given on Sun.

Marble reliefs symbolizing the Seven Islands surround a monument to the islands' union with Greece, while a **statue of Capodistrias** surveys the empty shell of the Ionian Lower House and Lord Guilford's Ionian Academy.

On the opposite side of the Spianada, numerous statues surround a Baroque likeness of *Count von der Schulenburg*, the town's successful defender in the siege of 1716.

Town Hall ⬚ ☆
Voulgareos. Closed to the public.

An attractive building decorated with sculptured medallions, it was begun in 1663 but not finished for 30yr. It began life as a club for the island's nobility, but was converted into a theatre in the mid-18thC, and has accommodated the town council since 1902. The adjoining **memorial to Admiral Morosini** is as mutilated as the Parthenon in Athens was after he commanded the infamous bombardment in 1867.

Other sights

Near the Halikiopoulou Lagoon, the ancient Hyllaic port, the Venetian San Salvatore Fortress, now ruined, was built; the French began the excavation (in 1812) of antique Korkyra (**remains of the lower city** still in evidence); and the **Temple of Artemis** was discovered 100yr later. This led to the excavation of a large **archaic temple** and two tiny **classical shrines**, one dedicated to Hermes, the other to Aphroditos, patron of transvestites. The moustached and bearded **clay statuettes of**

Aphrodite seem a curious anticipation of Lady Adam, the second High Commissioner's Corfiote wife, whose "beard on her upper lip would ornament an hussar", according to a contemporary. Her tastes were expansive as well as expensive, her lovers rivalling in number the many public works she instigated.

One of these is the large **Villa of Mon Repos**, barely 3.5km (2 miles) from the town palace, which was built for Sir Frederick Adam in 1824 and became the summer residence of the High Commissioners and later of the Greek kings. It was at 'Sir Frederick's Folly' that Prince Philip, Duke of Edinburgh, was born in 1921.

The road skirts the lovely park which covers most of the E of the headland. It continues through the village of Analipsi, built on the **site of ancient Palaeopolis**, of which there are some remains, then goes S to beautifully located **Kanoni** (Cannon), named after the gun battery installed by the French in 1798.

Sir Frederick Adam's aqueduct, which serves as a causeway (*pedestrians and cyclists only*) to Perama on the opposite shore, separates the iridescent stillness of the Halikiopoulou Lagoon from one of the loveliest bays in the Mediterranean, the inspiration for Böcklin's *Island of the Dead* and countless other paintings. A shorter breakwater (*pedestrians and cyclists only*) leads to the whitewashed **Convent of Vlaherna** with its Byzantine Chapel of the Saviour.

From here motorboats ply to **Pontikonissi** (Mouse Isle), a cypress-clad rock rising almost too romantically from the deep-blue sea; supposedly this was the Phaeacian ship that brought Odysseus to Ithaki, which was turned to stone by the angry Poseidon. Marble tablets in the 13thC **Byzantine chapel †** on the summit commemorate the visit of Empress Elisabeth of Austria and Archduke Rudolf, c.1880. In later years the tragic empress prayed for her unhappy son in this superb setting.

Hotels in Corfu town

Corfu Palace 🏨
Dimokratias Ave. ☎ *39–485/7*
📺 *332126* ▮▮▮ 🛏 *106* 🍽 🏧
🚗 🅰🅴 🅒🅑 🄲🄳 🆅🅸🅂🅰 ⚓
Location: Slightly set back from the boulevard, overlooking Garitsa Bay. 180m (200yd) from Mon Repos Beach, but the hotel bus takes guests to Miramare Beach, 18km (11 miles) away.
🏠 ◻ 🗡 ⟨⟨ ⚓

Suisse 🏨
Kapodistriou 13 ☎ *39–815* ◻
🗡 *32* 🚗
Location: On the Liston facing the Spianada. No lift or showers – but it has large, comfortable rooms, half with lovely views.

Also in town
🏨 **Atlantis** (*Xenofontos Stratigou* ☎ *35–560/2* ◻ 🛏 *58* 🍽 🚗 🏠 🗡), on port seafront;
Cavalieri (*Kapodistriou 4* ☎ *39–336* 📺 *332116* ▮▮▮ 🛏 *48* 🚗 🏠 🏧 🅰🅴 🅒🅑 🄲🄳 🆅🅸🅂🅰 🏠 🗡 ⚓ *on roof* ⟨⟨), at upper end

of the Spianada; **Ionion** (*Xenofontos Stratigou 46* ☎ *39–915* ◻ 🛏 *81* 🚗 🗡), in the port area; **King Alkinoos** (*Dimarhou Zafiropoulou 29* ☎ *39–300/2* ▮▮▮ 🛏 *61* 🚗 🗡 🄲🄳 🆅🅸🅂🅰 ⚓ *on roof*);
Olympic (*Doukissis Marias 4* ☎ *30–532/4* ▮▮▮ 🛏 *50* 🚗 🗡 🅰🅴 🅒🅑 🄲🄳 🆅🅸🅂🅰 🚗 ⚓).
Kanoni (*s of the town*)
Ariti (☎ *38–885/9* 📺 *332163* ▮▮▮ 🛏 *171* 🍽 🚗 🅰🅴 🅒🅑 🄲🄳 🄲🄳 🆅🅸🅂🅰 🗡 ⚓), facing the sea, with a funicular railway to its own beach; **Corfu Hilton** 🏨 (☎ *36–540/9* 📺 *332148* ▮▮▮ 🛏 *274* 🍽 🚗 🅰🅴 🅒🅑 🄲🄳 🆅🅸🅂🅰 🏠 🗡 🗡 ⟨⟨ 🚗 🗡 ⚓ ◻), hotel and bungalows; **Divani Corfu Palace** (☎ *38–996/8* 📺 *332103* ▮▮▮ 🛏 *165* 🍽 🚗 🅰🅴 🅒🅑 🄲🄳 🆅🅸🅂🅰 🗡 ⚓ ◻); **Royal** (☎ *37–512* ◻ 🛏 *114* 🚗 🗡 *on roof* ⚓ ◻); **Salvos** (☎ *31–693/4* 📺 *332153* ◻ 🛏 *92* 🚗 🚗 🗡 *on roof* ⚓ ◻).

Restaurants
Although the Venetian connection left more of an architectural than a culinary mark, the *sofríto* (veal with garlic and vinegar sauce) became an Ionian speciality which joined the nationwide Greek bill of fare. The outstanding local white wine is the slightly sparkling *Theotóki*, if you can get it; otherwise, try

Palóumbi or *Corifó*, the latter in both red and white. *Koum kouat* is a syrupy liqueur made from tiny Japanese oranges; and, of course, there is *tzíntzi bíra* (ginger beer), left by the British.

Aegli
Kapodistriou 23 ☎ *31 – 949* ▥
▱ ▤ ⊙ ⊚

The best of several attractive restaurants along the elegant Liston, each with many tables on a wide, tree-shaded pavement facing the Spianada and its cricket pitch.

Averof
Alipiou 4 ☎ *31 – 468* ▥ ▱ ⇔
▣ ⊙ ⊚

The restaurant is in a shady courtyard in the old port, and has

the widest choice of local dishes, with quick, efficient service.

Ⓡ Other restaurants: **Bella Napoli** (*Skaramanga 11* ☎ *33 – 338* ▥ ▱ ▣ ⊙ ⊚), has an attractive, vaguely Italian decor; **Kostas** ● (*Taxiarhon Sq.* ▱ ▱), in a maze of lanes, with authentic atmosphere and a small but tasty selection of local specialities; **Rex** (*Kapodistriou 66* ☎ *39 – 649* ▥ ▱ ⇔ ▣ ⊚).

Entertainment and nightlife
Entertainment revolves around the **Liston** in the Spianada, even at night. Eat ice-cream and watch the world go by from numerous cafes: the **Olympia** is the smartest. *Bouzóukia* orchestras are the main attractions at **Corfu by Night** (*Potamou, 2.5km (1.5 miles)* NW ☎ *38 – 123*) and the **Kastro** (*also in Potamou* ☎ *32 – 154*). Among the discotheques on the port road, try **Bora Bora** and **Koukouvaya**.

See also *Hotels* in *Corfu/The town*, many of which have discotheques.

Achillion ▥
In the village of Gastouri, in the hills 9km (5.5 miles) SW *of town* ☖ ☗
⇔ ◁◾

Baccarat, chemin-de-fer, roulette and sometimes blackjack are played. Passports required; men must wear jackets and ties. (See also *Sights* in *Corfu/The town*.)

Shopping
It is better to shop in town, where bargaining for locally-made articles is expected, than in hotel boutiques. Look out for attractive bowls and trays made from olive wood. Silver jewellery, plates and containers vary in quality and price, so it pays to pick and choose. Ceramics from the workshops on the road to Perama and Kontokali are cheaper than in the souvenir shops in town. Leather goods are similar in quality and price to the rest of Greece. Sponges are plentiful and relatively cheap, so bargain; the same is true for straw baskets and mats, and for Greek toy figures. Crystallized fruit, especially *koum kouat*, nougat, honey, and olive oil can all be purchased in the many tiny 'super markets'.

The southeast coast
The road S from town skirts the Halikiopoulou Lagoon and passes the airport on its way to **Perama**, 8km (5 miles), where several holiday villas are let. Corfu has about 400, ranging from simple cottages to luxuriously appointed homes, as well as a large number of rooms in private houses.

Benitses, 12km (7.5 miles) further S, is very touristy despite having an unsatisfactory, tiny beach. The road keeps close to the sea, passing the **Val Tour** luxury hotel and bungalows, part of the Club Méditerranée, on the way to **Moraïtika**, 18km (11 miles). Only 1.6km (1 mile) further is **Messongi**.

The road turns inland through the loveliest olive groves, near Corfu's only lake, **Limni Korission**, 25km (16 miles). **Lefkimi** is in the centre of the largest plain on the island and **Kavos**, 47km (29 miles), is the end of the road. It is a port of call for the Corfu-Paxi boat, and has several tavernas near an unexciting beach. Much better is the long, sandy strip at **Agios Georgios**, 34km (21 miles), on the sw coast.

Hotels on the southeast coast

Messongi Beach
Messongi ☎ 38–684/6 ▯▯▯ ▭ 684 ▭ ▭ ▭ ▣ ▣ ▣ ◉ ◉
Location: *20km (12 miles) from Corfu town)*. Well-positioned and the largest beach holiday complex on Corfu, the hotel also includes bungalows laid out in a sub-tropical garden. All forms of nautical sport are available.
▭ ☀ ≈ ◈ ⚬ ◉

Other hotels
Benitses *(12km (7.5 miles) from Corfu town)*
Corfu Maris (☎ 38–684 ▯▯ ▭ 31 ▭); **Corfu Summer Flats** (☎ 92–227 ▯▯▯ ▭ ⚬), furnished apartments; **Potomaki** (☎ 92–201 ▯▯▯ ▭ 149 ▭ ▭ ▭ ▣ ◉ ◉ ▭ ▭ on roof ≈ ◈ ◉); **San Stefano** (☎ 92–292 ▯▯▯ ▭ 288 ▭ ▭ ▭ ▣ ▣ ◉ ◉ ▣ ▭ ≈ ⚬), hotel and bungalows, 730m (800yd) from the beach.

Messongi *(20km (12 miles) from Corfu town)*
Melissa Beach (☎ 92–429 ▯▯ ▭ 32 ▭ ▭ ▭).
Moraïtika *(18km (11 miles) from Corfu town)*
Delfinia (☎ 30–318 ▯▯▯ ▭ 83 ▭ ▭ ▭ ▣ ▭ ≈) is rustic/modern; **Miramare Beach** ▯▯▯ (☎ 30–226/8 ◉ 332126 ▯▯▯ ▭ 149 ▭ ▭ ▭ ▣ ▣ ◉ ◉ ▣ ▭ ▭ ◈ ⚬), bungalows.
Perama *(8km (5 miles) from Corfu town)*
Aeolos Beach (☎ 33–132/4 ◉ 332165 ▯▯▯ ▭ 231 ▭ ▭ ▭ ▣ ▣ ◉ ◉ ▣ ≈ ▭ ▭ bungalows; **Akti** (☎ 39–445 ▯▯▯ ▭ 55 ▭ ▭ ▭ ☀ ≈ ◈ ▭), motel; **Alexandros** (☎ 36–855/7 ▯▯▯ ▭ 75 ▯▯▯ ▭ ▭ ▭ ▣ ▣ ◉ ◉ ▣ ▭ on roof ◈ ≈); **Oasis** (☎ 38–190 ▯▯ ▭ 66 ▭ ▭ ▭ ☀ on roof ◈ ≈ ◈ ◉).

The northeast coast
The coast road N from town passes through several hotel and holiday accommodation centres. These include **Alykes**, 3.2km (2 miles), really a suburb of the town, **Kontokali**, 6.5km (4 miles), and **Gouvia**, 8km (5 miles), with its large marina. The road is lined with an endless string of restaurants, souvenir shops, and hotels. Some are listed, at **Komeno**, 9.5km (6 miles), **Dafnila** 13km (8 miles) and **Dassia**, 11km (7 miles); the latter has the **Castello** hotel, in a converted 16thC castle.

On the lovely Bay of Ypsos, the village of **Ypsos**, 14km (9 miles), has numerous fish restaurants along its seafront; nearby is **Pyrgi**, 14km (9 miles).

At the apex of the bay, the road branches beneath **Mt. Pantokrator**. The inland road to the N coast at Anaharavi can be taken around the mountain, via **Spartilas**. Or you can head towards Kassiopi along the coast road, which is at its most dramatic as it passes along the flanks of Mt. Pantokrator.

On the coast at **Nissaki**, 22km (14 miles), the **Ilios** is another vast luxury hotel in the Club Mediterranée chain. The Durrells' **White House** taverna at **Kalami** offers simple, tasty food in a lovely position on the N end of the bay. **Kouloura**, 30km (19 miles), is blissfully unspoilt as there is barely enough space for a few fishing boats. Winding through the green foothills of Mt. Pantokrator, the road by-passes the NE promontory, separated from Albania by a 2.4km (1.5 miles) channel, then returns to the coast at **Kassiopi**, 36km (22.5 miles), a small fishing village sadly spoilt by unplanned development. *Bouzóukia* and electronic music are no improvement on the fiddling of Nero, who in AD66 supposedly gave a concert here.

Sights and places of interest

Mt. Pantokrátor ☆

From Spartilas, a rough branch off the inland road to Anaharavi zig-zags up to the magnificent views from the barren summit, 914m (2,972ft) high. An equally circuitous road descends to the N coast.

The Village ♣

2km (1.25 miles) from Gouvia on the coast, or (by direct route) 8km (5 miles) NW *of Corfu town* ⬚ ➡ *Open morning until late* ® *evenings* ♫ *evenings.*

The Village is a reconstruction of an island village as it would have been during the Venetian era, complete with recreations of contemporary crafts and occupations. The buildings include a small **museum** and there is an **olive press**. A variety of **restaurants** (all ⬛ ⬜ ⬜ ➡ AE CB ⊕ ⬜ VISA) and **nightclubs** (all ⬛ ⬜ ♪ ⬜ ⬜ ⬜ VISA) open in the evenings, the latter featuring Greek folk dancing. Handicrafts from the **National Welfare Organisation shop** (⬛ ⬜ AE CB ⊕ ⬜ VISA).

Hotels on the northeast coast

Castello ⬛

Dassia ☎ *93–201/2* ⬛ *332136* ⬛ 🛏 72 ⬜ 50 ⬜ ➡ AE CB ⊕ ⬜ VISA

Location: 12km (7.5 miles) N *of Corfu town.* Of all hotels and tavernas in this large concentration, by far the most original is the Castello, a 16thC castle dressed up in 'Seignorial Florentine' style at the turn of the century. It was a favourite residence of King George II of Greece during the few summers he was allowed to spend in his own country – he imparted the country-house atmosphere which the rather incongruous furniture preserves. ⬚ ⬜ 🌿 ⇌ ⬜ ✂ ♫

Lucciola Inn

Sgombou ☎ *91–419* ⬛ 🛏 10

Location: Inland, 5km (3 miles) NW *of Corfu town.* A safe home-from-home, cosy and run with gratifying attention to detail by the owner and his English wife. Set menu dinners are served promptly at 20.30. ⬚ ⬜ 🌿 ♫

Other hotels

Alykes *(3.2km (2 miles) from Corfu town, in the suburbs)*
Kerkyra Golf (☎ *31–785/7* ⬛ *332149* ⬜ 240 ➡ ⬜ ➡ AE CB ⊕ ⬜ ⬜ 🌿 on roof ⇌ ⬜ ✂ ♫ ○), despite its name, has nothing whatever to do with golf; **Salina** (☎ *36–782* ⬛ ⬜ 16 ➡ ⬜ ⇌).
Dafnila *(13km (8 miles) from Corfu town)*

Robinson Club (☎ *35–732* ⬛ *332185* ⬛ ⬜ 260 ➡ ⬜ ➡ ⬜ 🌿 🌿 ⇌ ⬜ ✂ ○), three main buildings with bungalows in terraced garden, on a headland.
Dassia *(11km (7 miles) from Corfu town)*
Chandris Corfu and **Chandris Dassia** (☎ *33–871/5* ⬛ *332151* ⬛ ⬜ 552 ⬜ ➡ ⬜ ➡ AE CB ⊕ ⬜ ⬜ 🌿 🌿 ⇌ ⬜ ✂ ○), two huge hotels, bungalows and villas, just off the main road, sharing the same switchboard; **Dassia** (☎ *93–224* ⬛ ⬜ 54 ➡ ⬜ ⇌ ⬜).
Gouvia *(8km (5 miles) from Corfu town)*
Corcyra Beach (☎ *30–770/2* ⬛ *332128* ⬛ ⬜ 252 ➡ ⬜ ➡ ⬜ ⊕ ⬜ VISA ⬜ 🌿 🌿 ○), two main buildings with bungalows, set in spacious grounds; **Feakion** (☎ *91–264* ⬛ ⬜ 24 ➡ ⬜ ⇌).
Komeno *(9.5km (6 miles) from Corfu town)*
Astir Palace ⬛ (☎ *91–481/6* ⬛ *332169* ⬛ ⬜ 308 ⬜ ➡ ⬜ ➡ AE CB ⊕ ⬜ VISA ⬜ 🌿 🌿 ⇌ ⬜ ✂ ○ ♫), hotel and bungalows in terraced garden on a headland; **Eva Palace** (☎ *91–286/7* ⬛ ⬜ 174 ⬜ ➡ ⬜ 🌿 🌿 ⇌ ⬜ ✂ ○).
Kontokali *(6.5km (4 miles) from Corfu town)*
Kontokali Palace ⬛ (☎ *38–736/9* ⬛ *332113* ⬛ ⬜ 238 ⬜ ➡ ⬜ ➡ AE CB ⊕ ⬜ VISA ⬜ 🌿 🌿 ⇌ ⬜ ✂ ○), hotel and bungalows on a small headland.

Nissaki *(22km (14 miles) from Corfu town)*
Nissaki Beach (☎ 91–232/3 📺 332155 ▮▮▮ �
240 … on roof …).

Pyrgi *(14.5km (9 miles) from Corfu town)*
Emerald (☎ 93–209 📺 332121 … 58 … on roof …).

Ypsos *(14km (9 miles) from Corfu town)*
Mega (☎ 93–208 … 32 …); **Ypsos Beach** (☎ 93–232 … 60 …).

Ⓡ **Dassia**
(On the coast, 11km (7 miles) NW of Corfu town)
Delfini (☎ 93–339 ▮▮▮ … 🖽 🖽 🖽 🖽).

The north coast

Along the eastern half of the N coast, the road, though rarely touching the rocky shore, is never very far from the sea. There is a 3km (2 miles) branch to the small, semi-circular, sandy beach at **Agios Spyridon**. The beach is connected by a channel to the Antinioti Lagoon where duck shooting is popular in the autumn. The beach at **Roda** is overdeveloped, but **Sidari**, 35 km (22 miles) NW of Corfu town, has remarkable **rock formations** on the *Canal d'Amour*, which requires a long but worthwhile detour inland.

Hotels on the north coast

Roda *(36km (23 miles) from Corfu town)*
Roda Beach (☎ 31–225 📺 332159 ▮▮▮ 🖽 360 … 🖽 🖽), two main buildings with bungalows; **Silver Beach** (☎ 31–357 … 33 …).
Sidari *(35km (22 miles) from Corfu town)*
There are three small, inexpensive and unremarkable hotels at Sidari: **Astoria**, **Mimosa** and **Three Brothers**.

The west coast

The best beaches are to be found here, although there is no continuous road linking them. Tourism has not yet disfigured the NW: another **Agios Georgios** (there are two on the island) is a beautiful sweep of sand with only two tavernas, and tourist development has only just begun at **Agios Stefanos**.

The small, whitewashed **Monastery of the Myrtiotissa** (Our Lady of the Myrtles) stands on a headland separating **Ermones**, 14km (9 miles), and **Glyfada**, 16km (10 miles). Beneath the monastery is a beautiful beach of the same name. Glyfada's beach is equally sandy but less romantic. There is an 18-hole golf course at Livadi Ropa (Ropas' Meadow) near Ermones.

Sights and places of interest
Paleokastrítsa ★
On the w coast, 23km (14 miles) from Corfu town.
The road from Corfu town was built in the 19thC by the Eleventh Regiment of Foot to reach a convalescent camp, which happened to be near Lady Adam's favourite picnic ground. Paleokastrítsa, despite numerous hotels, is still outstandingly beautiful. The trefoil-shaped harbour, separated by a rocky promontory from the enchanting bay, corresponds more closely to Homer's description of the Phaeacian capital than does Alkinoos' port near Palaeopolis, s of Corfu town. The palace would have stood on the **promontory of Agios Nikolaos**, now occupied by the 12thC **Monastery of the Panagia** (Our Lady). The rock visible far out to sea may be yet another version of Odysseus' petrified ship (see also **Pontikonissi** in *Corfu/The town* under *Other sights*), although the monks maintain that it is an Algerian pirate ship miraculously prevented from plundering the monastery.

Seaside restaurants serve *astakós*, wrongly translated as lobster: it is in fact clawless salt-water crayfish, but like lobster in taste and price.

163

Other sights

The fine view from the clifftop at Agios Nikolaos hardly compares with
the superb panorama from the 300m (1,000ft) high **Bella Vista** cafe ☆
reached by a 4km (2.5 miles) road through olive groves and located near
the village of Lakones.

The narrow road continues along a crest to Krini, where a steep,
30min climb brings you to **Angelokastro** ☆ which was the stronghold of
Michael I Angelos, Despot of Epiros, during his brief rule over Corfu in
the early 13thC.

Hotels on the west coast

Agios Gordis (*14km (9 miles) from Corfu town*)
Agios Gordis (☎ 36–723/5 ▥▥ ▭ 197 ⬤ ⌂ ⇆ ▱ ⇶ ⁂ ≈ ⋒ ℘ ◉),
in three large buildings reaching down to the sea.
Ermones (*14km (9 miles) from Corfu town*)
Ermones Beach (☎ 94–241/2 ▦ 332162 ▥▥ ▭ 272 ⬤ ⌂ ⇆ ⇶
CB ◉ ▱ VISA ⌂ ⇶ ⁂ ⟨⟨ ≈ ⋒ ℘), a main building with
bungalows.
Glyfada (*16km (10 miles) from Corfu town*)
Grand Hotel (☎ 94–201 ▦ 332107 ▥▥ ▭ 218 ▤ ⬤ ⌂ ⇆ AE CB
◉ ▱ VISA ⌂ ⇶ ⁂ ⟨⟨ ≈ ⋒ ℘ ◉), in three buildings.
Paleokastritsa (*23km (14 miles) from Corfu town*)
Akrotiri Beach (☎ 41–275/6 ▥▥ ▭ 126 ⬤ ⌂ ⇆ AE CB ◉ ▱
VISA ⌂ ⇶ ⁂ ⟨⟨ ≈ ⋒), set in its own grounds; Oceanis
(☎ 41–229/230 ▥▥ ▭ 71 ⬤ ⌂ ⇆ AE CB ◉ ▱ VISA ⌂ ⇶ ⟨⟨
⇶ ⋒) is on a terraced slope with steps to the beach; Odysseus
(☎ 41–209 ▥ ▭ 36 ⬤ ⌂ ⇆), in three buildings above the main
road; **Paleokastritsa** (☎ 41–207 ▥▥ ▭ 150 ⬤ ⌂ ⇆ ⇶ ⁂ ⟨⟨ ≈ ⋒
◉), 200m (220yd) above its own beach, in a main building with
bungalows.

Crete (*Kríti*) ★

*Map 12M9. In the s Aegean. 256km (160 miles) long by up to
60km (37.5 miles) wide. Getting there: By air, direct charter
flights from most European cities, scheduled flights from
Athens, Rhodes and Thira, all to Iraklio, and from Athens to
Hania; by ferry, from Piraeus to Hania and Iraklio, the
Cyclades to Iraklio, the Dodecanese to Agios Nikolaos, and
Gythio (Peloponnese) and Agia Pelagia (Kythira) to Kissamos.
Getting around: By bus to all sites and villages, and excursion
coaches. Car-hire agencies in all major towns. Taxi and
ample garage facilities available. Police: Akti Tombazi 6,
Hania ☎ 26–426. Population: 500,000 i GNTO –
see Iraklio and Hania.*

Both the Asian and African shores of the Mediterranean
contributed to the early development of the Minoan
civilization. Asia supplied the human material: in about 3000BC
the Neolithic ancestors of the Minoans from Asia Minor
conquered the earlier settlers of the island, who had probably
also come from Asia Minor, some 3,000yr before. But Egypt
provided the initial inspiration for the Minoans' artistic
development.

If the Linear A Script, found on clay tablets on many sites, is
indeed an Indo-European language akin to the Louvian spoken
in some parts of Asia Minor, it might be possible at last to
deduce the precise origin of the Minoans. Even this would
throw no light on their actual history, however, for the
innumerable clay tablets that have been found are almost
exclusively store inventories, and the occasional invocation.
This is true also of the Linear B Script which was deciphered in
the 1950s by the English expert Michael Ventris, who
discovered that it is Achaean Greek.

Crete is associated with Zeus, Minos and the labyrinth, and Sir Arthur Evans, the archaeologist – or was, before it was taken over by tour operators. The main Minoan deity was the Great Goddess, whose emblems were the *labrys* (the double axe) and the horns of the sacred bull, universally regarded as a symbol of fertility but in Crete additionally a symbol of earthquakes. The bull-leap performed in her honour was much more dangerous than any bullfight, for the youth or maiden would literally take the bull by the horns, and somersault over its back.

The bull theme continued even after the mainland Dorians had invaded the island and dethroned the Great Goddess. In the myth of Europa, Zeus, in the form of a bull, abducted her (see *Mainland/Thebes*), and carried her off to Crete, where she gave birth to the first Minos (whose name was taken by the rulers of Minoan Crete) and his brothers, Radamanthys and Sarpedon. The first two later became judges in Hades. Zeus probably felt very much at home in Crete, where in the generally accepted version of the myth he had spent his childhood in the cave on **Mt. Dikti** (see under *Crete/Nomos Lassithi*), under the care of the goat Amalthea (see *Mythology* in *Culture, history and background*). He was also reputed to retire to the islet of Dia, which lies offshore, opposite **Iraklio**, whenever Hera's tantrums made life on Olympos unbearable.

The bovine connection was resumed in the story of the wife of the last Minos, lascivious Pasiphae (daughter of Ilios, the Sun, and the nymph Crete, after whom the island is named) who fell victim to the family vice and developed an uncontrollable lust for a bull. For once, her passion was not inspired by a god lurking in animal form, and the desired union with the real-life bull was thus only consummated when Pasiphae concealed herself in a hollow wooden cow, made by the greatest craftsman of the day, Daedalos, a fugitive from Athens who was wanted there for murder. The fruit of this unusual mating was the Minotaur, the man-bull, who the surprisingly forbearing Minos put out of sight if not out of mind in a labyrinth, once again constructed by the ingenious Daedalos. The labyrinth was built near the sign of the *labrys*, under which the bull-leaping was performed. Gory speculations about the fate of the seven youths and seven maidens who were exacted annually by the Minoans as a strange blood tribute from Athens is explained by the sport they were required to perform; for although bulls are not man-eating, the bull-leaping was so dangerous that they were just as unlikely to last out the year.

Athenian Prince Theseus volunteered for the yearly tribute, slew the Minotaur and escaped from the labyrinth along a silk thread supplied by Minos' daughter Ariadne. Theseus quickly tired of her, however, then abandoned her on *Naxos*, and returned to Athens, but forgot to change the black sails on his ship to white, as he had promised his father, Aegeus, that he would do if the mission to Crete should be successful. Believing his son to be dead, Aegeus in despair committed suicide by his sensational leap off the Acropolis (see *Aegean Islands*).

The major Minoan eras are the Early Minoan (2600–1900BC) and Middle Minoan (1900–1550BC), the latter subdivided by the terrible earthquake around 1700 into the Palace Periods I and II. The discovery that Linear B is Achaean Greek gives substance to the legend that an Achaean chief (Theseus, returning in revenge) invaded the world's first maritime empire in about 1550BC. The usurper assumed the title of Minos which was continued by his successors until the total destruction which, it is thought, was caused 100yr later by a tidal wave and earthquake, following the explosion of the *Thira* volcano.

Feudal Mycenae literally rose from the ashes of the Minoan Empire. King Idomeneus, no longer entitled Minos, led a contingent against Troy from "Crete of the hundred cities", in the words of Homer. The political fragmentation of the island which this description suggests was accompanied by a steep artistic decline. In about 1100BC the Dorians drove the surviving Eteocretans (pure Cretans) into the inaccessible mountains. After its emergence from the ensuing Dark Ages, Crete remained politically too divided to play any significant part in classical Greece. But its mercenary soldiers were highly valued and the 6thC BC Law Code of **Gortys** (see under *Crete/Nomos Iraklio*) suggests a developed society.

Crete, having now become a base for pirates, was conquered by the Romans in 66BC and Gortys became the capital of the province of Crete and Cyrenaica. St Paul and his disciple St Titus converted it to Christianity and numerous large churches were constructed during the early Byzantine period. In AD823 Crete was occupied by the Saracens. The swift Moslem galleys terrorized the western Mediterranean until the Byzantine reconquest of the island by the Emperor Nikephoros Phokas in 961.

Following the Fourth Crusade, the Venetians ruled the island from 1210–1669, constructing mighty fortifications and building many churches. They encouraged the Cretan school of painting which left its mark on the work of Domenikos Theotokopoulos (El Greco) and was continued, after Crete fell to the Turks, by the Ionian school (see *Ionian Islands*). During this fertile period Kornaros wrote the epic romance *Erotokritos*.

After the heroic 24yr defence by the Venetians (1646–69) under Admiral Morosini (see also **Acropolis** in *Athens/Sights* and **Town Hall** in *Corfu/The town*) and the unsuccessful intervention of a relief squadron sent by Louis XIV, Iraklio finally fell to the Grand Vizier Ahmed Kiuprilu in 1669. Under Turkish rule of the island there were to be some 400 uprisings culminating in the war between Greece and Turkey in 1897, as a result of which Crete became autonomous under Prince George of Greece the following year. Union with Greece was accomplished in 1913. In 1941, Greek, British and ANZAC forces fought bravely but in vain against the German airborne invasion. The island was liberated in 1944.

Greece's largest island, Crete, is almost equidistant from the Peloponnese, the Cyclades, Rhodes and Libya. There are three towering mountain ranges, Dikti, 2,148m (7,045ft) in the E, Idi, 2,456m (8,060ft) in the centre, and Lefka Ori, 2,452m (8,045ft) in the w. Three of the four administrative regions into which the mountains divide the island are named after their respective main town; from E to w: **Nomos Iraklio**, **Nomos Rethymno** and **Nomos Hania**. The fourth, most eastern, administrative region, **Nomos Lassithi**, has **Agios Nikolaos** as its main town. All the major tourist complexes are on the N coast, connected by an excellent coastal road. There are several N–S roads, and others leading to important points in the mountains, but the southern E–W road only occasionally touches the less developed s coast and comes to a halt before the barrier of the Lefka Ori massif.

Small but fertile plains produce mainly olive oil, oranges and potatoes, but although tourism is by far the biggest industry,

much of the island has preserved its distinctive and attractive character.

The sights of Crete are arranged alphabetically after the main town, within the four administrative regions (see above) as a reasonable choice among several equally possible geographical divisions.

Events: There are strictly local festivals relating to agricultural products (oranges, raisins, wine, chestnuts), often in remote areas. The only significant one for tourists is the Wine Festival, July, in Rethymno.

Nomós Lassíthi
This has the most varied scenery of the four regions, ranging from palm trees on the E coast at **Vaï** to the hidden highland (to the w below Mt. Dikti, on the way to **Psihro**) where apples, potatoes and wheat are grown.

All distances given are from the main town, **Agios Nikolaos**.

Ágios Nikólaos
Map **13** *M10. 86km (54 miles) E of Iraklio, on the N coast. Port: Ferries to the Dodecanese. Population: summer, 10,000; winter, less than 5,000.*

A white-painted town on the w coast of **Mirabello Bay**, Agios Nikolaos is now overwhelmed by tourism and has rather lost the charm for which it was once famed. But the small, deep lake in the town centre (connected since 1907 to the sea), the brightly-coloured fishing boats in the small port, and the numerous open-air restaurants and cafes still give it a certain quaintness.

The **museum** (▨ *standard opening times*) contains finds from the region's archaeological sites. These include the islets of **Mohlos** and **Psira**, easily reached from the town by motorboat.

The many handicrafts and souvenir shops, especially those in the large hotels, are slightly more expensive than in other towns in the region. There are plenty of discotheques, both in the hotels and elsewhere.

Hotels

There are a large number of moderately-priced to cheap hotels in town, which are however at least 0.8km (0.5 mile) from the nearest small beach. The following are a selection.

Akratos (☎ 22–721/5 ▯ ▭ 31 ⬥ ⬜ ⇌ ☼ *on roof*); **Du Lac** (☎ 22–711/2 ▯ ▭ 74 ⬥); **Panorama** (☎ 28–890 ▯ ▭ 26 ⬥); **Rea** (☎ 28–321/3 ☏ 261109 ▥ ▭ 113 ⬥ ⬜ ⇌ ◉ ▯) is closest to the beach.

There are also numerous hotels within about 1.5km (less than 1 mile) of town, on their own beaches, including the following: **Ariadni Beach** (☎ 22–741/4 ☏ 262196 ▥ ▭ 76 ⬥ ⬜ ⇌ ◉ ◎ VISA ⌂ ⬥), bungalows; **Coral** (☎ 28–363/7 ☏ 262165 ▥ ▭ 170 ⬥ ⬜ ⇌ CB ◎ VISA ⌂ ⬥); **Minos Beach** ▥ (☎ 22–345/9 ☏ 262214 ▥ 118 ▭ ⬥ ⬜ ⇌ AE CB ◉ ◎ VISA ⌂ ▯ ☼ ⬥ ⬥ ℘), bungalows; **Mirabello** (☎ 28–400/5 ☏ 262166 ▥ ▭ 174 ▥ ⬥ ⬜ ⇌ AE CB ◉ ◎ VISA ☼ ⬥ ⬥ ℘); **Mirabello Village** ▥ ☎ 28–400/5 ☏ 262–166 ▥ ▭ 131 ⬥ ⬜ ⇌ AE CB ◉ ◎ VISA ▯ ⌂ ⬥ ⇌ ⬥ ℘), hotel and bungalows.

▣ All serving good fish and expensive by local standards, and all having ⬜ ⬥ ⬥ AE CB ◉ ◎ VISA); **Cretan** (*Iosif Koundourou 12* ▥); **Vassilis** (*Iosif Koundourou 16* ▥).

Very similar are **Avra** and **Rififi** (*on Akti Koundourou*).

Dikti, Cave of, (*Díkteo Ándro*)   See **Psihro** in *Crete/Nomos Lassíthi*.

Dreros   See **Elounda** in *Crete/Nomos Lassíthi*.

Elóunda

Map 13M10. 8km (5 miles) N, on the coast road.

A modern village on the w coast of the Mirabello Bay. Opposite it lies the island of **Spinalonga** ☆ separated from the promontory by a canal constructed by the Venetians, who in 1579 built there a large **fortress** ▥ which held out against the Turks until 1715. The ruins, still very impressive, served as a leper colony from 1912–52.

5km (3 miles) w lie the ruins of ancient **Dreros** with walls, an agora and a 7thC BC Temple of Apollo, in which the oldest Greek hammered-bronze statue was found.

Hotels

Elounda Beach ▥
☎ 41–412/3 ☏ 262192 ▥ ▭ 301 ⬥ ⬜ ⇌ AE CB ◉ ◎ VISA
Deservedly ranked among the best hotels in Greece, particularly for its tasteful harmonization with its superb environment.
▯ ⌂ ☼ ⇌ ⬥ ℘ ◉

▣ **Aristea** (☎ 41–300/5 ▯ ▭ 37 ⬥ ⬥ ℘); **Astir Palace Elounda** ▥ (☎ 41–580/5 ☏ 262215 ▥ ▭ 297 ▤ ⬥ ⬜ ⇌ AE CB ◉ ◎ VISA ▯ ⌂ ⬥ ⚓ ⬥), hotel and bungalows.

▣ **New Elounda** (▥ ⬜ ⬥ AE CB ◉ ◎ VISA).

Góurnia ☆
Map 13M10. 12km (7.5 miles) SE.

On a hill overlooking Mirabello Bay are the best-preserved **remains of a Minoan town** of about 1600BC in Crete. The smallness of the workshop and domestic quarters are remarkable. Vases and tools are in the **museum** in **Iraklio**.

Ierápetra
Map 13M10. 36km (22.5 miles) s, on the s coast road.
Population: 3,500.

The largest town on the s coast, on a fine, sandy beach, was founded by the Dorians. It became a prosperous town in the Hellenistic and Roman eras, and the Venetians built a strong **fortress** here. Among the Roman finds in the **museum** (⛨ *standard opening times*) is a superb sarcophagus.

At **Myrtos**, just 16km (10 miles) w, the British School of Archaeology in 1967–68 excavated an **Early Minoan settlement**, dating from 2500–2100BC.

Ⓗ Atlantis (☎ 28–555/7 📟 🛏 69 ▦ 🖾 🏠 ⇌ 🐟); Petra Mare (☎ 23–341/8 ▐▐▐ 220 ▦ 🚗 🏠 ⇌ AE CB ⊕ ⊙ VISA 🖾 ⚓ on roof ⇌ 🐟 ●).

Ítanos   See **Sitia** in *Crete/Nomos Lassithi.*

Kritsá ☆
Map 13M10. Inland, 36km (22.5 miles) sw.

Kritsa is described as an 'authentic mountain village'; its altitude, 580m (1,903ft), and position provide a splendid view over Mirabello Bay. About 1.5km (less than 1 mile) beyond is the **Church of Panagia Kera** ✝ with fine 14th and 15thC frescoes.

Myrtós   See **Ierapetra** in *Crete/Nomos Lassithi.*

Neapolis   See **Psihro** in *Crete/Nomos Lassithi.*

Paleokástro   See **Sitia** in *Crete/Nomos Lassithi.*

Pressós (*Praisos*)   See **Sitia** in *Crete/Nomos Lassithi.*

Psihró ☆
Map 13M9. Inland, 49km (31 miles) w.

Just before you reach the small town of **Neapolis**, where the schismatic Pope Alexander V was born in 1340, a road winds up into the Lassithi highland. The fertile plateau is irrigated by 6,000 white-sailed **water pumps** – an incredible sight in summer, though there are now 4,000 less than in the 15thC when the Venetians first introduced this practical system.

The road ends at a tourist pavilion (🍴) above the Cave of Dikti. There is a road down through **Tzermiado** (the only one of the 18 highland villages having an acceptable hotel) NW to either **Malia** or **Gouves**.

Sights

Cave of Dikti (*Díkteo Ándro*) ☆
⛨ 𝕏 🚗 *Standard opening times.*

A guide is needed for the rather difficult descent into the cave where Zeus was reared (see *Mythology* in *Culture, history and background*). It was excavated by the British School of Archaeology; the remains, dating from Middle Minoan to archaic times, are in the **museum** at **Iraklio**.

Sitía

*Map **13***M10. 69km (43 miles) E, on the coast road.
Population: 2,100.
Crete's easternmost port has pleasant seaside tavernas and a
sandy beach. It can be reached either on the N coast road along
Mirabello Bay, or from **Ierapetra** on the S coast.

Nearby sights and places of interest
By the inland road from Ierapetra, 16km (10 miles) s of Sitia, lies **Pressos**
(ancient Praisos), the capital of the Eteocretans, the triple acropolis of
which was destroyed in 155BC.

Taking the coast road E from Sitia, then branching left along the
peninsula at the NE extremity of Crete, leads to the 16thC fortified
Monastery of Toplou, 16km (10 miles) from Sitia. It contains a
beautiful *ikon, Lord, Thou Art Great*, painted in 1770 by Ioannis
Kornaros.

The road crosses the peninsula to the E coast, where the romantic
beach of **Vaï** is fringed by Europe's only natural palm grove (R ☂ *both
summer only*).

Almost at the tip of Cape Sideros, 6.4km (4miles) N of Vaï, are the
Hellenistic and Roman ruins of **Itanos**, built on the site of an Early
Minoan settlement.

8km (5 miles) s at **Paleokastro** is a **Late Minoan settlement**
overlooking the sea. Still further s, the road passes through the
picturesque village of **Zakros** and reaches **Kato Zakros**, 10km (6 miles)
from Paleokastro. Here the remains of a luxurious 17thC BC **Minoan
palace** ☆ were discovered in 1961 below a banana plantation. Of
traditional plan, it was the fourth largest palace and probably an
important naval base of the Minoan maritime empire.

Ⓗ **Itanos** (☎ 22–146 ▯☐ ▭ 72 ▦ 🚗 🏠 🚐 🛬), 45m (50yd) from
the beach; **Sitian Beach** (☎ 28–821/4 ⓣ 262102 ▥▥▥ ▭ 162 🚗 🏠 🚐
🅐🅔 🅒🅑 ⊕ 🅒🅓 🆅🆂🅰 🗗 ⇌ 🔥 ♨ ⦿), both in Sitia.

Spinalonga See **Elounda** in *Crete/Nomos Lassithi*.

Toplóu See **Sitia** in *Crete/Nomos Lassithi*.

Tzermiádo See **Psihro** in *Crete/Nomos Lassithi*.

Vaï See **Sitia** in *Crete/Nomos Lassithi*.

Zákros See **Sitia** in *Crete/Nomos Lassithi*.

Nomós Iráklio

The region contains the most important Minoan sites, at
Knossos, **Phaestos** and **Malia**; **Iraklio**, commercial centre of
the island; and numerous beach resorts.
All distances given are from **Iraklio**.

Iráklio (*Herakleion*) ☆
*Map **13***M9. On the N coast of Crete. Airport ☎ 282–025.
*Getting there: See Crete. Post office: Daskalyannis Sq.
Population: 60,000* ℹ *GNTO. Xanthoudidou 1* ☎ 222–487/8.
Crete's largest town and port has a singularly uninviting
waterfront, with hardly a taverna or cafe to be found. Only the
restored **fortress** ▥ on the jetty bears witness to the epic siege
from 1646–69, when 120,000 assailants fell before the mighty
ramparts that still surround the town. On the landward side it is
additionally protected by a moat (the *khandaq*) which the
Saracens dug in the 9thC. Possibly the port of Knossos, it was
still in use as a port in Byzantine times, but was renamed after
the Byzantine Emperor Heraklios. The Venetians changed the

Arabic form *Khandaq* into Candia, which was the Cretan
capital until the Turkish Pasha moved the capital to **Hania** in
1850. After Crete became independent it was rechristened
Iraklio and became the main commercial centre of the island.

It is the least attractive of the four main cities but possesses an
outstanding **Archaeological Museum** on the main Eleftherias
Sq. The **Venetian ramparts**, 4.3km (over 2.5 miles) long and
up to 29m (95ft) thick, are reinforced by 12 bastions, one of
which contains the **tomb of Nikos Kazantzakis**, modern
Greece's best-known author. More Venetian walls are to be seen
in the old port above the vaulted 16thC **Arsenals**.

The other Venetian buildings of note are on or near the small
central Venizelou Sq. They include the reconstructed copy of the
Renaissance **Loggia** 🏛 that was destroyed during World
War II, the 13thC **San Marco Basilica** 🏛 now an exhibition
hall, and the Baroque marble **Lion Fountain**, named after an
earlier Morosini, uncle of the famous defender of the city.
Much-restored **Agios Titos** now houses the head of the saint
which was returned in 1966 from St Mark's in Venice.

Off Kalokairinou, the long main shopping street, and next to
the large 19thC **Metropolis of Agios Minas**, the 16thC church
of **Agia Ekaterini** possesses six **ikons** by the chief exponent of
the Cretan school of painting, Mihalis Damaskinos, the first
teacher of Domenikos Theotokopoulos (El Greco).

Numerous discotheques on and near Eleftherias Sq. are
interspersed with handicrafts and jewellery shops. The nearest
beach, which gets very crowded in summer, is at **Karteros**,
5km (3 miles) to the E.

Sights and places of interest
Archaeological Museum ★
Eleftherias Sq. ☎ *282–305* 🗺 *Standard opening times.*
The museum houses the Minoan finds of Sir Arthur Evans and Frederick
Halbherr, constantly enriched from current excavations on old and new
sites, which comprise a uniquely complete collection of a whole
civilization.

The work of the potters illustrates superbly the sequence of
development and rise to splendid heights, followed by sensuous
decadence and final decline. There are examples of Proto-Geometric and
Geometric ceramics, vases in the Oriental, Polychrome, Marine or Floral
styles, and the magnificent ware named *Kamarés* after the cave where the
first delicate specimens were discovered. The **Phaestos disc** has circular
hieroglyphic inscriptions which are now also among those scripts
claimed to be Achaean Greek. There are statuettes of gods, humans and
animals, ranging from the primitive through the perfection of simplicity
to the elaborate.

Throughout the museum it is easy to follow the portrayals of the Great
Goddess in all shapes, sizes and materials. The second favourite subject
is the bulls, who played such a legendary part in the love life of the
Minoan royal family and in the sacred sport of bull-leaping. The latter,
alas not the former, is depicted in the magnificent **frescoes** on the upper
floor. There are ritual processions, scenes from the bull-ring, and
amazingly impressionistic court ladies, whose puffed sleeves framing
bare breasts over blue-flounced skirts earned them the name 'Les
Parisiennes', and there is the graceful *Prince of the Lilies*, followed by
large-eyed, broad-shouldered, slim-waisted youths.

There is also jewellery of every kind and description: necklaces on gold
and rock crystal, silver and alabaster vases, jasper and mother-of-pearl
goblets, delicately-carved ivories, and the sealstones with the Linear
Scripts that first attracted Evans' attention. The **painted sarcophagus
from Agia Triada** (see **Phaestos** in *Crete/Nomos Iraklio*) deserves
special mention.

Later civilizations are also represented, especially remains from
Roman **Gortys**.

Historical Museum

Akti Makariou. On the waterfront 🖭 *Standard opening times.*
After the treasures of the **Archaeological Museum**, the exhibits in the
Historical Museum, from the Byzantine, Venetian and Turkish periods
of Cretan history, are bound to be something of an anti-climax, and not
even the collections of folk art, local costumes, woven fabrics and
embroideries, and a **replica of a traditional Greek interior of a peasant
home** quite manage to dispel this impression.

Nearby sights

The **Vrondissi Convent**, which is passed on the way to **Valsamonero**,
47km (29 miles) sw of Iraklio on the slopes of Mt. Idi, and the **Church of
Agios Fanourios** ✝ in the tiny village, both have frescoes often attributed
to El Greco, but which are in fact 15thC. El Greco was born in 1541 in the
village of **Fodele** near the N coast, 24km (15 miles) w from Iraklio.

In 1978 the British School of Archaeology uncovered an **antique
cemetery** used from 1400BC–AD500, at the Cretan University's Medical
School along the road to Knossos.

Hotels

Asterion (*Ikarou Ave.* ☎ 224–981/3 [ ] ☐ 60 ☎ 🏠 ☰); **Astoria**
(*Eleftherias Sq. 5* ☎ 286–462/5 ☎262152 [ ] ☐ 141 ☐ ☎ ☎
AE CB ⊕ ⊙ VISA 🗠 ☎ ⊙) is on the noisy main square, so back rooms
are preferable; **Atlantis** (*Miravellou 2* ☎ 288–241/5 ☎262163 [ ]
164 ☐ 🏠 ☎ AE CB ⊕ ⊙ VISA 🗠 ☎ ⊻ *on roof* ☎ 💬);
Daedalos (*Daedalou 15* ☎ 224–391 [ ] ☐ 60 ☎ 🏠); **Galaxy**
(*Dimokratias 67* ☎ 236–421/6 ☎262301 [ ] ☐ 148 ☐ ☎ ☎
AE CB ⊕ ⊙ VISA 🗠 ☎); **Mediterranean** (*Smyrnis 1* ☎ 289–331/5
☎262115 [ ] ☐ 55 ☐ ☎ ☎ ⊕ ⊕ ⊙ VISA 🗠 ⊻ *on roof*).

Restaurants

Open-air restaurants in the pedestrianized zone on Venizelou Sq. and
Daedalou are numerous, inexpensive and undistinguished; among these
is the **Caprice** (AE CB ⊕ ⊙ VISA). **Maxim Fish Tavern** (*Koroneou 5*)
and **Ta Psaria** (*opposite the sea fortress*) serve fresh fish.

Beach resort hotels near Iráklio

Many hotels in this main tourist region of Crete are listed under
the individual towns, villages and sites. In addition, hotels are
available in a number of resorts, some of which are listed below.

Agia Pelagia (*16km (10 miles) NW,
just off the coast road to the w*)
Capsis Beach (☎ 233–395/7
☎262204 [ ] ☐ 509 ☐ ☎ 🏠
☰ ☎ CB ⊕ ⊙ VISA 🗠 ☎
☎ ⊙), hotel and bungalows.
Amoudara (*8km (5 miles) w, on the
coast road*)
Creta Beach (☎ 286–301/5
☎216896 [ ] ☐ 141 ☐ ☎ 🏠
☰ ☎ CB ⊕ ⊙ VISA 🗠 ☎
☎).
Gouves (*16km (10 miles) E, on the
coast road*)
Aphrodite (☎ 41–271/4
☎262321 [ ] ☐ 166 ☎ 🏠 ☎
☰ ☎ ☎ ☎; **Candia Beach**
(☎ 41–361/5 ☎262182 [ ]
197 ☎ ☎ ⊕ ⊕ ⊙ VISA 🗠 ☎
☎ ☎ ⊙); **Marina** (☎ 41–361/5
☎252182 [ ] ☐ 250 ☐ ☎
☰ ☎ CB ⊕ ⊙ VISA 🗠 ☎ ☎
☎ ⊙).

Hani Kokkini (*12km (7.5 miles) E,
on the coast road*)
Arina Sand (☎ 761–350 [ ] ☐
233 ☐ ☎ 🏠 ☎ AE CB ⊕ ⊙
VISA 🗠 ☎ ☎ ⊙), hotel and
bungalows; **Danaë** (☎ 761–375
[ ] ☐ 18 ☎ ☎ ☎ ☎);
Knossos Beach (☎ 288–450
☎262206 [ ] ☐ 106 ☎ ☎
AE CB ⊕ ⊙ VISA 🗠 ☎ ☎ ⊙),
hotel and bungalows.
Limenas Hersonissou (*25km (16
miles) E, on the coast road*)
Belvedere (☎ 22–010/5 [ ] ☐
296 ☎ 🗠 ☎ ☎ ☎ ⊙), hotel
and bungalows, 230m (250yd)
from the beach; **Creta Maris** 🏨
(☎ 22–115/130 ☎262233 [ ] ☐
516 ☐ ☎ ☎ 🏠 ☎ ☎ AE CB ⊕ ⊙
VISA 🗠 ☎ ☎ ⊙), hotel
and bungalows; **Eva** (☎ 22–090/2
[ ] ☐ 33 ☐ ☎ ☎ 🏠 ☎ 🗠 ☎
⊙); **Glaros** (☎ 22–106 [ ] ☐ 94

🏠); **Nora** (☎ *22–271/5* 🏳️ 🔲
181 🍴 🏠 ⇌ 🖼 ⇄ 🏠 ⅋ ⭕).
Linoperamata (*8km (5 miles) w, on
the coast road*)
Apolonnia Beach (☎ *223–766/9*
🅿️ *262224* 🏳️ 🔲 *261* 🍴 🏠
⇌ 🏠 ⅋ ⭕), hotel and
bungalows; **Zeus Beach**
(☎ *223–761/5* 🏳️ 🔲 *246* 🍴

🍴 🏠 ⇌ 🖼 🅒🅑 🕀 🔲 🎫 🖼
⚓ *on roof* ⇄ ⅋).
Stalida (*30km (19 miles) E, on the
coast road*)
Anthousa Beach (☎ *31–380/2*
🏳️ 🔲 *167* 🍴 🏠 🏠 🅒🅑
🕀 🔲 🎫 🖼 ⇄ 🏠 ⅋); **Blue
Sea** (☎ *31–371/4* 🏳️ 🔲 *197* 🏠
⇌ 🕀 🔲 🎫 🖼 ⇄ 🏠 ⭕).

Agía Triáda   See **Phaestos** in *Crete/Nomos Iraklio*.

Arhanés   See **Knossos** in *Crete/Nomos Iraklio*.

Fodéle   See **Iraklio** in *Crete/Nomos Iraklio*.

Górtys ☆
Map 13M9. Inland, 45km (28 miles) sw.

Inhabited from Neolithic times, Gortys wrested supremacy
from post-Minoan Knossos in the 6thC BC. At about this time,
the famous **Law Code** was written on marble slabs in the Doric
boustróphedon, named after the ox plough because the lines run
alternately left or right. The Romans incorporated this in the
circular portico of the 1stC BC **Odeon**.

By this time Gortys was capital of the Roman province of
Crete and Cyrenaica. Its main sanctuary, the 6thC BC **Temple
of Pythian Apollo**, enlarged during the Hellenistic era, had
been divided by the Romans into three colonnaded naves. The
Romans also built a **Temple of Isis and Serapis**, a **theatre**, an
aqueduct, **baths** and the **Praetorium**, the governor's residence.

The ubiquitous St Paul installed Agios Titos as the city's first
bishop. The 6thC **Basilica**, named after him, contained his
remains until its destruction by the Saracens in 823.

Karterós
Map 13M9. 8km (5 miles) E, on the coast road.

Important frescoes were found here in a villa from Amnissos,
which some think was the site of the Minoan port of **Knossos**
(the alternative theory supports **Iraklio**) from which Idomeneus
sailed for Troy. Modern Karteros has a long, sandy beach.

Ⓗ **Minoa Palace** (☎ *225–333/6* 🏳️ 🔲 *124* 🍴 🏠 🏠 ⇌ 🖼 🅒🅑
🕀 🔲 🎫 🖼 ⇄ 🏠); **Xenia** (☎ *281–841* 🏳️ 🔲 *42* 🚗 🏠 ⇌ 🖼
🅒🅑 🕀 🔲 🎫 🖼 🏠).

Knossós 🏛 ★
*Map 13M9. Inland, 5km (3 miles) SE. Getting there: By bus,
every 15min from Iraklio harbour* 🚌 Ⓡ ✗ *for organized tours*
🅿️ 🍴 *Standard opening times.*

As at *Mycenae* (see *Mainland A–Z*), it was belief in the
historical basis of Homer that led the great German
archaeologist Schliemann to the then unimpressive mound at
Knossos, shut off from the sea by low hills. But the greed of the
Turkish authorities was greater even than Schliemann's
financial means, and it was only in 1899, after Crete became
autonomous, that Arthur Evans was able to begin excavations.

The palace
The first palace, dating from about 1900BC, was destroyed by earthquake
some 200yr later, and superseded by a more elaborate four-storeyed
complex of halls, temples, rooms, corridors and stairways that might

173

indeed have seemed a sinister labyrinth to the simple Achaeans. Wooden columns, tapering downwards, and a timber framework are not the most solid of building materials, however, especially when charred by fire. When excavated, only rubble supported the remaining delicate fabric, so that concrete had to be used to preserve the **grand stairway** and the **throne room**, complete with its **gypsum throne**, as well as the **royal apartments** with their spacious bathrooms. Light-wells gave adequate illumination while shutting out the summer heat. The water supply from the hills was carried by pipes across a valley, and the system of drainage remained unequalled in the West until the Roman development of plumbing.

Sir Arthur Evans has been condemned by professional archaeologists for carrying out a partial reconstruction, on which he spent 250,000 British sovereigns. Yet to the layman there seems rather too little than too much restoration: the red, like congealing blood, and the intense blue and green stand badly in need of a new coat of paint.

Nearby sights

In 1979 the British School of Archaeology discovered, in a burnt-out 15thC BC house at Knossos, a jumbled, disarticulated pile of bones belonging to children aged between 8–15 which show knife marks comparable to those a butcher might make. This could be evidence of cannibalism, but at the least it confirms the discovery of human sacrifice in 17thC BC **Arhanes**, 10km (6 miles), further S, where many Minoan remains have been found among the extensive vineyards of this very attractive village.

4km (2.5 miles) further on, at **Vathypetro**, there are remains of a spacious **Minoan villa** which was equipped with wine and oil presses, weaving looms and a pottery furnace, of which some traces still remain.

Kommós See **Phaestos** in *Crete/Nomos Iraklio*.

Mália
Map 13M9. 35km (22 miles) E, on the coast road.
The justification for Evans' restoration of **Knossos** may be appreciated at this much lovelier site, where only some low walls mark the presence of a **Minoan palace**. Built on the site of the first palace which was destroyed by the earthquake of 1700BC, this was itself destroyed in 1450BC.

One of the finest beaches in all Crete is crowded with vast holiday complexes.

Ikaros Village (☎ 31–267/9 📞262191 ▥▥ 🛏 179 🚗 🏠 🚘 AE CB 🔟 ⓥ VISA 🗚 🏊 🎾) is the German idea of what a Cretan village is supposed to look like; Kernos Beach (☎ 31–421/5 📞262255 ▥▥ 🛏 246 🍴 🚗 🏠 🚘 AE CB 🔟 ⓙ 🔟 VISA 🗚 🏊 🎾 ⚓ ●); Malia Beach (☎ 31–301/3 📞 🛏 168 🚗 🏠 🚘 AE CB 🔟 🏊 🎾); Sirens Beach (☎ 31–321/5 📞262194 ▥▥ 🛏 228 🍴 🚗 🏠 🚘 AE CB 🔟 🔟 VISA 🗚 🏊 🎾 ⚓ ●); Sofokles Beach (☎ 31–348 ▯▯ 🛏 44 🚗 🏊).

Mátala
Map 12M8. 70km (44 miles) SW, on the S coast.
The ancient **tomb caves** (no longer a dormitory for hippies) dominate the superb beach at this thriving S coast village.

Matala Bay (☎ 22–100 ▯▯ 🛏 55 🚗 🏠 🚘 ⚓ ●).

Phaestos (*Festós*) ★
Map 12M8. 64km (40 miles) SW, off the S coast road 🍴 💻 🚗 Standard opening times.
Built on the levelled summit of a hill and following the layout of **Knossos** but on a smaller scale, the situation of this palace below Mt. Idi at the edge of the wide Messara plain is infinitely more attractive.

The palace

The Italian Frederic Halbherr started excavations some years before Evans for, unlike Knossos, Phaestos had never been forgotten. In place of the three-storey-high second palace, destroyed like all the others in the disaster of 1450BC, a **temple** was erected in classical times, dedicated to Rea as successor to the Great Goddess. Hellenistic houses overlooked the **eight-tiered stand** from which the bull-leaping was watched. A broad **staircase** led to the **central court**, the great **propylaea**, the **banqueting hall** and the **royal apartments**, traces of all of which can be seen.

Nearby sights

Agia Triada, just 3.2km (2 miles) NW, is named after a small Venetian church near to the small **palace**. The wealth of the jewellery and vases discovered suggest it may have been the summer residence of Minos himself. It continued as an important settlement in Late Minoan times.

At **Kommos**, 4km (2.5 miles) S, American and Canadian archaeologists since 1979 have been excavating the only Minoan port on the S coast. It was connected by a paved road to the two palaces at Knossos and Phaestos. A Proto-Geometric temple, probably unique, was succeeded here by an archaic and Hellenistic temple.

Ⓗ and Ⓡ A simple guesthouse at Phaestos offers two rooms without showers, for those who insist on ruins in the moonlight.

Valsamonéro See **Iraklio** in *Crete/Nomos Iraklio*.

Vathypétro See **Knossos** in *Crete/Nomos Iraklio*.

Nomós Réthymno

This region is the least popular with visitors and so has best preserved its authentic flavour. It is dominated by the island's highest mountain chain, Idi – ancient Mt. Ida.

All distances given are from the main town, **Rethymno**.

Réthymno

Map **12***M8. 79km (49 miles) W of Iraklio, on the N coast.*
Population: 8,000.

The town lies directly on a vast, sandy beach at the centre of a shallow bay. Minarets still rise over the Venetian houses near an elegant 17thC fountain. An imposing gate leads into the 16thC fortress, the **Fortezza** Ⅲ ☆ on a hill once occupied by the acropolis of antique Rithymna. The **museum** (🖼 *standard opening times*) in the late-16thC **Loggia** contains an interesting coin collection, besides the archaeological finds.

The annual Wine Festival (see events in introduction to *Crete*) is held in the second half of each July, under the tall trees in the Municipal Park.

Ⓗ **Braskos** (☎ 23–721/3 ⅢⅢ 🛏 78 ← ✏ ⌁ *on roof* 🅿 ●), 460m (500yd) from the beach; **Ideon** (☎ 28–667/9 ⅢⅢ 🛏 71 ← 🛆 🚬 Ⓔ ⬤ [VISA] ✏ 🅿), 45m (50yd) from the beach.

Agía Galíni

Map **12***M8. 61m (38 miles) SE, on the S coast road.*

As this is one of the few points where the E–W road along the S coast touches the Libyan Sea, this small fishing village has become overcrowded. Seafront tavernas abound.

A better, less crowded beach is to be found at **Plakias**, 35km (22 miles) from Rethymno on the S coast, NW of Agia Galini.

Ⓗ There are rooms to let in every house in Agia Galini, and numerous small, inexpensive hotels all providing only bed and breakfast. Within easy walking distance from the beach are the **Astoria** and **Candia**.

Arkádi

Map 12M8. Inland, 23km (14 miles) to the SE.

The monastery 🏛 ✝ ☆ dates from the 17thC, apart from the rustic 16thC **facade of a Venetian Baroque church**. On Nov 9, 1866, after a short siege, the Turks had just begun to enter the monastery when the Abbot Gabriel blew up one wing of the building, thereby killing 829 defenders and assailants. This is regarded as a national shrine at which annual celebrations of this historic event take place.

Pánormos

Map 12M8. 22km (14 miles) NE, on the coast road.

A 13thC **castle** stands on the mouth of the Milopotamos river, and there are ruins of a 5thC **basilica**. 3km (2 miles) to the S is the **Melidoni stalactite cave** (🏛 *standard opening times*).

⎣H⎦ **Lavris** (☎ 51–226/7 ▮▯▮ ▭ 28 ⇌ 🏠 ⇌ 🏊 ⇌ 🀫 ✤ ✿ ◑).

Plakiás   See **Agia Galini** in *Crete/Nomos Rethymno.*

Plataniás

Map 12M7. 8km (5 miles) E, on the coast road.

⎣H⎦ **El Greco** (☎ 71–281 🆅 291113 ▮▯▮ ▭ 310 🍴 ⇌ 🏠 ⇌ AE CB ⊕ ⊙ 🆅🆂🅰 🗗 ⇌ 🀫 ✿ ◑), hotel and bungalows; **Orion** (☎ 71–471 ▭ 73 ⇌ 🏠 ⇌ 🀫 on roof ✤), 140m (150yd) from the beach; **Rithymna** (☎ 29–491 🆅 291112 ▮▯▮ ▭ 392 🍴 ⇌ 🏠 ⇌ AE CB ⊕ ⊙ 🆅🆂🅰 🗗 ⇌ 🀫 ✿ ◑), hotel and bungalows.

Nomós Haniá

Some visitors might take comfort from the fact that this western part of Crete is slowly rising, while the eastern part is sinking – although the Lefka Ori (White Mountains), largest in extent of the Cretan mountain ranges, is still some way short of Mt. Idi, the island's highest peak. The roads E and W of the White Mountains lead through spectacular scenery to the loveliest, wildest and least developed parts of the S coast.

All distances given are from the main town, **Hania**.

Haniá

Map 12L7. 136km (85 miles) NW of Iraklio, on the N coast. Airport: At Akrotiri, 16km (10 miles) NE ☎ 63–264; flights to Athens. Port: At Souda, 7km (4 miles) SE; ferries to Piraeus. Population: 40,000 ℹ GNTO, Akti Tombazi 6 ☎ 26–426.

In 1252 the Venetians built a **fortress** 🏛 on the acropolis of ancient Kydonia, and some 300yr later surrounded the town below with ramparts and a moat. This proved of little avail against the Turks, who made their entry in 1645. To the tall, elegant houses in the narrow lanes behind the **old port** ☆ – Crete's most charming – the Turks added some mosques and fountains.

After the capital was transferred here from **Iraklio** in 1850, and especially after Crete became autonomous and then independent, villas spread along wide, tree-lined avenues towards the seafront suburb of Halepa, where Eleftherios Venizelos, modern Greece's most famous statesman, was born. Prince George of Greece, while High Commissioner, also resided there at the turn of the century.

Most discotheques are at or near the port. There are far fewer handicrafts and jewellery shops than in Iraklio.

Sights and places of interest

The **Archaeological Museum** 𝕸 ☆ (*Halidon* ☎ *24–418* 🖼 *standard opening times*) is the main repository for finds from Neolithic times to the recent past. It is located in the 13thC former **Church of St Francis** ✝ (the island's largest Venetian church). The **Historical Museum and City Archives** (*Sfakianaki* 🖼 *standard opening times*) is second only in importance to the State Archives in Athens. The **Naval Museum** is in the old port (🖼 *standard opening times*), and displays models of ships from antiquity onwards.

On the opposite side of the port to the Naval Museum is the **Mosque of the Janissaries** 𝕸 built in 1645, which now houses the GNTO office (🏛). Still standing are seven of the 23 arches of the **Venetian Arsenal**.

At **Akrotiri** (The Promontory), 7km (4 miles) NE on the way to the airport, are the simple **tombs of Venizelos, father and son**, both prime ministers of Greece. Further along the headland are two monasteries, one of which, **Agia Triada**, possesses a very impressive **Renaissance church** 𝕸 ✝

Hotels

Hania
Canea (*1866 Sq.* ☎ *24–673/5* ▯▯ 🖵 *50* 🛏); **Kydon** (*S. Venizelou Sq.* ☎ *26–190/4* ☎ *291146* ▥▥ 🖵 *117* 🛋 🍴 ⇄ AE CB ⊙ ⊙ VISA 🗗 ●); **Porto Veneziano** (*Akti Enosseos* ☎ *29–311/3* ▯▯ 🖵 *63* ▦▦ 🛋 ⇄ AE CB ⊙ ⊙ VISA 🗗) is in a converted Venetian mansion in the old port; **Xenia** (*Theotokopoulou* ☎ *24–561/2* ▯▯ 🖵 *44* 🛋 🍴 ⇄ AE CB ⊙ ⊙ VISA 🗗 ⇌ 🛏) is in the Venetian fortress.

Galatas (*5km (3 miles) w of Hania*)
Panorama (☎ *54–200/5* ☎ *291140* ▥▥ 🖵 *167* 🛋 🍴 ⇄ AE CB ⊙ ⊙ VISA 🗗 ⇌ 🛏 ●), 45m (50yd) from the beach.

Restaurants

Naturally the best seafood can be found at the numerous open-air, moderately priced establishments in the old port, but on the whole the setting is more pleasing than the food. Much the same can be said for the town's most original taverna and cafe, **Aposperida** (*in a lane behind the old port* ▯), which occupies several floors of a 17thC soap factory.

Agía Róumeli See **Omalos** in *Crete/Nomos Hania.*

Fournés See **Omalos** in *Crete/Nomos Hania.*

Gorge of Samaria See **Omalos** in *Crete/Nomos Hania.*

Kíssamos
Map **12***L7. 43km (27 miles) w, on the coast road. Port: Ferries to Gythio and Kythira. Population: 1,800.*
An ancient **temple** and **theatre** form the nucleus of the 16thC **Venetian castle** 𝕸 With its long, sandy beach, Kissamos is a convenient excursion centre for the w and s of Crete, but only limited, quite simple accommodation is available.

🏨 **Kastron** (☎ *22–140/1* ▯▯ 🖵 *11* 🛋 ⇄).

Kolymbári
Map **12***L7. 23km (14 miles) w, off the coast road.*
Kolymbari is at the w end of Kolpos Hanion (Bay of Hania), and at the base of the middle and most northerly of the three arms protruding from the w of Crete. It is the seat of the Orthodox Academy, the large hall of which, near the 15thC **Gonias Monastery**, 1.5km (less than 1 mile) N, is used for international congresses. There is good bathing.

Máleme
Map 12L7. 17km (11 miles) w, on the coast road.

The inhabitants of Maleme saw much of the heaviest fighting in the battle of Crete in 1941, when the German airborne forces invaded from Attica.

H **Crete Chandris** (☎ 91–221/8 ⊕ 291100 ▯▯▯ ▭ 416 ▤ ← ▱ ≕ ᴀᴇ ᴄʙ ⊕ ⊙ ᴠɪꜱᴀ ↗ ≋ ✦ ☞ ◉).

Omalós
Map 12M7. Inland, 37km (23 miles) sw.

An outstanding drive along a route that can also be followed by bus – and in a day if the earliest bus is taken – is from *Hania* (see *Crete/Nomos Hania*), through the orange groves around **Fournes**, 15km (9miles) sw, up to Omalos, where a tourist pavilion (▣) stands at the head of the 18km (11 miles) long **Gorge of Samaria** ☆ Wooden stairs and a footpath (*open Apr–Oct*) allow easy walking between the steep rock walls which rise 300–600m (1,000–2,000ft). At the end of the spectacular gorge is a good beach at Agia Roumeli, from which a motorboat (▤) carries passengers to **Sfakia**.

Paleohóra
Map 12M7. 77km (48 miles) sw, on the s coast.

From the N coast you are faced with a hard choice of two attractive roads to the s, either from **Maleme** or **Kissamos**. Both converge on Paleohora, an as yet unspoilt fishing village on one of the s coast's finest beaches.

H **Elman** (☎ 41–412/4 ▯▯▯ ▭ 16 ≕ ↗ ✦ ◉), 16 furnished flats.

Samaría Gorge   See **Omalos** in *Crete/Nomos Hania*.

Sfakía
Map 12M7. 73km (46 miles) se, on the s coast.

Southeast from Hania on the N coast road is a popular picnic spot, **Vrysses**, 25km (16 miles). From here, a branch turns s through an austere, barren, mountainous region to its capital village, Sfakia, on the Libyan Sea.

The population has now dwindled to some 300, but the racial characteristics of the tall, blond, blue-eyed Doric invaders of the 10thC BC have been preserved. Subsequent invaders never gained more than nominal sovereignty here, despite the 16thC **Venetian castle** standing on a hill, nor the nearby, much larger 14thC **Frangokastelo** ▥ ☆ on a lonely beach s of the coast road e towards Plakias.

At the latter, on May 17, 1828, 650 Cretan defenders were slain by the Turks. At each anniversary of the massacre, a phalanx of armed men has been seen marching from the ruined fortress into the sea, according to one of the world's most persistent ghost stories.

H **Xania** ▰ (☎ 91–202 ▯ ❧ 12 ← ▱ ≕).

Sóuda
Map 12L7. 7km (4 miles) se, on the coast road. Population: 1,200.

Around one of the Mediterranean's finest bays are Hania's modern port and an important naval base.

Nearby sights and places of interest
The **Venetian fortress** on the islet opposite held out against the Turks until 1715, despite psychological warfare by the enemy, who piled up 5,000 Christian heads around the ramparts.

The Turks built their own **fortress** to the s, below the ruins of ancient **Aptera** – the building materials of which were supplied by the **Doric and Hellenistic temples**, **Roman theatre** and **cistern**, still partly protected by walls.

Vrysses   See **Sfakia** in *Crete/Nomos Hania*.

Cyclades (*Kykládes*)

The 39 islands that make up the Cyclades form a rough circle, *kýklos* in Greek, around *Delos*, the religious centre of the archipelago. The islands were first settled before 6000BC from Karia in Asia Minor, and the Early Cycladic culture was developed some 3,000yr later by the Phoenicians. They were conquered and ruled by the Minoans during the Middle Cycladic period (2000–1450BC). In the late Cycladic period (1450–1100BC), the Minoan influence continued to prevail on some islands.

In the 10thC BC the Cyclades were colonized by the Ionians, and usually sided with the main Ionian state, Athens, in the following centuries. Later, they fell successively to the dominant powers in the Aegean, and in the time of the Crusades were split into feudal baronies owing allegiance to the Venetian Dukes of Naxos and Paros.

Catholicism, introduced under Venetian rule, survived the massacres committed under the Turkish admiral Khair-ed-din Barbarossa, a Greek converted to Islam. As a result, most island capitals have a Catholic as well as an Orthodox cathedral.

Though there is no lack of variety among them, the most popular of the Cyclades conform to the archetype of an Aegean Island, with dazzling white houses clustering in tiny villages on sun-drenched brown rocks rising from a deep-blue sea. Completing the image, white chapels are tucked into folds in the hills, or share prominent vantage points with equally romantic windmills.

The islands lie close together, making island-hopping an easy matter. An ever-growing number of tourists opt for Greek Island cruises, however, despite the relatively high cost compared with striking out on one's own. For the well-heeled individualist, the archipelago is ideal for yachting, despite the *meltémi*, the violent north wind which in the height of summer keeps the temperatures down but whips up the waves. Winters are mild, but often rainy.

The majority of the roughly 100,000 inhabitants are directly or indirectly employed by the tourist industry, which has greatly raised standards of living but largely destroyed the traditional way of life, except off the beaten track. However, fishermen still follow their age-old trade, and a dwindling number of islanders scratch a living from the stony, barren soil, growing figs, olives and wine grapes.

Some of the local handicrafts are attractive, especially the handwoven fabrics of **Mykonos**, though surely the entire population must be occupied weaving the endless fashionable stripes.

With the exception of *Delos*, only islands with adequate accommodation are given separate entries in the *Greek Islands A–Z: Andros, Ios, Kea, Kythnos, Milos, Mykonos, Naxos, Paros, Syros, Thira* and *Tinos*.

179

Delos

Other islands, such as **Amorgos, Anafi, Folegandros, Kimolos, Serifos, Sifnos** and **Sykinos** are relatively inaccessible with irregular ferry links. Accommodation is often sparse and basic, or if of a reasonable standard, almost certainly will have been long booked in advance by Greek tourists. They are advisable therefore only for independent travellers having some knowledge of the Greek language and a motive for visiting them, and it is essential to arrange accommodation in advance.

Officially – with rare exceptions – the capital towns or the villages bear their respective island's name, being known locally as the *Hóra*.

Delos (*Dílos*) ★
Map 12I8. 2.5km (1.5 miles) w of Mykonos. Area: 3.5sq.km (1.35sq. miles). Getting there: By motorboat (20min), from Mykonos: depart 9.00, return 12.30; cruise ships also call at Delos.

Neighbouring *Mykonos* sends its two- and four-legged flocks to Delos, a mere patch of land across a narrow channel at the centre of the Cyclades. The sheep – wisely – stay all year round. Visitors with motorboats to Mykonos or cruise ships to catch stay only for the morning, however, and so miss the spectacular sunsets to be witnessed from **Mt. Kynthos**, an easy 112m (368ft) ascent up a flight of stairs. In the marvellous evening clarity the view extends over islets and headlands separated by strips of deep-blue sea. Distant *Syros* in the w took over as the trading centre from Delos when the latter ceased to be the ancient centre of the Aegean world. *Naxos* and *Paros* still dominate by size in the s. To the N is the high ridge of *Tinos*, which has replaced Delos as the sacred island. Mykonos inherited the tourist trade and retains the only direct motorboat link with Delos. (See also *Cyclades*.)

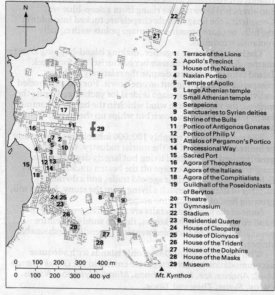

1 Terrace of the Lions
2 Apollo's Precinct
3 House of the Naxians
4 Naxian Portico
5 Temple of Apollo
6 Large Athenian temple
7 Small Athenian temple
8 Serapeions
9 Sanctuaries to Syrian deities
10 Shrine of the Bulls
11 Portico of Antigonos Gonatas
12 Portico of Philip V
13 Attalos of Pergamon's Portico
14 Processional Way
15 Sacred Port
16 Agora of Theophrastos
17 Agora of the Italians
18 Agora of the Compitialists
19 Guildhall of the Poseidoniasts of Berytos
20 Theatre
21 Gymnasium
22 Stadium
23 Residential Quarter
24 House of Cleopatra
25 House of Dionysos
26 House of the Trident
27 House of the Dolphins
28 House of the Masks
29 Museum

Mt. Kynthos

Sights and places of interest

In historical terms the riches of Delos are without bounds, although mostly no more than foundations remain. The island's sights are therefore best understood historically.

7thC BC–315BC

Apollo ruled over both the grandest landscape and seascape in all Greece, but although as a Dorian god he was a usurper at Delphi, as an Ionian god (see *Mythology* in *Culture, history and background*) Delos was his by birthright. In the 7thC BC this small island became the religious centre of the Ionian Greeks. The dominant power in the Cyclades, Naxos, dedicated to Apollo the **Terrace of the Lions ★** where five lean, vigilant beasts with tapering waists still crouch on their hind legs; the sixth of these heraldic guardians was carried off by the Venetians to stand sentinel before the Arsenal at Venice. Also dedicated by the Naxians was the colossal archaic statue of *Apollo* whose sheer size and weight foiled its medieval despoilers, though the torso was sawn in two; one **hand** is now in the local museum and there is a foot in the British Museum in London. The base, inscribed 'I am of the same marble, statue and base', stands at the entrance to **Apollo's Precinct** surrounded by porticos to which Doric propylaea were added in the 2ndC BC. To the right is the 6thC BC **House of the Naxians** with a central colonnade, and to the left, the sharp angle of its contemporary, the **Naxian Portico**.

In classical times it was decreed that no-one should give birth or die on the sacred island. Mothers near labour, the dying and even the coffins of the dead were taken by boat to the neighbouring island of **Rheneia**. In 530BC Polykrates of *Samos* attached the much larger Rheneia by a chain to Delos in token of its subjugation to the sacred island.

The first, 6thC BC Delian League was a purely Cycladic alliance dominated by Naxos. The second, 5thC BC Delian League stored its treasure in the 6thC BC **archaic Temple of Apollo** until the treasury's transfer to Athens in 454BC (see **Acropolis** in *Athens/Sights*). A **larger Athenian temple**, 29.5 by 13.5m (97 by 44ft), was begun in 476BC, the year the second Delian League expanded into a pan-Ionian alliance dominated by Athens, but the temple was only finished in the 3rdC BC. A **smaller Athenian temple** dates from 420BC, shortly after a purification decreed by the Athenians in 426BC which led to the entire population being expelled for blasphemy.

315–166BC

In the division of Alexander the Great's empire, Delos in 315BC became once more the seat of government of a Cycladic confederacy, under Egyptian protection. But all the Hellenistic kings vied with each other by constructing temples in both individual and collective honour of the 12 Olympian gods, the Egyptian Ptolemies building no less than three **Serapeions** as well as the **Sanctuaries to Syrian deities**, while Dimitrios Poliorkitis contributed the **Shrine of the Bulls** – a long portico with ornamentation recalling Cretan motifs.

The architectural emphasis shifted to the secular, with the 125m-long (410ft) **Portico of Antigonos Gonatas** and the 71m-long (234ft) **Portico of Philip V**, his successor as King of Macedonia, which faces **Attalos of Pergamon's Portico** across the **Processional Way** from the **Sacred Port**. The Delian Senate met in the Hypostyle Hall, lit through a lantern in a rectangular roof supported by Doric and Ionic columns.

From 166BC

In 166BC the Romans influenced Athens to annex the island and bring about the final expulsion of the native Delians to Achaea. An *epimelétes* (supervisor) was established on Delos under an *epimelétes* (supervisor). The **Agora of Theophrastos** was named after one of these, who ruled from 126–125BC, and was the first of the spacious, elegant agoras built during this period of commercial prosperity. After the destruction of Corinth in 146BC the Romans became the dominant commercial power in the Aegean, so naturally the **Agora of the Italians** was the largest, with a quadrangle measuring 100 by 70m (328 by 230ft) and an interior Doric arcade which supported the Ionic columns of the first floor. Freemen and slaves traded in the **Agora of the Compitialists** at the commercial port, Roman bankers met in the Guildhall of the Hermaïsts, and Phoenician ship-owners in the imposing **Guildhall of the Poseidoniasts of Berytos** (Beirut), while Phoenician Jews built one of the few synagogues in ancient Greece.

The 43-tier **theatre**, **Gymnasium** and the **Stadium** catered for entertainment and sport, and were located beyond the **residential quarter ★** where the walls of luxurious villas bright with painted stucco rise to a height of 3m (10ft) round the restored colonnaded courts. The **House of Cleopatra** is named after a fine **statue of an Athenian matron** in flowing drapery, the others after their lovely **floor mosaics**. In the **House of Dionysos** the god, crowned with ivy, rides a tiger; the central mosaic in the **House of the Trident** contains some delicate, small pictures; the mosaics of the **House of the Dolphins** and the **House of the Masks** are both equally remarkable.

In the first Mithridatic War, Delos sided with the Romans against King Mithridates of Pontus and in 88BC his fleet massacred all 20,000 of the island's community – an incredible number of inhabitants in so small an area. Rome's attempts to revive the island with new settlers came to nothing when pirates raided and sold them into slavery 20yr later. The emporium reverted to its ancient role of sanctuary, but eventually became, like *Delphi* (see *Mainland A–Z*), a museum visited by Roman tourists. When neighbouring islanders and barbarian invaders began using the magnificent Parian marble from the buildings as a convenient quarry, the sacred island's historic role was at an end.

The museum

📷 *Standard opening times* 💷 *housed in the tourist pavilion* ▥▥

At the entrance stands a bust of the *Duc de Loubat*, who financed the excavations begun by the French School of Archaeology in 1873. Though the most important finds have been removed to the **National Archaeological Museum** in *Athens*, the superb **collection of *kouroi* and *korae* ★** is second only to that in the **Acropolis Museum** (see *Athens/Sights*). As well as Hellenistic and Roman sculptures, jewellery and bronzes, there is the **Mycenaean treasure** found in the archaic Temple of Artemis on the island.

Ⓗ **Xenia** offers four basic rooms. (See also *Mykonos* for accommodation.)

Dodecanese (*Dodekánissa*)

Although they are called the 'Twelve Islands', there are at least 13 of the Dodecanese, not counting the numerous islets scattered over the SE Aegean. So far, only four – *Kalymnos*, *Kos*, *Patmos* and *Rhodes*, each listed separately in the *Greek Islands A–Z* – are equipped to receive tourists in any number. In the case of Rhodes, this is true with a vengeance; only Athens has slightly more hotels, but not so tightly concentrated. *Karpathos*, between Crete and Rhodes, has good ferry and air communications but relatively little hotel accommodation.

The other islands, such as **Astypalea**, **Kassos**, **Kastelorizo** (Megisti), **Leros**, **Nissyros**, **Symi** and **Tilos** have irregular ferry links and are relatively inaccessible. Accommodation is either sparse and basic, or where of a reasonable standard, it will almost certainly have been booked long in advance by Greek tourists. They are therefore advisable only for independent travellers with some Greek and a reasonable motive for visiting them; it is essential to arrange accommodation in advance.

The proximity of the Dodecanese to Asia Minor determined their historical position as an outpost of Europe. Like the *Cyclades*, they were probably first ruled by Minoan princes under the overlordship of Crete. Then came the Achaeans followed by the Dorians, under whom they played a minor part in the Delian League.

The Dodecanese enjoyed two great periods, naturally most in evidence on the largest island, *Rhodes*. The first was the Hellenistic period when, under the benevolent sovereignty of the Egyptian Ptolemies, they were both commercially and

artistically pre-eminent in the Aegean. The second was the
period of rule by the Order of St John, following the Knights'
expulsion from Jerusalem by the Saracens in 1291 and their
temporary exile in Cyprus. In 1306 they purchased the islands
from the Genoese Admiral Vignolo de' Vignoli, but the
Byzantine Emperor Andronikos II refused to abide by this, and
it took 4yr of hard fighting for the Knights to secure control of
the archipelago.

The Order of St John consisted of knights, priests and
serving brothers (hospitallers) organized into seven national
divisions, or 'Languages' as they were known, under a Grand
Master elected for life by the General Chapter. Of the 19 Grand
Masters who resided on Rhodes, 14 were French. Dieudonné
de Gozon (1346–53) is said to have gained office by slaying the
best authenticated dragon, which was "the size of a moderate
horse, covered with hard and scaly skin, the head of a serpent
and legs like a crocodile". Pierre d'Aubusson successfully
resisted the 70,000 Turks of Mohammed II in 1480 and was
made a cardinal by Pope Innocent VIII. Villiers de l'Isle Adam,
with only 650 knights, about 1,000 Italians and 6,000
Rhodians, resisted the 200,000 men of Suleiman the
Magnificent for six months and only surrendered at Christmas
1522 after being granted free passage with his 180 survivors.

Turkish occupation of the islands lasted until 1912. It was
followed by Italian domination until World War II, when
British troops prepared the way for union with Greece in 1948.

In all cases the name of the island and its capital is the same.

Égina (Aegina) ☆

*Map 8H7. 33km (21 miles) sw of Piraeus. Getting there: By
hydrofoil, from Zea Harbour and ferry from the main harbour
in Piraeus, and from the other Argo-Saronic Islands and the
se Peloponnese; by motorboat, from the Angistri and Moni
Islets. Getting around: By bus to all villages. Taxi and garage
facilities available. Population: 7,000.*

Zeus and the nymph Aegina (after whom this island in the
Argo-Saronic group is named) were the parents of Aeakos, who
became the grandfather of Achilles and Ajax before he was
appointed jointly with his Cretan stepbrothers Minos and
Radamanthys as a judge in the Underworld (see *Mythology* in
Culture, history and background).

The first settlement on the fertile plain on the island's w coast
dates from the fourth millenium BC. By 1800BC a maritime city
was trading on the site of the modern town, **Egina**. In 650BC
Egina minted the first European coins which for a century were
the standard silver currency throughout Greece.

The rise of Athens led to protracted hostilities until in 456BC
Perikles occupied 'the eyesore of the Piraeus'. On the outbreak
of the Peloponnesian War in 431BC, the Aeginetans were
deported by the Athenians but were returned to their island by
the victorious Spartans in 404BC.

Control of Egina thereafter passed from one dominant power
to another. The most beneficial were the kings of Pergamon
who were awarded possession by the Romans in 210BC.
Although they started their rule unpromisingly by
appropriating the famous indigenous 6th and 5thC BC
sculptures, later they built a stadium and theatre below the
5thC BC Doric **Temple of Apollo**. These splendid buildings
were used as quarries by subsequent conquerors, who included
such plunderers as Khair-ed-din Barbarossa and Morosini.

Even Capodistrias, during the Greek government's short stay on Egina in 1828, used the temple's ancient marbles to construct the quay, so that now only one of the 36 columns is left standing. In compensation, however, he built the first high school, now the **museum** ☆ (🖾 *standard opening times*), containing local archaeological finds, and the orphanage, now a prison for capital offenders. He also published the island's first newspaper, and fittingly, in view of Egina's history, issued the first modern drachme.

The jetty of the harbour, lined with brightly-painted caiques, ends at a dazzlingly white church, by which the excellent Aeginetan pistachio nuts are sold. Porous clay jugs are an even older export but, superb in antiquity, they are now crude.

The nearest good beach to the town of Egina is at **Perdika**, 8km (5 miles) s. The best beach on the E coast is at **Agia Marina**, 16km (10 miles).

Although the frequency of ferries to the island makes it easy to bring a car, cycling is popular. But the main excursions (see below) are rather far and easier by bus. See also *Poros, Spetses* and *Ydra*.

Sights and places of interest

Temple of Aphaia 🏛 ★

On the E coast, 12km (7.5 miles) from Egina town. Getting there: By bus 🖾 Standard opening times.

The magnificent Doric Temple of Aphaia dominates the E coast from a pine-covered crest, from which the view extends over Egina and the sea as far as the Acropolis in Athens and Akro-Corinth, each against its mountain backdrop – on days when the Piraeus smog clears briefly.

The limestone peripteral temple is the best-preserved in all the Greek Islands, having 25 of the original 32 columns still standing. It was built with spoils of the Battle of Salamis in honour of Aphaia, the third child of Leto. Local tradition maintains that she threw herself hereabouts into the sea to escape the pursuing Minos, a legend that demonstrates the historic fact of a Minoan attack on the island becoming enshrined in myth.

The pediments of Parian marble were purchased in 1813 by Crown Prince Louis of Bavaria, the philhellenic father of Greece's first king, and are still in Munich.

Other sights

The single-vaulted frescoed **nave of Omorfi Ekklesia** (Beautiful Church) 🏛 ✝ was built in 1289 on the road leading to the medieval capital, **Paleohora** ☆ which was abandoned and all the houses removed stone by stone for the re-building of the capital on the antique (and present) site, leaving only the 27 churches as lesser examples of Byzantine architecture. Below their empty shells is the **convent** where Agios Nektarios, Bishop of African Tripolis, ended his days in great sanctity in 1920. His embalmed body continues to work miracles, as testified by the enormous number of *ex-votos*.

Hotels on Égina

Egina town
Avra (☎ 22–303 🔲 🔲 33 🎏 🖾 🏠 ⇌); **Nafsika** (☎ 22–333 🔲🔲 🔲 34 🏠 ⇌ 🖾 ⇌ ◁), bungalows, on the nearest beach.

Agia Marina (*On the E coast, 16km (10 miles) from Egina town*)
Ammoudia (☎ 32–313 🔲 🔲 14 🖾 ⇌ 🏠 🍴); **Apollo** (☎ 32–271/4 🔲🔲 🔲 107 🚗 🖾 ⇌ 🖾 AE CB ⊙ 🔘 VISA 🖾 ⇌ 🏠 ◔); **Argo** (☎ 32–471/3 ☎214540 🔲🔲 🔲 60 🎏 🚗 🖾 ⇌ 🖾 ⇌ ◔).

Perdika (*8km (5 miles) s of Egina town*)
Aegina Maris (☎ 25–130/2 🔲 🔲 165 🎏 🚗 🖾 ⇌ AE CB ⊙ VISA 🖾 ⇌ 🍴 ◔), hotel and bungalows; **Moondy Bay** (☎ 25–146/7 🔲 🔲 72 🚗 🏠 ⇌ 🖾 ⇌ 🍴 ◔), bungalows.

Évia *(Euboea)* ☆

Map 8G7. Alongside the eastern coast of Boeotia, 88km (55 miles) N of Athens. 175km (109 miles) long by 6–50km (4–31 miles) wide. Getting there: By ferry, from Skala Oropou to Eretria, Agia Marina to Nea Styra, Rafina to Karystos, Arkitsa to Edipsos, and Glyfa to Agiokampos; by bus, from Athens to Halkida, Edipsos and Limni. Getting around: By bus throughout the island. Taxi, car-hire and garage facilities available. Population: 170,000.

Halkida (Chalkis), the capital of Greece's second-largest island, is connected with mainland Boeotia by a bridge over the **Evripos** (Euripus) channel. Legend has it that Aristotle drowned himself there, in despair over his inability to understand the still unexplained reason for the frequent changes of direction of the channel's current. Mountain chains, densely wooded, fill most of the island, the highest point being Mt. Dirfis, 1,745m (5,725ft) high.

The spectacular road s occasionally affords views over the Euboean Channel to the w and the open sea to the E. It ends at **Karystos**, 124km (78 miles) from Halkida, which is connected by daily ferry to Rafina.

The road N to **Edipsos**, 151km (94 miles) from Halkida, is also lovely. The town is connected by ferry to Arkitsa.

The islands of *Skiathos*, **Skopelos** and **Skyros**, all in the *Sporades*, can be reached by ferry from **Kymi** on the E coast.

Sights and places of interest

The 35,000 inhabitants of **Halkida**, which is built both on the island and the mainland, have taken to modernity in a big way, and what there is left of antiquity, which as recorded by Homer goes back to the Trojan War, is in the **Archaeological Museum** (📷 *standard opening times*). Most of what remains of the Middle Ages is to be seen in the **museum** (📷 *standard opening times*) in the restored **Turkish Mosque**. The Byzantine **Basilica of Agia Paraskevi †** – transformed into a Crusader cathedral in the 14thC – is near the **Turkish fortress** on the site of the ancient acropolis, on the mainland.

The coastal road s passes **Lefkanti** where a **9thC BC building**, 50 by 10m (164 by 33ft), was unearthed in 1980. It rivals a similar excavation at Kommos in Crete for seniority among Greek temples.

Eretria, 22km (14 miles) s from Halkida, was the only city state rash enough to join Athens in the Ionian expedition for which it was destroyed in revenge by the Persians before they sailed to their defeat at Marathon in 490BC. However, so advantageous a position was soon reoccupied, as is clear from the ruins of a **theatre**, the **Temples of Apollo** and **Dionysos**, **fortifications** on the acropolis, and the finds in the town's **Archaeological Museum** (📷 *standard opening times*).

To the N, **Edipsos** was already known as a spa to Aristotle, and its hot sulphur springs were appreciated as much by the ancient Romans as they are now by modern Athenians.

Hotels on Évia

Halkida
Hara (☎ 25–541/2 🔲 🔲 47 🍴); **Paliria** (☎ 28–001/7 ☎ 272149 🔲 🔲 118 ▦ 🍴 AE CB ① ⦿ VISA 🔲), on the waterfront.

Agios Minas *(14km (9 miles) N on the mainland)*
Saint Minas Beach (☎ 98–411 🔲 🔲 80 ▦ 🍴 ⚓ 🛥 ☰ ☑ ⚓ ⚘ ⦿).

Amarynthos *(On the coast SE of Halkida)*
Amarynthos (☎ 72–241 🔲 🔲 36 🏠 ⚓ ⥤ ⚘ *on roof* ⚘); **Blue Beach** (☎ 22–467 🔲 🔲 210 ▦ 🍴 ⚓ 🏠 ☰ ≈ ⚘ ⚘ ⦿).

Edipsos *(On the coast in the NW of the island)*
At Edipsos, hotels in the moderately expensive and comfortable categories (see *Accommodation* in *Planning*) are also the oldest and, although most have been modernized, half of the rooms are still without

private baths. This is therefore the one place in Greece where the
inexpensive hotels are better value, of which the following are a selection.
Capri (☎ 23–296/7 ⟏ ▭ 45, 2 suites ⊂⊃ ☎ ▼ on roof),
180m (200yd) from the beach; **Galini** (☎ 22–488 ⟏ ▭ 36 ⊂⊃ ☎
⁂); **Knossos** (☎ 22–460 ⟏ ▭ 37 ⊂⊃), 90m (100yd) from the
beach.

Eretria (On the coast, 22km (14 miles) SE of Halkida)
Among several holiday complexes and all having ▤ ⊂⊃ ☎ ≕ ⟦⟧ ≋
⁂ ⚯ ● **Golden Beach** (☎ 61–012 ⚈ 219181 ⟏ ▭ 130); **Holiday
Club Olympia** (☎ 62–411/4 ⟏ ▭ 234), hotel and bungalows.

Karystos (At the s of the island)
All on good beaches nearby: **Amalia** (☎ 23–311/4 ⚈ 272174 ⟏ ▭
158 ⁂); **Apollon Resort** (☎ 22–045/9 ⚈ 272100 ⟏ ▭ 79 ⊂⊃ ☎
≕ ⟦⟧ ⁂); **Galaxy** (☎ 22–600/3 ⟏ ▭ 72 ▤ ⊂⊃ ☎ ▼ on
roof ⁂); **Karystos Beach** (☎ 23–141/4 ⟏ ▭ 85 ▤ ⊂⊃ ☎ ⟦⟧ ≋
⁂ ⚯ ●).

Restaurants in Halkida

There are an unusually large number of excellent fish restaurants along
the waterfront, although no singling out is justified; they are all
expensive and offer dining à la carte.

Folégandros See Cyclades.

Híos (Chíos) ☆

*Map 9G10. Off the w coast of Asia Minor (Turkey), 56km (35
miles) s of Lesvos; 284km (177 miles) NE of Piraeus. 48km
(30 miles) long by 13–24km (8–15 miles) wide. Getting
there: By ferry, from Piraeus, Rafina, Lesvos, Samos, and
Tsesme (Turkey); by air, from Athens. Getting around: By
bus to all villages. Taxi and garage facilities available.
Population: 60,000.*

The landscape of the island of Hios varies from barren rocks, in
some regions, with no visible vegetation to four distinct, fertile
plains, with a densely wooded mountain range rising to the
1,297m (4,255ft) of Mt. Pelineo. The plain around the capital is
well irrigated and luxurious gardens surround the 19thC
mansions.

The old quarter of **Hios town** lies within the Byzantine
fortress that was repaired by the Genoese Giustiniani, who was
granted the island by the Emperor Michael Palaeologos in 1261
in gratitude for assisting in the reconquest of Byzantium. In the
old quarter there is a ruined mosque and a tiny **prison**, where
Bishop Platanos and 75 leading citizens of the island were held
before being hanged by the Turks in 1822 in reprisal for
rebelling at the beginning of the War of Independence. This
event formed part of the massacre of 30,000 of the islanders and
the enslavement of a further 45,000, depicted in the famous
painting *The Massacre of Chios* by Delacroix and also described
in a poem by Victor Hugo.

On the main square, another mosque is surrounded by cafes
and pastry shops. On the waterfront, the **Archaeological
Museum** (▨ *standard opening times*) contains interesting local
finds, many of which are marked with the Chian Sphinx,
symbol of the island.

At **Karfas**, 13km (8 miles) s, there is a much better beach
than the small one at the town, and the tavernas serve fresh fish.

There are direct ferry links with neighbouring *Lesvos* and
Samos and, further afield, with *Patmos* in the *Cyclades*.

Event: Prize-winning parade of ship models, Dec 31, well
attended by locals.

Sights and places of interest

Híos: Homer's birthplace?

Vrontados, 13km (8 miles) N of the town, is the seat of the International Society of Homeric Studies. The bard is said to have taught his epic poems to wandering minstrels, from the **Petra Omirou** (Homer's Stone) on the far side of the port, although in fact it was a shrine of the Asian goddess Cybele, who is portrayed with her two lions.

If indeed Homer was from Híos, he was most likely born in the medieval village of **Pitios** (in the mountains above the northern port of Kardamyla) where his supposed house and olive grove can be visited.

The mastic villages ☆
In the sw of the island.

The mastic villages have long prospered from gathering the gum of the *terebinth lentisk* bushes which is made into a liqueur as well as being served as a sticky sweet. The gum, very popular in the harems of Constantinople, became a monopoly of the sultans during the Turkish occupation from 1566–1912, and as a result the mastic district was exempted from the massacre of 1822.

Medieval ramparts surround **Pyrgi**, the main village, where in the maze of narrow lanes native life and costumes remain unchanged. At **Mesta**, some of the old houses have been converted into guest houses.

Néa Moní (*New Monastery*) ★
In the mountains, 13.5km (8.5 miles) w of the town.

In 1042 the Virgin Mary is said to have revealed to some shepherds the hiding place of her miraculous **ikon**, high up on Mt. Provatio which rises w of Híos town. She also prophesied the ascent to the imperial throne of the Byzantine general Konstantinos Monomachos, which took place when he became the third husband of the Empress Zoe. In gratitude, the new emperor built this splendid monastery which in the importance of its architecture and mosaics equals *Daphni* and *Ossios Loukas* (see *Mainland A–Z*).

Despite the ravages of time and the earthquake of 1881, the **mosaics** are superb, their mobility of design and their daring colouring being most unusual. The **central cupola on corner pendentives** is a reconstruction. A few nuns have replaced the 600 monks of the past.

Hotels on Híos

Híos town
Chandris Chios (☎ 25–761/8 ☎ 294113 ⬛⬛ ◻ 156 ⬛⬛ ⬛ ⬛ ⬛ 🅰🅴 🅲🅱 ⓪ ⬛ 🆅🆂🅰 ◉), on the waterfront, 90m (100yd) from the town's small beach; **Kyma** (☎ 25–551/3 ◻ ◻ 59 ⬛), also on the waterfront.

Kardamyla (*On the N coast*)
Cardamyla (☎ 21–378 ⬛⬛ ◻ 32 ⬛⬛ ⬛ ⬛ ⬛ 🅰🅴 🆂 ◉).

Ikaría

Map 13/10. 20km (12.5 miles) sw of Samos; 269km (168 miles) se of Piraeus. Getting there: By ferry, from Kavala, Piraeus, Thessaloniki, Híos, Lesvos, Samos and the Dodecanese. Population: 9,000.

The island is named after Ikaros who, according to the myth of Daedalos and Ikaros, fell to his death there. Usually visited for its spas, it is also known as the 'Island of Radium', with ten hot springs that are the most radioactive in Europe.

Ⓗ **Toula** (☎ 22–298 ⬛⬛ ⬛ 151 ⬛ ⬛ ⬛ 🅰🅴 🅲🅱 ⓪ ⬛ 🆅🆂🅰 ⬛ 🆂 🆂 ◉), at Therma Lefkados, one of the spas – hotel and bungalows.

Ionian Islands

The Ionian Islands, from N to S, are *Corfu, Paxi, Lefkada, Ithaki, Kefalonia* and *Zakynthos*, strung along the western shore of Greece, and a seventh, *Kythira*, far to the S and close to the eastern promontory of the Peloponnese. Each is listed separately in the *Greek Islands A–Z*.

In mythology, Io was changed by Zeus into a heifer to protect her from his wife's jealousy. Undeceived, Hera caused a gadfly to sting the transformed Io who, maddened by pain, plunged into the sea which thereafter bore her name.

The next unexpected visitor from the sea was Aphrodite, who rose from the waves near Kythira. Perhaps her protection, rather than its distance from the other islands, accounts for Kythira's more tranquil history.

The northern islands, first settled by Illyrians in the Stone Age, form stepping-stones between Greece and Italy, and have shared in both countries' civilizations, histories and religions. Ruins of Mycenaean dwellings support Homer's account that the realm of Odysseus, King of Ithaki, extended far to the south. Lefkada was named after Leukadias, the brother of Odysseus' wife, Penelope, and Alkinoos ruled 'the hospitable Phaeacians' on Corfu.

This bond of Homeric association between the northern islands survived the fall of the Mycenaean kings in the 12thC BC and their colonization by Corinth in the 8th–7thC BC, but in 665BC Corfu became a great maritime and commercial power in its own right. The islands were divided in the Peloponnesian War.

The architecture of the town is Venetian; the houses above the old port are built up elegantly into slim tiers with narrow alleys and colonnades running between them; red, yellow, pink, umber – a jumble of pastel shades which the moonlight transforms into a dazzling white city built for a wedding cake.

Lawrence Durrell, *Prospero's Cell*

In the ensuing centuries all six northern islands changed sides and hands in the best Greek tradition, falling in turn to Syrakuse, Epiros and Macedonia, and were pillaged by Illyrian pirates. The Romans occupied Corfu c.200BC, and subsequently the other islands, assuring 500yr of *Pax Romana*.

With the rest of Greece the islands became part of the Byzantine Empire but, as this began to break up, they once again fell prey to raiders from the sea, beginning with the Vandals and culminating in AD562 with the Ostrogoths, who savagely destroyed the ancient towns and monuments.

Invasions by Slavs, repelled in 933, and by Normans from Sicily between 1080 and 1185, interrupted Byzantine influence periodically until in 1204 the islands, with the Peloponnese, were awarded to Venice. Despite this, for a time the Norman Counts Palatine of Kefalonia ruled the southern islands and the Despots of *Epiros* (see *Mainland A–Z*) governed Corfu.

Venetian rule proper, which was to last for over 400yr, began on Corfu in 1386 and was gradually extended to the other islands, although the latter were from time to time occupied by the Turks. Only Corfu escaped being conquered, resisting bravely in 1537, and again in 1716 when its forces were commanded by the German mercenary Count von der Schulenburg. Corfu was, as a result, the only part of Greece never subjugated by the Ottomans.

Culturally the islands flourished in the Venetian era. After the fall of Crete in 1669, Corfu and Zakynthos welcomed the painters Moskhos, Tzanes and Poulakis, who founded an Ionian school of painting in which Cretan starkness was overlaid increasingly by a Baroque voluptuousness, culminating in the harmonious blend seen in the works of Doxaras, father and son.

The most lasting benefit of the Venetian governors, known as the Proveditors, was a result of the cash bonus they paid to planters of olive trees. These still cover the islands in magnificent groves: there are some ten million knotted and gnarled trunks, many 500yr old. Extensive orange and lemon orchards, acacia, oleander and plane trees complement the luxuriant natural vegetation, all sustained by generous rain.

By the Treaty of Campo Formio in 1797 the Venetian domains, including the Ionian Islands, were transferred to the French Republic. But though Napoleon declared that "the greatest misfortune which could befall me is the loss of Corfu", lost it was, in 1799 to a Turko-Russian army. The Republic of the Seven Isles, as it became known, was first an Ottoman protectorate, then a Russian one, but was finally returned to France by the Treaty of Tilsit in 1807.

In 1809 the British occupied four of the islands, but could only blockade Corfu. In 1814, however, the Treaty of Paris placed the United States of the Ionian Islands under British protection. Despite the enlightened but paternalistic rule of the Lord High Commissioners, tension exploded into open rebellion on Kefalonia in 1849, as nationalists agitated for union with Greece. As part of the negotiations for union, Britain secured the election of Prince William of Denmark as King George I of Greece, and in June 1864 he made his triumphal entry into Corfu. The British left behind some graceful buildings, as well as cricket, ginger beer and chutney.

In Dec 1916 the remains of the Serbian army, together with its king, the Crown Prince and the government, were ferried from Albania by the French, who occupied Corfu during World War I. This influx of 150,000 men, considerably more than the island's normal population, caused appalling overcrowding and an outbreak of the plague. About one third of the Serbs had died before the reorganized troops were able to return to the Balkan front.

Mussolini ordered the temporary occupation of Corfu in 1923, then occupied the island again during World War II, creating a separate Ionian state which lasted from Apr 1941 to Sept 1943, when German occupying forces abolished this unwanted separation.

Although Corfu town suffered irreparable damage from German and Italian bombing it still remains uniquely attractive. Not so, alas, Ithaki, Kefalonia and Zakynthos, where the earthquake of 1953 levelled the lovely Venetian houses of the capitals.

Íos

Map 12J9. 24km (15 miles) SE of Paros; 209km (131 miles) SE of Piraeus. 18km (11 miles) long by 10km (6 miles) wide. Getting there: By ferry, from Piraeus, Paros and Thira. Population: 1,300.

The increasing number of visitors to Íos, one of the Cyclades, visit the hills covered with olive groves and vineyards above two excellent beaches, one of which is at **Gialos** next to the small harbour, from which the white houses of **Íos town** (locally the *Hóra*) are visible. Homer's supposed tomb is at **Plakoto**, at the N of the island, where a monastery commands an enchanting view. The *Hóra* contains many fine Cycladic houses; 12 windmills remain on higher ground.

The island is linked by ferry with neighbouring *Paros* and *Thira* and other islands in the group can also conveniently be reached (see *Cyclades*).

Hotels on Íos

Armadoros (☎ *91–201* ⬛⬛ 🔲 *27* 🛏 ⚊ 🔺), 180m (200yd) from the beach, is the best of the many inexpensive hotels between town and sea; **Sea Breeze** (☎ *91–285* ⬛⬛ 🔲 *14*) is by the harbour; **Manganari** (☎ *91–215* ⬛⬛⬛ 🔲 *31* 🛏 ⚊ ▱ 🔺⬤), bungalows, 275m (300yd) from the beach, on the s promontory, reached by motorboat.

Itháki (*Ithaka*)

Map 6G3. Off NE Kefalonia; 11km (7 miles) s of Lefkada; 139km (87 miles) NW of Patra. Getting there: By ferry, from Patra, Sami (Kefalonia) and Lefkada; by air to Kefalonia, then by ferry. Getting around: By bus to all villages. Taxi and garage facilities available. Population: 5,000.

Homer described the Ionian Island of Ithaki as "a precipitous isle, unfit for horses . . . good for goats", but its numerous natural harbours and inlets made it the obvious centre for the island kingdom of Odysseus. A deep inlet divides the northern highland of Anoi, 828m (2,716ft), from the southern highland of Stefani, 641m (2,104ft). The excellent harbour of Vathy, as the capital is locally known (officially **Ithaki**), attracts a large number of yachts, but hotel accommodation is limited. The entrance to the harbour is protected by the Lazaretto inlet, flanked by two ruined Venetian fortresses. There are roads to all the well-kept villages on the island, but the absence of beaches discourages visitors.

Homer enthusiasts have to be content with the accuracy of the poet's descriptions of the island rather than the scanty Mycenaean relics kept in the small **Archaeological Museum** (▨ *standard opening times*) in the capital. And although Schliemann excavated a 7thC BC town high up on Mt. Aëtos, and named the Cyclopean walls **Odysseus' Castle**, in fact it was nothing more sensational than the acropolis of medieval Alkaklomena.

See also *Ionian Islands* and the other northern islands in the group: *Kefalonia* and *Lefkada* (direct ferry links with both), *Corfu*, *Paxi* and *Zakynthos*.

Event: Theatre Festival, Aug–Sept.

H **Mentor** (☎ *32–433* ⬛⬛ 🔲 *36* 🍴🛏⚊) has clean but simple rooms to let, 460m (500yd) from the town beach.

Kálymnos ☆

Map 13J12. 13km (8 miles) NW of Kos; 347km (217 miles) SE of Piraeus. 21km (13 miles) long by up to 13km (8 miles) wide. Getting there: By ferry, from Piraeus, Kos, Leros, Patmos, Rhodes, the other Dodecanese Islands, the Cyclades and Samos. Getting around: By bus to all villages. Taxi and garage facilities available. Population: 12,000.

Kalymnos, in the Dodecanese, is rocky and barren, with only a few patches of olive and fruit trees. Sponge fishing is still the main source of income for nearly all 3,000 of its active male population, who sail away each year after Easter, for at least four months. Among the houses of **Kalymnos**, the capital, painted all in different shades of blue, will be found the school for divers which is attended by many of the American sponge divers of Tampa, Florida, who are mainly descendants of Kalymnians.

The better beaches are on the w coast, perhaps the best being at **Massouri**. You will find everywhere simple tavernas with a very limited menu, although the fish is freshly caught.

Kalymnos combines well with a visit to several Aegean islands, and reference to *Kos*, *Patmos*, *Rhodes* and *Samos* may provide ideas. There are also ferry links with other *Dodecanese* islands and with several of the *Cyclades*.

Sights and places of interest

The road to the w coast passes the **medieval Hóra** below the **Castle of the Knights of St John** 🏰 whose arms are displayed on the **Church of the Panagia Hryssoheria** (Our Lady of the Golden Hand) † At the central valley's narrowest point are the **ruins of Mycenaean Damos** and the apse of the large 4thC **Basilica of Christ of Jerusalem**.

The road reaches the coast at **Panormos**, then turns N towards **Myrties** (The Myrtles) from which caiques make the 15min trip (🚤) to the islet of **Telendos**, which split off from the main island in an earthquake in the 6thC AD.

Hotels on Kálymnos

Kalymnos town
Olympic (☎ 28–801/3 🏨 ▭ 42 🍴), 230m (250yd) from the beach.
Massouri (*On the w coast*)
Armeos Beach (☎ 47–488 🏨 ▭ 34 🛏 ⇌ 🍴).
Myrties (*On the w coast*)
Delfini (☎ 28–914 🏨 ▭ 18 🛏 ⇌ 🍴).
Panormos (*On the w coast*)
Drossos (☎ 47–301 🏨 ▭ 51 🛏 ⇌ 🍴).

Kárpathos

Map 5L13. Between Crete, 80km (50 miles), and Rhodes, 50km (31 miles). Getting there: By ferry, from Rhodes and the s Dodecanese, Crete and Thira; by air, from Rhodes (summer only). Population: 1,360.

This rugged Dodecanese island is divided into the wild northern highland and the cultivated south, where several villages are scattered among the hills encircling a wide bay. Here the capital, **Karpathos**, was built near the insignificant **remains of ancient Poseidonion**.

H **Romantica** (☎ 22–460 🏨 ▭ 20), just outside Karpathos town, 90m (100yd) from the beach.

Kássos   *See Dodecanese.*

Kastelórizo *(Megísti)*   *See Dodecanese.*

Kéa *(Tzía)*

Map 9I8. 21km (13 miles) SE of Cape Sounio; 78km (49 miles) SE of Piraeus. 19km (12 miles) long by 9.5km (6 miles) wide. Getting there: By ferry, from Lavrio and Kythnos to Korissia. Getting around: By bus, from Korissia to Kea town. Population: 1,700.

Kea, a barren, hilly island, is the closest of the Cyclades to Attica, which faces the harbour at **Korissia**. This is near an archaeological site where Minoan ruins and the foundations of **Apollo's temple** have been uncovered, from which a road climbs through the sun-baked brown rocks towards **Kea town** (locally the *Hóra*) in the interior. Stone arches cross the cobbled lanes of the capital, leading to numerous chapels and churches. The colossal **lion** among the olive trees higher up the hillside was carved out of the rock in antiquity. At **Pisses** in the w, a fine 5thC BC **tower** has been preserved at the **Monastery of Agia Marina**.

There is a ferry link with neighbouring *Kythnos*. See also *Cyclades*.

Hotels on Kéa

Kea town
Ioulis (☎ *21 – 577* ▯▯ ▭ *11*).
Korissia (*On the NW coast*)
Karthea (☎ *31 – 222* ▯▯ ▭ *35* ⊞ ⇌ ⏴), 18m (20yd) from the beach.
Koundouros (*s of Kea town*)
Kea Beach (☎ *22 – 144* ▯▯▯ ▭ *80* ⊞ ⇌ ≈ ⏴ ●).

Kefaloía (*Cephallonia*)

Map 6G2. 107km (67 miles) w of Patra, between Lefkada and Zakynthos. Getting there: By ferry, from Patra, Astakos, Mitikas and Ithaki to Sami, and Vassiliki (Lefkada) to Fiskardo; by air, from Athens. Getting around: By bus to all villages. Taxi, car-hire and garage facilities available. Population: 37,000 ℹ GNTO, Argostoli ☎ 22 – 847.

The fertile plains of this largest among the Ionian Islands are divided by barren mountain ranges rising to the peak of Mt. Aïnos, 1,619m (5,313ft) high. The attractive N of the island is fairly thickly wooded; its dark fir trees are unique. The most interesting sights, however, are in the SE.

Argostoli, the only Ionian Island capital whose official name is not the same as its island, was completely rebuilt after the devastating earthquake of 1953. It is situated on an inlet branching off the deep Linadi Bay which divides the island into two very unequal parts. The **Archaeological Museum** (▨ *standard opening times*) contains discoveries from the four ancient cities which were founded by the sons of the legendary King Kephalos. The deep **subterranean tunnels** in the coastal cliffs, constantly filled and emptied by the sea, are remarkable, but less spectacular than they were before the 1953 earthquake caused a marked reduction in water volume. The hotels and restaurants of the capital are mediocre, but accommodation at the nearby beaches to the s is more pleasant.

Hotel accommodation is of a low standard at the lovely fishing villages ☆ of **Agia Evfimia**, **Assos** and **Fiskardo** on the N promontory. In any case, the small, simple hotels and the few private rooms are fully booked in season, but a day excursion is well worthwhile.

See also *Ionian Islands* and the other northern islands in the group: *Ithaki, Lefkada* and *Paxi* (direct ferry links with both), *Corfu* and *Zakynthos*.

Sight
Ágios Géorgios ☆
25km (16 miles) s of Argostoli.
This site was once the Byzantine and Venetian capital of the islands, with 15,000 inhabitants. The derelict shells of its buildings surround the ramparts of the **Kastro** (Castle), the seat of the Counts Palatine, which was captured by the Turks in 1483 but retaken in 1500 by the Venetians and Spaniards. It was reconstructed after the devastating earthquake of 1636, but was abandoned in 1757 in favour of its port, Argostoli.

Other sights

To the SE of Argostoli, the **Cyclopean Walls** ☆ are the impressive
remains of ancient Krani, one of the four original cities. At **Mazarakata**,
vases and ornaments have been found in 83 **Mycenaean tombs** ☆ –
partly beehive, partly carved into the rock. Byron wrote *Don Juan* at
Metaxata, in the fertile, rolling plains in the S, before going on to die in
Messolongi (see *Mainland A–Z*). **Kourkoumelata**, destroyed by the
1953 earthquake, was rebuilt as a modern model village. The **Convent of
Agios Andreas** has some relics of the Apostle Andrew and fine murals.

In the central plain due E of Agios Georgios, site of the old capital, is
the **Monastery of Agios Gerasimos**, the patron saint of Kefalonia. The
road from the monastery ascends through tall fir trees to the top of **Mt.
Ainos** ☆ from which the splendid view takes in all the islands.

Above **Sami**, the main port on the E coast, are some **ancient
fortifications**. The **Melissani stalactite cave** ☆ 3.5km (2 miles) W, and
the **Drongarati cave** ☆ further inland, are the region's main attractions
(*both* 🔲 *open all day*).

Hotels on Kefalonia

In Argostoli, hotels include **Aenos**, **Agios Gerasimos** and
Cephalonia Star, all undistinguished but inexpensive, and
moderately-priced **Xenia** which has a restaurant. There are
only four noteworthy hotels on Kefalonia, all outside Argostoli.

Agia Pelagia (*10km (6 miles) s of Argostoli*)
Irinna (☎ 41–285/7 ⫿⫿ 🔲 169 ← 🚗 🍴 ⫽ 📺 💷 📷 ↝ 🍴 ↝ 🎾 ∿).

Lassi (*2km (1.25 miles) s of Argostoli*)
Méditerranée (☎ 28–760/4 ⫿⫿⫿ 🔲 227 ▦ ← 🍴 ⫽ 📷 ↝ ∿ 🎾 ∿ ●).

Platys Gialos (*3km (2 miles) s of Argostoli*)
P.L.M. White Rocks (☎ 28–332/4 ⫿⫿⫿ 🔲 102 ▦ ← 🍴 ⫽ 📷 📺 💷 📷 ↝ 🎾 ●).

Sami (*On the E coast*)
Ionion (☎ 21–235 ⫿ 🔲 16 ←).

Restaurants

Among those on the waterfront in Argostoli are **Ainos**, **Kephalos**,
Limenaki and **Lorensatos**, all serving the very drinkable white *Rómbola*
wine but uninteresting food – despite the fine local cheeses and nougat.

Kérkyra   See *Corfu*.

Kímolos   See *Cyclades*.

Kos ★

*Map 5J12. SW of Kalymnos; 85km (53 miles) NW of Rhodes;
370km (231 miles) SE of Piraeus. 45km (28 miles) long by up
to 11km (7 miles) wide. Getting there: By ferry, from Piraeus,
Kalymnos, Leros, Patmos, Rhodes, the other Dodecanese
Islands, the Cyclades and Samos; by air, from Athens and
(summer only) Rhodes. Getting around: By bus to all
villages; also sightseeing buses. Taxi, car-hire and garage
facilities available. Population: 9,000 ℹ GNTO, Akti
Koundourioti ☎ 28–724.*

No longer 'the poor man's Rhodes', this elongated, fertile
island in the Dodecanese, divided by a central range rising to
Dikaios Christos (Christ the Just), 685m (2,250ft) high,
competes successfully with its larger rival both in scenery and
architecture. Although perhaps its medieval remains are minor,
its antique remains are of major importance. There is a wide
choice of accommodation, though none as yet in the luxury

class, but the food sadly is as uninteresting as on Rhodes.

The ancient capital, Astypalaea, was on the sea to the w, near the ruined 4thC **Basilica of Agios Stefanos**. It was destroyed by an earthquake in 412BC and sacked soon after by the Spartans. The **town of Kos** was founded in 366BC on a wide bay facing N. It became a favourite residence of the Ptolemies, who encouraged the local school of pastoral poetry. Its founder, Philetas, was tutor to Ptolemy II Philadelphos who himself was born in Kos, and its greatest exponent, the Sicilian Theokritos, visited the island several times.

The best fish tavernas are in the port, but the pleasantly situated restaurants under the trees along the town's beach serve indifferent food.

Visitors to Kos will probably want to take in *Rhodes* as well, and reference to *Kalymnos*, *Patmos* and *Samos* may provide further ideas. There are also ferry links with others of the *Dodecanese* and with several of the *Cyclades*.

Event: Hippokratia Festival, Aug – performances of ancient drama, re-enactment of the Hippokratic Oath, flower show, athletic competition.

Sights and places of interest

Asklipiíon ☆
4km (2.5 miles) sw of the town 🔲 *Standard opening times.*

A cypress avenue leads from the town to the sanctuary of the god of healing and the renowned medical school built after Hippokrates' death. If the dates of his birth and death, 460–357BC, are indeed authentic, he was excellent proof of the efficacy of his own cures, so very different from those practised at *Epidaurus* (see *Mainland A–Z*).

The three terraces rise up a hillside and are connected by a **monumental staircase**. The Italians restored, on the lowest terrace, the **stoa** and **bath** above the curative iron and sulphur springs; on the middle terrace, an **Ionic temple**, the oldest in the sanctuary, and a **Roman temple**, which flanked the **great altar**; on the upper terrace, the main **Doric temple**.

Higher up, the sacred spring of Vourina still supplies the town with water from a vaulted reservoir, but the medical centre ceased to function in AD554. An Institute for Prophylactic Medicine is under construction, founded by the South African surgeon Dr. Christian Barnard.

Castle of the Knights 🏛 ☆
On the port 🔲 *Standard opening times.*

The town's excellent port is guarded by the imposing 15thC Castle of the Knights, surrounded by two ramparts separated by a moat. Antique bas-reliefs have been incorporated into the walls next to medieval coats of arms. Inside the fortress are numerous Hellenistic finds.

Tree of Hippokrates
Hippokratous Sq.

A bridge spans Finikon (Palm Road) which links the port with the coastal avenue, leading to the delightful square named after Kos' most famous son. Hippokrates is supposed to have taught under the enormous plane tree, the 12m (39ft) circumference of which is shored up with marble. In fact, apart from the impossibility of a tree living for some 2,500yr, Hippokrates was born in 460BC in Astypalaea, long before the foundation of Kos.

Other sights

From the elegant **Loggia Mosque** 🏛 – a three-storey building entered on the first floor by a staircase with a canopied porch – the view extends over the vast Agora to central Eleftherias Sq, where the **museum** (🔲 *standard opening times*), containing the island's most important archaeological finds, faces the 18thC **Defterdar Mosque**. Hellenistic and Roman temples and baths are scattered among the one-storey white houses, built after the devastating shock of 1933.

On the outskirts are the **Odeon** where ancient tragedies are occasionally performed, the **Gymnasium**, the small **Temple of Dionysos**, and the reconstructed **Casa Romana** with fine floor mosaics.

Hotels on Kos

In or near Kos town

In the town centre: **Alexandra** (☎ 28–301/4 ⌨ 292188 ▯▯ 🖵 79 🏠 ⇌ 📺 ●); **Oscar** (☎ 28–090/1 ▯ 🖵 108 🏠 ⇌ ⤋ *on roof*).

On the town's most pebbly beach: **Kos** (☎ 22–480/1 ▯▯ 🖵 137 🏠 ⇌ 📺 🏖); **Theoxenia** (☎ 22–310/2 ▯▯ 🖵 42 🏠 ⇌ 📺 🏖); **Zephyros** (☎ 22–245 ▯▯ 🖵 🏠).

Comfortable hotels on nearby beaches within 3km (2 miles) and offering ▦ 🏠 ⇌ AE CB ⓓ ● VISA 📺 ⇌ 🏖 ⤴ **Atlantis** (☎ 41–291/4 ⌨ 292182 ▯▯▯), hotel and bungalows; **Continental Palace** (☎ 22–737 ▯▯▯); **Ramira Beach** (☎ 28–489 ▯▯▯).

Agios Fokas (*7.5km (4.5 miles) s of Kos town*)
Dimitra Beach (☎ 28–581/2 ⌨ 292207 ▯▯ 🖵 134 🏠 ⇌ AE CB ⓓ ⓔ ● VISA 📺 ⇌ 🏖 ⤴ ●), hotel and bungalows.

Marmari (*17km (11 miles) w of Kos town*)
Caravia Beach (☎ 41–291/4 ⌨ 292196 ▯▯ 🖵 347 ▦ 🏠 ⇌ AE CB ⓓ ⓔ ● VISA 📺 ⇌ 🏖 ⤴ ●), hotel and bungalows.

Kríti   See *Crete*.

Kykládes   See *Cyclades*.

Kýthira (*Kythera*)

*Map **11**K6. 12km (7.5 miles) s of the eastern promontory of the Peloponnese, 187km (117 miles) sw of Piraeus. 32km (20 miles) long by 19km (12 miles) wide. Getting there: By hydrofoil, from Piraeus to Agia Pelagia; by ferry, from Neapoli, Gythio and Kissamos (Crete); by air, from Athens. Getting around: By bus all over the island. Taxi and garage facilities available. Population: 10,000.*

Kythira's history is linked with the *Ionian Islands*, to which it was annexed by the Venetians in 1717, although geographically it is in the Aegean. Watteau's painting *Embarquement à Cythère* gives a misleading impression; present day visitors who flood the island are mostly former natives or their descendants, returning for a holiday from Australia where over something like 100,000 now live.

The capital, **Kythira**, is known locally as the *Hóra*, as so often in the Aegean. The capital has no hotels, nor is there one at its port at Kapsali, a 20min walk, 275m (900ft) below. The only one is in the NE at **Agia Pelagia**, the hydrofoil port. Elsewhere, private rooms will have to suffice. There is a weekly ferry link with *Crete*.

There are several good beaches on the island.

Sights and places of interest

The Venetian **Kastro** (Castle) rises above the blue and white houses of the capital in which there are also ten Venetian mansions and the small **museum** (🏛 *standard opening times*).

On the w coast of the shrub-covered central plateau, the **ikon of the Virgin and Child** attracts large crowds of pilgrims to the **Monastery of the Panagia Myrtidion**.

To the N is the pretty village of **Milopotamo**, criss-crossed by streams of clear water, above another 16thC Venetian fortress, **Kato Hora**. The **Cave of Agia Sofia**, by the sea, contains frescoes and small lakes, as well as stalactites and stalagmites.

Boat excursions (🚤) can be made to the little island of **Antikythira**, about 37km (23 miles) SE of Kythira, and can make a very pleasant day trip for the tourist.

Ⓗ **Kytheria** (☎ 33–321 ▯▯ 🖵 10 🚗 ⇌ 📺), at Agia Pelagia, on the NE coast.

Kýthnos

Kýthnos

Map 9I8. 8km (5 miles) s of Kea; 100km (62 miles) SE of Piraeus. Getting there: By ferry, from Lavrio and Kea to Merihas. Getting around: By bus to the four villages. Population: 1,600.

Kythnos offers a truly Cycladic setting of treeless rocks in a deep-blue sea, its port, **Merihas**, being in the centre of the W coast. On the NE coast, **Loutra** (Baths), the only spa in the Cyclades, is visited for rheumatic ailments. Half way between the two is the capital, **Kythnos** (locally called the *Hóra*), the white houses of which ascend the barren slopes of a hill. There are approximately 700 **frescoes** painted by a local artist in the several churches, and the two **Monasteries of the Panagia** (Our Lady) are interesting.

There is a ferry link with *Kea*. See also *Cyclades*.

Hotels on Kýthnos

Loutra (*On the NE coast*)
Xenia Anagenissis (☎ 31–217 ⫽□ ⫼ 46 ⌂ ⇌ ☜).
Merihas (*On the W coast*)
Possidonion (☎ 31–244 ⫽□ ⫼ 83 ⌂ ⇌ ☜).

Lefkáda (*Lefkas*)

Map 6F3. Off the mainland coast, 59km (37 miles) W from Amfilohia. 32km (20 miles) long by between 8km (5 miles) and 13km (8 miles) wide. Getting there: By chain ferry ▣ (5 min), from the mainland; by ferry, from Mitikas, Ithaki and Kefalonia; by air, to Aktio, 18km (11 miles) away; by bus, from Athens and Patra. Getting around: By bus to all villages. Taxi and garage facilities available. Population: 28,000.

Had not the Corinthian colonizers dug a canal through the mudbanks in 640BC, the Ionian island of Lefkada would be a peninsula, an extension of the mainland mountains to the N. The Emperor Augustus restored the **canal**, which had become silted up through centuries of war and neglect, and bridged the mudbanks by a 4km-long (2.5 miles) **causeway**. The Franks added an **aqueduct** of 260 arches in the 13thC. These three great feats of engineering are still in use. The Frankish **Fortress of Santa Maura** (Agia Mavra) – where Helen Palaeologos, the mother of the last Byzantine emperor, founded a monastery in 1453 after the fall of Constantinople – still guards the embarkation point for the chain ferry at the entrance to the huge lagoon, where the capital, **Lefkada**, is situated.

The capital was badly damaged by the earthquakes of 1867 and 1958. Some decaying Venetian churches look incongruous among the strange corrugated upper floors (a necessary precaution against the ever-present earthquake danger) of most of the houses.

A circular road follows most of the coast. Locally-made handwoven fabrics and embroidery are available. See also *Ionian Islands* and the other northern islands in the group: *Ithaki* and *Kefalonia* (direct ferry links with both), *Paxi*, *Corfu* and *Zakynthos*.

Events: Prose and Arts Festival, Aug, with concerts, lectures, theatre and folk performances.

Sights and places of interest
Temple of Apollo
Near the modern lighthouse on the s promontory.
From the temple, those accused of crimes could prove their innocence by

attempting the Lefkadian leap, a dive of 72m (236ft) into the sea.
Disappointed lovers also leapt from the cliffs and it was here that the
poetess Sappho met her death. The priests of Apollo perfected their
jumping techniques as part of a ritual, and the Romans devised a way of
breaking their fall using feather wings.

Other sights

The **museum** (📷 *standard opening times*) in Lefkada contains
Mycenaean finds. There is a fine view from the **Faneromeni monastery**,
3.2km (2 miles) to the w of the town.

🄷 Lefkas (☎ *23 – 916/8* 🏢🍴 🛏 *93* 🚗 🏠 ⚍ 🖬) is the only
recommendable hotel in town; Nirikos (☎ *24 – 132/3* ☎ *312244* 🏢
🛏 *39* 🚗 ⚍ 🖬), near town but in a more pleasant position on the
sandy strip which separates the lagoon from the open sea.

Léros   See *Dodecanese.*

Lésvos (*Lesbos*) ☆

*Map 9F10. Off the w coast of Asia Minor (Turkey), 56km (35
miles) N of Hios; 348km (217 miles) NE of Piraeus. 69km (43
miles) long by up to 45km (28 miles) wide. Getting there: By
ferry, from Kavala, Piraeus, Hios, Limnos, Samos and
(summer only) Ayvali (Turkey); by air, from Athens. Getting
around: By bus to all villages. Taxi, car-hire and garage
facilities available. Population: 112,000.*

According to Homer, Lesvos, the third-largest island in
Greece, belonged to Troy, on the coastal plain of Asia Minor
across the straits. The Achaeans attacked Lesvos, Achilles
carried off the girl Briseïs, who was then claimed by
Agamemnon, and the resulting row is an important theme in
the *Iliad.*

By the 8thC BC, Lesvos had become the centre of the Aetolian
Greeks. It was unified by the tyrant Pittakos, one of the Seven
Wise Men of antiquity. In the following century, a highly
original school of poets flourished in Mytilini, the prosperous
capital: Aesop's fables are still read today, Alkaeos lyrically
praised the joys of high living, while the poetess Sappho
expressed her love for the girls in Aphrodite's sanctuary so
passionately that 'lesbian' has become a universal term for that
particular inclination.

The island encloses two deep gulfs, the Gulf of Kalloni in the
s and the Gulf of Gera in the SE. The interior is mountainous,
with fertile, dense olive plantations in the E. The beautiful
scenery and excellent beaches make Lesvos an attractive
holiday island.

Lesvos can be reached by ferry from *Kavala* (see *Mainland
A–Z*) in Macedonia, and there are useful ferry links with other
islands: *Hios*, *Limnos* (and thence *Samothraki*), and *Samos.*

Sights and places of interest

Mytilíni ☆

On the E coast. Airport: 9.5km (6 miles) s. Population: 25,000.
Modern Mytilini, the island's capital, is a pleasant, thriving town. Most
of its 19thC mansions, including the one housing the small
Archaeological Museum (📷 *standard opening times*), are on or near the
larger central harbour. This is divided from the little-used northern
harbour by a rocky promontory where a 14thC **Genoese fortress** 🏰
replaced the temples of the antique acropolis.

The finest view across the 11km-wide (7 miles) straits dividing Lesvos
from Asia Minor is from the **Hellenistic theatre**, which is near the
ancient walls and the **Chapel of Agia Kyriaki** ✝ on a wooded hill behind
the town.

Límnos

There is a lovely ikonostasis in the 16thC **Cathedral of Agios Athanasios ✝** The **Popular Museum** (▓ *standard opening times*) in the town centre contains folk art and costumes. Much more interesting is the **Theophilos Museum ☆** (▓ *standard opening times*) which is outside the town at **Varia**, on the road s leading to the airport. It contains numerous paintings by Theophilos Hatzimihail (1867–1934), the primitive painter and a true original among the native sons of Lesvos.

Restaurants and bars serving the excellent local *oúzo* can be found on the lively central harbour.

Eressós ☆
88km (55 miles) w of Mytilíni.

This is the likely birthplace of Sappho, sheltered by cliffs in a fertile valley. A **Byzantine castle** and ruins of two three-naved 6thC **basilicas** are nearby. In summer everyone deserts it for the sandy seashore at **Skala**, 3km (2 miles) s.

To the w is the **petrified forest** – trees covered by volcanic action 800,000 to a million years ago – but, depite its local fame, this is hardly worth the long walk.

Mithýmna ☆
62km (39 miles) NW of Mytilíni.

Remains reaching back to the Trojan War lie scattered around this attractive red-roofed village on a hillside crowned by a strong **castle** ▥ This was courageously defended in the 15thC by Onetta d'Oria, wife of the Genoese lord of the castle, who donned armour and repulsed the besiegers, and it is she therefore, not Sappho, who in the strictly geographical sense is the locally honoured Lesbian. However, the castle eventually fell to Mohammed the Conqueror in 1462.

On the main square there are a number of inexpensive restaurants with a fairly good choice of food, in addition to the usual fish.

Pétra
55km (36 miles) NW of Mytilíni.

The 18thC **Church of the Panagia Glykofiloussa** (Our Sweet-Kissing Lady) ✝ stands on the huge black rock from which this fishing village on a sandy beach takes its name.

Hotels on Lésvos

Mytilíni
All 180m (200yd) from the unexceptional beach: **Blue Sea** (☎ 23–994/5 ▥▥ 🖵 56 ⬤ 🖻 ⟺ 🖾 ⦿), on the seafront; **Sappho** (☎ 28–415 ▥ 🖵 31 ⬤); **Xenia** (☎ 22–713 ▥▥ 🖵 74 ⬤ 🖻 ⟺ 🖾 ⬤).

Mithýmna (62km (39 miles) NW of Mytilíni)
Delfinia I (☎ 71–315 ▥▥ ⟿ 50, *some with bathrooms* ⬤ 🖻 ⟺ ⟿ ⬤), on a long but pebbly beach.

Petra (55km (36 miles) NW of Mytilíni)
Petra (☎ 41–257 ▥ 🖵 18 ⬤), on the central square.

Límnos

Map 4E9. Between Lesvos, 70km (44 miles) to the SE and Thassos to the NW; 347km (217 miles) NE from Piraeus. Getting there: By ferry, from Kavala, Thassos, Alexandroupoli, Lesvos and Samothraki; by air, from Athens and Thessaloniki. Getting around: By bus to all villages. Taxi and garage facilities available. Population: 4,000.

This lowest-lying of all the Aegean Islands concentrates on agriculture and livestock grazing, but is bare of trees because of fierce gales which sweep down from the Dardanelles in winter. The deep gulf of Moudros Bay on the s coast, which in World War I served as a base for the ill-fated Gallipoli expedition, and the much shallower inlet of Bounia Bay on the N coast together almost bisect the island.

When Zeus hurled one of his few legitimate sons from Olympos (see *Mythology* in *Culture, history and background*), Hephaestos was lucky only to break both his legs when he fell on Limnos. Lamed for life, he decided to set up his forge there, conveniently near to the now extinct volcanoes. The island's ancient capital took his name, and the ugliest of the Olympians was so popular that when his wife Aphrodite cuckolded him in favour of his better-looking brother Ares, the righteous women of Limnos stopped worshipping the goddess of love. In retaliation, Aphrodite afflicted them with halitosis and bodily odours. Their husbands not unnaturally came to prefer captive Thracian women, and for their unfaithfulness their wives drugged them and slit their throats. But the Argonauts happened to pass by on their quest for the Golden Fleece and the unsavoury-smelling women were thus assured of descendants.

Limnos can be easily reached by ferry from *Kavala* (see *Mainland A–Z*) in Macedonia and less frequently from *Alexandroupoli* (see *Mainland A–Z*) in Thrace, and there are services to neighbouring *Lesvos* and *Samothraki*.

Sights and places of interest

The **ruins of antique Hephaestia** are to be found on the coast of Bounia Bay. At **Paliohni** on the SE coast, the Italian School of Archaeology has excavated four layers of settlements, the oldest dating from c.3500BC.

The capital, **Myrina**, is divided by a precipitous cliff which is crowned by a **Genoese castle** 🏰 erected on Classical foundations. The **Archaeological Museum** ☆ (🔳 *standard opening times*) is located in the mansion of the Turkish Pasha, and is remarkable for its prehistoric exhibits.

🅷 1km (0.6 mile) N of town, on a private beach: **Myrina Beach** 🏨 (☎ 22–681/4 🖭 294173 ⬛⬛⬛ 📶 🏧 🆎 🆑 🅾 💲 🆅🅸🆂🅰 ▢ 🗠 ⇌ ⤵), bungalows. Both in town: **Lemnos** (☎ 22–153 ▯ 🗠 29, *some with bathrooms*); **Sevdalis** (☎ 22–691 ▯ 🗠 36, *some with bathrooms*).

Megísti   An alternative name for Kastelorizo; see *Dodecanese.*

Mílos
Map 12J8. 24km (15 miles) SW of Sifnos; 167km (104 miles) SE of Piraeus. Roughly 21km (13 miles) long by 13km (8 miles) wide. Getting there: By ferry, from Piraeus and Lavrio. Getting around: By bus to the main villages. Taxi and garage facilities available. Population: 4,500.

The strange, white volcanic soil attracted the earliest Neolithic settlers in the Cyclades to Milos, the most southwestern of the group. Tourist development is concentrated at **Adamas**, one of the best harbours in the Mediterranean. See also *Cyclades.*

Sights and places of interest

A ruined **Frankish castle**, a **Byzantine church** ✝ an **Archaeological Museum** (🔳 *standard opening times*) and a **Folklore Museum** (🔳 *standard opening times*) are to be found in the capital, **Milos**, or Plaka as it is known locally, 5km (3 miles) inland.

A short walk away, at **Tripiti**, are extensive 1stC **Christian catacombs** (🔳) with long corridors and arched tombs. Nearby, in 1820, a farmer discovered the famous statue of the *Venus de Milo*, sold to the French and now in the Louvre in Paris. At the well-preserved **Roman theatre** 🏰 plays are sometimes performed during the summer months.

The remains of three successive towns, the earliest dating from 3500BC, have been excavated at **Fylakopi** near **Apolonia** on the NE coast.

🅷 At Adamas: **Korali** (☎ 41–800 ▯ 🖭 16 🐾), 180m (200yd) from the beach; **Venus Village** (☎ 41–770 ▯▮ 🖭 91 🎛 🏧 🛏 ⇌ 🗠 ⇌ 🐾 🅾), hotel and bungalows, also in town.

Mýkonos ★

Map 12I9. 2.5km (1.5 miles) E of Delos; 10km (6 miles) SE of Tinos; 174km (109 miles) SE of Piraeus. Getting there: By ferry, from Piraeus, Tinos, and most of the Cyclades; by air, from Athens. Getting around: By local and hotel buses. Taxi and garage facilities available. Population: 4,000.

Until the 1950s, Mykonos, one of the Cyclades, was merely the starting point for a visit to *Delos*. But then the jet-set discovered its 'quaint' town of cubic houses of dazzling whiteness enhanced by the strong blues and greens of the shutters and doors. There are 365 tiny churches, with painted cupolas in delicate pastel shades. A walk through the winding lanes, compulsorily whitewashed twice a year, reveals little gardens with red hibiscus, pink oleanders, acacia, eucalyptus and pepper trees. The **Chapels of the Paraportiani** (Our Lady by the Port) † are lopsidedly stuck together like a honeycomb, near the jetty, and seven tiny churches cluster round the square named after them. On another square, any maiden who drinks from each of the **Three Wells** is reputedly guaranteed to find a husband.

It is all still as quaint as ever, although the jet-set have long since departed for more secluded haunts. Even the most picturesque row of old houses – rather grandiloquently called Enetia (Venice) because the wooden balconies project over an inlet of the sea – is now occupied by restaurants, tavernas, bars and discotheques.

Although the larger hotels are on beaches outside the capital, **Mykonos**, or have joined the chapels, dovecots and windmills scattered over the ochre hillsides, the island is simply too small for the annual influx of visitors. The atmosphere is as cosmopolitan and claustrophobic as anywhere on the Mediterranean, even on one of Greece's few naturist beaches. The island, incidentally, is the holiday headquarters for the gay fraternity.

Mykonos is the launching pad for day trips to Delos, and *Tinos* is also very near. It is conveniently central for many of the *Cyclades* and there is a direct ferry link with *Samos*.

Sights and places of interest

The **museum** (*on the outskirts of Mykonos* 🕮 *standard opening times*) contains mostly finds from the necropolis discovered on the uninhabited island of **Rheneia** (on the opposite side of neighbouring *Delos*) to which were taken coffins exhumed from the sacred island during the purification of 426BC by the Athenians.

At **Ano Mera**, 8km (5 miles) E, indeed the 'Place Above' as its name indicates, is the 15thC **Tourliani Monastery**.

Hotels on Mýkonos

In Mykonos

Despotika (☎ 22–009 ▥▯ ▦ 21 ▦ ▨ ☜), 275m (300yd) from the beach; **Konhyli** (☎ 22–107 ▥▯ ▦ 29 ☜ ▨ ☜), 460m (500yd) from the beach, closed Nov–Mar; **Leto** (☎ 22–207 ▥▥ ▦ 25 ☜ ☜ ☜ ☜ ☜).

Agios Stefanos Beach (*3km (2 miles) from Mykonos*)

Alkistis (☎ 22–332/3 ▥▯ ▦ 102 ☜ ☜ ☜ AE CB ④ ⑩ VISA ▨ ☜ on roof ☜), bungalows.

Ano Mera (*8km (5 miles) E of Mykonos*)

Ano Mera (☎ 71–215 ⑨ 293161 ▥▥ ▦ 67 ▦ ☜ ☜ ☜ AE CB ④ ⑩ VISA ▨ ◄€ ●).

Kalafati Beach (*12km (7.5 miles) from Mykonos*)

Afroditi (☎ 71–367/8 ▥▯ ▦ 95 ☜ ☜ ☜ ▨ ≈ ☜ ⅋ ✺ ●), bungalows.

Ornos (3.5km (2 miles) from Mykonos)
Paralos Beach (☎ 22–500 ▥ ◰ 40 🚗 🏠 ➠).

Restaurants

As expected because of the high tourist count, prices are among the highest in Greece, but nowhere does this coincide with superior quality.

In Mykonos
Georgos (▥ ▭ 🐴); **Marko Polo** (▥ ▭ 🐴).
At Agia Triada (Near Mykonos)
El Greco (▥ ▭ 🐴 💲 💳 VISA); **Katerini** (▥ ▭ 🐴 💲 💳 VISA), adequate restaurants.

Nightlife

Among the numerous discotheques the two most popular are **Nine Muses** and **Remezzo**.

Náxos ☆
Map **12**J9. 6km (3.75 miles) E of Paros; 194km (121 miles) SE of Piraeus. 29km (18 miles) long by 19km (12 miles) wide. Getting there: By ferry, from Piraeus, Mykonos, Paros, Syros and Thira. Getting around: By bus to all villages. Taxi and garage facilities available. Population: 14,000.

Escaping from Crete, Theseus abandoned Ariadne on Naxos, the largest of the Cyclades. But Minos' daughter was able to progress from being merely a mortal lover to being a divine one by granting her favours to the god Dionysos as he made his triumphal progress through the Aegean (see Mythology in Culture, history and background). So real to Greeks is their mythology that the islet reached from the harbour by an ancient jetty is called **Palatia**, after the legendary site of Ariadne's palace, despite the fact that its **marble gate** which stands out as the harbour is entered belongs to a temple begun only in 522BC.

The Venetian adventurer Marco Sanudo conquered the Byzantine fortress in 1207 and founded the Duchy of Naxos. This endured even after the Turkish conquest of 1564, although it was obliged to pay tribute to the sultans. Only a tower and a few walls remain of the **ducal palace** in **Naxos town**, but the long period of Latin rule left an unusual blend of Venetian and Cycladic architectural features in the buildings below the fortress, while the blank white walls of the lower town are reminiscent of Africa.

The **museum** (🔄 standard opening times) contains local finds. The nearer beaches are disappointing, but there is a choice of excursions along the two roads, to the N coast at **Apolonas** or to the E coast at **Moutsouna**. In the E is the hill village of **Apirinthos** below the highest peak in the Cyclades.

From Naxos, neighbouring Mykonos (and from there Delos) and Paros may be visited by frequent ferries. The further islands of Syros and Thira are also well served by ferry. See also Cyclades.

🏨 Among the numerous inexpensive hotels in Naxos town, the closest to the Agios Georgios beach are: **Akroyali** (☎ 22–922 ▥ ◰ 15); **Ariadne** (☎ 22–452 ▥ ◰ 24); **Koronis** (☎ 22–626 ▥ ◰ 32); **Naxos Beach** (☎ 22–928 ▥ ◰ 25).

Níssyros See Dodecanese.

Páros ☆

*Map 12J9. 6km (3.75 miles) w of Naxos; 167km (104 miles)
SE of Piraeus. 23km (14 miles) long by 16km (10 miles) wide.
Getting there: By ferry, from Piraeus, Ios, Naxos, Syros,
Thira and the s Cyclades. Getting around: By bus to all
villages. Population: 6,800.*

The capital and main port, **Paros**, or locally Parikia, is situated
on the only bay on the w coast of this Cycladic island. It was
known as Minoa until it was conquered by the semi-legendary
Paros of Arcadia. Most traces of antiquity have disappeared
under the cobbled lanes leading to the Aegean's most
impressive church, **Panagia Ekatontapyliani.**

There are hotels in Paros town and on a good beach on the
northern **Bay of Naoussa**, reached by a road from the capital.

There are frequent ferries to *Ios, Naxos* and *Syros*, while
Thira is also within reasonable distance. See also *Cyclades.*

Events: Feast of the Virgin's Assumption, Aug 15, Paros
town; Pirates' Raid pageant, Aug, Bay of Naoussa.

Sights and places of interest

Church of Panagía Ekatontapyliani (*Our Lady of the Hundred
Gates*) ﬍ ✝ ★

The church was commissioned by the Emperor Justinian, designed by
the architect of St Sophia in Constantinople and built by his master
builder, Ignatios, in the 6thC. The small **Agios Nikolaos** at the church's
E and the S **baptistry** were added to the fine cruciform main church. A
17thC restoration inserted Baroque arches to support a vaulted nave and
100yr later the addition of an elegant entablature completed the
transformation.

Other sights

Nearby are the ruins of the classical **Asklipiion** and the **museum** (🏛
standard opening times). The finest ikons are in the blue-domed **Church
of Agios Konstantinos** ✝ which stands on a rock on the waterfront.

Crossing the barren central mountain range is a road to the famous
Parian white marble quarries which since time immemorial have
assured the prosperity of the island. The road turns s at the pretty village
of Lefkes and descends to the Venetian **Castle of Marpissa** situated on
the E coast.

Hotels on Páros

Paros town
Argo (☎ 21–367 ▥ ▱ 44 ⬟); **Xenia** (☎ 21–394 ▥▥▱ 23 ⬟
⬟▱ ◳ ⬟).
Along the northern Bay of Naoussa
Ippokambos (☎ 51–223/4 ▥▥ ▱ 49 ⬟ ⬟ ⊐ ◳ ⬟), bungalows;
Kalypso (☎ 51–488 ▥ ▱ 24 ⬟ ⬟ ⊐ ⬟).

▣ Both in Paros town: **Livadia** (▥ ▱ ⬟); **Pandrosos** (▥ ▱ ⬟).

Pátmos ☆

*Map 13I11. 34km (21 miles) sw of Samos; 278km (173 miles)
SE of Piraeus. Getting there: By ferry, from Piraeus,
Kalymnos, Kos, Patmos, Rhodes, Samos, the Cyclades and
Hios. Getting around: By bus to the two villages. Taxis
available. Population: 2,500.*

The rocky island of Patmos, one of the Dodecanese, succeeded
Delos as the Aegean's sacred island after AD95, when St John
the Evangelist was exiled there by the Emperor Domitian. It
has never been swamped by pilgrims like *Tinos*, but tourists are
eroding the atmosphere of patriarchal piety.

The port is at **Skala**, site of the ancient capital which was abandoned because of fierce pirate raids, and only re-appeared under its present name after independence. In the narrow lanes of **Patmos**, locally called the *Hóra*, several of the fine 18th and 19thC mansions have been bought and restored by foreigners.

Patmos may be reached daily by ferry from *Kalymnos*, *Kos*, *Rhodes* and *Samos*, all reasonably close. There are also ferry links with *Hios* and many of the *Cyclades*.

Events: Feasts of St John, May 8 and Sept 26; Feast of the Assumption of the Virgin, Aug 15.

Sights and places of interest
Monastery of Agíou Ioánni Theológou (*St John the Theologian*)
In Patmos ☒ *Standard opening times.*
In the 11thC, a saintly hermit, Blessed Christodoulos, successfully foretold Alexis Komnenos' ascent to the Byzantine throne, and the new emperor granted him the island of Patmos and provided the means to build the monastery, on the site of a temple of Artemis which as usual provided a convenient quarry. The construction of a formidable array of cupolas, belfries and battlements was begun on a 210m-high (689ft) ridge in 1088. Effectively it is a medieval fortress which provided protection against pirates, opening on to a serenely peaceful court where a profusion of purple hydrangeas smothers the well and the staircase to the arcaded gallery.

In the inner narthex is the 11thC **ikon of St John**, a gift from Alexis I to Blessed Christodoulos, whose embalmed body lies in a silver shrine. There are Russian and Byzantine imperial gifts in the **Treasury** unequalled outside *Mt. Athos* (see *Mainland A–Z*). The magnificent library contains, besides precious manuscripts and illuminated gospels, the **33 leaves of the Codex Porphyrius** containing St Mark's Gospel, with the text in silver and the holy names in gold on purple vellum. The British Museum has four leaves; others are in the Vatican, Vienna and Leningrad. The **frescoes** in the **Chapel of the Panagia** date from 1210–20.
The Sacred Cave
Half-way up the hillside s above Skala.
The Apostle John landed at the ancient capital and port of Skala. He withdrew to a grotto above the town, where he wrote his *Revelation* (*The Apocalypse*), said to have been made by the voice of God through a triple rift which it opened in the roof. A silver halo marks the rock he used as a pillow. A small 17thC church marks the entrance to the Sacred Cave.

Hotels on Pátmos

Skala (*On the E coast*)
Chris (☎ *31–001* ☒ ☒ *26* ☜) is the closest of the several inexpensive hotels to the beach.
Grikos (*4km (2.5 miles) s of Skala*)
Xenia (☎ *31–219* ☒ ☒ *35* ☒ ☒ ☒ ☜), on a much better beach than at Skala.

Paxí (*Paxos*) ☆
Map 6F2. 18.5km (11.5 miles) SE of Corfu; 13km (8 miles) W of the coast of Epiros off Parga. 16km (10 miles) long by 3.2km (2 miles) wide. Getting there: By ferry, from Corfu town via Kavos, Patra via Kefalonia, and Parga. Getting around: One bus and five taxis. Boat- and bicycle/moped-hire available. Population: 2,000.
Paxi and neighbouring **Antipaxi** are two verdant Ionian Islands which make a delightful excursion from *Corfu*.
Accommodation is restricted but this means they have remained happily unspoilt. There are spectacular **sea caves** on the W coast. The island also produces superlative olive oil.

The locals insist on the name Gaios (officially **Paxi**) for the port and main village on the E coast.

See also *Ionian Islands* and the other northern islands in the group: *Corfu* and *Kefalonia* (ferry links with both), *Ithaki*, *Lefkada* and *Zakynthos*.

H **Paxos Beach** (☎ 31–211 ▮▮ ▭ 27 ▱ ⇌ ▱ ⊛ ⬤), 3km (2 miles) s of the main village.

Póros

*Map 8*l7. *s of Egina, 57km (36 miles) sw of Piraeus. Length from E–W: 9.5km (6 miles). Getting there: By hydrofoil, from Zea Harbour, Piraeus; by ferry, from the main harbour, Piraeus; continuous ferry from Galatas on the Peloponnese. Getting around: By bus on the only road. Taxis and garage facilities available. Population: 4,300.*

The approach to Poros, one of the *Argo-Saronic* group, is particularly attractive: the many-coloured houses of the island town, **Poros**, and the village of **Galatas** on the Peloponnese face each other across a narrow strip of water, constantly crossed by ferries, and it seems as though the island's beaches and pine forests are an extension of the copious orange and lemon groves of the mainland.

Theseus brought his Cretan wife Phaedra (see *Crete*) – after previously abandoning her sister Ariadne on *Naxos* – to the ancient city of **Troezen** (Trizina), which he inherited from his mother, 9km (5.5 miles) w of Poros town. A true daughter of the dissolute Pasiphae, Phaedra fell passionately for her chaste step-son Hippolytos, as dramatized in the works of Euripides and Racine.

Except for fish, the island's food is uninteresting; it is at its best in the many seaside tavernas which are overcrowded in summer. See also *Egina*, *Spetses* and *Ydra*.

Sights and places of interest

The only road on the island leads from the town to the 18thC **Monastery of the Virgin**, 4km (2.5 miles) E. From here a path continues to the **Temple of Poseidon**, where the god fathered Theseus by the daughter of the king of Troezen. In 322BC the Athenian orator and demagogue, Demosthenes, sought sanctuary at the temple in vain and poisoned himself to avoid capture by the approaching Macedonian soldiers.

Hotels on Póros

Latsi (☎ 22–392 ▮▮ ▭ 39 ▱ ▱ ⇌ ▱) is among the noisy hotels on the town waterfront; **Poros** (☎ 22–216/8 ▮▮ ▭ 91 ▱ ▱ ⇌ AE CB ⊙ ⊙ VISA ▱ ⟨⟨ ⊛ ⬤), much quieter, 2km (1.25 miles) NW on the main island; **Neon Aegli** (☎ 22–372 ▮▮ ▭ 72 ▱ ▱ ⇌ ▱ ⊛), also 2km (1.25 miles) away but E; **Sirene** (☎ 22–741 ▮▮ ▭ 120 ▱ ▱ ⇌ AE CB ⊙ ⊙ VISA ▱ ⇌ ⊛ ⬤), at the end of the only road, 4km (2.5 miles) E.

Rhodes (*Ródos*) ★

*Map 5*K14. *11km (7 miles) off the sw coast of Asia Minor (Turkey); 495km (309 miles) SE of Piraeus. 77km (48 miles) long by 35km (22 miles) wide. Getting there: By ferry, from Piraeus, all the Dodecanese, and several of the Cyclades; included in most Aegean cruises; by air, from Athens, Crete and (summer only) Karpathos and Kos, and direct flights, mostly charter, from main European cities. Getting around: By bus to all villages; also sightseeing tours by hotel buses. Taxi, car-hire and garage facilities available. Population: 53,000. i GNTO, Makariou 5 ☎ 23–655.*

The flora and fauna of Rhodes, largest of the Dodecanese, are as varied as on the neighbouring coast of Asia Minor. Deer, fox, hare and partridge abound in the luxuriant valleys and wooded hills round central Mt. Ataviros, 1,215m (3,985ft) high. Much closer to town, cedars and pine trees on Mt. Profitis Ilias, 720m (2,362ft) high, combine with meadows watered by fast-flowing brooks to form a surprisingly alpine landscape. Everywhere you see the pink and white *roses lauriers* (oleanders) of the 'Island of Roses'.

In the *Iliad* Homer identifies Tlepolemos as a leader from Rhodes, although he also describes him as a Heraklid or Achaean. And his fatal combat with Sarpedon of Lycia reflects their rivalry for mastery of the seas, which was a more likely cause of the Trojan War than Helen's fading charms.

Tlepolemos was, however, the leader of the later Dorian invaders of the Dodecanese, where they were less destructive than elsewhere and founded, or at least preserved, the ancient cities of Lindos, Ialysos and Kamiros. Alternative theories suggest a Phoenician origin for the cities; and local legend has it that they perpetuate three of three of the 50 daughters of Danaos who died on Rhodes and so escaped their sisters' unenviable fate at *Argos* (see *Mainland A–Z*).

The three cities prospered within a Dorian *Hexapolis* (confederacy of six cities) during a period of Persian rule and then as part of the Delian League. In the closing phase of the Peloponnesian War they deserted Athens and jointly established a new capital, Rhodes, in the N. In 408BC the architect Hippodamos, who had planned Piraeus (see *Athens/Sights*), drew up the chequerboard plan for the capital of which the geographer Strabo wrote: "Harbour, roads, walls and buildings so much surpass other cities that we know of none equal, much less superior to it."

In the 4thC BC, Rhodes became dominant in the Aegean and received support from Alexander the Great. In the struggle for his succession, the capital was besieged in 305–304BC by Dimitrios Poliorkitis (the Besieger) until both sides grew weary and arrived at a compromise.

Dimitrios' formidable siege engines were melted down for the colossal 30m-high (100ft) statue of Ilios, the sun god and lover of the nymph Rodos, by then identified with Apollo, that straddled the **Mandraki harbour**. It took Timochares of Lindos 12yr to cast the bronze *Colossus*, one of the Seven Wonders of the ancient world. It was felled by the terrible earthquake of 227BC, and, although the 80,000 inhabitants of the town were quickly rehoused with the generous help of Hellenistic kings, re-erection of the statue was prevented by technical difficulties. The bronze was broken up by Saracen pirates in AD654 and shipped to Syria where, according to the Emperor Konstantine Porphyrogenitos, 900 camels were required to carry the ponderous debris to its Jewish purchaser.

The *Colossus* was merely the largest product of the Rhodian school of sculpture, founded by Alexander the Great's court artist, Lysippos, whose *Quadriga of the Sun*, with Ilios in the likeness of the king, was considered equal to Phidias' statue of *Zeus* at *Olympia* (see *Mainland A–Z*). Yet in contrast to the serene idealized beauty of the sculpture of the two preceding centuries, the work of the Rhodian school emphasized size and dramatic movement. Important examples included Timochares' bas-relief on the cliff at **Lindos**, Philiskos' *Nine Muses* which was carried off to decorate the portico of Octavia in Rome, Appolonios' superb *Laokoon*, also carried off to Rome, which was excavated in 1506 and is now in the Vatican, and the *Winged Victory* excavated on *Samothraki* in 1856 and now in the Louvre.

Rhodes' contribution to the ancient world extended into both cultural and practical affairs. Its School of Rhetoric rivalled that of Athens (see introduction to *Athens*) in the number of senatorial youth it attracted. Rhodes' progressive commercial and maritime code was chosen by Augustus as the standard for the whole Roman Empire.

The island was visited by St Paul in AD43. In the Middle Ages it suffered its fair share of vicissitudes, and in 1191 was visited by King Richard Coeur de Lion who viewed "with profound astonishment the splendid remains of mighty works of art". In 1310, against the objections of Andronikos II, the Knights of the Order of St John (see *Dodecanese Islands*) entered the town of Rhodes on a dark, misty night by concealing themselves in a flock of sheep. The Order made the town the strongest bulwark of Christendom until it fell to the Turks in 1522, each 'Language' being responsible for the defence of a section of the tremendous ramparts they built.

From 1522, Rhodes shared the fate of the other Dodecanese.

The smaller villages are surrounded by vineyards producing some very drinkable white, rosé and red wines, notably *Chevalier de Rhodes* and *Líndos*. Surprisingly, in view of the pressures of tourism, some of the smaller villages have preserved their traditional lifestyle, at least in the less accessible S of the island.

One of Greece's four casinos is at the **Grand Hotel Astir Palace**, which will be found under *Hotels in Rhodes town*. There are organized tours of **Rhodes town**, **Lindos** and of the whole island.

Although Rhodes has more than enough to offer as a holiday island in its own right, those with island wanderlust may pick up ideas by referring to *Kalymnos*, *Kos* and *Patmos*, all easily reached by ferry. There are also ferry services to other *Dodecanese* islands, *Samos*, several of the *Cyclades* including *Mykonos*, and daily flights to *Crete*.

Events: Son-et-lumière, Apr–Oct, Residence of the Grand Masters, Rhodes town; Wine Festival, July–Sept, park of Rodini, 3.2km (2 miles) S of the town, with a varied programme of folkloric events; folk dancing all year.

The town

At the N end of the island. Population: 33,000.

The town of Rhodes is divided into two distinct parts, the old and the new. The **old town**, the only complete medieval town in Greece, is contained within the fortified walls built by the Knights of St John and encloses to its NE the main port. Outside are newer areas – mostly hotels – almost all built since the late 1950s. They cover the whole **north promontory** where Mandraki, the second and smaller port, is located, and the area west of the old town, which also includes the acropolis and site of the **antique town**.

Sights and places of interest

The old town ★

The best introduction to the town is by way of the 5km (3 miles) circuit of the **battlements** 🏛 which are largely the work of Basilio dalla Scuola, military engineer to the Emperor Maximilian I. This provides excellent views of the old town's mixture of Byzantine, Latin and Turkish architecture, topped by several narrow minarets and framed by the scarlet hibiscus, purple bougainvillea and pink and white oleander of the lovely gardens laid out across the moat by the Italians.

On entering by either the **Marine Gate** (Pyli Navarhiou) or the **Freedom Gate** (Pyli Eleftherias), the main concentration of sights in the town is clearly signposted: the foundations of the 3rdC BC **Temple of Aphrodite**, the **Inn of Auvergne** 🏛 and the **Palace of the Armeria** (Admiralty), which accommodates the Library, the **Museum of Popular Decorative Arts** (🔲 *standard opening times*) and the **Byzantine Museum** (🔲 *standard opening times*) housed in a deconsecrated 13thC church.

The **Street of the Knights** (Ton Ippoton) follows the antique road which led from the port to the acropolis. All the **Residences of the Seven Languages** that line the street have been restored. They were built in the late Gothic order, with some national stylistic features providing variety. Among them is the **Inn of England** 🏛

Opposite is the austere facade of the **Knights' Hospital** 🏛 hiding a handsome court with upper and lower arcades of rounded arches. It was built between 1440–89 on the lower corner of the Street of the Knights. The spacious **infirmary** upstairs with its projecting apsidal chapel is divided by seven octagonal pillars into two naves, and houses the **Archaeological Museum** (🔲 *standard opening times*). There are finds from the Mycenaean to Roman periods, with the emphasis on Hellenistic sculptures such as the 3rdC BC *Bashful Aphrodite*. There are also medieval exhibits which overflow into the elegant **refectory**.

An archway from the Street of the Knights opens on to the Palace Sq., with the reconstructed **Lodge of St John** 🏛 and remains of the **Burial Church of the Grand Masters**.

Also in the square is the **Residence of the Grand Masters** 🏛 (🔲 *standard opening times*), built by Helion de Villeneuve, Grand Master from 1319–46, in imitation of the papal palace at Avignon in his native Provence. The building was used by the Turks as a prison and wrecked by an explosion in 1856. In 1940 the last Italian governor of Rhodes finished building the present passably convincing replica, improved by trees, some ancient mosaic pavements from the island of Kos, and statues and vases from Lindos. It looks its best in summer during the nightly son-et-lumière spectacle (see events in introduction to *Rhodes*).

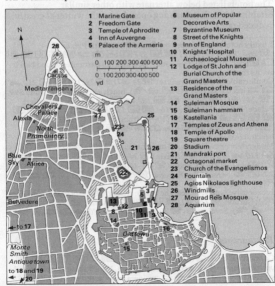

1 Marine Gate	6 Museum of Popular
2 Freedom Gate	Decorative Arts
3 Temple of Aphrodite	7 Byzantine Museum
4 Inn of Auvergne	8 Street of the Knights
5 Palace of the Armeria	9 Inn of England
	10 Knights' Hospital
	11 Archaeological Museum
	12 Lodge of St John and
	Burial Church of the
	Grand Masters
	13 Residence of the
	Grand Masters
	14 Suleiman Mosque
	15 Suleiman hammam
	16 Kastellania
	17 Temples of Zeus and Athena
	18 Temple of Apollo
	19 Square theatre
	20 Stadium
	21 Mandraki port
	22 Octagonal market
	23 Church of the Evangelismos
	24 Fountain
	25 Agios Nikolaos lighthouse
	26 Windmills
	27 Mourad Reïs Mosque
	28 Aquarium

Narrow lanes, spanned by arches or supported by flying buttresses against the recurrent earthquakes, are darkened by tiled eaves and overhanging wooden balconies with intricately latticed shutters. The lanes lead to tiny, attractive squares where huge plane trees shade the fountains. The 16thC **Suleiman Mosque** 🏛 is noteworthy with its added **Venetian portico**, while the same Sultan's **hammam** (hot baths) 🏛 is distinguished by its plaster work. The high lanterns and cupolas of Byzantine churches vie with the domes of mosques on the way down to the lower town, where the fine 16thC **Kastellania** on Hippokratous Sq. was the Order of St John's commercial court.

The antique town ☆
The antique town extended over the eastern slope of Monte Smith, 110m (360ft) in height, named after Admiral Sir Sydney Smith who watched the movements of Napoleon's fleet from the hill. On the acropolis are some columns of the 3rdC BC **Temples of Zeus** and **Athena**, and rather more of the **Temple of Apollo**. Among the olive trees are the restored **Stadium** and the oddly-shaped **square theatre** where classical tragedies are performed in summer.

The north promontory
From sea to sea this is taken up by the densest concentration of hotels imaginable. Only along the **Mandraki port**, where in the early 20thC the Italians alternated pseudo-Venetian with pseudo-Roman public buildings, is there any relief. The most pleasing are the **octagonal market** and the three-naved **Church of the Evangelismos** (Annunciation) ✝ The **fountain** outside its w end is a copy of the Fontana Grande of Viterbo. At the head of the long breakwater stands the circular **Agios Nikolaos lighthouse** and three disused **windmills**.

Only the **Mourad Reis Mosque** surrounded by derelict Turkish tombs adds a picturesque touch on the way to the **Aquarium** (🏛 *standard opening times*) on the N point.

Other sights near the town
Beyond the old town, a ruined **aqueduct**, probably Roman, and a **Hellenistic funeral monument** are reflected in the waterlily pond of the vast **Park of Rodini**, 3.2km (2 miles) s, where the Wine Festival is held annually (see events in introduction to *Rhodes*).

Hotels in Rhodes town
The hotels listed below alternate with other similar establishments in remaining open during the winter at greatly reduced rates.

Luxury hotel housing a casino: **Grand Hotel Astir Palace** 🏨 (☎ 26–284/94 🕿 292121 ▯▯▯ 🖂 377 ▦ 🖼 🛏 ⇌ AE CB ⊙ ⊙ VISA ▯ 🖂 ⇌ ⌘ ☺ ●), fine hotel, but with a not particularly good beach across the road.
Comfortable hotels: **Belvedere** (☎ 24–471/4 🕿 292120 ▯▯▯ 🖂 212 🚗 🛏 ⇌ AE CB ⊙ ⊙ ⊙ VISA ⌘ ⇌ ⇌), beach across the road; **Blue Sky** (☎ 24–091/3 🕿 292160 ▯▯▯ 🖂 182 🚗 🖂 ⇌ ⌘ ●); **Chevaliers Palace** (☎ 22–781/4 🕿 292163 ▯▯▯ 🖂 153 ▦ 🚗 🛏 ⇌ AE CB ⊙ ⊙ VISA ⌘ ⇌ ⌘ ●), 90m (100yd) from the beach; **Mediterranean** (☎ 24–661/5 ▯▯ 🖂 154 🚗 🛏 ⇌ AE CB ⊙ ⊙ VISA ⌘ ⇌), beach across the road.
Moderately priced hotels, all near the beach: **Aglaia** (☎ 24–061/3 ▯▯ 🖂 110 🚗 ⌘ ⇌ ⌘); **Alexia** (☎ 24–061/3 ▯▯ 🖂 135 🚗 🛏 ⇌ ⌘ ⬇ on roof ⌘); **Cactus** (☎ 26–100 🕿 292235 ▯▯ 🖂 177 🚗 🛏 ⇌ ⌘ ⬇ on roof ⌘); **Esperia** (☎ 23–941/3 ▯▯ 🖂 191 🛏 ⇌ ⌘ ⌘).
Inexpensive hotels, all near the beach: **Africa** (☎ 24–979 ▯ 🖂 75 🚗 ⌘); **Carina** (☎ 22–381/2 ▯ 🖂 59 ⌘); **Marie** (☎ 22–751 ▯ 🖂 79 ⇌ ⌘ ⇌ ⌘); **Semiramis** (☎ 20–741/2 ▯ 🖂 120 🚗 🛏 ⇌ ⇌ ⌘).

Restaurants

Captain's House 🍴 (*Zervou 5* ☎ 21–275 ▯▯▯ ⌘ AE CB ⊙ ⊙ VISA *open evenings only*), in a converted mansion, has a quiet atmosphere and serves Greek and international cuisine; **Casa Castelana** (*Aristotelous 33*

☎ *28–803* ▥ ▢ ◠ AE CB ⊡ ⊙ VISA), in a 15thC building of the Knights, serves everything from snacks to full meals; **Kon Tiki** (*Limin Mandrakiou* ☎ *22–477* ▥ ▢ AE CB ⊡ ⊙ VISA *open evenings only*), on a boat in the old port, serves good seafood; **Neorion** (*Neoriou Sq.* ☎ *24–644* ▥ ▢ AE CB ⊡ ⊙ VISA) is a cafe-restaurant.

Along the Mandraki port, the inexpensive restaurants offer open-air dining, but they are unremarkable. So too is the food in hotels, except those in the luxury category.

Shopping

The best handicrafts shops, as well as some jewellers, are in Sokratous in the old town. They have counterparts in the luxury hotels but naturally these are more expensive. Look out for the local pottery and embroidery, some of which is good. Shopping in Rhodes needs discrimination, however, for much of what is available is aimed at the mass tourist market.

The west coast

The coastal road from town, Ialyssou Ave., is lined along the whole of its 8km (5 miles) length with vast hotels. It leads to Trianda, now renamed Iallysos, from which various sights inland can be reached. (All distances are from **Rhodes town**.)

Sights and places of interest

At **Iallysos**, the 18thC **Church of the Dormition** (Theotokou) † possesses a beautifully carved **ikonostasis**. From here, a road branching left winds 8km (5 miles) inland through pine trees to ancient Ialysos.

The **Acropolis of Ialysos** ☆ – site of one of the three ancient cities – commands a splendid view over the island and sea. The **Knights' 14thC church and monastery** were restored by Franciscan monks who left with the Italians. The **baptismal font** of a 5thC church stands on the foundations of the Hellenistic **Temple of Athena**. In the **Chapel of Agios Georgios** † there are 14th and 15thC **frescoes**. A restored 4thC BC **Doric fountain** is reached by descending 134 steps.

The next left branch off the coast road leads inland to the **Vale of Petaloudes** (Butterflies) ☆ which is a narrow valley, 1.5km (less than 1 mile) long, where rustic bridges cross brooks shaded by enormous plane trees. Between June – Sept clouds of golden moths fill the air and settle on the *amber orientalis* trees.

Further s are the remains of another of the ancient cities, **Kamiros** ☆ (▨ *standard opening times*). An impressive **Doric stoa** has been reconstructed near the foundations of the **Temple of Athena**, and there is an aqueduct and some houses of the ancient city on the slope of a hill facing the sea.

Hotels on the west coast

Hotels along the coastal road from town (Ialyssou Ave.) all close Nov – Mar.

Luxury hotels, both having ▦ ▭ ▢ ⇌ AE CB ⊡ ⊙ VISA ▢ ▱ ⇌ ☜ ♫ ♪ **Olympic Palace** ▥ (☎ *28–755* ☏ *292138* ▥ *338*); **Rodos Palace** ▥ (☎ *25–222/32* ☏ *292212* ▥ *610*), hotel and bungalows.
Comfortable hotels, all having ▦ ◠ ▢ ⇌ AE CB ⊡ ⊙ VISA ▱ ⇌ ☜ ♪ ● **Avra Beach** (☎ *25–284/5* ☏ *292214* ▥ *186*), hotel and bungalows; **Blue Bay** (☎ *92–352* ☏ *292243* ▥ *237*); **Electra Palace** (☎ *92–521/5* ▥ *216*); **Metropolitan Capsis** (☎ *25–015/25* ☏ *292165* ▥ *649*).
Moderately priced hotels: **Leto** (☎ *23–511/2* ▥ *97* ◠ ▢ ⇌ ▱ ⇌ ☜); **Vellois** (☎ *24–615* ▥ *51* ▢ ⇌ ▱ ▢), 140m (150yd) from the beach.

The east coast

There are fine beaches along the road from town to **Kallithea**,

10km (6 miles), a pretty spa, the reopening of which has been announced so often that no-one believes it any more. **Faliraki**, 13km (8 miles), has one of the finest beaches, lined with hotels and restaurants. (Distances from **Rhodes town**.)

The white village of **Afandou** (Invisible), 19km (12 miles), is indeed hidden, but the road to the 18-hole golf course passes the interesting old **Church of the Panagia I Katholiki** (The Catholic Virgin) † Further s, the village of **Arhangelos** (Archangel) is dominated by the handsome **Castle of the Knights**, but the **Castle of Faraklos**, on a hill closer to the sea s, is more impressive.

The coast road continues to **Lindos**, site of the third of the ancient cities.

Sights and places of interest
Líndos ★
On the E coast, 56km (35 miles) from Rhodes town.

Located on a precipitous promontory rising to a height of 114m (375ft) between a larger bay and a tiny landlocked port, Lindos is probably the Aegean's most remarkable blend of nature, antiquity and the Middle Ages. It was there that St Paul landed to fulminate against the worship of Athena *Líndia*, whose mantle was worn by Alexander the Great at the decisive battle of Arbela in 331 BC.

A long stairway passes the ruined 27-tier **theatre** and Timochares' colossal 4.5 by 5m (15 by 17ft) **bas-relief of a ship and its captain** (see introduction to *Rhodes*). It ends at the 5thC BC **stoa**, 20 of the 42 columns of which have been re-erected. This stands in front of the small but elegant 14thC BC Doric **Temple of Athena Lindia** ㏌ ★ on the edge of the cliff. The Knights used the sanctuary as a quarry for their impressive 15thC **castle** ㏌ but enough was left for an admirably restrained reconstruction by the Italians, who tastefully blended antique, Byzantine, Frankish and Turkish elements.

The narrow lanes, lined with whitewashed 17thC houses with pebbled courtyards, climb from the splendid sweep of sand of the bay to the foot of the castle rock. In some places, lovely early 'Rhodian' plates are embedded in the walls, remnants of 16th and 17thC ware from Asia Minor. Numerous souvenir shops offer modern imitations of this which, though of harsher design and colouring, are reasonable value.

In the 15thC **Church of the Panagia** † there are 18thC frescoes rather poorly restored in 1929, although they provide a restful contrast to the dazzling white exterior.

Hotels on the east coast
All hotels on the E coast close Nov–Mar.

Kallithea
Comfortable hotels, all having ⊷ ㏕ ⇒ AE CB ⊕ ⊙ VISA ≈ ⬚
♨ **Eden Roc** (☎ 23–851/3 ⊗ 292116 ▮▮▮ ▭ 376 ▤), hotel and bungalows; **Paradise** (☎ 29–220 ⊗ 292174 ▮▮▮ ▭ 455 ▤ ●); **Sunwing** (☎ 28–600/8 ⊗ 292252 ▮▮▮ ▭ 389 ●).
Faliraki
Luxury hotels, all having ▤ ⊷ ㏕ ⇒ AE CB ⊕ ⊙ VISA ☐ ◺ ≈
㏌ ♨ **Apollo Beach** (☎ 28–781 ⊗ 292220 ▮▮▮ ▭ 293.); **Blue Sea** (☎ 29–271/3 ⊗ 292241 ▮▮▮ ▭ 296 ●); **Faliraki Beach** (☎ 85–301/3 ⊗ 292219 ▮▮▮ ▭ 298 ●); **Rodos Beach** (☎ 85–471/4 ⊗ 292104 ▮▮▮ ▭ 280 ●).
Inexpensive hotels: **Dimitra** (☎ 25–674 ☐ ▭ 38 ⬚); **Edelweiss** (☎ 85–442 ☐ ▭ 51 ⊷ ⬚).
Afandou
Xenia Golf (☎ 51–121 ☐ ▭ 26 ▨ ㏕ ⇒ ◺ ≈ ⬚).
Lindos
Lindos Bay (☎ 31–212 ▮▮▮ ▭ 192 ▤ ▨ ㏕ ⇒ AE CB ⊕ ⊙ VISA ◺ ≈ ⬚ ♨ ●), at Vlyha Bay, set back to keep the view unrestricted.

Salamis See *Argo-Saronic Islands*.

Sámos ☆

Map 13H10. 2km (1.25 miles) off the w coast of Asia Minor (Turkey); 70km (44 miles) SE of Hios; 322km (201 miles) E of Piraeus. 46km (29 miles) long by up to 19km (12 miles) wide. Getting there: By ferry, from Piraeus, Hios, Kalymnos, Kos, Leros, Lesvos, Mykonos, Patmos, Rhodes, Syros and Kusadasi (Turkey); by air, from Athens. Getting around: By bus to all villages. Taxi and garage facilities available. Population: 33,000.

Samos is the closest Greek island to Asia Minor, separated by a mere 2km (1.25 miles) from Cape Mykale under whose twin peaks the Greek fleet, in 479BC, won a decisive victory over the Persians. It is mountainous and well-wooded with an abundance of superb scenery. The rocky N coast has steep cliffs while the S coast has numerous fine beaches. The island's red *Moschato* wine, though praised by Byron, is too sweet for most tastes.

Visitors to Samos may also wish to explore some of the wide choice of nearby islands. There are twice-weekly ferries to *Hios* and *Lesvos*, and ferries to *Kalymnos*, *Kos*, *Patmos* and *Rhodes* in the Dodecanese. *Mykonos* and *Syros* in the Cyclades can also be reached.

Hera spent her extended honeymoon (see *Mythology* in *Culture, history and background*) on this island and the original Pelasgian settlers even pretended that she was born by the River Imbrassos, where the legendary King Angaeos, one of the Argonauts, built her first temple. Her worship was continued there by the Ionians after their conquest in the 11thC BC.

Fill high the cup with Samian wine!

Byron, *Don Juan*

In 535BC the ruling oligarchy was overthrown by Polykrates and his two brothers. Polykrates then murdered one, exiled the other, and ruled Samos alone. During the tyrant's reign, his capital (present-day **Pythagorio**) flourished, becoming what Herodotos declared to be "the first among all Hellenic and barbaric cities". Great buildings and fortifications were constructed, outstanding poets such as Anakreon and Ibykos gathered in the city, and Polykrates held court in a splendid palace, high above the city on Mt. Ambelos, where later Antony and Cleopatra would entertain the kings and princes of the East before sailing to their doom at *Actium* (see *Mainland A–Z*). Only the mathematician and philosopher Pythagoras reversed the general trend; wishing to put into practice his stern moral code, he left his native island to found Krotona in southern Italy. Modern Pythagorio is named after him.

By open piracy and with the help of the largest fleet in the Aegean, Polykrates amassed an empire. Amasis of Egypt, his ally, became frightened by such persistent good luck and recommended that a most precious possession should be sacrificed to placate the potential jealousy of the gods. So a ring engraved by the court jeweller Theodoros was thrown into the sea, only to be returned by Poseidon in the belly of a fish served up at Polykrates' table. According to Herodotos, the Pharaoh then renounced the alliance, but in reality it was terminated by Polykrates who sent his fleet to help the Persians in their conquest of Egypt. Eventually Polykrates' luck did run out and in 522 BC he was captured and crucified by the Persians.

There are impressive remains of this great period in Samian

history at or near Pythagorio, but there is much more to see besides. The road around most of the island provides a rewarding circular trip which takes in the principal sights and offers greatly varied scenery.

Sights and places of interest

Vathý and Sámos ☆
On the N coast. Main port of Samos. Population: 9,500.

In 1854 the Christian princes who had ruled the island under Turkish suzerainty since 1834 moved the capital to Vathy (Deep) which, as its name indicates, lies at the head of a deep, narrow bay. To complicate matters, the old upper town still bears this name, while the port is called Samos.

In an unusually disparate jumble, public buildings, restaurants and some hotels are grouped round central Pythagora Sq. In the Town Hall, the princes until 1912 presided over the Autonomous Council. The main gate of the public garden with its minute zoo still bears the **escutcheon** of the former principality. Behind it is the interesting **Archaeological Museum** ☆ (📷 *standard opening times*) in which all the island's more important finds are stored. The **Byzantine Museum** (📷 *standard opening times*) is near the port. There are a number of hotels on Themistokli Sofouli, named after the Samian politician who brought about union with Greece in 1912 and in his 90s became the Greek Prime Minister after World War I.

Kokari, 8km (5 miles) w, has a fine sandy beach and hotels.

The Heraion ★
8km (5 miles) sw of Pythagorio.

Left off the coast road w from Pythagorio (see below) and close to a fine sandy beach rises the sole **column** still left standing of what was once the Great Heraion (Temple of Hera), one of 'the three mighty works of the Samians'. It was built near the legendary birthplace of the goddess by Polykrates, shortly after he became tyrant of Samos. Greece's largest temple, it was connected by a Sacred Way, once lined with statues, to the tyrant's capital.

The column is surrounded by foundations which range from Mycenaean to Roman times. Continuing excavations by the German School of Archaeology brought to light in 1980 the largest antique *kouros*, 5m (16.5ft) high, which dates from 570–560BC. It is now in the Archaeological Museum at Samos.

Hóra
5km (3 miles) W of Pythagorio.

A branch right off the coast road just w from Pythagorio (see below) leads up to Hora, now a quiet village but capital of Samos from 1560–1854, when the island's population gradually plucked up courage and ventured back after taking refuge on Hios in the wake of the Turkish conquest of 1453.

Karlovassi
33km (21 miles) w of Samos. Port: Ferries to Piraeus. Population: 5,000.

The second town and port of Samos has old houses which extend out to two monasteries, the 10thC **Panagia tou Potamou** (Our Lady of the River) and **Profitis Ilias**, founded in 1703. A tanning factory often pollutes the air, but inland is rich in vines, and good walks are possible on nearby Mt. Kirkis.

Pythagório ★
On the SE coast. Airport: 6.5km (4 miles) w. Population: 1,700.

The attractive town of Pythagorio was once Polykrates' capital. He enclosed it within 6,500m (7,100yd) of **ramparts** ☆ strengthened by towers, which can still be followed on the slopes of a barren spur of Mt. Ambelos, 1,033m (3,389ft) high.

The mountain is pierced by a 900m-long (1,000yd) **tunnel** ☆ through which water was brought to the town from mountain springs. The tunnel, the first of 'the three mighty works of the Samians', was built by the Megarian Efpalinos, the leading architect of Samos from 6thC BC, who tunnelled from opposite ends until the aqueduct's galleries met with astonishing accuracy in the middle. From the entrance, which is near the ruined **theatre**, the tunnel can be followed deep into the mountain with the help of a flashlight.

Higher up is a **stalactite cave** with a pool, and the **Chapel of the Panagia Spiliani** (Our Lady of the Grotto) †

The second of the 'three mighty works', also by Efpalinos, was the long **breakwater** he built to shelter the Aegean's largest fleet. It was partly used as a foundation for the present shorter mole, and more of the huge blocks can be discerned far out under the water.

The small **museum** (▨ *standard opening times*) contains various lesser finds – the major ones being at Samos. There are restaurants on the waterfront.

The 6km (4 miles) road leading w starts at the romantic **fort** built by Lykourgos Logothetis during the War of Independence, and continues over the island's only plain towards the airport, the village of Hora and the nearby Heraion.

Hotels on Sámos

Samos town (*On the N coast*)
Samos (☎ *28 – 377/8* ❚❚❘ ▭ *83* ➹ ⇨ ≍ ❖ *on roof*); **Samos Bay** (☎ *22 – 101/4* ❚❚❘ ▭ *40* ➹ ◿); **Xenia** (☎ *27 – 463* ❚❚❘ ▭ *31* ▦ ➹ ⇨ ≍ ◿).

Karlovassi (*33km (21 miles) w of Samos*)
Merope (☎ *32 – 650/2* ❚❚❘ ▭ *80* ➹ ⇨ ≍ ◿), 1.6km (1 mile) from the next beach.

Kokari (*8km (5 miles) w of Samos*)
Afroditi (☎ *22 – 504/5* ❚❘ ▭ *42* ➹ ⇨ ≍), 140m (150yd) from the beach; **Kokkari Beach** (☎ *28 – 538* ❚❘ ▭ *45* ➹ ⇨ ≍ ☎).

Pythagorio (*On the SE coast*)
Doryssa Bay (☎ *61 – 360* ☎ *294165* ❚❚❘ ▭ *176* ▦ ➹ ⇨ ≍ ◿ ≈ ☎ ♪); **Glicorisa Beach** (☎ *61 – 305* ❚❘ ▭ *48* ☎); **Polyxeni** (☎ *61 – 359* ❚❘ ▭ *23*).

Samothráki (*Samothrace*) ☆
Map 5D10. 32km (20 miles) SW of Alexandroupoli. 22km (14 miles) long by 13km (8 miles) wide. Getting there: By ferry, from Alexandroupoli and Kavala. Getting around: By bus, to villages and archaeological sites. Taxi and garage facilities available. Population: 3,000.

Samothraki owed its importance in antiquity to its strategic position at the entrance to the Dardanelles. The craggy island rises to the 1,676m (5,500ft) central summit of Fengari (Mountain of the Moon), snow-covered throughout the harsh winter, which affords so spectacular a view that Poseidon chose it as a vantage point from which to watch the Trojan War. The open anchorage at **Kamariotissa** on the more accessible W coast is protected by a breakwater. From here, the road towards the ruins of the ancient city at **Paleopolis** skirts the N coast beaches.

Paleopolis was the site of the sanctuary of the Thracian *Kabiri*, the Great Gods of Samothraki. They were gods of the Underworld who were invoked against the perils of the sea in a cult that centred on a particularly unpleasant aspect of the universal Great Goddess, the form of Hekate, goddess of the night and witchcraft. Initiation into the mysteries of this cult was nearly as sought after as that at *Eleusis* (see *Mainland A–Z*). Philip of Macedonia, for example, met his future wife, Olympias of Epiros, at the annual summer rites at the sanctuary.

There is practically no accommodation for visitors on the island, apart from a small hotel mainly intended for archaeologists at Paleopolis.

Samothraki is reached by daily ferry from *Alexandroupoli* (see *Mainland A–Z*) on the nearby Thracian coast and twice weekly from *Kavala* (see *Mainland A–Z*) in Macedonia. There is a ferry service to neighbouring *Limnos* to the s.

Sights and places of interest
Paleópolis ☆
On the N coast, reached by road (bus) from Kamariotissa.

The finest building on Samothraki was dedicated by a queen, Arsinoë II, who had once fled to the sanctuary. Her fortunes were revived by her marriage to her brother, Ptolemy II Philadelphos (see *Kos*) with whom she ruled Egypt until 270BC. The building she dedicated in gratitude was the largest Greek **rotunda**, with a diameter of 20m (66ft) built for the reception of VIPs, and a huge **stoa** – partially restored.

In 1856 French archaeologists began excavations which 7yr later unearthed the superb *Winged Victory*, a votive offering by Dimitrios Poliorkitis, now in the Louvre.

Continued diggings by a team from New York University have brought to light the graceful **Hellenistic Hieron** with six columns of Parian marble – all other buildings are of inferior marble from *Thassos*.

Among the olive groves which cover the site, the long 4thC BC **walls of the antique city**, constructed of polygonal blocks, mount from the sea to two Genoese towers built from ancient material.

The **museum** ☆ (■ *standard opening times*) is small but interesting.

Other sights
Hora, now officially called **Samothraki**, is inland on a spur of Fengari. Its houses are built in the mainland Thracian style with tiled roofs and overhanging balconies, below a Byzantine-Genoese **castle**. From Hora, the ascent of **Fengari** takes at least 4hr.

An easier excursion is by boat ■ s from Kamariotissa to the lovely **Ammos** beach, where a waterfall cascades from a sheer cliff into the sea.

Ⓗ The only accommodation, mainly for archaeologists, is at Paleopolis: **Xenia** (☎ 41–230 ▥ ▭ 7 ⊂ ↩ ◿).

Santoríni   See *Thira.*

Sérifos   See *Cyclades.*

Sífnos   See *Cyclades.*

Skíathos
*Map **8**F7. Off the coast of Thessaly, 44km (27 miles) SE of Volos. 12km (7.5 miles) long by up to 6km (4 miles) wide. Getting there: By ferry, from Agios Konstantinos, Volos, the other Sporades and Kymi (Evia); by air, from Athens. Getting around: By bus to all villages; also hotel buses. Taxi and garage facilities available. Population: 3,900.*

Skiathos means 'Shadow of Athos', although the title might equally be claimed by several of the other northern Sporades of which it is geographically a member. It lies at the entrance of the Pagassitic Gulf, closest to the Thessalian coast. It is hilly and densely wooded, with some 70 sandy inlets, several bays and three harbours, and has long been a favourite with the British.

White-walled, red-roofed **Skiathos**, the capital, built in 1830 on two low hills, is the setting for most of the stories by its most distinguished son, the writer Alexandros Papadiamantis (1855–1911). A bridge leads to the **Bourtzi islet**, on which the medieval **fort** has been turned into a discotheque. Below are the colourful caiques for exploring the beaches and sights in the N.

Accommodation in town is badly wanting, but there are many hotels strung along the 12km (7.5 miles) of the only road that hugs the S coast to the W of the town. Listed are a selection from several beaches. One of the most beautiful of these is at **Koukounaries**, where the hotels listed are located among the tall stone-pines which give the beach its name.

See also *Sporades* and separate entry on neighbouring *Evia.*

Sights and places of interest

Kastro

Two hours on foot, N of the town.

The former capital, now deserted, was built on an impregnable rock jutting into the sea when the island was occupied by the Turks in the 16thC. Rough steps have replaced the drawbridge to the cliff platform upon which only **Christ Church** with its fine frescoes and an 18thC ikonostasis is left standing among the sad ruins.

Hotels on Skíathos

Skiathos town

The best hotel in town is **Koukounaries** (☎ 42–048 ☎ 282114 ▮▯ ▭ 17), 180m (200yd) from the beach.

All the following hotels are on beaches on the S coast along the road leading W from the town.

Ammoudia
Alkyon (☎ 42–298/5 ☎ 216187 ▮▯ ▭ 80 ▦ ☗ ⇌ ◿ ♨ ◉).

Ahladies
Esperides (☎ 42–245/6 ☎ 282144 ▮▮▮ ▭ 162 ▦ ☗ ⇌ ◿ ≋ ♨ ✤◉).

Tzaneria
Nostos (☎ 42–420/5 ▮▮▮ ▭ 104 ☗ ⇌ ◿ ≋ ♨ ✤ ✔◉).

Koukounaries
Skiathos Palace ▥ (☎ 42–242/3 ☎ 282108 ▮▮▮ ▭ 201 ▦ ☗ ⇌
AE CB ◉ ◉ VISA ◿ ≋ ♨ ✤ ◗); Xenia (☎ 42–041/2
☎ 282114 ▮▮ ▭ 32 ☗ ⇌ ◿ ✤).

Skópelos See *Sporades*.

Skýros See *Sporades*.

Spétses

*Map 8I6. 8km (5 miles) S of Portoheli, on the Peloponnese;
98km (61 miles) SW of Piraeus. Getting there: By hydrofoil,
from Zea Harbour, Piraeus; by ferry, from the main harbour,
Piraeus, and the SE Peloponnese; by motorboat, from Kosta
on the Peloponnese. Getting around: By hotel bus only. Taxis
available. Population: 3,500.*

Furthest of the *Argo-Saronic Islands*, at the mouth of the Saronic Gulf, Spetses is a favourite with Athenians but little visited by foreigners. Some streets in the main town, **Spetses**, are paved with black and white pebble mosaics, but all are practically car-free. Stately progress is made instead by horse-drawn carriage.

The **museum** (▧ *standard opening times*), in a large mansion, is taken up mainly with mementos of the War of Independence.

The dense pine forests of the island waft their perfume out to sea. The most popular beach is at **Kosta** opposite, on the Peloponnese mainland and reached by motorboat. Spetses has plenty of discotheques, less noisy than those on Ydra. See also *Egina*, *Poros* and *Ydra*.

Hotels on Spétses

Spetses town
Faros (☎ 72–613/4 ▮▯ ▭ 47), on the central square; **Kasteli**
(☎ 72–311/3 ▮▮ ▭ 72 ☗ ⇌ ⬇ on roof ✤), hotel and
bungalows; **Roumanis** (☎ 72–244 ▮▮ ▭ 35 ◿), 140m (150yd) from
the beach; **Spetses** (☎ 72–602/4 ▮▮▮ ▭ 77 ▦ ☗ ⇌ AE CB ◉ ◉
VISA ◿ ⬇ on roof ✤).

▣ Among the fish restaurants in the Old Port of the town: **Trehandiri**
(▮▮ ▯ ☗).

Sporades

The Sporades, "the sprinkled isles", form an archipelago just outside the Pagassitic Gulf. They are most easily reached from Volos, except for Skyros which is a mere 46km (29 miles) NE of Kymi on Evia.

The four largest attract ever increasing numbers of visitors. **Alonissos**, reached by motorboat, is oblong in shape and hilly, with a precipitous NW coast. **Skopelos** is a green, fertile island, famed for its plums which are first dried in the sun, then slowly baked into delicious prunes; the colourfully painted houses in the capital rise in an amphitheatre from the sea.

The sprinkled isles,
Lily on lily that o'erlace the sea

Browning, *Cleon*

Skyros, the largest, where in World War I the English poet Rupert Brooke died of fever, lies far to the SE and is almost divided by a narrow waist which accentuates the contrast between the green, wooded north and the barren, mountainous south with sparse olive and fig trees. Its capital is built on a steep rock. Although the island has one of the Aegean's finest beaches, accommodation is insufficient and of a generally low standard.

Skiathos, the most popular, is described in detail.

Sýkinos   See *Cyclades.*

Sými   See *Dodecanese.*

Sýros

Map 12I9. 22km (14 miles) SW of Tinos; 14km (9.6 miles) SE of Piraeus. 22km (14 miles) long by up to 9km (5.5 miles) wide. Getting there: By ferry, from Piraeus, Lavrio, the Cyclades, Ikaria and Samos. Getting around: By bus to all villages. Taxi and garage facilities available. Population: 19,000.

Under French protection Syros, one of the Cyclades, remained neutral during the War of Independence, offering refuge to other islanders who helped to make the capital **Ermoupoli** (Town of Hermes, god of commerce) Greece's main port until 1870, when it was overtaken by Piraeus. Even now, in its decline, the administrative capital and by far the largest town and busiest port of the Cyclades shows signs of its past glory.

On the shady, raised central square a **statue of the patriot Admiral Miaoulis** and a bandstand where performances are given on Sun afternoons, in front of the **Town Hall** and the **Archaeological Museum** (■ *standard opening times*). The **Apollo Theatre**, where opera once used to be performed, is modelled on La Scala in Milan, and there are several attractive Othonian mansions. The grandest of the many churches, **Agios Nikolaos** † ☆ contains a fine *Last Supper*.

Each of the two conical hills is crowned by a large cathedral: **Anastasis** (Resurrection) † on the predominantly Orthodox hill of Vrontado; Neo-Baroque **Agios Georgios** † on the predominantly Catholic Ano Syros, where the Capuchin Monastery of St Jean was founded by Louis XIII of France in 1535 in the medieval Venetian town.

The great local speciality, *loukoumia* (Turkish Delight), is sold from stalls in the port.

Island-hoppers may refer for ideas to the entries on *Delos* (via *Mykonos*), *Naxos*, *Paros* and *Tinos* and, further afield, other islands in the *Cyclades*, especially *Thira*, all connected to Syros by ferry, as is *Samos* in the eastern Aegean.

Hotels on Sýros

Ermoupoli
Hermes (☎ 23–011/2 ▯▯ ▭ 28 ☞ ▭ ☰ ◪); **Nissaki** (☎ 28–200/1 ▯▯ ▭ 42 ☞).
Finikas (*On the w coast, 12km (7.5 miles) from Ermoupoli*)
Hotel Olympia (☎ 42–212 ▯▯ ▭ 30 ▤ ☞ ▭ ☰ ◱).
Megas Gialos (*On the E coast, 12km (7.5 miles) from Ermoupoli*)
Alexandra (☎ 42–540 ▯▯ ▭ 30 ☞ ▭ ☰ ◱).
Vari (*On the E coast, 8km (5 miles) from Ermoupoli*)
Romantica (☎ 22–704 ▯▯ ▭ 30 ☞ ▭ ☰ ◱).

Thássos ☆
Map 4C8. 30km (19 miles) SE of Kavala. 24km (15 miles) long by 19km (12 miles) wide. Getting there: By ferry, from Keramoti and Kavala. Getting around: By bus to all villages. Taxi and garage facilities available. Population: 10,000.
The vales and mountains of Thassos are thickly wooded, with chestnuts, plane trees, pines and firs climbing almost all the way up the 1,203m (3,947ft) of Mt. Ypsario. Geologically, botanically and climatically they are part of Macedonia rather than of the Aegean, a continuation of Mt. Symvolo which rises behind the mainland town of *Kavala* (see *Mainland A–Z*), formerly a colony of Thassos, and of distant Mt. Pangeo, whence came its gold and resulting prosperity. The island was colonized from Paros in 750BC.

The closest good beach to **Thassos**, the main village, is 3km (2 miles) to the E at **Makry Ammos** (Long Sand) but most of it is reserved for the Makry Ammos bungalows (see over).

A scenic circular road makes the entire coast easily accessible and frequent car ferries encourage the bringing of cars; there is also an adequate bus service. There is accommodation in all the numerous seaside villages. Those listed – **Glyfada**, **Skala Rahoniou** and **Skala Prinou** on the w of the island; **Panagia** on the E – are the best equipped with hotels.

Skala Prinou, w, is the port of Greece's only off-shore oil-field. There are also ferry-ports at Thassos and **Limenasia** in the SW.

Sights and places of interest
Thássos ★
On the N coast. Main port of the island. Population: 900.
The two fortified ancient ports are still used, but much of the modern village lies outside the 5km (3 miles) of **ancient ramparts**. They were finished in 494BC, dismantled by the Persians in 491 and then by the Athenians in 464BC, only to be rebuilt, and they now remain as the best-preserved 5thC BC fortifications in Europe. Twelve towers defend the gates from which the bas-reliefs of protecting deities have been taken to Greek, French and Turkish museums, except for a **satyr** which remains on the main land-gate.

The walls ascend steeply from the commercial port to the 4thC BC **theatre**, converted by the Romans in the 2ndC BC into a gladiatorial arena, but now once again the site for performances of classical tragedies.

The 5thC BC **temple** on the pine-clad acropolis may have been dedicated to Athena *Polióuchos* (Protectress of the Town) or to the Delphic Apollo, whose oracle directed the first colonizers from *Paros* in c.750BC. The Venetians in the 13thC and the Genoese in the 15thC used ancient materials for the nearby **fortress**.

The prosperity that maintained the island's sound defences overlaid the antique town with Hellenistic, Roman, Byzantine, Frankish and Turkish buildings. The five chambers of the 5thC BC Ionic **Temple of Herakles** were enlarged with a ritual hall 200yr later. The circular **memorial to Telesikles**, the Parian leader, was restored in 200BC when the **Agora** (🔲 *standard opening times*) began to be surrounded by marble porticos. The **propylaea** faced the **Hellenistic altar** and **Temple of Zeus Agoraios** (Of the Market). Two better-preserved **choragic monuments** were added to the **Temple of Dionysos**, and beside the older **shrines of Artemis** and **Poseidon** there was one to foreign gods. The Romans contributed an **odeon** and the unfinished **Triumphal Arch of the Emperor Caracalla** (c.AD 213), and the pious Byzantines left a **basilica**, of which there are foundations on the main square.

Although the outstanding finds from the island are in the Louvre, the **museum** ☆ (🔲 *standard opening times*) has so many periods upon which to draw that it overflows into the garden where there are monumental sculptures of a **recumbent lion**, an **ornamental bird** and a **Roman emperor**. The most remarkable exhibits are the 6thC BC *Kriophóros*, a *kouros* with a ram slung over his shoulders; a **relief of griffons slaying a deer**; 5thC BC **heads of horses** from the Temple of Herakles; and **statues of Dionysos with Comedy and Tragedy** from the god's 3rdC BC temple.

Hotels on Thássos

In Thassos
Angelika (☎ *22–387* 💴 📺 *26* 🚗), on the town's uninviting beach;
Timoleon (☎ *22–177* 💴 📺 *30* 🚗 ✒), 45m (50yd) from beach.
Glyfada (*5km (3 miles) from Thassos*)
Glyfada (☎ *22–164* 💴 📺 *52* 🚗 ⬛ ✒).
Makry Ammos (*3km (2 miles) E of Thassos*)
Makry Ammos (☎ *22–101* 🅥 *452107* 💴 📺 *206* 🚗 ⬛ ═ AE CB ⬛ 🅓 VISA ⬛ ⬛ 🏊 ⬛), bungalows.
Panagia (*8km (5 miles) from Thassos*)
Faedra (☎ *22–319* 💴 📺 *11* 🚗 ⬛ ═).
Skala Prinou (*6km (4 miles) from Thassos*)
Crystal (☎ *71–272* 💴 📺 *13* 🚗).
Skala Rahoniou (*5km (3 miles) from Thassos*)
Argyro (☎ *22–563* 💴 📺 *29* 🚗 ✒).

Thíra (Santoríni) ☆

Map **12**K9. *20km (12.5 miles) s of Ios; 237km (148 miles) SE of Piraeus. 18km (11 miles) long by about 7km (4.5 miles) wide. Getting there: By ferry, from Piraeus, Crete, Naxos, Paros, Syros and the Dodecanese; by most Aegean cruises; by air, from Athens and (summer only) Rhodes. Getting around: By bus to all villages. Taxis and garage facilities available. Population: 6,400.*

One of the world's strangest islands, the southernmost of the Cyclades has changed its name twice and its shape several times. Kallisti, rightly named the Loveliest, was renamed Thira after the town founded by the Dorian Thiras in the 9thC BC, and renamed again Santorini, elided from St Irene of Thessaloniki, the island's patroness who died here in exile in AD304. Its changes of shape followed shattering geological convulsions: a major earthquake in 1956 destroyed the island's capital.

In c.1450BC the most devastating eruption of the volcano, which first rose in prehistoric times, opened a wide gap in the SW perimeter. The sea poured through this into the crater, submerging the centre of the island and creating a tidal wave which probably hastened the collapse of the Minoan Empire (see *Crete*) and certainly buried the Cretan palaces of Knossos and Phaestos in pumice and ash.

Lava followed upon this deadly combination and covered a prosperous Minoan city on Thira's s promontory, **Akrotiri** ☆

(*standard opening times*). Recently this has been partly excavated, after the late Professor Marinatos put forward his theory, based on an ingenious interpretation of Plato's *Kritias*, that this was the site of fabled Atlantis. The discovery of stately houses decorated with superb frescoes, and a wealth of artistic objects – housed in the **National Archaeological Museum** at Athens (see *Athens/Sights*) until completion of a museum on the site – lend a certain credibility to this theory.

A path zig-zags up an awesome cliff, iridescent against the basic black of the lava, to the white houses on **Thira**, the capital ☆ It has been rebuilt on the cliff's edge, although some houses have been transferred to the gentler slope of the outer rim. The position of the town between the eerie crater and the luxuriant gardens of the eastern district is startling.

Restaurants are indifferent, but the local wines are distinctive and sweet, especially *Nihtéri* and *Vissánto* (Vino Santo). These are grown on the wonderfully fertile SE plain, through which several roads lead to beaches of black volcanic sand.

Thira is served by ferries from *Crete, Ios, Naxos* and *Paros*, all reasonably near, and further afield it can be reached from *Syros* and some of the *Dodecanese*. See also *Cyclades*.

Sights and places of interest

An eruption in 236BC caused the western island of **Thirassia** to splinter off, and since then mini-volcanoes have risen and sunk in the great gulf on the w of the island, lying within the broken rim of the crater. **The Kamenes** (The Burnt Islands) ☆ appeared in 1573 and 1868. They provide a favourite boat excursion () for the more adventurous, for they are still active, especially after one of the frequent earth tremors.

The finest of the beaches on the SE coast is at **Perissa**. Here a large, circular white **Church of the Holy Cross** † with eight flying buttresses supporting four cupolas round a central dome was designed by a local architect in the 1840s.

On the Mesavouno (Middle Mountain), 369m (1,211ft) high, above Perissa, the Dorians settled in the 9thC BC and, 600yr later, the Egyptian Ptolemies placed a garrison on the top of the barren ridge. This large town, **ancient Thira** ☆ occupied an area measuring 800 by 147m (2,625 by 482ft). The Doric and Ptolemaic elements were blended in the **Gymnasium of the Ephebes** where once naked boys danced and sang paeans in praise of Apollo. The Romans added a small **theatre**.

Kamari, N coast, was also an ancient town, but few traces remain.

The small **museum** in Thira town (*standard opening times*) contains finds from ancient Thira and Akrotiri.

Hotels on Thíra

Thira town
Atlantis (*22–232* ▪▪▪ ▭ *25* ⌂ ⇌ ▱ ◁€); **Theoxenia** (*22–740* ▮▯ ▭ *11* ◁€).
Kamari (*On the N coast*)
Kamari (*31–234* ▮▯ ▭ *55* ⌂ ⇌ ⇌ ⬧ ⚲ ●).

Tílos See *Dodecanese*.

Tínos ☆

Map 12|9. Between Andros to the NW and Mykonos, 10km (6 miles) to the SE; 158km (99 miles) SE of Piraeus. 27km (17 miles) long by 12km (7.5 miles) wide. Getting there: By ferry, from Piraeus, Andros, Mykonos, and Syros. Getting around: By bus to all villages. Taxi and garage facilities available. Population: 8,300.

The long Venetian occupation of Tinos, from 1207–1715, left a strong Catholic element, but the discovery in 1822 of a

miraculous ikon of the Panagia (Our Lady) created an
Orthodox equivalent of Lourdes on this Cycladic island. The
Marian Feasts of the Annunciation, Mar 25, and the
Assumption, Aug 15, attract enormous crowds of pilgrims. All
island boats are diverted from their schedules to ferry the sick,
who then lie on the route of the procession while the ikon is
borne by sailors over the prostrate bodies.

There are frequent ferry services from *Andros*, *Mykonos*
and *Syros*. See also *Cyclades*.

Sights and places of interest

In the nave of the small **Church of Panagia Evangelistra ✝** in Tinos
town, there is a faithful queue to kiss the **Megalohari ikon** (ikon of Our
Great and Gracious Lady) ✰ encrusted with diamonds and pearls, and
surrounded by *ex-votos* of precious metals and hundreds of lighted
candles. In the white marble stoas round the vast courtyard are a **Picture
Gallery**, a **Sculpture Museum** and a **Byzantine Museum** (*all* 🖾
standard opening times).

The **Archaeological Museum** (🖾 *standard opening times*) is in the
wider of the two streets leading up from the harbour, the narrower being
lined with shops selling religious articles and souvenirs.

The Orthodox **Kehrovouni Convent** above the town was a favourite
retreat of Princess Andrew of Greece, mother of Prince Philip, Duke of
Edinburgh. The nuns sell embroideries.

Inland on Mt. Exobourgo to the N is the site of the **ancient city** ✰ the
second built there. It became one of the strongest Venetian fortresses in
the Cyclades, **Santa Helena** 🏰 which was attacked 11 times but never
taken by the Turks.

The island boasts 1,200 chapels, and 600 **dovecots** – characteristic of
many of the Cyclades but most common here and on *Andros*.

Ĥ **Asteria** (☎ 22–132 ⬛ ▭ 48 ⬅), in Tinos town; **PLM Tinos
Beach** (☎ 22–626/8 ▥ ▭ 204 ⬅ ☐ ⊶ AE CB ⓓ ⑩ VISA ⬜ ⇝
⬅ ⤋ ⓞ), hotel and bungalows, 2km (1.25 miles) NW of Tinos town.

Tzía   See *Kea*.

Ýdra (Hydra) ✰

*Map 8 I7. 21km (13 miles) SE of Ermioni; 70km (44 miles) SW
of Piraeus. 14km (9 miles) long by 3km (1.9 miles) wide.
Getting there: By hydrofoil, from Zea Harbour, Piraeus; by
ferry, from the main harbour, Piraeus, and the SE
Peloponnese; by motorboat, from Ermioni. Population:
2,500.*

Ýdra is the next stop after Poros for the hydrofoil and ferries
which link the *Argo-Saronic Islands* with Piraeus and the SE
Peloponnese. Its brightly coloured 18th and 19thC houses
climb steeply up the barren, elongated mountainside, forming a
picture-postcard island town, for the houses of the sea captains
who grew rich running the British blockade during the
Napoleonic Wars have been preserved by tourism. There is a
small foreign colony of artists and writers, though the phoney
greatly outnumber the genuine.

The beaches are a long way out of **Ydra town** and are
accessible only on foot or by boat. Accommodation is quite
insufficient, being mostly in converted mansions with faulty
plumbing. A safer bet are the various holiday complexes around
Ermioni (see *Mainland A–Z*) on the Peloponnese opposite.

The numerous restaurants and discotheques of Ydra are
extremely lively. Although it seems over-priced, **La
Grenouille** ᴿ serves the best food in town.

See also *Egina*, *Poros* and *Spetses*.

Event: *Miaoulia* (Naval competition), June 20.

Hotels on Ýdra

Hydroussa (☎ *52–217* ▮▮ ❧ *36, some with bathrooms* 🚪 ⇌ 🖭) is typical of the hotels in town in converted mansions; **Miramare** (☎ *52–300/1* ▮▮ ▭ *28* 🚪 ⇌ 🖭 🍴), 3km (1.25 miles) s, is preferable.

Zákynthos (*Zante*) ☆

*Map **10**H3. s of Kefalonia; 31km (19 miles) sw from Kylini. 40km (25 miles) long by 19km (12 miles) wide. Getting there: By hydrofoil, from Patra; by ferry, from Kylini, reached by rail and bus from Athens and Patra; by air, direct charter flights from several European cities, and domestic flights from Athens. Getting around: By bus throughout the island. Taxi and garage facilities available. Population: 28,000.*

This Ionian island was named after the legendary hero Zakynthos, who in the 15thC BC built a fort on the same hill, now occupied by the **medieval fortress** above the town. The 'Flower of the Levant' rivals *Corfu* for natural beauty, but the Venetian mansions were lost in the 1953 earthquake.

The capital, **Zakynthos**, seems unnecessarily utilitarian, even the once charmingly arcaded streets, so useful against the summer sun and winter rains, now being of rectangular uniformity. The Strata Marina is a popular seaside promenade, opening on to two squares which have open-air restaurants and pastry shops. The **Museum of Byzantine Art** ☆ (▨ *standard opening times*) on Solomou Sq. contains 16th and 17thC ikons from the island's ruined churches, and major works of the Ionian school of painting. The **Solomos Museum** (▨ *standard opening times*) on Agiou Markou Sq. is dedicated to the local poets Dionysios Solomos and Andreas Kalvos. The mortal remains of the patron saint, Agios Dionysios, lie surrounded by gold and silver *ex-votos* in the huge **church** †

Food is slightly better than average for the islands. The white *Verdéa* wine is pleasant, and *mandaláto* (white nougat with peanuts) and *pastéli* (a sort of pretzel with sesame seeds) are specialities of Zakynthos.

The better beaches, with adequate hotels, include, to the s, **Argassi**, 4km (2.5 miles) and **Laganas**, 8km (5 miles) and to the N, **Alykes**, 16km (10 miles) and **Planos**, 5km (3 miles).

See also *Ionian Islands* and the other northern islands in the group: *Corfu, Ithaki, Kefalonia, Lefkada* and *Paxi*.

Events: International Meeting of Medieval and Popular Theatre, Aug; procession in honour of St Dionysios, Aug 24.

Hotels on Zákynthos

Zakynthos town
Diana (☎ *28–547* ▮▮ ▭ *36* ☕); **Phoenix** (☎ *22–719* ▮▮ ▭ *38*);
Strada Marina (☎ *22–761* ▮▮ ▭ *56* ☕ 🚪 ⇌ AE CB ⊕ ⊙ VISA 🖭 ⚓ *on roof*).
Alykes (16km (10 miles) N of Zakynthos town)
Levante (☎ *83–245* ▮▮ ▭ *63* ☕ 🖭 🍴); **Montreal** (☎ *83–341/2* ▮▮ ▭ *31* 🚪 ⇌ 🍴⊙).
Argassi (4km (2.5 miles) s of Zakynthos town)
Chryssi Akti (☎ *28–022* ▮▮ ▭ *61* ☕ 🚪 ⇌ 🖭 🍴 ♨); **Mimosa Beach** (☎ *22–588* ▮▮ ▭ *32* ☕ 🚪 ⇌ 🍽 🍴), bungalows.
Laganas (8km (5 miles) s of Zakynthos town)
Galaxy (☎ *72–271* ▮▮ ▭ *80* ☕ 🚪 ⇌ 🖭 🍴); **Zante Beach** (☎ *78–870/1* ▮▮ ▭ *252* ☕ 🚪 ⇌ 🖭 AE CB ⊕ ⊙ VISA 🖭 ⚓ ♒), hotel and bungalows.
Planos (5km (3 miles) N of Zakynthos town)
Tsilivi (☎ *23–109/110* ▮▮ ▭ *55* ☕ 🍽 🍴).

A guide to Greek

Sokrates' avowal "I know that I know nothing" could be an entirely appropriate reaction to the intricacies of modern Greek, particularly where place and street names are concerned. Yet when he made this superbly humble statement in the 5thC BC, he was not referring to his language, the Ionic dialect's Attic form. The classical Greek poets spoke and wrote various Ionic, Aeolic and Doric dialects more or less indifferently, all employing the same alphabetical basis, which was subsequently standardized by the great Hellenistic grammarians in the form that is used today. This literature and speech spread through the empire of Alexander the Great and the succeeding Hellenistic kingdoms. The *koiné* of the Bible was the second language of the Roman empire, before becoming the first in the thousand years of the Byzantine civilization, and then slowly evolving into the *katharévousa* of the Konstantinopolitan Greeks. The peasants and serfs of Greece, cut off from all education, developed a vernacular of their own, the *dimotikí*.

Even before independence, a fierce struggle raged between the adherents of these two versions, which not only differ in vocabulary, but are equally at variance in grammar. Like most things in Greece, it soon became a political issue, the educated aristocrats naturally inclining towards the traditional *katharévousa*, the often illiterate revolutionaries restricted to the various dialects of *dimotikí*. The battle continued for 150yr, and the sensible compromise of the *kathomilouméni*, which combined elements of both extremes, was rejected by the fanatical right and left alike, although it was used by the few serious newspapers.

In 1976, however, the right-wing government imposed *dimotikí* as the official language and the only one that would be taught henceforth in schools – a levelling down reminiscent of Mao's high-handed treatment of Chinese.

Though conjugations, declensions and other grammatical frills have been ruthlessly simplified, spelling based on the 24 letters of the antique alphabet has remained unchanged, giving, for instance, five ways to render the *i* (as in *give*) sound: I/ι, H/η, Y/υ, EI/ει and OI/οι. The ancient Greeks were known for the richness of their language and these alternatives must have originated in different pronunciations, as followed in classical studies throughout the world. Unfortunately this diversity has been rejected by modern Greeks.

Place names

Place names, as well as street names (see opposite), present a special problem in Greece. Many rivers, mountains and villages have two names, the local, often Slav or Albanian, name and the antique name that is now official again. The preferred style in this book is to give only the latter, except for the most recent reversions, where the local name, as the only one used by the inhabitants, is given in brackets.

In complete contradiction to this understandable return to a proud past, however, is the imposition of *dimotikí* on names that have reverberated through world history for millennia. Athens itself is no longer *Athíne*, as it has been for 4,000yr, but *Athína*. Even *pólis* (town) has not been spared and has been reduced to *póli*. Generally the word endings -n and -s have been dropped with gay abandon, but almost as many have been added where there were none before. Most signs, moreover, are still in the pre-reform spelling, giving a happy mix of Agrinion with Agrinio, Patras with Patra, Pireefs with Pireas, or Thive with Thiva. Ruins of famous antique towns, where there is no modern settlement, added a further complication, thus Dion is still as frequent as Dio, Nikopolis as Nikopoli.

These variations quite gratuitously aggravated officialdom's already formidable task of making signposts and maps comprehensible to tourists from all nations. As conventionally romanized forms in English differ considerably from those used in French or German, the decision to use phonetic rendering – simply changing the Greek into roman characters – was the obvious solution. To avoid confusion this practice has been followed here, with the exception of world-renowned names that have been left in the familiar anglicized form in the text, with the romanized phonetic Greek in brackets. Thus: Athens (*Athina*), Corinth (*Korinthos*) and Thebes (*Thiva*).

For lesser-known names, where there is nevertheless a known anglicized form, it is more appropriate to give the romanized phonetic Greek first with the alternative spelling in brackets. Thus: Hios (*Chios*), Kefalonia (*Cephalonia*), Zakynthos (*Zante*).

For the majority only the romanized phonetic Greek is given.

Rules of spelling still vary, particularly in place names. There is no official consistency regarding -nt- and -nd-, but the former is less eccentric and is preferred; thus Konstantinos and Penteli rather than Konstandinos or Pendeli. In place names the Greek Y/υ was, for a time, romanized as I/i, rather than Y/y as in *dimotikí*, except for Olympia and Mount Olympos which remained sacrosanct. The current trend, however, shows a triumphant return of Y/y in tourist leaflets and hotel lists and this is reflected here. Thus one finds again Mykonos and Ydra, although some publications still feature Mikonos and Idra. Double-l (LL/ll) suffered in the reform, and so one reads Apolonia and Apolonas, to the chagrin of Apollo, but generally double consonants appear in romanized Greek as they do in the original. The letter C, illogically, does appear in some place names, in contradiction to the rule that it does not exist in Greek. Porto Carras retains the name of its owner. Following an older precedent the most familiar spelling of Acropolis and Mycenae have been retained, although not in Akro-Nafplio, and only in half the compound Akro-Corinth.

One further complication bedevils motorists. When giving directions, Greeks use the objective case, saying "Delfous" while pointing to the road you think leads to Delphi. But never fear, the name has not changed – you will find Delphi on arrival.

Street names

In most larger towns and resorts these are signposted in both Greek and roman letters. *Odós* (street) is omitted, but usually *leofóros* (avenue) and *platía* (square) remain. In smaller towns, however, where street names appear only in Greek, *odós* (οδός) is written.

Street names also change, but commonly the old is kept with the new, for a time at least. Although streets named after Churchill and Roosevelt in gratitude after World War II have reverted quietly to Stadiou and Akadimias, Athens retains the prime example of this changeability in its main thoroughfare, which used to be named Panepistimiou, after the University; it is still known by many as such, although officially it is called Venizelou, in honour of Greece's famous statesman Venizelos.

Words and phrases

Pronunciation

In romanized Greek (see alphabet below), A/a, E/e, I/i, K/k, M/m, N/n, O/o, T/t, Y/y and Z/z are pronounced as in English and present no difficulty. Greek *víta* (B/β), when romanized, is written and pronounced as V/v. English C and H sounds do not exist in Greek, although the letter C was used as a substitute for K for a time. Modern scholars have reverted to the original K in almost all cases; thus Kimon, Konstantine, Perikles, and Sokrates. *Ita* (H/η) in Greek is pronounced as I/i. *Délta* (Δ/δ) is pronounced as a soft TH, but is written in romanized Greek as D/d. *Thíta* (Θ/θ) is a strong TH/th. *Lámda* (Λ/λ) is L/l. *Sígma* (Σ/σ) is S/s. Both *oméga* (Ω/ω) and *ómikron* (O/o) are written and pronounced as O/o.

More difficult are the sounds that do not exist in English. The slightly guttural *gamma* (Γ/γ) used to be rendered as GH, but now is simply G/g. The strongly guttural *hi* (X/χ) used to be CH or KH but is now H/h, except after S/s where, for clarity's sake, it remains KH/kh; it is no less guttural than before. *Fi* (Φ/φ), formerly PH, is now F/f. *Ro* (P/ρ) should be rendered R/r. *Pi* (Π/π) is P/p. *Xi* (Ξ/ξ) is X/x, and should not be confused with *hi. Psi* (Ψ/ψ) is PS/ps. M Π/μπ (MP/mp) is pronounced B. The diphthongs AE/αε and AI/αι are written and pronounced as E/e (as in Elizabeth). EI/ει and OI/οι are as I/i (as in give); OY/ου as U/u (pronounced -oo-); AY/αυ is pronounced -af-; EY/ευ is pronounced -ev-. When the first letter of a diphthong carries an accent, the two letters are pronounced separately.

Greek alphabet		Romanized letters	Pronunciation
A/α	άλφα (*álfa*)	A/a	as a in father
B/β	βήτα (*víta*)	V/v	as v in victory
Γ/γ	γάμμα (*gámma*)	G/g	as guttural g
Δ/δ	δέλτα (*délta*)	D/d	as th in then
E/ε	έψιλον (*épsilon*)	E/e	as e in get
Z/ζ	ζήτα (*zíta*)	Z/z	as z in zoo
H/η	ήτα (*íta*)	I/i	as i in is
Θ/θ	θήτα (*thíta*)	TH/th	as th in thorough
I/ι	γιώτα (*yóta*)	I/i	as i in is
K/κ	κάππα (*káppa*)	K/k	as k in king
Λ/λ	λάμδα (*lámda*)	L/l	as l in love
M/μ	μί (*mi*)	M/m	as m in mother
N/ν	νί (*ni*)	N/n	as n in nice
Ξ/ξ	ξί (*xi*)	X/x	as x in axis
O/o	όμικρον (*ómikron*)	O/o	as o in hot
Π/π	πί (*pi*)	P/p	as p in pick
P/ρ	ρώ (*ro*)	R/r	as r in rod
Σ/σ	σίγμα (*sígma*)	S/s	as s in soft
T/τ	ταῦ (*taf*)	T/t	as t in tap
Y/υ	ύψιλον (*ípsilon*)	Y/y	as y in mystery
Φ/φ	φί (*fi*)	F/f	as f in fox
X/χ	χί (*hi*)	H/h	as ch in Bach
Ψ/ψ	ψί (*psi*)	PS/ps	as ps in lapse
Ω/ω	ώμέγα (*oméga*)	O/o	as o in hot

Reference words

Monday	Deftéra	Friday	Paraskeví
Tuesday	Tríti	Saturday	Sávvato
Wednesday	Tetárti	Sunday	Kyriakí
Thursday	Pémpti		

January	Ianouários	July	Ioúlios
February	Fevrouários	August	Ávgoustos
March	Mártios	September	Septémvrios
April	Aprílios	October	Októvrios
May	Máios	November	Noémvrios
June	Ioúnios	December	Dekémvrios

1	éna	11	éndeka	21	ikossiéna
2	dýo	12	dódeka	22	ikossidío
3	tría	13	dékatria	30	triánda
4	téssera	14	dékatéssera	40	saránda
5	pénde	15	dékapénde	50	penínda
6	éxi	16	dékaéxi	60	exínda
7	eptá	17	dékaeptá	70	evdomínda
8	októ	18	dékaoktó	80	ogdónda
9	ennéa	19	dékaennéa	90	enenínda
10	déka	20	íkossi	100	ekató

First	prótos	Quarter past . . . . ke tétarto
Second	défteros	Half past . . . . ke missí
Third	trítos	Quarter to . . . . pará tétarto
Fourth	tétartos	Quarter to six éxi pará tétarto

Mr	kýrios	Ladies	ginekón
Mrs	kyría	Gents	andrón
Miss	despinís		

Red	kókkino	Blue	blé
Yellow	kítrino	Black	mávro
Green	prássino	White	áspro

Basic communication

Yes ne
No óhi
Please parakaló
Thank you efharistó
I'm very sorry lipáme polí
Excuse me signómi
Not at all/you're
  welcome parakaló
Hello yiá sou
Good morning kaliméra
Good afternoon kalispéra
Good night kaliníhta
Goodbye adío
Morning proí
Afternoon apógevma
Evening vrádi
Night níhta
Yesterday htés
Today símera
Tomorrow ávrio
Next week tin álli evdomáda
Last week tin perasméni
  evdomáda
. . . . days ago prin apó . . . .
  méres
Month mínas
Year hrónos
Here edó
There ekí
Big megálo
Small mikró
Hot zestó
Cold krýo
Good kaló
Bad kakó
Beautiful oréo
With me me
And ke
But allá
Open aniktó
Closed klistó
Entrance íssodos
Exit éxodos
Free tzámpa
Left aristerá

Right dexiá
Straight on issia embrós
Near kontá
Far makriá
Above apó páno
Below apó káto
Front embrós
Behind písso
Early norís
Late argá
Pleased to meet you. Hárika pou
  sas gnórissa/héro polý.
How are you? Pos iste?
Very well, thank you. Polí kalá,
  efharistó.
Do you speak English? Miláte
  Angliká?
I don't understand. Den
  katalavéno.
Please explain. Parakaló exigíste.
Please speak more
  slowly. Parkaló milíste pió
  argá.
My name is . . . . To onomá mou
  íne . . . .
I am English/American. Íme
  Ánglos/Amerikanós.
Where is/are . . ? Poú íne . . ?
Is there a . . ? Ypárkhi éna . . ?
What? Ti?
When? Póte?
How much? Pósso?
That's too much. Íne pára pollá.
Expensive akrivó
Cheap fthinó
I would like . . . . Tha íthela . . . .
Do you have . . . ? Éhete . . . ?
Where is the toilet? Poú íne i
  toualéta?
Where is the telephone? Poú íne
  to tiléfono?
That's fine/OK. Polý oréa/O.K.
I don't know. Den xéro.
What time is it? Ti óra íne?
I feel ill. Den esthánome kalá.

225

Words and phrases

Shopping

Where is the nearest/a good . . . . ?   Poú íne to plisiéstero/éna kaló . . . . ?

Can you help me/show me some . . . . ?   Boríte na me voithíssete/na mou díxete meriká . . . . ?

I'm just looking.   Aplós kyttázo.

Do you accept credit cards/travellers cheques?   Pérnete credit cards/travellers cheques?

Can you deliver to . . . . ?   Boríte na to meteférete sto . . . . ?

I'll take it.   Tha to páro.

I'll leave it.   Tha to afísso.

Can I have it tax-free for export?   Boró na to páro aforológito giá exagoghí?

This is faulty. Can I have a replacement/refund?   Aftó éhi elátoma. Boró na to alláxo/na páro tá leftá písso?

I don't want to spend more than . . . .   Den thélo na xodépso perissótera apó . . . .

I'll give you . . . . for it.   Tha sas dósso . . . . gi' aftó.

Can I have a stamp for . . . . ?   Boró naého éna gramatóssimo giá . . . . ?

Shops

Antique shop antíkes	Grocer bakáliko
Art gallery gallerí érgon téhnis	Haberdasher psilikatzídiko
Baker foúrnos	Hairdresser kommotírio
Bank trápeza	Jeweller kosmimatopolío
Beauty salon institoúto kallonís	Market agorá
Bookshop vivliopolío	Newsagent efimeridopólis
Butcher (and variants) kreopolío	Optician optikós
Cake stop zaharoplastío	Photographic shop fotografío
Chemist/pharmacy farmakío	Post office tahidromío
Clothes shop katástima idón rouhismoú	Shoe shop katástima ypodimáton
Dairy galaktopolío	Supermarket super market
Department store megálo katástima	Tailor rafío
	Tobacconist kapnopolío
Fishmonger psarádiko	Tourist office touristikó grafío
Florist anthopolío	Toy shop katástima pehnidíon
Greengrocer manáviko	Travel agent touristikos práktor

Some useful goods

Antiseptic cream antisiptikí kréma	Soap sapoúni
Aspirin aspirínes	Sticking plaster lefkoplástis
Bandages epídesmi	Sunburn cream kréma giá engávmata apó ton ílio
Cotton wool vamváki	Sunglasses gialiá ilíou
Diarrhoea/upset stomach pills diárria/hápia giá stomahikí diatarahí	Suntan cream/oil kréma/ládi mavrísmatos
Indigestion tablets hápia giá dyspepsía	Tampons tampón
Insect repellant ygró giá éntoma	Tissues hartomándila
Sanitary towels serviétes ygías	Toothbrush odontóvourtsa
Shampoo sampouán	Toothpaste odontókrema
Shaving cream kréma xyrísmatos	Travel sickness pills hápia giá naftía

Bra soutién	Shoes papoútsia
Coat paltó	Skirt foústa
Dress fórema	Socks káltses
Jacket sakkáki	Stockings/tights káltses nylon/kalson
Ladies panties kulóttes	Swimsuit mayó
Pullover poulóver	Trousers pantelóni
Shirt poukámiso	

Film film	Postcard kart postál
Letter grámma	Stamp grammatósimo
Money order émvasma	Telegram tilegráfima

Motoring

Service station stathmós venzínis

Fill it up.   Gemíste to.

Give me . . . . drachmes worth.   Válte moú venzíni . . . . drahmón.

I would like . . . . litres of petrol. Tha íthela . . . . lítra venzíni.
Can you check the . . . . ? Boríte na kittaxete to . . . . ?
There is something wrong with the . . . . Káti den pái kalá me to . . . .
Battery bataría
Brakes fréna
Engine mihaní
Exhaust exátmissi
Lights fóta
Oil ládia
Tyres lástiha
Water neró
Windscreen par-bríz
My car won't start. To aftokínito dén xekinái.
I have had a puncture. Émina apó lástiho.
How long will it take to repair? Se pósso keró tha íne étimo?

Other methods of transport

Aircraft aeropláno
Airport aerodrómio
Bus leofório
Bus stop stássi leoforíou
Coach poúlman
Ferry/boat ferry/plío
Ferry port limáni ferry boat
Hydrofoil yptámeno delfíni
Station stathmós
Train tréno
Ticket issitírio
Ticket office grafío isstiríon
Single monó
Return met' epistrofís
Half fare missó issitírio
First/second/economy próti/ défteri/tríti
Sleeper/couchette me krevváti/ kousétta

Food and drink

Have you a table for . . . . ? Éhete éna trapézi giá . . . . ?
I want to reserve a table for . . . . at . . . . Thélo na klísso éna trapézi giá . . . . stis . . . .
A quiet table. Éna íssiho trapézi.
A table near the window. Ena trapézi kondá sto paráthiro.
Could we have another table? Boroúme na éhoume állo trapézi?
I only want a snack. Thélo káti elafró.
The menu, please. Ton katálogo parakaló.
I'll have . . . . Tha páro . . . .
Can I see the wine list? Tón katálogo tón krassión parakaló?
I would like . . . . Thélo . . . .
What do you recommend? Tí moú synistáte ná páro?
What do you want to drink? Tí thá piíte?
I did not order this. Den to parángila aftó.
This is bad. Avtó íne halasméno.
Can this be changed? Boríté ná tó alláxete?
Lunch/dinner Gévma/dípno
Bring me another. Férte mou állo éna.
The bill please. Tón logariasmó parakaló.
Is service included? To servís perilamvánete?
Restaurant estiatório
Taverna tavérna
Hot zestó
Cold krýo
Glass potíri
Bottle boukáli
Half-bottle missó boukáli
Beer/lager bíra/láger
Orange/lemon squash mía porto kaláda/lemonáda
Water neró
Iced . . . . pagoméno
Mineral water emfialoméno neró
Fizzy/still me anthrakikó/ horís anthrakikó
Flask/carafe karáfa
Red wine kókkino krassí
White wine áspro krassí
Cheers! Stín ygiá sas!
Sweet glykó
Salt aláti
Pepper pipéri
Mustard moustárda
Oil ládi
Vinegar xídi
Bread psomí (ártos when written)
Butter voútyro
Cheese tyrí
Egg avgó
Milk gála
Pastry shop zaharoplastío
Coffee house kafenío
Coffee kafé
Greek (Turkish) coffee ellinikó kafé
without sugar skéto
moderately sweet métrio
very sweet varý glykó
Ice cream pagotá
Chocolate sokoláta
Honey méli
Sugar záhari
Tea tsái
Steak filéto
well done kalopsiméno
medium métrio
rare senián

227

Words and phrases

Most menus are written in Greek and English, but even in the all-Greek taverna they keep approximately the same layout.

ΚΟΥΒΕΡ/kouvér   cover charge
ΑΡΤΟΣ/ártos   bread
ΟΡΕΚΤΙΚΑ/orektiká   appetizers
ΣΟΥΠΕΣ/soúpes   soups
ΖΥΜΑΡΙΚΑ/zymariká   pasta
ΨΑΡΙΑ/psária   fish
ΘΑΛΑΣΣΙΝΑ/thalassiná   seafood
ΛΑΔΕΡΑ/laderá   vegetables cooked in oil
ΚΥΜΑΔΕΣ/kymádes   minced meat
ΕΝΤΡΑΔΕΣ/entrádes   entrees, esp. meat dishes
ΨΗΤΑ/psitá   grills
ΤΗΣ ΩΡΑΣ/tis óras   à la minute/while you wait
ΣΑΛΑΤΕΣ/salátes   salads
ΤΥΡΙΑ/tyriá   cheeses
ΦΡΟΥΤΑ/froúta   fruit
ΓΛΥΚΑ/glyká   sweets
ΠΟΤΑ/potá   drinks
ΟΙΝΟΙ ΛΕΥΚΟΙ/ΕΡΥΘΡΟΙ/ΚΟΚΚΙΝΕΛΙ/óinoi
    leykói/erythrói/kokkinéli   white/red/rosé wines (written in
    katharévousa)
ΜΠΥΡΕΣ/býres   beers
ΑΝΑΨΥΚΤΙΚΑ/anapsyktiká   soft drinks
When the menu is handwritten and illegible, go into the kitchen and look in the pots (it's that kind of place).

Agináres á lá políta   small artichokes cooked in a white onion and celery sauce
Ahinós   sea urchin
Ahládi   pear
Amygdalotó   baked mixture of ground almonds, orange flower water, semolina and sugar, coated with icing sugar
Angóuri   cucumber
Araká   green peas
Arnáki gálaktos   baby lamb
Arní   lamb
    exohikó   baked country style with peas, potatoes and cheese in flaky pastry
    frikasé   sauteed with lettuce, spring onions and dill in egg and lemon
Astakós   crayfish/lobster
Avgolémono   chicken broth with rice, lemon and egg
Bakaliáros   fried salt cod usually served with *skordaliá*
Baklavá   thin pastry layers stuffed with nuts and spices, doused in syrup
Bámies   okra, lady's fingers
Barboúnia   red mullet, possibly the best Greek fish
Bon filé   fillet steak
Bougátsa   custard tart
Bourekákia   tiny stuffed flaky pastry pasties
Brík   red caviar
Brizóla   chop, cutlet
Damáskina   plums
Dolmádes   vine or cabbage leaves rolled and stuffed with meat and/or rice
Dolmadákia   tiny *dolmádes*

Eliés   olives—best from Delphi (large purple) and Kalamata (pointed black)
Fakiés   lentils, often in soup
Fasólia   white beans, often a soup base with other vegetables
Fasólia fréska   French beans
Fáva   split pea, onion, oil and lemon purée—a Lentan speciality from Thira
Féta   most popular Greek cheese, salty and white, made from ewes' or goats' milk
Fráoules   strawberries
Galaktoboúreko   flaky pastry with a custard filling, doused in syrup
Galopoula   turkey
Garídes   prawns
Gígantes   broad beans
Giuvétsi   (with) pasta
Glóssa   sole
Gourounópoulo gálaktos   sucking pig, often roasted whole
Granitá   sorbets
Graviéra   Greek gruyère
Grép   grapefruit
Halvá   sesame seed sweet
Hirinó   pork, usually lean and tender
Horiátiki   peasant salad with cucumber, tomato, onion, olives and *féta*
Hórta   bitter leaves like dandelion
Hortósoupa   vegetable soup, usually with carrots and peas
Imám bayildí   "the priest fainted"—aubergines stuffed with tomatoes and onions
Kadaïfi   shredded wheat pastry with nuts, soaked in syrup
Kakaviá   fish stew

228

Kalamarákia   young squid excellent when deep fried

Kapamá   with potatoes and onions in a tomato sauce

Karavídes   langoustine

Karpoúzi   watermelon

Karýdia   walnuts

Katsíki   goat, often tough

Katsikáki   baby goat

Keftedákia   tiny meat balls, served hot or cold

Keftédes tiganités (skáras)   fried (or grilled) meatballs

Kerássia   cherries

Kokorétsi   kidneys, tripe and liver, bound with intestines and grilled on the spit

Kolokýthia tiganitá   fried sliced courgettes

Kopenháï   sweet of flaky pastry, honey and nuts

Kotópoulo   chicken

Kotósoupa   chicken soup

Kounéli   rabbit

Kounoupídi   cauliflower

Kourabiédes   white biscuits

Krassáto   cooked in wine

Kreatópitta   triangular flaky pastry containing minced meat

Krem karamelé   cream caramel, fairly ubiquitous

Ladolémono   olive oil and lemon juice

Lagós   hare

Láhano   cabbage

Lemóni   lemon

Lithrínia   sea bream

Loukániko   sausage

Loukoumádes   hot honey fritters sprinkled with cinnamon

Loukoúmi   Turkish delight, best from Syros

Magirítsa   soup of lamb's liver, heart, lungs and intestines with spring onions, rice, egg and lemon – for Easter

Makarónia   ubiquitous but not as good as Italian pasta

Manoúri   bland Cretan cheese

Marídes   fried whitebait

Melitzánes   aubergines

Melitzanosaláta   baked aubergine, puréed with garlic, onion and tomato. Nearly always excellent

Melomakárona   honey cake

Melópitta   honey pie

Mílo   apple

Miloradákino   nectarine

Moskhári   veal kokinistó   in tomato sauce

Moussaká   mince and aubergine layers topped with béchamel and cheese sauce

Myalá salatá   boiled brains served cold with lemon

Mýdia   mussels, best from Thessaloniki

Myzíthra   bland Cretan cheese

Nefrá   kidneys

Oktapódi   octopus

Pagotá   milk ices

Païdákia   chops, usually lamb

Pápia   duck

Pastítsio   macaroni, cheese and mince pie

Patátes   potatoes

Pepóni   melon

Piláfi   Middle Eastern pilaff

Piperiá   green pepper

Piperiés   stuffed peppers

Pitsoúnia   pigeon

Portokáli   orange

Prókola   broccoli

Psári plakí   fish steak baked in a tomato, garlic and onion sauce

Psarósoupa   fish soup

Psitó   roast

Radíkia   bitter leaves, usually boiled and served cold

Revýthia   chick peas

Rodákino (yarmádes)   yellow peaches

Ryzógalo   cold rice pudding sprinkled with cinnamon

Skordaliá   garlic and potato purée

Soupiá   cuttlefish

Souvláki   meat kebab grilled on skewers – watch out for street stalls, sometimes dire

Soúvlas   spit-roasted

Souzoukákia   meat and rice balls with tomato or white sauce

Spaghétti   like makarónia, often served, but not as good as Italian pasta

Spanakópitta   triangular spinach and féta flaky pastries

Stafída   small seedless grapes, black or white

Stafýlia   grapes

Stifádo   meat stew with tomatoes, onions, herbs and red wine

Strídia   oysters – rather risky

Sýka   fig

Sykóti   liver

Synagrída spetsiótiko   sea bass baked in a tomato and white wine sauce

Sykotáki tiganitá   liver fried with lemon and origan

Taramosaláta   cod's roe purée

Tomátes gemistés   stuffed tomatoes

Tsatsíki   cucumber, garlic and yoghurt salad

Tyrópitta   flaky pastry cheese pasties

Verýkoka   apricots

Vísina   black sour cherries

Vlíta   delicate variety of radíkia

Xiphías   swordfish, best when grilled

Yaoúrti   yoghurt, especially with honey – insist on próvio, made from ewes' milk

Guide to road signs

Some major places on the mainland and islands are given below in both Greek and English.

Index

Every topic covered in the book, together with each town and village mentioned in the text, is listed in the index. Important sights and places of interest are listed under their own name, as well as in general categories specially selected for their practical usefulness (eg Venetian architecture, Caves). Major historical and mythological figures, artists etc. are also listed.

Page numbers in bold indicate the main entry. Map references are to the maps at the end of the book. Page numbers given in italics denote an illustration or plan.

Index

Index

Index

Index

Index

GREECE

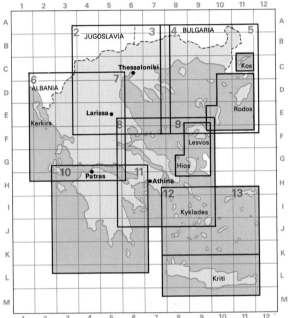

LEGEND

Area maps

0   10   20   30   40   50 Km

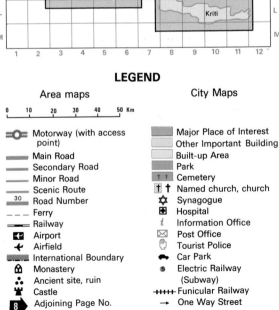

- Motorway (with access point)
- Main Road
- Secondary Road
- Minor Road
- Scenic Route
- 30   Road Number
- Ferry
- Railway
- Airport
- Airfield
- International Boundary
- Monastery
- Ancient site, ruin
- Castle
- 8   Adjoining Page No.

City Maps

- Major Place of Interest
- Other Important Building
- Built-up Area
- Park
- Cemetery
- Named church, church
- Synagogue
- Hospital
- Information Office
- Post Office
- Tourist Police
- Car Park
- Electric Railway (Subway)
- Funicular Railway
- One Way Street

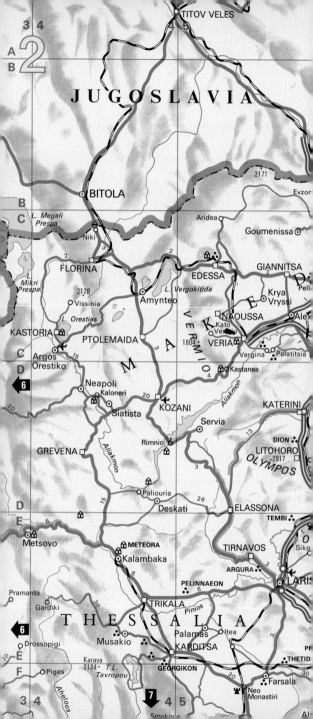

A 4

B

BULGA

RODOPI

1950

Kula
1827

FALAKRO
2232

DRAMA

Prossotsani

Stavroupoli

Ehinos

XANTHI

KO

B

FILIPI

KAVALA

Hrissoupoli

Lagos

Eleftheroupoli

AVDIRA

Fanari

PANGEO

Keramoti

Nea
Peramos   Skala
Rahoniou

Nestos

Agios
Haralan

Skala Prinou

Thassos

Panagia

Makry Ammos

Potamia

Theologos

KINYRA

Limeni
Potos

Alyki

C

THASSOS

D

THRAKIKO

Kamariotissa

PELAGOS

SAMOT

11

12   1

13

Ouranoupoli

2   14

15

5 4

Karves

ATHOS

6   16

3

19

Dafni

18

7   8   9

20

10

Athos
2033

LIMNOS

D

E

Mt. Athos Monasteries

1. Zografou
2. Konstamonitou
3. Dohiariou
4. Xenofontos
5. Ag. Panteleimonos
6. Xiropotamou
7. Simonos Petras
8. Ossiou Grigoriou
9. Dionyssiou
10. Ag. Pavlou

11. Esfigmenou
12. Hiliandariou
13. Vatopediou
14. Pantokratoros
15. Stavronikita
16. Koutloumoussiou
17. Iviron
18. Filotheou
19. Karakalou
20. Meg. Lavras

HEPH

Myrina

PALIOHNI

Moudros

3

Agios
Efstratios

AGIOS
EFSTRATIOS

SKYROS

LESVOS

GIOURA

E

F

KYRA
PANAGIA

PIPERI

9

7   8

8   9

LIMNOS

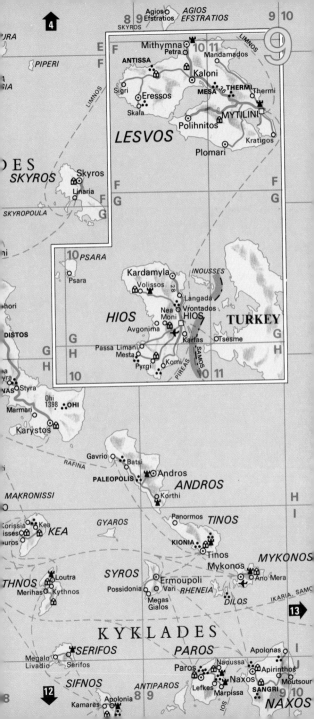

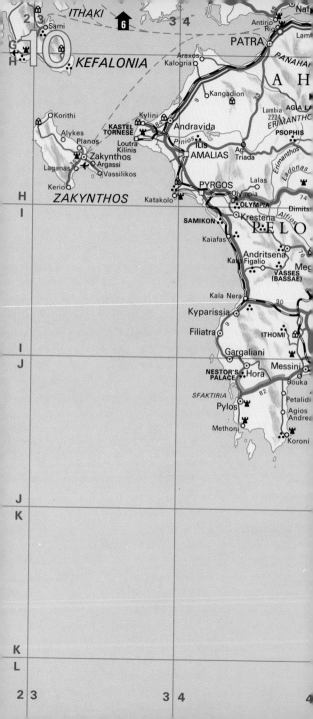

ATHENS

14

0   250   500m

- Athens Station
- Peloponnisos Station
- PLATIA KARESKAKI
- PLATIA OMONIA
- OMONIA
- National Theatre (Ethniko Theatro)
- Town Hall (Dimarhio Kotzia)
- PLATIA ELEFTHERIAS
- Agios Ioannis Kolonna
- Agli Theodori
- PLATIA KLAFTHMONOS
- Town of Athens Museum
- Synagogue
- THISSION
- MONASTIRAKI
- PLATIA MONASTIRAKI
- Kapnikarea
- Cathedral (Mitropolis)
- Old Mitropolis
- Thission
- AGORA
- Stoa of Attalos
- Agi Apostoli
- Tower of the Winds
- PLAK
- Observatory
- Barathron
- AREOPAGOS (HILL OF ARES)
- Kanelopoulos Museum
- Mus. of Gr Popular A
- ACROPOLIS
- Acropolis Museum
- PNYX
- HILL OF THE NYMPHS (LOFOS NIMFON)
- Odeon of Herodes Atticus
- Parthenon
- Dionyssos Theatre
- Lysikrates Mon.
- Agia Aikateri
- St. P
- Arch of Hadrian
- PHILOPAPPOS (HILL OF THE MUSES)
- Theatre of Philopappos
- Philopappos Monument
- Tem
- Olymp (Olymp

Street names
PARASIOU, KAPANEOS, ISMINIS, ARISTOFANOUS, DERIGNY, ALKAMENOUS, PEONIOU, HEIDEN, FERRON, VIC, SAMOU, LIVANIOU, IPHIOU, SEPTEMVRIOU, PATI, METAXA, MICHAIL VODA, AHARNON, FYLIS, PALEOLOGOU, KRITIS, SOUMELI, ARISTOTELOUS, MARNI, STOURNARI, FAVIEROU, MARNI, VERANZEROU, VATHIS, 28th, HALKOKONDYLI, MANGIS, KAN, AGIOU KONSTANTINOU, ZINONOS, EMM, BENAKI, PIREOS, SOFOKLEOUS, STADIOU, SOFOKLEOUS, EOLOU, National (Vivlio, EVRIPIDOU, SAHTOURI, EVRIPIDOU, STADIOU, DIPILOU, KERAMIKOS, ERMOU, KALAMIDA, ADRIANOU, ERMOU, PERIKLEOUS, MITROPOL, APOLLONOS, IRAKLIDON, APOSTOLOU, FESSA, KIDONON, KYDATHINEON, DIONYSIOU, R. GALI, AREOPAGITOU, R. GALI, VIRONOS, G. GARIBALDI, HATZIHRISTOU, DIAKOU, EREHTHIOU, DIMITRAKOPOULOU, VEIKOU, LEOFOROS, KALLIRROIS, FILOPAPPOU, VOUTIE, VEIKOU, DRAKOU, SYNGROU, KALLIRROIS